Women and Employment

Women and Employment

Changing Lives and New Challenges

Edited by

Jacqueline Scott

Professor of Empirical Sociology, University of Cambridge, UK

Shirley Dex

Professor of Longitudinal Social Research in Education, Centre for Longitudinal Studies, Institute of Education, University of London, UK

Heather Joshi

Professor of Economic and Developmental Demography, Centre for Longitudinal Studies, Institute of Education, University of London, UK

Edward Elgar
Cheltenham, UK • Northampton, MA, USA

Published by
Edward Elgar Publishing Limited
The Lypiatts
15 Lansdown Road
Cheltenham
Glos GL50 2JA
UK

Edward Elgar Publishing, Inc.
William Pratt House
9 Dewey Court
Northampton
Massachusetts 01060
USA

A catalogue record for this book
is available from the British Library

Library of Congress Control Number: 2008927973

ISBN 978 1 84720 249 9 (cased)

Printed and bound in Great Britain by MPG Books Ltd, Bodmin, Cornwall

Contents

v

Contributors

Adina Batnitzky is a Postdoctoral Research Fellow in the School of Geography at the University of Oxford. Dr Batnitzky holds a BA with honours from Barnard College, Columbia University and an MA and PhD in Sociology from Brown University, where she was a trainee in demography at the Population Studies Training Center. She is currently working on an Economic and Social Research Council (ESRC) Gender Equality Network funded research project entitled 'Gender, Ethnicity, Migration and Service Sector Employment'. Her doctoral thesis examined the health consequences of unequal divisions of household labour on women's health in Morocco.

Rosemary Crompton is Professor of Sociology at City University, London. Her most recent book is *Employment and the Family*, published by Cambridge University Press in 2006. Other books include *Restructuring Gender Relations and Employment* (Oxford University Press, 1999), *Women and Work in Modern Britain* (Oxford University Press, 1998) and *Class and Stratification* (Polity, 2008). She is currently Principal Investigator on the ESRC project, 'Class, gender, employment and family' linked to the GeNet Research Network (www.genet.ac.uk).

Angela Dale is Professor of Quantitative Social Research at the Cathie Marsh Centre for Census and Survey Research (CCSR) at the University of Manchester. She was CCSR's founding director from 1995 to 2002 when she was appointed Director of the ESRC Research Methods Programme. From 1993 to 2006 she led the CCSR team providing academic access and support for microdata samples (Samples of Anonymised Records) from the UK Census of Population. Research interests centre around gender and the labour market, with a particular emphasis on ethnic differences and the life course.

Simon Deakin is Professor of Law at the University of Cambridge and a Fellow of Peterhouse. He is the director of a programme of interdisciplinary research on corporate governance at the Centre for Business Research and is a senior research associate of the Judge Business School at Cambridge. He has recently been a visiting professor at Columbia University and the EUI, Florence, and is currently a visiting fellow at the Institute for

Technology, Enterprise and Competitiveness at Doshisha University, Kyoto. He is the author, with Frank Wilkinson, of *The Law of the Labour Market: Industrialization, Employment and Legal Evolution* (Oxford University Press, 2005) and, with Gillian Morris, of *Labour Law* (4th edn, Hart Publishing, 2005). He was elected a Fellow of the British Academy in 2005.

Shirley Dex is Professor of Longitudinal Social Research and Head of the Bedford Group of Lifecourse and Statistical Studies at the Institute of Education, University of London. She has held posts at the Judge Business School, University of Cambridge, the Institute for Social and Economic Research at the University of Essex, and the Economics Department at the University of Keele. From 1998 to 2003 she was Research Advisor to the Joseph Rowntree Foundation's Work and Family Life Programme. She has published many books and articles on women's employment and cross-national comparative research, equal opportunities, families and work, ethnic minorities and employment, flexible working arrangements in organisations, work and care and family policy. Recent books include *Families and Work in the 21st Century* (York Publishing Services and Joseph Rowntree Foundation, 2003) and with H. Joshi (eds) *Children of the 21st Century* (Policy Press, 2005).

Sarah Dyer is a lecturer in Human Geography at the University of Oxford. She is currently undertaking research with Linda McDowell and Adina Batnitzky exploring gender, ethnicity, migration and service sector employment. She also has research interests in ethics and the relationship between science and society. Sarah has previously worked as a lecturer at King's College, London.

Peter Elias is a Professor in Employment Research at the University of Warwick. As a full-time researcher based at Warwick since 1975, he has developed a number of research interests and worked on a wide variety of employment-related research projects. These range from the evaluation of large-scale government programmes designed to affect labour market behaviour, statistical monitoring of the status of particular groups in the labour market, the study of occupational change and research on the relationship between further and higher education, vocational training and labour market outcomes. Related to these research themes, he has developed methods for the measurement and analysis of labour market dynamics and has an interest in the classification of labour market activities. He has published his research extensively in a wide variety of journals, book, research reports and papers. He is a Fellow of the Royal Statistical

Society and from 1998 to 2002 he was a member of the ESRC Research Resources Board. In October 2004 he was appointed as the ESRC Strategic Advisor for Data Resources.

John Ermisch is a Professor of Economics at the Institute for Social and Economic Research, University of Essex and a Fellow of the British Academy. Formerly, he was Bonar-Macfie Professor in the Department of Political Economy at the University of Glasgow (1991–94), and a senior research officer at the National Institute of Economic and Social Research. From 1991 to 2001, he was one of the co-editors of the *Journal of Population Economics*, and was President of the European Society for Population Economics in 1989. His research is broadly concerned with how the family and markets interact. He is the author of *An Economic Analysis of the Family* (Princeton University Press, 2003), *Lone Parenthood: An Economic Analysis* (Cambridge University Press, 1991) and *The Political Economy of Demographic Change* (Heinemann, 1983), as well as numerous articles in economic and demographic journals.

Colette Fagan is Professor of Sociology at the University of Manchester and co-Director of the University's European Work and Employment Research Centre. Between 2004 and 2007 she was a co-ordinator of the European Commission's Expert Group on Gender, Social Inclusion and Employment. Her research focuses on gender relations in employment and domestic life, with a particular focus on cross-national comparative analysis and working time. She has recently co-edited *Gender Divisions and Working Time in the New Economy: Public Policy and Changing Patterns of Work in Europe and North America* (Edward Elgar, 2006) and co-authored 'Patterns of labour market integration in Europe – a life course perspective on time policies' in *Socio-Economic Review* (2006).

Susan Harkness is a Senior Lecturer in the Department of Social and Policy Sciences at the University of Bath. Her research interests include women and employment; lone parent employment and well-being; and child poverty and outcomes. She has previously worked as a lecturer in the Department of Economics at the Universities of Bristol and Sussex, and as a researcher at the Centre for Economic Performance at the London School of Economics.

Susan Himmelweit is Professor of Economics at the Open University. Her research is on gender issues in economics, particularly those to do with work–life balance and care, including currently a joint study that forms part of the GeNet on 'Within Household Inequalities and Public Policy', and a recently published report *Supporting Parent and Carer*, written jointly with

Professor Hilary Land for the Equal Opportunities Commission. She is a member and past chair of the UK Women's Budget Group, a think tank monitoring and advising government on the gender aspects of social and economic policy. She is on the editorial board of *Women, Politics and Policy* and an Associate Editor of the journal *Feminist Economics* of which she was joint guest editor of special issues on 'Lone Mothers' (2004) and 'Children and Family Policy' (2000). She is the president-elect of the International Association for Feminist Economics.

Heather Joshi is Professor of Economic and Developmental Demography at the Institute of Education, University of London, where she is also the Director of the Centre for Longitudinal Studies, the department which houses three national birth cohort studies of 1958, 1970 and the Millennium, resources for the research community. Her own research at the intersection of economic and demographic issues has covered gender, family, lifetime earnings, co-education, health inequalities, migration and neighbourhood effects. Publications include *Unequal Pay for Women and Men: evidence from the British Birth Cohort Studies* (with Pirella Paci, MIT Press, 1998), *Children of the 21st Century: From Birth to Nine Months* (contributor and editor with Shirley Dex, Policy Press, 2005) and 'Production, Reproduction and Education: women, children and work in contemporary Britain', in *Population and Development Review*, **28**(3), in 2002. She was one of the first economists to analyse the Women and Employment Survey in 1984 which opened a vein of research on women's lifetime incomes which lead to the award of an Officer of the Order of the British Empire (OBE) in 2002.

Jane Lewis is Professor of Social Policy at the London School of Economics and Political Science (LSE). She has a longstanding interest in gender and social policy, and in the comparative study of welfare regimes. Her recent books include *Should we Worry about Family Change* (2003) and *The End of Marriage? Individualism and Intimate Relations* (2001).

Joanne Lindley is a Senior Lecturer in Economics at the University of Sheffield. Her research interests include the economics of education, migration, labour market discrimination and the effect of globalisation on mobility and labour market adjustment.

Clare Lyonette is a research officer working in the Department of Sociology at City University, London. Since completing her PhD, she has been working with Professor Rosemary Crompton on a series of cross-national comparative studies, funded by the ESRC, and is currently working on the project 'Class, Gender, Employment and Family', which is part of the

ESRC-funded GeNet research project (http://www.genet.ac.uk). Her main research interests are in gender, women's employment, and caring responsibilities, and her published work includes both work and elder-care and work–life conflict issues. She recently co-edited (with Professor Crompton and Professor Suzan Lewis) a book entitled *Women, Men, Work and Family in Europe*, published by Palgrave Macmillan (2007).

Jean Martin is a Senior Research Fellow in the Department of Sociology, University of Oxford where she teaches survey methods. She retired in 2005 from the Office for National Statistics where she was Director of the Social Analysis and Reporting Division. She was responsible for designing, managing and analysing many large-scale social surveys, including the 1980 Women and Employment survey. She has specialised in survey methodology, heading the Data Methodology and Evaluation Division at the Office for National Statistics (ONS). She is a Visiting Professor at the University of Surrey and an Honorary Fellow at the University of Bristol.

Linda McDowell is Professor of Human Geography at the University of Oxford and a Fellow of St John's College, where she is the director of the St John's Research Centre. Her interests are in gender divisions of labour, economic and social change in the UK, migration and feminist theory. Her most recent books are *Redundant Masculinities?* (Blackwell, 2003) and *Hard Labour* (UCL Press, 2005). She currently holds a Leverhulme Major Research Fellowship (until October 2008) and is writing a book about bodies at work. As well as the GeNet project on migrant workers in the service sector in Greater London, she has an Australian Humanities Research Council (AHRC) grant to investigate Asian women's political action in the UK since 1976.

Colm McLaughlin is Lecturer in Industrial Relations and Human Resources at University College Dublin and a Research Associate of the Centre for Business Research at the University of Cambridge. His former positions include Lecturer at the University of Auckland and ESRC Postdoctoral Research Fellow at the University of Cambridge. He is currently working on the ESRC GeNet project 'Addressing Gender Inequality through Corporate Governance'. His research interests include labour market equity; labour market protections and low-paid work; reflexive governance; and comparative industrial relations.

Susan McRae is Professor of Sociology (Emeritus) at Oxford Brookes University, where she was formerly Dean of Social Sciences and Pro Vice-Chancellor for Research and Graduate Studies. From 1994 to 1999, she was

Director of the ESRC Programme on Population and Household Change. Her research interests include women's employment, family and household change, and inequality. She is the author of *Cross-Class Families* (1986), *Maternity Rights in Britain* (1989), *Cohabiting Mothers* (1993) and editor of *Changing Britain: Familes and Households in the 1990s* (1999).

Diane Perrons is the Director of the Gender Institute at the London School of Economics. Her main publications include *Globalization and Social Change; People and Places in a Divided World* (Routledge, 2004) and the anthology *Gender Divisions and Working Time in the New Economy Changing Patterns of Work, Care and Public Policy in Europe and North America* (Edward Elgar, 2006) with Colette Fagan, Linda McDowell, Kathryn Ray and Kevin Ward. Diane's research focuses on the social and spatial implications of global economic restructuring, paying particular attention to inequality and intersectionality between different dimensions of inequality, changing employment composition and social reproduction of daily life.

Kate Purcell is a sociologist and Professor in Employment Research at the University of Warwick having returned to the Institute for Employment Research in September 2006, after seven years as Professor and Director of the Employment Studies Research Unit at the University of the West of England. She has researched and written widely on gender, employment and labour market change and has increasingly focused on policy-related research on the socio-economic impact of higher education expansion. She is currently Director of the biggest-ever investigation of the relationship between higher education and employment – the Higher Education Careers Services Unit (HECSU)-funded Futuretrack six-year longitudinal study of 2006 Universities and Colleges Admissions Service (UCAS) applicants – where the 130 000 respondents to the first stage are being surveyed at six points between 2006 and 2012 to track their experiences, career-relevant decisions, and early career outcomes.

Anthony Rafferty is a Research Associate at the Cathie Marsh Centre for Census and Survey Research (CCSR), Manchester University. Prior to joining CCSR, he worked as a researcher at Birkbeck College, University of London, acting as a Regional Officer for the National Evaluation of the Sure Start government early years programme. He has also worked as a researcher and teaching assistant at Nottingham Policy Centre, Nottingham University, and as a research assistant in the School of Psychology, Cardiff University.

Kathryn Ray is a Research Fellow at the Policy Studies Institute. Her research interests focus around intersections of gender and race in inequalities and identities. Her current work focuses on the employment–family interface and work–life balance issues, and changing racisms and identities in contemporary Britain. She is co-editor of *Gender Divisions and Working Time in the New Economy* (Edward Elgar, 2006), and co-author of *Social Cohesion in Diverse Communities* (JRF, 2007).

Ceridwen Roberts is a Senior Research Fellow in the Department of Social Policy and Social Work at the University of Oxford. She was formerly Director of the Family Policy Studies Centre (FPSC) for eight years until 2001. Prior to joining the FPSC she held research and research management posts in the UK Department of Employment and academia as an industrial sociologist. While in government she developed and managed an extensive programme of research on women in the labour market. From 1998 to 2004 she was the UK expert on the European Commission's Observatory on the Social Situation, Demography and Family. She has lectured, published and appeared on television and radio in a wide range of family policy issues and currently has research projects on family policy issues and grand-parenting as well as a project in the ESRC Gender Equality Network on 'Tackling Inequalities in Work and Care: Policy Initiatives and Actors at the EU and UK levels'. She is an Academician of the Academy of Social Sciences and sits on its Council, was chair of the Social Research Association 2001–05 and is currently its vice-chair and a member of the ESRC Research Strategy Board.

Jill Rubery is Professor of Comparative Employment Systems and Deputy Director for Human Resources, at Manchester Business School, University of Manchester. She is a co-director of the European Work and Employment Research Centre at Manchester and has co-ordinated for 15 years the European Commission's expert group on gender and employment. Her research interests include segmented labour markets, comparative employment systems, theories of pay and the influence of gender on the organisation of the labour market. She was elected a fellow of the British Academy in 2006 and is an emeritus fellow of New Hall, Cambridge. Recent publications include with M. Marchington, J. Grimshaw, J. Rubery and H. Willmott (eds), *Fragmenting Work: Blurring Organisational Boundaries and Disordering Hierarchies* (Oxford University Press, 2005) and J. Rubery and D. Grimshaw, *The Organisation of Employment: an International Perspective* (Palgrave, 2003).

Jacqueline Scott is Professor in Empirical Sociology at the University of Cambridge and a Fellow of Queens' College. She directs the Economic and Social Research Council's Research Network on Gender Inequalities in

Production and Reproduction. Her former positions include Director of Research at the ESRC Centre for Micro Social Change at the University of Essex, where she was involved in the original design and implementation of the British Household Panel Study. Her research interests include life-course research; gender-role change; attitudinal research; and ageing and well-being. She has recently co-edited the *Blackwell Companion to the Sociology of Families* (2004); and the Sage Benchmark Series on Quantitative Sociology (2005).

Kelly Ward is a Data Manager at the National Centre for Social Research (NatCen) and works on two major surveys, the Health Survey for England (HSE) and Longitudinal Study of Young People in England (LSYPE). She was formerly a Research Officer at the Centre for Longitudinal Studies examining the changing occupational careers of women and men, using the birth cohort studies National Child Development Study (NCDS), British Cohort Study 1970 (BCS70), National Survey of Health Development (NSHD) and Millennium Cohort Study (MCS). Her research interests include data linkage, survey methodology; occupational histories and life-course trajectories.

Kevin Ward is Professor of Human Geography and Co-Director of the European Work and Employment Research Centre at the University of Manchester. He has written over 60 articles and book chapters on state reorganisation, the politics of urban and regional development and social reproduction and labour market restructuring, which have appeared in journals including: *Antipode, Area, Environment & Planning A, Environment & Planning C, Geoforum, Sociological Review, Transactions of the Institute of British Geographers, Urban Studies and Work, Employment and Society.* He currently serves on the editorial boards of *Geography Compass* and *Antipode*, is the Editor of the RGS-IBG (Human Geography) Book Series, and he has recently co-edited. *Neo-liberalization; States, Networks, Peoples* (with Kim England, Blackwell, 2007).

Acknowledgements

We gratefully acknowledge support for this research from a grant by the Economic and Social Research Council (RES-225-25-1001) which funds the ESRC Research Priority Network on Gender Inequalities. We also thank the Women and Equality Unit and the Cambridge Research Centre for the Arts, Humanities and Social Sciences for their support for the conference 'Celebrating the 25th Anniversary of the Women and Employment Survey: Changes in Women's Employment 1980–2005' on which this book is based.

Introduction: changing lives and new challenges

Jacqueline Scott, Shirley Dex, Heather Joshi, Kate Purcell and Peter Elias

There have been enormous changes in women's lives in the UK in the past 25 years. The proportion of women in the labour market has grown markedly; the pay gap has narrowed; notions that a woman's place is in the home have eroded further; women have overtaken men in numbers pursuing higher education; and women have made inroads into some previously male-dominated employment sectors. In other areas, earlier inequalities have proved very resistant to change, with women continuing to be more likely than men to reap adverse job-related penalties associated with child-rearing and family care; conditions of part-time work continue to enhance gender inequality; and work–family or work–life balance remains very different for men and women.

In this book we examine different aspects of women and employment, and discuss how labour market experiences have not only changed the lives of women and their families, but also brought new challenges. These not only differ for women and men but also differ across the life course. Even before adulthood, young girls and boys have very different expectations and aspirations concerning their work and family lives. In the post-retirement phase, the gendered consequences of inequalities in the workplace are visible in terms of the dramatically lower pension entitlements of women who have taken 'time out' of paid work for child-raising and family care. The challenges also affect institutions. For example, employers are struggling to implement rather than just pay lip-service to family friendly policies, from childcare provision to flexible work hours; and schools and career advisory services are attempting to break down the stereotypes that contribute to the gender segregation of the labour force, including the worrying dearth of women entering careers in science, engineering and technology. Policy-makers are sometimes caught unawares by the speed with which women's work and home lives are changing, as well as the extent of change. Indeed, changing patterns of women's and men's employment and family roles have to be set in the wider context of socio-economic changes

1

including demographic changes, migration processes, educational expansion, transnational labour markets, technological advances, and the global economy.

We tackle a range of questions that are relevant to understanding the changing nature of women and employment and look ahead to likely changes to come. How are women faring in the labour market in comparison to men, and how has this changed over time? What do we know and what do we need to know about how ethnic diversity impinges on equality in the workplace? How well is Britain doing on equality issues compared with other countries? Can we disentangle the influence of preferences and constraints on the different priorities of men and women concerning family and employment? What does work–family or work–life balance *mean*? How far do the time pressures on dual earners differ across employment sectors and class? How will migration and the enlarged European Union (EU) affect the employment opportunities of women and men in the future? The authors use both qualitative and quantitative data at local, national and cross-national levels to provide empirical evidence for how women's employment lives are changing.

The book builds on a collection of original papers given at a high profile conference hosted by the UK Women and Equality Unit. The conference celebrated the twenty-fifth anniversary of the Women and Employment Survey (WES), which was carried out in 1980 jointly by the Office for Population Census and Surveys and the Department of Employment. The main aims of the survey were to establish what factors determine whether or not women are in paid work and to identify the degree to which domestic factors, or more broadly the gender division of labour, shapes women's lifetime labour market involvement. Full information was collected about the type of work women do, their pay and conditions of employment, as well as the way women behave when in the labour market, when they leave jobs or look for work. The study also set out to determine the importance of work to women and their job priorities. It was the first time detailed work histories, covering the whole of women's lives, were collected and such data allow for analysis of how earlier events such as the timing of childbirth affects women's job transitions and career trajectories.

THE CONTEXT FOR THE 1980 WOMEN AND EMPLOYMENT SURVEY

The WES survey supported analysis that sought to investigate and understand the extent of women's labour market activity and to find out the reasons why women were not in the labour market (Martin and Roberts 1984). The survey was the cornerstone of a whole raft of studies that looked at questions about maternity provision, women's pay and other issues (for example, Dex and Shaw 1986; Main and Elias 1987; Wright and Ermisch 1991). These were key concerns because there had been major changes in the level and nature of women's economic activity. In addition there had been a series of legislative initiatives concerning sex discrimination, equal pay and maternity provision that were designed to address the all too glaring inequalities in employment experiences of women and men.

Large-scale social surveys, such as the 1980 Women and Employment Survey, have an invaluable role in informing research on the social and economic changes that impact upon, and shape, the way we live and work. It is important, though, to recognise that these research instruments are themselves influenced by prevailing cultural norms and contemporary perceptions of social roles.

In this book we step back to the early 1980s and reflect upon research conducted at that time, based upon the 1980 Women and Employment Survey and its predecessor, the 1968 Survey of Women's Employment. What were the gender and equality issues that preoccupied us 25 years ago? How were these shaped by social and economic trends and the changing legal environment of that time? More importantly, when the 'evidence' was interpreted and extrapolated to envisage the future, how well did we predict the changes that would take place over the next 25 years? What do the prospects for equality look like a quarter of a century on?

Two features of the UK economy stood out in the period around 1980: the move towards mass unemployment as the economy encountered fundamental restructuring from heavy, male-dominated labour-intensive physical production to an economy based upon the production and exchange of information and the provision of business and consumer services, and the strong growth in part-time working associated with the latter. It seemed quite natural to interpret these related economic developments in terms of their implications for men and women. Many men were losing full-time jobs in industries such as coal mining and steel production, vehicle production and assembly, and appeared to have little chance of regaining full-time employment. At the same time, women's employment in part-time jobs continued to expand rapidly, albeit in fairly low-paid occupations. The combined supply-side and demand-side influences on women's labour force participation, arising from pressures to maintain family incomes and to satisfy the burgeoning demand for flexible labour in the service sector, were drawing many women back into employment after a period of family formation.

CHANGES IN THE LABOUR MARKET SINCE 1980

In 1980 just under half of all married women and two-thirds of single women were working in employment outside the home. Just over 40 per cent of mothers with dependent children were working. The gender pay gap was just under 30 per cent.

Many changes have taken place in the labour market since 1980. Figure I.1 shows the trends in male and female employment over the past two decades, distinguishing between those in full-time and part-time employment. The decline in male full-time employment in the late 1980s and early 1990s is distinctive, as is the growth in part-time working. Given that the rise in female labour force participation was associated with the return to paid work after a period of family formation, researchers were expressing concern that this would lead to a growing mismatch between the prior skills and work experience of these 'women returners' and the quality of the part-time work to which they were returning (Elias and Purcell 1988). While the outlook was not optimistic for women who worked part-time, policy and legislation changes over this period have ameliorated some of the potential effects that were being predicted. The European Union Part-time Working Directive, the Parental Leave Directive, and provision of day and after-school care for children have gone some way to improve working conditions of part-time jobs, and offer women returners better employment prospects that more nearly match their preferences for job security, reduced hours and better career prospects.

In retrospect, while improvements of part-time working conditions were necessary to facilitate equality, they were not sufficient to address some of the more deep-seated problems that affect men and women's opportunities in employment more generally. From the mid-1990s, full-time employment for both men and women continued to grow steadily. This is apparent in Figure I.1, which shows that for women, the growth in full-time employment from the mid 1990s onwards was stronger than the growth in part-time employment.

What research in the 1980s failed to anticipate was the subsequent large changes in the occupational structure of the economy that has had a major impact on the employment opportunities for both men and women. Some indication of the dramatic nature of these changes can be gained from Figure I. 2, in which we distinguish between the two major groups of occupations. The first of these covers Groups 1, 2 and 3 of the 2000 Standard Occupational Classification (SOC). This broad group covers managerial, professional and associate professional occupations, essentially those which are strongly connected with the growth of the 'knowledge economy' – jobs linked to the production and utilisation of knowledge rather than

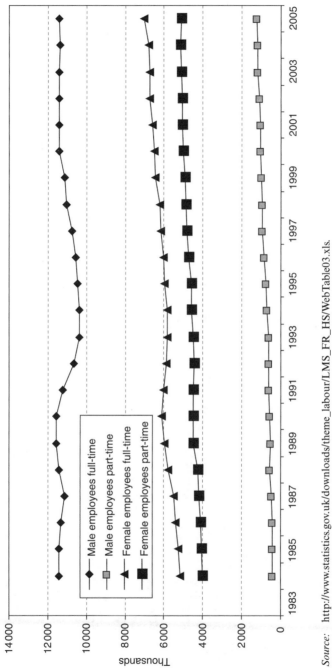

Source: http://www.statistics.gov.uk/downloads/theme_labour/LMS_FR_HS/WebTable03.xls.

Figure I.1   Trends in employees in employment by hours worked and gender, Great Britain, 1984–2005

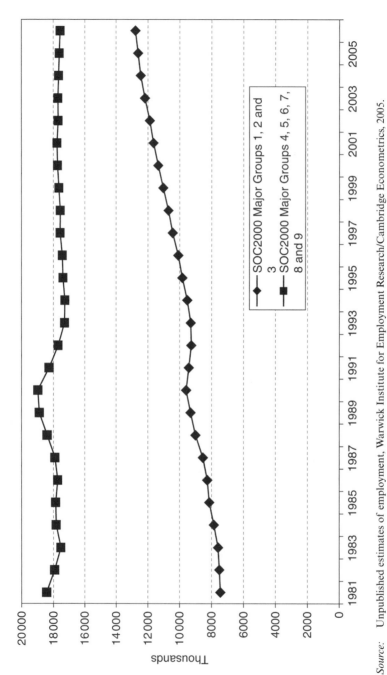

Source: Unpublished estimates of employment, Warwick Institute for Employment Research/Cambridge Econometrics, 2005.

Figure I.2   Changing structure of occupations, UK, 1981–2006

physical goods and low-level services. From a base of approximately 8 million jobs in the late 1980s, this group of occupations now covers over 12 million jobs in 2005. It is clear that the growth in the group of high level occupations is linked to the growth in full-time employment more generally.

Women were under-represented in the group of high level occupations in the early 1980s (Figure I. 3). Only 25 per cent of women were employed in this group in 1984, compared with 35 per cent of men. Since then, women have been catching up fast, with the corresponding ratios at 44 per cent for men and 38 per cent for women by 2004. Projections of employment by occupation indicate that this 'catch-up' is likely to continue, at least through the next decade.

Such growth would not have been possible without a corresponding increase in the acquisition of high-level qualifications associated with many of the jobs in this group of occupations. This coincided with the expansion of higher education generated by successive UK government and EU policies to raise skill levels, on the assumption that knowledge and technological sophistication rather than material resources will be the key to future success in the global economy (Figure I.4). The extent to which women would increasingly acquire the credentials to enable them to access these jobs was not anticipated in the 1980s.

The rate of increase of women's participation in higher education has been more than double that for men, such that women now outnumber men in part-time and full-time undergraduate and postgraduate studies (Table I.1).

With the benefit of hindsight, the quality of part-time employment as a significant constraint on women's employment opportunities was short-sighted. While underutilisation of part-time employees' skills remains a problem and a key research issue (see Chapter 2 in this volume; Grant et al. 2005), recent and ongoing research on graduate employment enables us to reassess the prospects for equality for women who have acquired the credentials to compete for opportunities in the 'knowledge economy'. It is here that we see the rapid growth in employment opportunities in general, with the growth of female full-time employment exceeding that for males.

The gaining of qualifications has been very noticeable among women in minority ethnic groups. Twenty-five years ago, it was not possible to examine minority ethnic differences in employment because of the shortage of data containing sufficient sample sizes of smaller minority ethnic groups. Recently, it has become possible to examine the separate minority ethnic groups' employment experiences, using Quarterly Labour Force Surveys (QLFS).

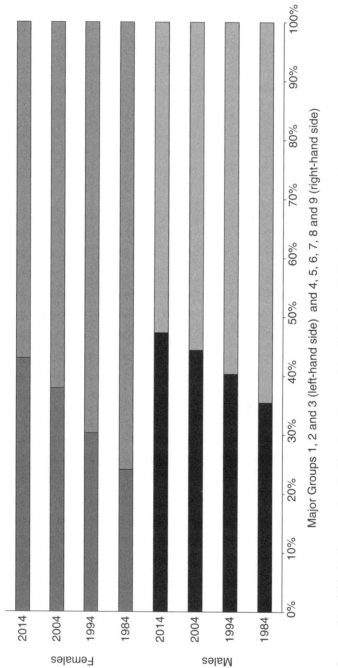

Major Groups 1, 2 and 3 (left-hand side) and 4, 5, 6, 7, 8 and 9 (right-hand side)

Source: Unpublished estimates and projections of employment, Warwick Institute for Employment Research/Cambridge Econometrics, 2005.

Figure I.3   Changing proportions of higher- and lower-level occupations by gender, 1984–2014

Note: *The Age Participation Index (API) measures the number of home-domiciled young (aged under 21) initial entrants to full-time and sandwich undergraduate courses, expressed as a proportion of the average 18- to 19-year-old Great Britain population.

Source: Elias and Purcell (2004).

Figure I. 4   Participation by young people in higher education, Age Participation Index (API),* Great Britain, 1961–2005

We are now able to see that enormous increases have taken place in the percentages of minority ethnic women of all groups, gaining degrees from the early 1990s to the early 2000s (Table I.2) . This has had a large knock-on effect to the overall employment rates of the higher qualified women from minority ethnic groups (Table I.3). It is clear that highly qualified women from minority ethnic groups have always had high employment rates relative to their unqualified peers. However, Black African women and Pakistani and Bangladeshi women also show large increases in the percentages employed over the 1990s decade, even when they were highly qualified.

WHERE ARE WE NOW?

In the first decade of the twenty-first century, we see a rather different picture: there is little difference in the percentage of married women (64 per cent) versus non-married women (62 per cent) in employment outside the home and almost 70 per cent of mothers with dependent children are working. Women now make up 45 per cent of the workforce, up from 38 per cent in 1971. The Equal Pay Act and the Sex Discrimination Act in the 1970s were important milestones in breaking down the barriers to women's participation in the labour market. But wages remain low in many occupations dominated by women and there is still a gap in mean hourly

Women and employment

Table I.1   *Students[1] in higher education:[2] by type of course and gender*
             (UK, 1970/71–2000/01) (000s)

| | Undergraduate | | Postgraduate | | All in higher education |
	Full-time	Part-time	Full-time	Part-time	
Males					
1970/71	241	127	33	15	416
1980/81	277	176	41	32	526
1990/91	345	193	50	50	638
2000/01	511	228	82	118	940
Change 1970/71–2000/01	212%	180%	248%	787%	226%
Females					
1970/71	173	19	10	3	205
1980/81	196	71	21	13	301
1990/91	319	148	34	36	537
2000/01	602	320	81	124	1128
Change 1970/71–2000/01	348%	1684%	810%	4133%	550%

Notes:
1   Home and overseas students.
2   At December each year. Includes Open University.

Sources: Department for Education and Skills; National Assembly for Wales; Scottish
Executive; Northern Ireland Department for Employment and Learning.

earnings between men and women of 18 per cent for full-time workers and
40 per cent for those women working part-time.

As the Fawcett Society report *Are We There Yet? 30 Years of Closing the
Gap between Men and Women* (2005) noted, women still experience 'sticky
floors', meaning they get stuck at the bottom on the employment ladder
clustered in low-paid jobs. So-called women's work such as caring, cleaning and catering is not valued, not paid well and has limited opportunities
for training and promotion. Women also still experience 'glass ceilings'.
The lack of acceptance that senior jobs can be done on a flexible basis combines with discrimination to stop women with family responsibilities reaching senior positions.

However, the picture is complex. Increasing proportions of women have
been gaining educational qualifications, with women's participation levels
in UK higher education now exceeding men's. Graduates now work in a
much wider range of occupations than was the case 25 years ago and a high

Table I.2   Percentage of women in each ethnic group (a) with a degree and (b) without any qualifications, 1992 to 2003

	1992–95			2000–03		
	With a degree	No qualifications	Number	With a Degree	No qualifications	Number
White	17.7	30.9	134 136	26.8	19.7	115 290
Black Caribbean and Other	19.3	28.4	1 650	28.4	14.8	1 558
Black African	22.2	23.4	603	33.7	17.0	941
Indian	15.4	40.9	2 297	28.5	23.8	2 194
Pakistani and Bangladeshi	5.7	61.5	1 469	13.1	46.8	1 769
Chinese and other	22.3	28.5	1 649	31.4	18.5	2 472
Total	17.7	31.3	141 804	26.8	20.1	124 224

Notes: For women age 19–60, excluding full-time student. Data are unweighted. 'Degree' refers to first or higher degree or equivalent.

Source: Quarterly Labour Force Survey Spring Quarters for GB, from Lindley et al. (2006).

proportion of these occupations involve the production, management or transfer of knowledge or information. To a large extent, this is because the nature of work has changed in ways that have both stimulated and accommodated the substantial expansion in higher education. In some areas of work this reflects the growth of sectors and occupations that make use of graduates (for example, the information and communication technology sector, environmental and social welfare occupations). In other areas it relates to the perceived need within organisations to recruit those who have relevant high-level qualifications into occupations where no such pool of highly qualified labour previously existed (for example, the wide range of junior and middle management and administrative jobs for which graduates are now recruited). In part it stems from the growth of particular occupational specialisms (for example, in many areas of health care, education, construction, engineering and technical sales). A pathway through higher education is becoming the *de facto* standard for entry into these occupations. Nevertheless, the longitudinal evidence in the paper by Purcell and Elias in this volume (Chapter 1) indicates that work–life balance choices and organisational obstacles continue to restrict the career progression of many highly qualified women.

Table I.3 Percentage of women employed by minority ethnic group and degree/without a degree

| | 1992–95 | | | 2000–03 | | |
	With a degree	Without a degree	All	With a degree	Without a degree	All
White	84.5*	65.4*	68.8	87.2*	68.2*	73.3*
Black Caribbean and other	84.6	58.6	63.6	85.3	59.3	66.7
Black African	70.9	45.8	51.4	79.8	47.0	58.0*
Indian	84.1	55.6	60.0	84.4	56.4	64.4*
Pakistani and Bangladeshi	55.9*	16.97	19.2	72.0*	17.6	24.8*
Chinese and other	79.4	48.3	55.3	77.2	48.8	57.7
Total	84.2*	64.3*	67.8	86.8*	66.5*	71.9*

Notes:
For women age 19–60, excluding full time students. Data are unweighted.
'Degree' refers to first or higher degree or equivalent.
* Denotes a statistical significance between the two means for period 1992–95 and period 2000–03.

Source: QLFS Spring Quarters for GB, reproduced from Lindley et al. (2006).

WHERE TO NEXT?

The Women and Work Commission (2006) concluded its report *Shaping a Fairer Future*, with several recommendations regarding ways of increasing employment opportunities for women and reducing the gender pay gap, including flexible working, affordable childcare and quality part-time work. Some felt the Commission 'lacked teeth' in not recommending the mandatory monitoring of gender pay and promotion (see Deakin and McLaughlin, Chapter 13 in this volume) but the Commission does applaud the new Gender Duty that requires the public sector to actively promote gender equality. The Commission emphasised that making progress on the gender pay gap is a key priority not only because barriers that prevent the utilisation of women's talent and skills in the labour market are economically costly for the UK economy, but also because women have the right to expect a fair deal in the labour market.

In this book we try to break down some of the artificial barriers that have plagued the understanding of changing women's lives. One such

So what is the way forward? In the Part IV, Rubery showcases best practice from a range of European countries that have sought to modernise labour market institutions to enhance greater gender equality. Deakin and McLaughlin examine, with reference to the gender pay gap, how far 'reflexive law', which relies on self-regulatory mechanisms rather than mandatory legislation, is likely to achieve greater equality. McDowell et al. illustrate the way transnational movements in employment are changing the experience of women workers at the start of the new millennium. Himmelweit looks specifically at whether policies on care help or hinder gender equality and she illustrates the potential dilemmas, for example, when affordable care for some women means low pay for other women who provide care. Policies often adopt a position of gender neutrality, but the realities of women's and men's experiences of paid and unpaid work make it clear that gender equality remains a pressing challenge.

REFERENCES

Dex, S. and L. Shaw (1986), *British and American Women at Work: Do Equal Opportunities Policies matter?*, London: Macmillan.

Elias, P. and K. Purcell (1988), 'Women and paid work: prospects for equality', in A. Hunt (ed.), *Women and Paid Work*, Basingstoke: Macmillan.

Fawcett Society (2005), *Are We There Yet? 30 Years of Closing the Gap between Men and Women*, London: Fawcett Society.

Grant, L., S. Yeandle and L. Buckner (2005), 'Working below potential: women and part-time work', Equal Opportunities Commission, Working Paper No. 40, EOC, Manchester.

Lindley, J., A. Dale and S. Dex (2006), 'Ethnic differences in women's employment: the changing role of qualifications', *Oxford Economic Papers*, **58**(2), 351–78.

Main, B. and P. Elias (1987), 'Women returning to paid employment', *International Review of Applied Economics*, **1**(1), 86–108.

Martin, J. and C. Roberts (1984), *Women and Employment – a Life Time Perspective*, London: HMSO.

Portes, A. (2000), 'Presidential address: the hidden abode: sociology as analysis of the unexpected', *American Sociological Review*, **65**(1), 1–18.

Scott, J. (2004), 'Gender inequality in production and reproduction: a new priority research network', GeNet Working Papers, No. 1. Available at www.genet.ac.uk/workpapers/GeNet2004p1.pdf (accessed 7 January 2008).

Women and Work Commission (2006), *Shaping a Fairer Future*, London: Women and Equality Unit.

Wright, R. and J. Ermisch (1991), 'Gender discrimination in the British labour market: a reassessment', *Economic Journal*, **101**(406), 508–22.

PART I

Women and Employment: Assessing Progress
on Equality

1. Achieving equality in the knowledge economy

Kate Purcell and Peter Elias

INTRODUCTION

In an earlier attempt to assess and further predict progress towards equality at the end of the 1980s (Elias and Purcell 1988), we were influenced by the social implications of the economic trends prevailing in the late 1970s and early 1980s. Two features of the UK economy stood out in this period: industrial restructuring and the strong growth in part-time working associated with the shift from manufacturing to services, and an increase in women's economic activity over the life cycle. We understood that the labour market map was being redrawn, skills required by employers changing, and the construction of jobs evolving to take account of industrial, commercial and technological changes as well as change in the labour supply. However, we underestimated the impact that the changing occupational structure of the economy would have on opportunities for both men and women to participate in employment. Crucially, we did not foresee the expansion of higher education that would be stimulated by successive UK government policies that, in line with international trends, have been predicated upon the belief that in the twenty-first century, successful economies will rely more upon knowledge than material resources to maintain competitiveness in the 'knowledge-intensive' global economy (DfEE 1998; European Commission 2004; Leadbetter 1999; OECD 1996).

One of the biggest differences between the generation surveyed in 1980 for the Women and Employment Survey (WES) and that represented by later cohort studies is the relative ratios of men and women entering graduate employment. Contingent differences include the extent to which women graduates' early careers run parallel to men's, their postponement of family-building – and (it might be assumed) the consequently very different gender contexts and expectations that they encounter. Highly qualified women surveyed in WES had a greater propensity than women generally to have continuous or less disrupted employment careers and experienced less gender disadvantage, in terms of earnings and other

conditions of employment. Graduate women's career development consequently might be expected to represent a useful indication of the efficacy
of equal opportunities legislation and the extent of related cultural
change.

In this chapter, we use both survey and interview data, drawing on mixed
methods research that we have been engaged on over more than 10 years
to move beyond the consideration of trends and statistical analyses. Our
aim is to obtain a better understanding of the relationship between the
attitudes, experiences and choices made by graduates in the transition
from higher education and young adulthood to the career establishment
and family formation life stage. The latter has traditionally been a stage
characterised by gender role divergence. Our use of mixed methods in this
longitudinal study is reflexive. It has involved subjecting relationships
between observed survey variables to scrutiny in the light of qualitative
evidence collected in the interviews and in developing survey questions
subsequently that were informed by patterns revealed by semi-structured
qualitative interviews. We take it as axiomatic that observed outcomes and
patterns of behaviour may or may not reflect preferences or constraints,
and that this is a question that mixed-methods research can address
effectively.

GRADUATE EARNINGS, CAREER DEVELOPMENT AND GENDER: EQUAL OPPORTUNITIES?

Gender differences in earnings are, in general, well researched[1] and form an
important theme of this volume, but questions remain about the processes
through which they arise and the mechanisms that perpetuate them.
Human capital theory posits a relationship between expected lifetime
labour market experience, education and earnings, suggesting that women
will invest less in human capital if they expect to withdraw from the labour
market for reasons of family formation or caring responsibilities. Related
to this theory, it has also been argued that women's preferences for paid
work are different from those of men, affecting their investment in
careers and, consequently, their earnings (Hakim 2000, 2004). Others have
argued that the reward structure reflects historically embedded differences
in the value accorded to women's and men's work. These reflect female
dependency, established gendered divisions of labour (Cockburn 1991;
Crompton and Sanderson 1986; Phillips and Taylor 1980) and gendered
constraints arising from social roles and expectations. These act to restrict
women's abilities to take advantage of employment and career development opportunities (Ginn et al. 1996; McRae 2003).

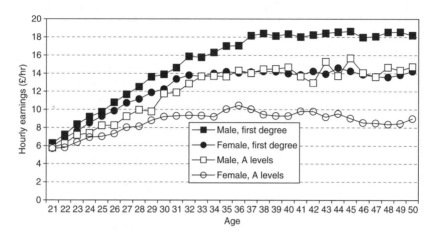

Source: Labour Force Surveys, 1999–2003.

Figure 1.1 *Average hourly earnings of graduates (first degree only) and non-graduates (A levels only), by age and gender*

The gender gap in hourly earnings varies with age, beginning to appear in the early 20s and reaching a maximum in the mid-40s (Figure 1.1). While graduates at any age earn significantly more than non-graduates, the emergence of the gender pay gap arises in a similar fashion for graduates and for non-graduates. We note also that the period covering the first 10 years after graduation is critical. A gender difference is apparent even for the youngest graduates, initially at about 10 per cent, but rising to about 25 per cent by the time graduates reach their mid-40s.

Thus, we observe an apparent widening of the gender pay gap with age, but this does not necessarily indicate the existence of a life-cycle phenomenon. These data are cross-sectional – that is, they arise from respondents across the range of ages shown and over a specific time period (Labour Force Survey earnings information collected between 1999 and 2003). They give a picture of the average situation prevailing in this period for all age groups, but they do not reveal earning paths through which these average values arose. In the cross-sectional picture (Figure 1.1), most of those in their early 40s had graduated 20 years earlier and could be on a different labour market trajectory to those who graduated more recently. Women who had graduated recently might be expected to have benefited from legislation-stimulated commitment to equal opportunities in recruitment and promotion. To advance understanding, longitudinal information – observations from the same individuals collected at successive points in time – is required.

A Longitudinal Study of Gender Differences in Earnings

We make use of data derived from a longitudinal study of a national sample of graduates who gained their first degrees in 1995. These graduates were first contacted in winter 1998–99, approximately three and a half years after graduation. A total of 11 125 responses were collected (response rate of 27 per cent, 6157 female and 4968 male graduates) in 1998–99.[2] A second contact was made in 2002–03, seven years after graduation, with the 70 per cent of respondents who had previously given permission to be recontacted. In total, 3447 responses were obtained in 2002–03, a response rate of 50 per cent. As part of the 'seven years on' investigation, detailed tape-recorded interviews were undertaken with a sub-sample of 200 of the 2002–03 survey respondents immediately following their survey participation, and subsequently, in 2005–06, those interviewees who had been identified as 'high flyers' with ambitious career plans were interviewed again approximately 10 years after completing their first degree.[3]

The graduates surveyed were predominantly aged between 24 and 28 at the time of the 1998/99 survey and few had children. The impact of family formation and childcare responsibilities on career patterns was, therefore, likely to be less significant for this sample than for women more generally. It was consequently surprising to find a significant gender gap in earnings at this early stage in the career development of these 1995 graduates. Figure 1.2 shows the evolution of the gender gap in pay among 1995 graduates in full-time employment:[4] for their first main job after graduating in 1995 (as long as the job was started before January 1996), at the time of the first survey of this cohort (1998–99) and at the time of the second survey (2002–03).[5]

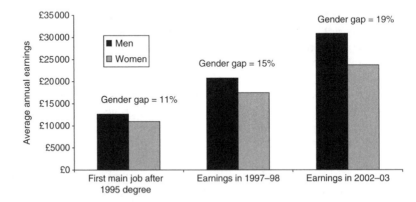

Source: Seven Years On: A Survey of the Career Paths of 1995 Graduates.

Figure 1.2   Average annual gross earnings of 1995 graduates, by gender

These comparisons reveal that the unadjusted earnings gap (without taking account of gender differences in subject studied, social class background, entry level qualifications, class of degree obtained, etc.) has been increasing steadily as careers evolve over the seven and a half year period since graduation. Women graduates reported full-time annual gross earnings in their first job after graduation that were, on average, 11 per cent less than those of male graduates. Three and a half years later the gap had risen to 15 per cent, then to 19 per cent by 2002–03.

As a first approach to gaining a better understanding of the factors underlying the gender difference in gross annual earnings, we present in Appendix Table 1A.1 results from a detailed multivariate analysis of the earnings of 1995 graduates, including only those in full-time employment, seven years after graduating with their first degree. This analysis reveals that, although a number of factors show a powerful association with annual earnings, they do not necessarily contribute to a better understanding of the gender difference in pay.[6] Gender differences in earnings do, however, appear to be associated with a number of factors which vary significantly between men and women. The most important among these, which we consider below in turn, are:

- gender differences in weekly hours worked
- the sectoral distribution of graduate jobs and public/private sector location
- the extent to which graduates are employed in workplaces where the type of job they do is segregated by gender
- gender differences in subject studied for their 1995 degree.

Weekly Hours Worked

The relationship found between annual earnings and hours worked per week is, as expected, positive – as working hours increase, so do annual earnings. The regression coefficient shown in Appendix Table 1A.1 implies that each additional weekly hour worked contributes to a 1 per cent increase in annual earnings. This may not seem large, but the young male graduates in our sample reported weekly hours that were significantly higher than those for the women,[7] as Figure 1.3 shows.

While some may argue that higher male earnings consequently simply reflect fair compensation for longer hours of working, this raises the important question of why men work significantly longer hours and whether or not women's hours are more constrained than men's due to the gendered division of non-paid work. These are issues to which we return later in this chapter.

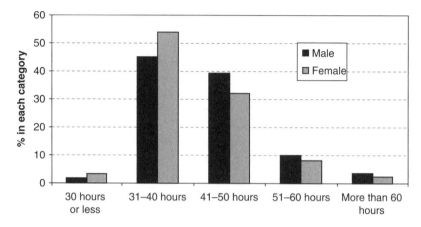

Source: Seven Years On: A Survey of the Career Paths of 1995 Graduates.

Figure 1.3   Weekly hours worked by 1995 graduates seven years after
graduating, by gender

The Sectoral Distribution of Graduate Jobs

Average annual earnings vary by industry sector and this is clearly related to
the observed gender pay gap among the graduate sample. The reasons
behind this are complex and varied, and may well reflect differential access
to sectors of employment by men and women. The distribution of graduate
employment by sector undoubtedly reflects choices made at an early stage in
the development of graduate career paths. Part of the explanation of sectoral
pay differentials lies in the demand for and supply of particular skills. The
information and communications sector is a good example of a sector where
jobs, until recently, were in relatively short supply, leading to higher pay for
those working in the sector. Additionally, public sector jobs typically pay less
than equivalent private sector posts – although they typically also provide a
different balance of non-wage costs and benefits, as will be discussed later.

These factors combine to have a significant impact upon the pay of men
and women. For example, graduates who worked in banking, insurance,
finance, the information and communications sector and business services
had annual earnings which are approximately 15 per cent higher than the
average. Figure 1.4 reveals that men were more likely than women to work
in higher paying and women were more likely than men to be in lower-
paying sectors.

Conversely, public sector earnings were approximately 10 per cent lower
than private sector jobs, after having taken account of the sector in which

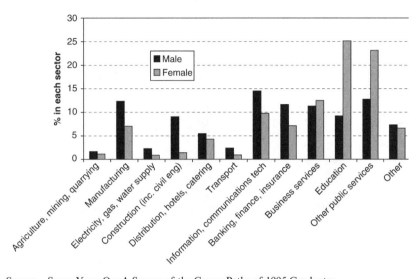

Source: Seven Years On: A Survey of the Career Paths of 1995 Graduates.

Figure 1.4 *Industry of graduates' current job seven years after graduating, by gender*

a person works. Figure 1.5 shows that over half of the female graduates in full-time employment seven years after graduation were employed in the public or 'not-for-profit' sector, compared with only one-third of male graduates. Elsewhere, we have discussed the intrinsic differences in job characteristics and job quality of the highest-achieving male and female graduates who had access to the full-range of opportunities, which suggests that women may be 'trading off' high earnings for job security, other terms and conditions of employment that include family-friendly policies, and job satisfaction (Purcell et al. 2006).

Access to occupations is clearly restricted, if not substantially determined, by subject and discipline choices made at school and in higher education and the consequent skills developed. Boys' and girls' secondary education subject choices and achievements at GCSE, A level and equivalent public examinations are gendered, with boys more likely to have chosen science and numeracy-based subjects than girls and more likely to have gone on to higher education courses that require such a foundation (DfES 2002). Seven years after graduation, choice of subject studied at the undergraduate level remains a key factor that aids our understanding of the gender difference in earnings.

Figure 1.6 shows the higher proportion of male graduates who had studied the quantitative-based engineering, mathematics and computing,

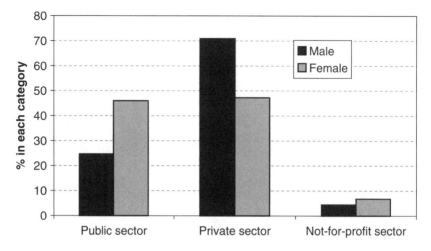

Source: Seven Years On: A Survey of the Career Paths of 1995 Graduates.

Figure 1.5 Graduates' location in public/private sector seven years after graduating, by gender

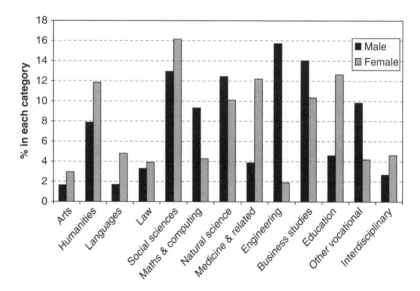

Source: Seven Years On: A Survey of the Career Paths of 1995 Graduates.

Figure 1.6 Subject studied at undergraduate level, by gender

and other vocational subjects, with women studying in higher proportions in arts, humanities, languages, social sciences, medicine and related subjects and education. The detailed multivariate analysis shown at Appendix Table 1A.1 shows that those who took an arts degree earned 17 per cent less seven years later than law, social sciences, engineering, business studies or education graduates. In contrast, mathematics and computing graduates and those who studied engineering recorded annual earnings which were 10–12 per cent higher than law, social sciences, engineering, business studies or education graduates at this point.

It is often assumed, not unreasonably, that degree subject studied is indicative of aptitudes and skills developed. It is perhaps less reasonably assumed that specialisation in numeracy-based skills is likely to be correlated with low development of a literacy-based skill-set, and vice versa. Skills, and the market values they are accorded are socially constructed and it is very clear in our graduate sample that possession of different types of degree is rewarded differentially. Thus, subject differences clearly go some way towards explaining the gender pay gap.

Workplace Segregation by Gender

The extent of gender segregation at the workplace was revealed in the 1980 Women and Employment Survey (Martin and Roberts 1984) and we find that this persists. To investigate whether or not this was an important factor influencing 1995 graduates' earnings we included the following question in the seven years on survey:

In your workplace, is your type of job done . . .

    . . . mainly by men?
    . . . by a fairly equal mixture of men and women?
    . . . mainly by women?
    . . . almost exclusively by women?

Figure 1.7 shows the response to this question, revealing the extent of occupational gender segregation at the workplace for all graduates in full-time employment (aged under 30 at the time of the survey).

While only 5 per cent of women were employed in workplaces where their type of job was undertaken almost exclusively by males, the corresponding figure for men was 20 per cent. In total, over half of the young male graduates in employment in the seven years on survey in 2002–03 were working in contexts where their jobs were exclusively or mainly done by men. Over 40 per cent of women were working in jobs exclusively or mainly done by women in their workplace. In Table 1A.1 we show that, all other things

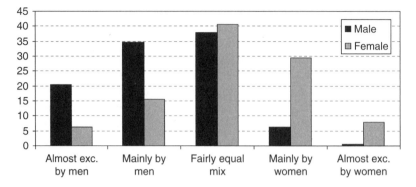

Source: Seven Years On: A Survey of the Career Paths of 1995 Graduates.

*Figure 1.7   Occupational workplace segregation for 1995 graduates seven
              years after graduating, by gender*

being equal, working in a workplace 'where my type of work is done almost
exclusively by women' has a 13 per cent pay penalty relative to working in
an exclusively male workplace environment.

Our qualitative interview data provide illustrations of the impact of gendered occupational contexts on career development. An example of a
female professional working in a female-dominated workplace is provided
by a natural sciences graduate with a PhD in addition to her first degree,
who had moved from the food manufacturing industry to a post working
for a government agency as a civil servant:

I   *Have you experienced any obstacles in your career so far? Problems in career
       development or getting jobs you felt were suitable for you?*
R   I think that if I had been not a woman then in [my last company] they would
       certainly have rewarded me more because the role I was taking was project
       management . . .
I   *Was it a male-dominated organisation?*
R   It was predominantly female but it was predominantly junior administra-
       tive staff and the managing director was male, the finance director was
       male, the research manager was male, the production manager was male
       and there was nobody female on the board of directors . . . so overall, the
       figures looked like it was equality – in fact going the other way, because
       they had more women employed than men. But most of [the women] were
       part-time; most of them were in secretarial or junior administrative roles.
       I certainly feel that for the salary I was getting, I had a lot of responsibil-
       ity and I was given a lot of opportunities that I wouldn't have expected,
       based on the job title and the salary that I was earning. (Female
       food science research team leader currently employed in a public sector
       organisation.)[8]

Further exploration of why we find highly qualified women and men working in contexts where 'people who do their jobs' are the same sex, revealed that those with androgynous occupational skills are more likely to be recruited to 'gender appropriate' vacancies: males and females both become human resource managers, but relatively well-paid human resource management (HRM) posts in manufacturing industry are more likely to be filled by men, and somewhat less highly paid public sector HRM posts by women even among young graduates (Purcell et al. 2006).

The Combined Effects on the Gender Difference in Pay

The combined influence on the gender difference in annual pay of the factors outlined above is shown in Figure 1.8. The uppermost bar on this chart shows the unadjusted difference in the annual earnings of male and female graduates in full-time employment seven years after graduation, as was shown in Figure 1.2. Each bar beneath this shows the effect on the gender difference in pay of introducing statistical controls for various factors. Controlling for weekly hours alone reduces the gender differential to about 16 per cent from over 18 per cent. Next, controls are added for the sector of employment (Standard Industrial Classification [SIC] divisions and the public/private sector distinction) which together with hours, reduces the gender difference further to nearly 11 per cent. Finally, the additional impact of gender segmentation at the workplace as a major force in the gender difference in earnings, brings the gender difference down a further 4 percentage points to 7 per cent. The final bar in this chart is the gender difference remaining after all the variables shown in the regression estimates in Appendix Table 1A.1 have been added. This is slightly higher than the gender difference adjusted simply for hours, sectors and workplace segmentation, reflecting women's higher average entrance qualifications for university and their better degree results.

An interesting finding from the analysis described above relates to the relative effects of subject studied and sector of employment. While these two factors are clearly related, we anticipated that subject studied would appear as the most important factor in helping us to understand the gender difference in pay. In fact, it turns out that the opposite is true – sector of employment and the public/private sector distinction are better predictors of the gender difference in earnings than subject of study, although the two are clearly interrelated when we look at the occupational distribution.

Differences in weekly hours worked and the different sectors in which men and women graduates are employed alone 'account for' half of the gender difference in the earnings of young 1995 graduates in full-time

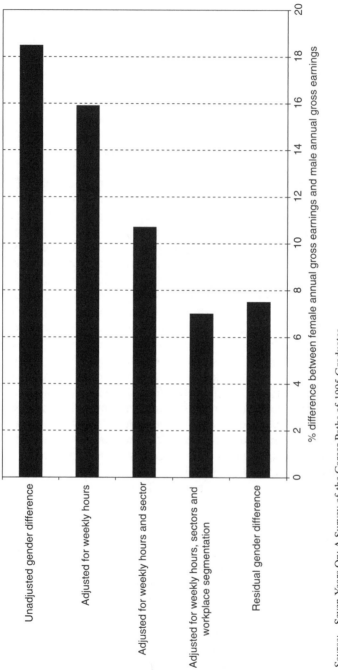

Source: Seven Years On: A Survey of the Career Paths of 1995 Graduates.

Figure 1.8 *The combined effects of various factors on the gender difference in annual earnings of 1995 graduates seven years after graduation*

employment seven years after gaining a first degree. Clearly this does not 'explain' the gender difference, given that working hours arrangements, occupational outcomes and access to employment in the public or private sector are likely to be influenced by subjects studied and may well reflect gender-based constraints on opportunities to vary working hours or access particular employment options. However, a very interesting result illustrated at the macro level of this national study is that the gender difference in earnings relates also to the gendered nature of the work environment. Women graduates tended to work in jobs where people who did their kinds of job tend to be primarily other women, and these jobs paid less than jobs in male dominated workplaces, a finding that reinforces earlier sociological studies of gender segmentation at the workplace and its association with gender inequalities in pay and promotion profiles (Cockburn 1991; Kanter 1977; Wilson 1998).

Moving Beyond Patterns to Understand Processes

How can we move beyond these interesting differences in the earnings profiles of male and female 1995 graduate populations in the early stages of their careers to a better understanding of how they have evolved and are perpetuated or challenged? Detailed qualitative interviews were carried out with 200 survey respondents seven and 10 years after graduation. These qualitative data provide evidence of *how* gendered differences in the work environment are being perpetuated. In our attempts to deepen our understanding of the relationships between work-related gender dynamics and the practical and psychological overlap between employment and wider societal gender roles and responsibilities, we draw, below, on further analyses of the survey data as well as integrating insights from the qualitative interviews.

In an earlier paper (Purcell and Elias 2004) we made a first attempt to explore further, by quantitative analysis, the complexities underlying the unexplained residual gender difference in average earnings by focusing in more closely on different subject choices and workplace contexts. Comparing women and men who had studied engineering, law and humanities degrees within each discipline group and across the discipline boundaries, it became apparent that the gender pay gap differed according to degree obtained – and the survey evidence provided some clues as to why this might be. The gap was narrowest for engineering graduates and widest for law graduates, and when we looked more closely at the kinds of jobs they had obtained, it appeared that not only salaries, but the use of disciplinary skills and knowledge in employment was different (Table 1.1).

Table 1.1   Career outcomes for 1995 graduates by degree subject

Subject studied	Humanities		Law		Engineering	
	Males	Females	Males	Females	Males	Females
Subject gender ratios	44:56		50:50		90:10	
Average annual earnings (£)	30 033	24 114	43 458	33 824	31 837	28 789
Gender pay gap (%)	20		22		10	
% using degree subject knowledge	31	37	85	79	75	50
% using degree skills	69	74	94	89	86	75

Note: These data relate to those in full-time employment, excluding respondents who were 30 or older when they completed their undergraduate degree.

Source: Seven Years On. A Survey of the Career Paths of 1995 Graduates.

The law graduates, who had the biggest gender pay gap, earned most, and the women were less likely than men to be using their legal skills and knowledge; the humanities graduates earned least, but had a similarly above-average gender pay gap, with the women more likely than men to be using their undergraduate skills and knowledge; and among the engineering graduates, with the lowest gender pay gap, the women were far less likely than men to be working in mainstream engineering jobs.

Further analysis of the qualitative interviews reinforced and explicated these patterns, revealing that women with law degrees reported difficulty in accessing legal professional vacancies and were less likely to be in the highest-paying occupational specialisms; male humanities degree holders were less likely than their female peers to work in the public sector and, particularly, to be in teaching jobs; and women in engineering reported substantial incidence of direct and indirect discrimination in the workplace, which in several cases had led them to move into less woman-unfriendly occupations (Purcell and Elias 2004.). Only in the last case of engineering, however, is there a clear explanatory element to assist us in assessing why equal opportunities have not led to greater equality of outcomes. In law and humanities, the question remains of why gendered differences in career development persist among this highly qualified sample? We need to shift our attention to the more difficult-to-research areas of orientations to work and non-work considerations if we are to move closer to being able to understand the unexplained gender gap in earnings.

GENDERED ORIENTATIONS TO WORK?

Seven years after graduation there was some indication from the survey and interview data that gendered attitudes and expectations – their own and, more often, those of their employers and others with whom they came into contact – had affected work experiences and career trajectories. This reflects Cockburn's (1991) finding that 'soft' ideological variables can present a greater obstacle to change than apparently 'harder' material variables such as technology. Highly qualified women have historically been more likely than non-graduates to have continuous employment careers, reflecting both greater intrinsic commitment to employment, greater earning power and the ability to purchase domestic and childcare services to facilitate their participation in paid work. Women's dependency, where they have worked for 'second-earner' rather than breadwinner wages, has been a fundamental brake on the achievement of greater equity between men and women in general. However, the graduate women in our sample had accessed equal opportunities to earn above-average wages and many earned high wages; some higher than their partners. Yet the average 'unaccounted' gender gap remains. Do female graduates, even where they have made similar choices of higher education course or career direction to their male peers, have fundamentally different career aspirations that go some way towards explaining different outcomes and earnings? Are women making rational choices to trade earnings for other advantages, in ways that reflect a different orientation to employment, career development, and the centrality of family roles (Hakim 2000), or are they accommodating to practical obstacles to the achievement of equal outcomes (Crompton and Lyonette 2005; Ginn et al. 1996; McRae 2003). Whatever the ratio of structural, biological or ideological elements in the explanatory equation, how much closer are the young women in our 1995 graduate sample in accessing equal opportunities and achieving equality of outcomes than members of the equivalent age group surveyed in 1980?

When we contacted these 1995 graduates in 2002–03, seven years after graduation, we asked a number of questions which relate to perceptions of their personalities. An interesting difference was evident between the male and female graduates concerning the extent to which they perceived themselves as ambitious. The question asked was simply 'How far do you agree or disagree with the following statement? *I am extremely ambitious*'. Respondents were asked to reply on a five-point scale: 'Agree strongly'; 'Agree somewhat'; 'Not sure'; 'Disagree somewhat'; 'Disagree strongly'. Seventy per cent of the young male graduates stated that they 'agreed strongly' or 'agreed somewhat' with this statement, compared with 59 per cent of young female graduates. While the direction of causality is questionable, we wanted to see whether or not this difference in perceived ambition correlates with the gender difference in earnings described in the preceding section. To achieve this, we estimated the coefficients of the same regression model;[9] with the addition of a binary variable describing those who answered that they agreed strongly or agreed somewhat with the statement that they were extremely ambitious. Interestingly, although this variable correlates strongly with earnings, it does little to reduce the residual gender difference in earnings, bringing it down from 7.5 per cent to 7.2 per cent. In other words, we find little statistical support for the notion that the gender gap in earnings is essentially a function of differences between male and female graduates in their stated views on the extent to which they consider themselves ambitious.

In the survey, we also included a series of questions about reasons for taking current job and longer term values related to – and with implications for – work and career development. We found remarkably little difference in the work orientations and work-related aspirations of these highly qualified males and females. The most popular reasons for taking their current jobs for both men and women were that it provided interesting work, was exactly the kind of work they wanted, and location. The fourth most frequently mentioned reason for both was that the salary level had attracted them but (not surprisingly perhaps, given the preceding evidence about the gender pay gap) this reason was given by a significantly higher proportion of the men than women. Women in this sample, although more satisfied with their current jobs and careers to date than men, were less satisfied with their earnings and promotion prospects. Compatibility with partners' careers was regarded as an important variable for 10 per cent of the women and 8 per cent of the men. Seven years after graduation the majority of survey respondents were living with a partner, although only 16 per cent had embarked upon parenthood. We found in discussion with the interview sub-sample that career decisions including, crucially, decisions not to change jobs, accept promotions or apply for jobs that involved location change, were made as a couple rather than as individuals. We realised that careers are consequently rarely as individual as the career literature suggests, even among young graduates at the outset of their careers who, at different stages of what sometimes turned out to be serial monogamy, were making decisions that maximised shared rather than individual utilities.

However, in these couples, in general, the partners were equally likely to be highly qualified and have similar potential for career development. In the interviews, we asked respondents whether they regarded their own career or their partner's as more important, or whether they considered them of equal importance. Among these mostly pre-family-building

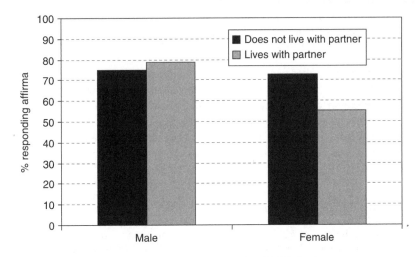

Source: Seven Years On: A Survey of the Career Paths of 1995 Graduates.

Figure 1.9 *Whether respondents expected to achieve a higher position within the next five years, by gender and whether or not had a partner*

respondents, the most common response was that both careers were of equal importance. However, returning to the survey data (Figure 1.9) illustrates how living with a partner appeared to be correlated with lower expectations of career development for women, and had, if anything, a slight positive impact on men's expectations. This iteration between survey and qualitative interview data uncovered some interesting inconsistencies.

The qualitative interviews revealed further gendered nuances in the priority of one or other person's careers. Where men were the higher earners, they tended to regard this as an obvious explanation for why their careers took precedence – but where men reported that their partners earned more, they tended to distinguish between 'financial importance' and other aspects of career. The following example illustrates this point:

> That's a hard question. I think they are equally important. Financially, obviously not! Maybe she doesn't see it the same way as I do. In terms of allowances that both of us make for each other's career and in terms of either of us saying – 'I need to work late on this . . .' – they are equally important. She earns a lot more money than I do. We could survive if I lost my job, our lifestyle would continue in exactly the same way as it does now, but if she lost hers we would have to sell the house and do something else . . . the mortgage dwarfs my salary. I couldn't pay it on my own, my wife can just about pay it on her own, but we want

> to have children in a couple of years time, so . . . That's the pressure in terms of future career development, so I have to move forward quickly. (Male journalist married to HRM manager)

The women of higher-earning partners also more often tended to accord priority to their partner's career (although almost always with the proviso that their career was also important or that this was not necessarily a stable situation), whereas where women were the higher earners, as was the case in a substantial minority of partnerships, they tended to see the two careers as equally important, as illustrated by the following example:

> They're equally important in terms of . . . well . . . on one level, mine tends to be more important in terms of a regular wage: I've always been the main bread-winner. But, certainly in the sense of career, they're both equally important. In fact, I'd say that probably his is more important because that's all he can do, music, whereas I can transfer my skills to just about anything, just about any kind of business sector. (Female ICT business manager married to musician)

We found cases where the woman was the sole breadwinner, but this was seen as temporary – a reflection of complementary careers where the partners had found that they could effectively alternate as breadwinner and, in one case, homemaker. In one case, there were no children and the male partner was taking time out to 'do up' a property that they had invested in while his scientist wife maintained the breadwinner role. In another, the husband of a senior public sector manager was made redundant while she was expecting their first child so had taken on primary parenting responsibilities. At the time of the most recent interview, he had returned to work while she took maternity leave with a second pregnancy, on a temporary basis, but the plan is that he will revert to the homemaker role when she returns to work 'because it works well'. It was, however, clearly regarded by the (female) respondent as a negotiable balance rather than a long-term division of labour.

HOW IMPORTANT ARE GENDERED VALUES?

As some of the quotes cited above show, women's and men's decisions about employment and career were facilitated and constrained by the contexts within which they were posed. How far did long-term values concerning career development, job satisfaction, high financial reward, personal growth and family development affect choices in career decision-making? We asked survey respondents about the importance to them of these, on a scale of 1 (meaning 'unimportant') to 5 (meaning 'very important'), and again the order of importance was remarkably similar for women and men, but there were two interesting differences. Men were significantly more likely to consider high financial reward as very important, and women were significantly more likely to put a high value on doing socially useful work. Both of these variables, of course, relate to the women's significantly greater propensity to be employed in the public sector: but are they cause or effect? The findings so far are almost eerily reminiscent of findings from an earlier sample of 1960 graduates in the way they reveal women's lesser concern with 'extrinsic' rewards and greater concern with social values – 'human contact and being able to help people' (Fogarty et al. 1971: 231). They also illustrate well-established socio-psychological findings about differences between women's and men's propensity to 'generativity' – concern with creativity and responsibility in both the public and private spheres (Erikson 1964; Stewart and Vandewater 1998) and socialised tendency to be 'other-directed' (Gilligan 1982). Related to this we found evidence that greater gender awareness on the part of women coexisted with similar career-centred gender identities when we asked respondents about the relative importance of various aspects of their identity 'in terms of how you feel about yourself, as a person': social class, educational level, job or employment plans, family relationships/being a parent, ethnicity and gender. Gender was a significantly more important component of identity for women than men, family relationships/being a parent were slightly more often very important for the women, but the responses on the other dimensions – including job or employment plans – were similar for both gender groups.

The somewhat unexpected finding from the questions about job characteristics and long-term values, though, was the proportion (6 per cent) of survey respondents who took the opportunity of selecting the 'Other: PLEASE SPECIFY' category in both the questions discussed above to note either that one of the characteristics provided by their current job, or one of the long-term values that were important to them, was 'work–life balance'. It also almost certainly reflects the stage which these graduates had reached in their careers and the growing realisation that graduate jobs tend to be occupations that spill over from work time into non-work time, and make significant demands on their incumbents that may not be compatible with other responsibilities and 'own life' activities. Analysing the seven years on qualitative interview findings, we found respondents in high-flying jobs citing that their current workloads were not sustainable and would not be compatible with the lives they envisaged leading in the future (Purcell and Elias 2004). Analysing the 1995 graduates' qualitative interviews 10 years on, when several more of those we spoke to earlier had become parents, we found this anticipation had proved accurate.

GRADUATE CAREERS 10 YEARS ON, 2005

Ten years after graduation, the 1995 cohort being studied were mainly in their early 30s, mainly living with a partner, and at an age when major life plans about career and family development are on their agenda. They have reached adulthood in a socio-political context within which equal opportunities in education and employment are taken for granted – but uneasily, within a highly gendered culture – and in which distinct differences between male and female career profiles remain evident and, as we have seen, a gender pay gap persists.

Most of the 'high flyers' identified in the seven years on interview sample were still in employment 10 years on. All the women interviewed had either had their first child, were expecting their first child or stated that having children was something they envisaged doing in the future, although a few women saw it as a possibility rather than something they definitely aspired to do. Several of the men had become fathers and only one male respondent stated that parenthood was definitely not something on the agenda for himself or his wife. Several of the women who had not yet had their first child expressed concern about research findings and related media concern that women who postpone childbearing beyond the age of 35 risk difficulty in conceiving children and infertility.

THE IMPACT OF PARENTHOOD IN DUAL-CAREER PARTNERSHIPS

Dual-career partnerships are not, of course, a new phenomenon, but previous research has invariably revealed that female partners have made significantly more accommodations to their career development than males as the family life cycle proceeded (Hochschild 1997; Herz 1986; Moen 2003; Rapoport and Rapoport 1978). Women in previous generations very often adapted to their partner's careers by developing flexible, secondary careers that were characterised by adaptability and horizontal rather than vertical career progression, resulting in women's 'asynchronous' career development to cope with life-stage transitions (Sekaran and Hall 1989), essentially reflecting 'trade offs' to complement the more 'conventionally synchronised' linear career of the breadwinner (Bonney and Love 1991; Bruegel 1996). Previous research on dual-career households has unanimously indicated that women in such partnerships took on the primary childcare and homemaker roles except in a very small minority of cases. 'Career women' routinely appear to have made career concessions to accommodate these responsibilities (Karambaya and Reilly 1992), and male partners' careers have traditionally taken priority over those of the female partners (Green and Canny 2003; Valcour and Tolbert 2003). It might be expected that the women in this generation of young adults, who have grown up in a context where equal opportunities are enshrined in legislation and they have been encouraged (rather successfully!) to compete on equal terms with their male peers, and that they would be resistant to reverting to a more gendered division of household labour.

As Moen and Sweet (2003) have pointed out, in two-parent households, parenthood (as well as being a relationship) is a watershed challenge to partnerships, replacing two jobs – his and hers – with an inescapable third set of responsibilities which, in effect, constitute a third job (culturally assumed to be allocated primarily to the mother). Moen (2003) has discussed how the challenge presented is concerned with the management of time, and, in analysing data from dual-earner couples in the USA, presents a strong case for a rethinking of working hours and responsibilities that allow for greater flexibility in household divisions of labour. The American study identified a range of different work–life balance arrangements and divisions of labour among the couples sampled, and we found similar diversity among the 1995 young graduate parents. At both seven and 10 years after graduation, we interviewed graduates who had become parents, including full-time homemakers, parents of both sexes who had reduced their working hours, mothers who had become self-employed and mothers who had remained in full-time employment. We also interviewed women who were ambivalent about becoming mothers, although none had ruled it out as a possible option.

As Moen and her contributors (Moen 2003) discuss in detail, managing dual-career households is essentially about managing time and timing: of family formation, making decisions about paid working hours and patterns of work, day-to-day balancing of public and private responsibilities and scheduling of conflicting demands on time – but it is also about managing two careers. In terms of family formation, Cramer (1980) argued that the amount of time women spend in the labour force affects their propensity to have children and there is some evidence that delayed childbearing has contributed to the reduction in the birth rates of most developed countries, particularly among highly qualified women (Altucher and Williams 2003; Hewlett 2002; Rendall and Smallwood 2003). We found evidence that illustrates the complex way in which women's and couple's decisions to start a family were directly related to work patterns, and what they perceived as available or appropriate options for their subsequent household division of labour. Women told us about longer-term strategies and shorter-term tactics they were adopting to what they perceived to be satisfactory work–life balances, and these had implications for earnings in both the short and long term. For example, a very ambitious 29-year-old, earning between £40 000 and £49 000 per annum in 2002, was on maternity leave expecting her first baby at the time of the seven years on interview. She told us:

> At the point I am at now, if I wasn't having a baby, I may well have looked or be looking for another job in the next 6 months, purely because I've been promoted from within and they . . . never give you the same salary as they would if they recruited externally. I am dissatisfied with my salary at the moment, but I can't really say anything to the people I work with because I am on maternity leave and they've known I would be going on maternity leave for quite some time. It's going to be something I am going to have to address when I get back. I am away now during both the appraisal period and the pay review period. I don't want to be stuck with a standard 2½–3% just because I am not there to stand my corner. I am going to go back in and discuss the fact that I am not particularly happy with my salary. I have seen huge increases, but retail is quite well paid and I know if I move to another company I could probably get about a £15 000 pay rise. (Female business studies graduate, manager for multinational retail company)

We interviewed several women who had 'put their careers on the back burner' to concentrate on motherhood and who expressed their ambivalence and their perception of an interrupted rather than discontinuous career graphically.

> I'd kept my options open initially. When I'd had the babies [twins] I wasn't at all sure . . . I'd worked very hard at [my company] and . . . I realised I couldn't invest that amount of attention and energy to work in the short term, while my babies needed me. I was working on a really interesting project at the [European] Commission, representing [the company I worked for] and I really loved it, it was just the kind of work I wanted to do and yes, I guess the intellectual stimulus, the debates we had in the meetings . . . it was stretching me and I enjoyed it. But I think that just because I've stopped doesn't mean I won't be able to start again. I have that confidence, I feel I might have to start off a bit lower down the rungs and work my way up, but that doesn't worry me . . . (Female homemaker, formerly product manager, international finance company)

The significance of options available and the context within which choices were made – the reflexiveness of work–life decisions – was also apparent. Another graduate who had taken the decision to exit employment while her children were very young began by explaining that although she had loved her job as a teacher, she had felt that it was important to prioritise her family – but in the course of the interview, it became clear that her decision had been influenced by her negative experience of the response to her pregnancy at work, and illustrates the reflexive relationship between work and household considerations in making work–life balance decisions.

> At the second school I'd been at, the one I left after having a baby, I felt totally and utterly unvalued by my employer. [The Head] was very autocratic . . . [whereas] at my first school the principal was so supportive; he was just the other end of the spectrum from her. I think now, well, if I was at my first school and I'd had my son, would I have been tempted to go back part-time there? Well possibly I would've done, because I know they are supportive of families – whereas this Head, she didn't seem to appreciate people's family commitment and concerns. (Female primary school teacher, married to GP)

All of the women cited above made it clear that they expected to return to employment within a few years, although only the teacher was clear that she would return to the same career, both others making reference to the desire to move to more socially useful, generative work (as discussed above) as well as less 'greedy' occupations (Coser 1974).

All of the men were in full-time employment, although we found several examples of men who had modified their career aspirations or adapted their working hours to accommodate their partner's career or to share childcare; for example, the respondent who told us:

> I work flexibly . . . for example, if I work nine till twelve or nine till one then I'm willing to go back in at four o'clock in the afternoon and work in till the evening then that's quite a popular option and it means I can do some childcare in the afternoon . . . Both of us would put the children quite high up the agenda and if it means that our careers suffer a little bit then so be it, family comes first I would say. (Male medical laboratory scientific officer, married to part-time primary school teacher)

Could reported household divisions be read as an indication of the relative importance of the partners' careers? We interviewed both men and women who regarded themselves as part of a joint household career enterprise, but where one partner's career (normally that of the male partner) was regarded as more important – normally because of greater earning power.

> I'm not thinking of going back to work at least until [my child] goes to school, so that's a good four or five years and then if we have more children that's going to be a few years after that. So all that time his career is going to be the most important one and I guess mine is on the back burner at the moment. I don't really know about the future. I can't imagine me going back into something that was earning the money that I was earning when I was working at [ICT company] . . . it's more likely going to be back into the kind of social services side of things, which is part time and not as well paid as the commercial side of things. (Female full-time homemaker, formerly sales and marketing director, married to accountant)

However, the majority of the high-flying female graduates interviewed for the 10 years on investigation so far have continued in employment and aspire to continue their career development, as is discussed below. A substantial minority earned as much as, or more than, their partners, and this included some who had become mothers. It is important to note that all of those who were successfully balancing motherhood and employment were invariably doing so in contexts where they (normally) or their partners had been able to modify their work patterns in the jobs they had held prior to childbirth, by negotiating a measure of flexibility with their employers: an option rarely available to previous generations. This appeared to be enabling some respondents who aspired to a relatively traditional linear career to accommodate parenthood with minimal career disruption in the short term – although it would, of course, contribute to the short-term widening of the gender pay gap in the cohort.

FAMILY-FRIENDLY EMPLOYMENT?

In this penultimate section, we explore the descriptions provided by successful female graduates who defined themselves as ambitious and intended to remain in continuous employment for the foreseeable future. In pursuit of an acceptable work–life balance, all interviewees who had recently had children had taken advantage of the right to return to work with reduced hours. Some had found their employers more receptive to this suggestion than others, and although it was clear from the accounts given that the role-balancing involved in maintaining demanding careers and parenthood is never easy, some organisations have made the prospects for women who aspire to break through 'the glass ceiling' less daunting than others. One manager described how her employer had agreed to a change from a 35- to a 32-hour contract and work a four-day week as opposed to a five-day week.

> *If anything, I think . . . they've valued me more since I've gone back, or it feels like that, with pay increases and this promotion – than when I was there doing a full-time job. I get the feeling that they value me. There's quite a good amount of flexibility and understanding.*

I Was that something you knew about the organisation before you had your son and before you went on maternity leave?

> *Yes I knew there would be the ability to have flexibility but I didn't realise they were quite so accommodating. I put that down to my line manager, he's very good and he's a family man himself and understands the commitments. I know that when I spoke to you* [last time] *I was going on maternity leave and I was going to see how things went, there was the intention to go back to work, but I've actually become more focused on what I want and the career is what I want. They're saying I have the talent to get to a senior management role . . . I am expecting my second* [child and] *if I have to work harder when I get back to get there, then that's fine. I don't want to be taken off the radar because I'm going back on maternity leave.* (Female pensions manager, manufacturing)

Another manager in financial services was enthusiastic about the way in which her employer had facilitated her employment continuity and enabled her to modify her work patterns to accommodate motherhood. Her account nevertheless hints at an element of frustration in the difficulties of making relatively demanding and responsible part-time employment work:

[My employer is] really flexible on these kinds of things, I think I probably had about 2 or 3 weeks just doing 2 days and then went to 3 days. They really have a good policy for maternity returners to work flexibly. I have times when I do need to bring work home, but things go on without you on the days that you're not there. In the majority of cases you work round it, but sometimes things . . . you don't get involved in things you should have been involved in. So I guess overall you have to make it work . . . There are times I've had to be flexible in terms of doing a different day off in the week just to try and get meetings arranged and that kind of thing, but it's not been to the point that it really, really bothers . . . and in terms of how they've probably viewed me, I got one of the biggest projects the department gets in the year to manage when I went back, so there's never been a question of give them all the duff stuff because you're only in three days a week! It's very much project-based, you only do as many projects as you can do in your three days . . . things maybe stand still a bit, but then I . . . well, I have been annoyed at that I suppose at times, but then you balance that with 'I do want the work/life balance' . . . My husband's probably listening in at the background thinking, 'That's not what you said half an hour ago!' (Female reward manager, finance)

For other women, self-employment had provided a solution to the difficulties of continuing to operate at a high level in industry or commerce. The director and joint owner of a growing public relations company had been able to negotiate with her business partner to work four days a week on her return from maternity leave and was enthusiastic about the quality of life that being self-employed afforded, in terms of flexibility and not having to report to anyone, and being her own boss. Emphasising the significance of partnership, her flexibility was further enhanced by her husband's occupation, in the police force, which meant that his shift-working frequently allowed him to be responsible for childcare during 'office hours'.

However, it is worth considering the accounts of two of the highest paid and most successful women interviewed in the course of the 10 years on investigation, who provide alternative perspectives on the gap between equal opportunities policy and practice. The first of these worked for one of the 'big four' financial consultancies as a senior manager. In response to the question 'Would it be possible to do your job on a part time basis?', she said:

Impossible because . . . well . . . yes, I believe it would be impossible [respondent's emphasis]. We do have a female senior manager who is actually on maternity leave at the moment with her second baby. After the first one, she came back in January after maternity leave and has now gone off on the second. She worked for us about nine months between the two pregnancies on a part-time basis – she worked full days, but did 8–4, because 8–4 and 9–5 on paper appears to be the same job, but she was quite strict on her 8–4 where there's huge flexibility on our 9–5. She probably felt it worked, but the rest of the team didn't. It meant that she had to be local as well [that is, she couldn't be away from the office for extended periods].

I   She wasn't actually part time, was she? In theory, that a full time job?
Well she worked 8–4, but we probably do another 4–5 hours a day on top of that, which is why I was saying it wasn't quite . . . In theory it was a full-time job: in reality, compared to other senior team members, it was part time hours.

The second example, which illustrates the issue from the perspective of such a 'part-time' worker is a woman who had just been promoted to a director-level post at an international retail company (in fact, the business studies graduate whose seven years on was cited on p. 40). At the age of 32, having had her first child at 30, she was expecting her second at the time of the 10 years on interview. Asked how satisfied she was with her current job, she was initially enthusiastic.

Umm, I'm pretty satisfied. I really enjoy my job. My challenge is my work–life balance, that's always very difficult. Part of me wishes that I wasn't quite as senior, because when I got this promotion, if I hadn't had a family I think I would have been ecstatic because it would have been – 'How far can I go?'
I am on a four-day week. I always say 'I will do everything I can, but . . . you have to give me time to plan it.' I cannot be spontaneous. Lots of my peers now don't have children and that, sometimes I find quite difficult because over the years I've put in a lot of hours and worked very late and lots of the guys in my team work very long hours, but I have to leave by 5:45 every night at the latest, *so I do sometimes feel I am leaving them in the lurch* . . . [researchers' emphasis] I know when I've worked very late at their kind of level, anybody who gets to leave before you, you get a bit kind of miffed! But I wouldn't have got promoted if I hadn't been satisfying the requirements of the role. This week, for example, I have to get one late night in, so I have to get my husband one night a week to give me an opportunity [*sic*] to work late and then I will work until about eight o'clock at night just to make up for all the other bits, and I work on a Sunday night for a couple of hours and I usually do a couple of hours on a Friday night, just picking up emails and responding to the team . . . I get weeks when I think I'm keeping ahead and other weeks where I feel like I'm drowning . . . my only thing is *a more personal aspect* [researchers' emphasis] because I think . . . I don't know how I am going to be able to do this with two children. My husband works away a lot as well and his job is doing really well and he travels quite a lot. So a lot of the time I am doing that on my own.

This female manager provides an example of the pattern described by Wajcman (1998) of a woman in a demanding job with a partner in an equally demanding job, working largely alongside male peers who tend to be supported by non-working or part-time working partners who obviate their need for family-friendly hours of work. Other researchers have drawn attention to the relatively longer hours and inflexibility of management work compared to professional work (Moen and Sweet 2003) and it is apparent from our findings that the pressures on successful women pursuing traditional organisationally bounded careers are similar to those of earlier generations (Kanter 1977; Marshall 1994) and not easily compatible with responsible parenting.

CONCLUSIONS

Young women currently developing careers in management and the professions have grown up in an environment where they were encouraged to take for granted equal opportunities in education and employment. It is disconcerting that they do not appear, even in their early career development, to have achieved equal earnings and that the gender pay gap among graduates increases as graduate careers develop. The survey data enabled us to identify some elements of the explanation for this – gendered skill development, differences in the sectors where men and women work, the occupations that they adopt, the work contexts where they were employed, the average hours that they worked and some interesting attitudinal differences. The interview data throw further light on why women find some work contexts less attractive, and employment in them less sustainable than in others – and why their working hours can be more restricted than men's, especially once they embark upon family formation. They also illustrate the ambivalence experienced by women in the choices they make, and the extent to which expediency and longer-term strategy underlie choices, which most often reflect a complex balance of preference and constraint.

In the interviews with male graduates and the accounts provided by women of their partnerships, we find that, on the whole, most aspired to be parents and these highly qualified young adults largely continue to accept that women will be the primary parents and men more often take primary responsibility for earning – but we also find that neither regard partnership and parenthood as an alternative career for women, but rather as relationships with implications for managing their careers. Many of the young graduate males were also concerned to promote and take advantage of work–life balance employment policies. Most took it for granted, as the graduate women themselves did, that careers and employment played, and would continue to play, a significant role in women's identities and would require to be taken account of in their own career decision-making.

The implications of these findings are that, in the medium term at least, there is unlikely to be a dramatic change in gender divisions of labour in the private or public sphere, or in gender expectations or aspirations, that are likely to lead to greater achievement of equal outcomes. Indeed, for this graduate cohort at least, it might be expected that the graduate earnings gap will continue to grow over the next few years as more of the female graduates have children and make career adjustments to facilitate this. However, the positive findings are that for the majority of them, their skills, knowledge and career development are important dimensions of their identities and it is possible for those who aspire to it, to continue in employment and to negotiate working conditions that make this feasible. We found examples of good practice: high-quality part-time work, with part-time workers valued and promoted and provided with opportunities for career development, in the same sectors where employees in other organisations had met with obstacles more related to company culture than commercial imperatives. In the latter cases, the greatest obstacles to women's ability to modify their working patterns at the early stages of their children's lives were not the formal but the informal pressures generated by custom and practice in particular organisational cultures. As more women develop successful careers prior to family formation and organisations make it possible for women to develop careers via 'non-traditional' working patterns, it might be assumed that the slow progress that we have observed towards greater accessing of equal opportunities and the even slower progress towards greater male responsibility for the work associated with parenting might continue to proceed. If the women who have not yet had children continue to postpone doing so, or reject parenthood, the social implications may precipitate policy-makers into more creative attempts to persuade employers to improve the effectiveness of their work–life balance provision.

NOTES

1. See, for example, Walby and Olsen (2003), Blundell et al. (2000), Harkness (1996) and Sorensen (1989).
2. For further details of the research methodology, response rates and survey data weighting, see Elias et al. (1999).
3. This final interview programme was funded by the UK Higher Education European Social Fund Programme. See Purcell et al. (2006).
4. For this and all subsequent analyses, our data are restricted to those who stated that they were in full-time employment in 2002–03 and who were aged less than 30 years at the time they graduated in 1995. The exclusion of those aged over 30 years at the time of

graduation was undertaken because of the lack of information in the survey about work experience prior to graduation.
5. Sample attrition is a major problem with longitudinal surveys and can lead to significant bias in the characteristics of respondents. We conducted tests to determine whether or not the respondents at the second survey (2002–03) are systematically different from those who responded at the first survey (1998–99). We found little evidence of any systematic differences.
6. For example, graduates working in inner London gained a 25 per cent premium on their earnings, reflecting the higher wages paid by inner London employers to take account of higher living costs, so if male graduates had a greater propensity to obtain inner London employment, this could be a factor in the gender pay gap. However, there is little gender difference in regional dispersion, so location of employment and the pay differential associated with it is not, therefore, a factor underlying the gender difference in graduate earnings.
7. Variations in weekly hours are shown for those in full-time employment only.
8. I = Interviewer, R = Respondent.
9. This model has the logarithm of annual gross earnings as the dependent variable, plus all of the factors included as shown in Appendix Table A1.1.

REFERENCES

Altucher, C. and L. Williams (2003), 'Family clocks: timing parenthood', in P.H. Moen (ed.), *It's About Time*, Ithaca, NY: Cornell University Press.

Blundell, R., L. Dearden, A. Goodman and H. Reed (2000), 'The returns to higher education in Britain: evidence from a British cohort', *The Economic Journal*, **110**, 82–99.

Bonney, N. and J. Love (1991), 'Gender and migration: the wife's sacrifice', *Sociological Review*, **39**, 335–48.

Bruegel, I. (1996), 'The trailing wife: a declining breed? Careers, geographical mobility and household conflict in Britain 1970–89', in R. Crompton, D. Gallie and K. Purcell (eds), *Changing Forms of Employment*, London: Routledge.

Cockburn, C. (1991), *In the Way of Women: Men's Resistance to Sex Equality in Organisations*, Basingstoke: Macmillan.

Coser, L.M. (1974), *Greedy Institutions*, New York: Free Press.

Cramer, J. (1980), 'Fertility and female employment: problems of causal direction', *American Sociological Review*, **45**, 167–90.

Crompton, R. and C. Lyonette (2005), 'The new gender essentialism – domestic and family "choices" and their relation to attitudes', *British Journal of Sociology*, **56**(4), 601–20.

Crompton, R. and K. Sanderson (1986), 'Credentials and careers: some implications of the increase in professional qualifications amongst women', *Sociology*, **20**(1), 25–43.

Department for Education and Employment (DfEE) (1998), *Higher Education in the 21st Century*, Sheffield: Department of Education and Employment.

Department for Education and Skills (DfES) (2002), *Education and Training Statistics for the UK*, Sheffield: Department for Education and Skills.

Elias, P. and K. Purcell (1988), 'Women and paid work: prospects for equality', in A. Hunt (ed.), *Women and Paid Work*, Basingstoke: Macmillan.

Elias, P., K. Purcell, A. McKnight, C. Simm and J. Pitcher (1999), *Moving On: Graduate Careers Three Years after Graduation*, Manchester: HECSU.

Erikson, E.H. (1964), *Insight and Responsibility*, New York: Norton.

European Commission (2004), *Facing the Challenge: The Lisbon Strategy for Growth and Employment*, report from the High Level Group chaired by Wim Kok, November.

Fogarty, M., R. Rapoport and R.N. Rapoport (1971), *Sex, Career and Family*, London: George Allen and Unwin.

Gilligan, C. (1982), *In a Different Voice*, Cambridge, MA: Harvard University Press.

Ginn, J., S. Arber, J. Brannen, A. Dale, S. Dex, P. Elias, P. Moss, J. Pahl, C. Roberts and J. Rubery (1996), 'Feminist fallacies: a reply to Hakim on women's employment', *British Journal of Sociology*, **47**(1), 167–74.

Green, A.E. and A. Canny (2003), *Geographical Mobility: Family Impacts*, Bristol: Policy Press.

Hakim, C. (2000), *Work–Lifestyle Choices in the 21st Century*, Oxford: Oxford University Press.

Hakim, C. (2004), *Key Issues in Women's Work*, London: GlassHouse Press.

Harkness, S. (1996), 'The gender earnings gap: evidence from the UK', *Fiscal Studies*, **17**(2): 1–36.

Herz, R. (1986), *More Equal than Others: Women and Men in Dual-career Marriages*, Berkeley and Los Angeles, CA: University of California Press.

Hewlett, S.A. (2002), *Creating a Life: Professional Women and the Quest for Children*, New York: Hyperion.

Hochschild, A. (1997), *The Time Bind: When Work Becomes Home and Home Becomes Work*, New York: Metropolitan Books.

Kanter, R. (1977), *Men and Women of the Corporation*, New York: Basic Books.

Karambaya, R. and A. Reilly (1992), 'Dual career couples. Attitudes and activity in restructuring work for family', *Journal of Organisational Behaviour*, **13**(6), 585–601.

Leadbetter, F. (1999), *Living on Thin Air: The New Economy*, London: Viking.

Marshall, J. (1994), 'Why women leave management jobs', in M. Tanton (ed.), *Women in Management: A Developing Presence*, London: Routledge.

Martin, J. and C. Roberts (1984), *Women and Employment: A Lifetime Perspective*, DE/OPCS, London: HMSO.

McRae, S. (2003), 'Constraints and choices in mothers' employment careers', *British Journal of Sociology*, **53**(3), 317–38.

Moen, P.H. (ed.) (2003), *It's About Time*, Ithaca, NY: Cornell University Press.

Moen, P. and S. Sweet (2003), 'Time clocks: work-hour strategies', in P. Moen (ed.), *It's About Time*, Ithaca, NY: Cornell University Press.

Organisation for Economic Co-operation and Development (OECD) (1996), *The Knowledge-based Economy*, Paris: Organisation for Economic Co-operation and Development.

Phillips, A. and B. Taylor (1980), 'Sex and skill: notes towards a feminist economics', *Feminist Review*, **6**, 78–88.

Purcell, K. and P. Elias (2004), 'Higher education and gendered career development', Research Paper No. 4, (Seven years on: graduates in the changing labour market), www.uwe.ac.uk/bbs/research/esru/rp4.pdf (accessed 15 January 2008).

Purcell, K., P. Elias and N. Wilton (2006), *Looking Through the Glass Ceiling: A Detailed Investigation of the Factors that Contribute to Gendered Career Inequalities*, Liverpool: UK Higher Education European Social Fund, www.warwick.ac.uk/go/glmf (accessed 15 January 2008).

Rapoport, R. and R.N. Rapoport (1978), *Dual Career Families re-examined*, London: Martin Robertson.

Rendall, M. and S. Smallwood (2003), 'An examination of the relationship between the attainment of higher educational qualifications and later entry to motherhood and how these are associated with the pace of subsequent childbearing', *Population Trends*, **111**, 18–26.

Sekaran, U. and D. Hall (1989), 'Asynchronism in dual-career and family linkages', in M. Arthur, D. Hall and B. Lawrence (eds), *Handbook of Career Theory*, Cambridge: Cambridge University Press.

Sorensen, E. (1989), 'Measuring the pay disparity between typically female occupations and other jobs: a bivariate selectivity approach', *Industrial and Labor Relations Review*, July, 624–39.

Stewart, A. and E. Vandewater (1998), 'The course of generativity', in D.P. McAdams and E. de St Aubin (eds), *Generativity and Adult Development: How and Why We Care for the Next Generation*, Washington, DC: American Psychological Association.

Valcour, M.P. and P.S. Tolbert (2003), 'Gender, family and career in the era of the boundaryless career', *Journal of Human Resource Management*, **14**(5), 768–87.

Wajcman, J. (1998), *Managing Like a Man*, Cambridge: Polity Press.

Walby, S. and W. Olsen (2003), 'The gendered pay gap and women's work histories', paper presented to the Conference of the British Household Panel study, Institute for Social and Economic Research, University of Essex, July.

Wilson, E. (1998), 'Gendered career paths', *Personnel Review*, **27**(5), 396–411.

APPENDIX

Table 1A.1   *Factors associated with the annual earnings of 1995 graduates in full-time employment seven years after graduation*

	Coeff.	Std. Error	Sig.	Mean	
				Males	Females
Hours per week (exc. breaks but inc. o/t, unpaid)	0.009	0.000	0.000	44.2	42.3
Contractual basis of current job				(%)	
Permanent/open-ended	ref.			84.8	82.1
Fixed term contract	0.020	0.005	0.000	8.7	9.9
Probationary	−0.033	0.011	0.002	1.1	1.6
Self-employed	0.080	0.008	0.000	3.9	3.8
Temp (agency)	0.140	0.015	0.000	0.4	1.0
Other temporary or casual	−0.109	0.024	0.000	0.0	0.5
Other (not permanent)	−0.097	0.020	0.000	0.3	0.5
Degree was required to obtain current job	0.157	0.003	0.000	64.3	69.8
Sector of current job					
Agriculture, mining	−0.109	0.012	0.000	1.6	1.1
Manufacturing	−0.121	0.006	0.000	12.2	6.9
Electricity, gas, water	−0.084	0.011	0.000	2.3	0.9
Construction	−0.168	0.008	0.000	8.9	1.4
Distribution	−0.108	0.007	0.000	5.4	4.2
Transport	−0.142	0.011	0.000	2.4	0.9
Information and communications	0.005	0.005	0.384	14.3	9.6
Banking, finance and insurance	ref.			11.5	7.0
Business services	−0.027	0.006	0.000	11.2	12.3
Education	−0.135	0.007	0.000	9.1	24.8
Other public services	−0.141	0.007	0.000	12.6	22.8
Other	−0.151	0.007	0.000	7.2	6.5
Private sector	ref.			70.2	46.8
Public sector	−0.096	0.005	0.000	24.4	45.6
Not for profit sector	−0.158	0.006	0.000	4.4	6.7
In my workplace, my type of work is done					
Exclusively by men	ref.			20.2	6.3
Mainly by men	0.022	0.004	0.000	34.2	15.4
By equal mixture of men and women	−0.049	0.004	0.000	37.5	40.3
Mainly by women	−0.109	0.005	0.000	6.3	29.1
Exclusively by women	−0.126	0.008	0.000	0.5	8.0

Table 1A.1 (continued)

	Coeff.	Std. Error	Sig.	Mean	
				Males	Females
After first started this job, to learn to do it reasonably well took				(%)	
< 1 week	−0.030	0.006	0.000	6.1	3.4
1 week to 1 month	−0.022	0.004	0.000	11.4	11.5
1–3 months	−0.055	0.003	0.000	24.3	24.7
Over 3 months	ref.			58.2	60.4
Use of computers in current job					
Do not use computers in job	ref.			1.9	3.4
Routine use of computers in job	0.199	0.008	0.000	51.7	70.0
Complex use of computers in job	0.166	0.008	0.000	28.8	21.1
Advanced use of computers in job	0.257	0.009	0.000	16.9	5.1
No employed by the organisation works for					
< 10 employees	ref.			5.1	5.4
10–24 employees	0.142	0.008	0.000	5.7	6.8
25–49 employees	0.145	0.008	0.000	5.7	8.7
50–199 employees	0.151	0.007	0.000	15.2	15.2
200–499 employees	0.175	0.008	0.000	9.9	8.5
500–999 employees	0.171	0.008	0.000	6.3	8.3
1000+ employees	0.233	0.007	0.000	51.4	46.1
SOC(HE) classification of current job					
Traditional graduate job	0.152	0.005	0.000	20.0	26.0
Modern graduate job	0.102	0.005	0.000	21.1	21.1
New graduate job	0.201	0.005	0.000	20.0	18.5
Niche graduate job	0.136	0.005	0.000	23.2	20.5
Nongraduate job	ref.			11.5	10.8
Not classified	0.088	0.008	0.000	4.1	3.2
Currently employed in					
Inner London	0.252	0.004	0.000	17.2	16.8
Outer London	0.184	0.005	0.000	7.0	5.8
South East	0.089	0.004	0.000	14.8	13.1
Elsewhere	ref.				
Male	0.075	0.003	0.000		
				(not %)	
Age	0.113	0.013	0.000	29.5	29.1
Age squared	−0.002	0.000	0.000	871.8	852.5
				(%)	
Disability	−0.089	0.010	0.000	1.7	1.4

Table 1A.1   (continued)

	Coeff.	Std. Error	Sig.	Mean Males	Females
Other work limiting factor	−0.105	0.008	0.000	2.1	2.7
Lives with partner and children	0.031	0.004	0.000	14.0	7.9
Lives with parents	−0.200	0.004	0.000	11.4	7.7
Shared accommodation	−0.100	0.004	0.000	12.1	9.4
Lives alone	ref.			62.5	75.0
Has children age 6–11	0.042	0.010	0.000	2.4	1.2
Fee paying school	0.039	0.004	0.000	16.2	14.5
Class of degree obtained in 1995					
First class degree	ref.			10.6	8.0
Upper second	−0.030	0.003	0.000	43.2	51.0
Lower second	−0.050	0.004	0.000	29.6	29.3
Third	−0.115	0.007	0.000	4.5	2.4
Subject area of 1995 degree					
Arts	−0.181	0.009	0.000	1.7	3.2
Humanities	−0.122	0.006	0.000	7.8	11.8
Languages	−0.108	0.008	0.000	1.4	5.7
Law	0.029	0.008	0.000	3.4	4.1
Social sciences	−0.037	0.005	0.000	12.9	16.6
Maths and computing	0.051	0.006	0.000	10.1	4.5
Natural sciences	−0.093	0.005	0.000	12.8	11.1
Medicine and related	0.057	0.007	0.000	3.9	9.7
Engineering	−0.018	0.006	0.002	16.8	2.3
Business studies	ref.			14.0	11.3
Education	−0.018	0.007	0.008	2.7	10.5
Other vocational	−0.070	0.006	0.000	9.7	4.6
Interdisciplinary	−0.105	0.008	0.000	2.7	4.5
Entry qualifications for 1995 degree					
24+ UCAS points	0.003	0.004	0.451	17.6	20.7
16–23 UCAS points	ref.			18.7	25.1
Less than 16 UCAS points	−0.052	0.004	0.000	17.8	18.3
Scottish or Irish Highers	−0.002	0.005	0.753	8.8	8.7
Access qualifications	−0.208	0.014	0.000	1.0	0.6
Foundation course	0.039	0.014	0.005	0.8	1.0
HND/HNC	−0.026	0.005	0.000	10.6	4.0
GNVQ or equiv.	0.097	0.015	0.000	0.9	0.6
Int. baccalaureate	0.118	0.023	0.000	0.4	0.1
O levels	0.153	0.026	0.000	0.3	0.2
BTEC, OND, ONC	−0.064	0.008	0.000	2.9	2.4
First degree	−0.254	0.018	0.000	0.3	0.7

Table 1A.1   (continued)

	Coeff.	Std.	Sig.	Mean	
		Error		Males	Females
Postgrad qual.	−0.374	0.126	0.003	0.0	0.0
Other qual.	−0.117	0.009	0.000	2.0	1.7
Further education and training since 1995					
Short course(s)	−0.032	0.003	0.000	24.8	32.0
Undergraduate degree	0.018	0.008	0.019	3.2	2.2
Postgraduate cert. or dip.	−0.019	0.003	0.000	16.0	31.7
Professional qualification	0.055	0.003	0.000	22.7	23.5
Master's degree	−0.040	0.003	0.000	16.1	19.1
PhD programme	−0.127	0.006	0.000	5.8	5.6
Other	−0.020	0.005	0.000	6.9	10.4
None	ref.				
Moved between regions (pre-degree home and current employment)	0.014	0.003	0.000	51.9	48.4
Parental socio-economic class:					
Managerial and professional occupations	ref.			46.7	45.6
Intermediate occupations	−0.033	0.004	0.000	11.2	11.3
Small employers and own account workers	0.023	0.004	0.000	15.2	17.6
Lower supervisory and technical occupations	−0.016	0.006	0.004	6.0	4.6
Semi-routine and routine occupations	−0.027	0.004	0.000	11.4	9.7
Neither parent in paid employment	−0.089	0.009	0.000	1.9	1.8
Not determined	0.018	0.005	0.000	7.6	9.5
Constant	0.201				

Adjusted $R^2 = 0.502$
Weighted N = 59 956
Unweighted N = 3286

Notes:
All independent variables are represented by 0, 1 values, except for age, age squared and weekly hours worked which are continuous. With the exception of these variables, mean values of the variables are displayed as the percentage in each category coded to the value 1. The dependent variable is the natural logarithm of annual gross earnings. The coefficients associated with each variable can be regarded as the percentage change in earnings associated with each variable, relative to the reference variable in each set (denoted by 'ref.').

2. Changes in women's occupations and occupational mobility over 25 years

Shirley Dex, Kelly Ward and Heather Joshi

INTRODUCTION

The collection of employment histories in the Women and Employment Survey (WES) in 1980 started to break down the stereotypes still around in the 1970s about women's careers. The tendency had been to think that a woman's main role was as a mother, working at domestic tasks. Relatively few women were expected to have employment careers. The term 'career woman' was commonly used to describe the few, mainly thought to be single women, in professional occupations and viewed as freaks. What the WES helped to show was that the majority (90 per cent) of women were returning to employment after childbirth and many were attached to their occupations in a way that could be described as having occupational careers, although they were not always able to return to their original occupation after an employment break for childbirth. The WES employment histories also showed that women had a sizeable amount of downward occupational mobility across the break from work for childbirth and this was more likely, the longer they stayed out of work at this point, and if they returned to a part-time job. In the 25 years since the WES was collected and analysed much has changed in the UK labour market. It is time to take stock.

This chapter reviews the enormous changes in women's occupational status that occurred between 1980 and 2005. Cross-sectional data show the extent of this as there were far more women in top occupations in 2001 compared with 1980. The distribution of employed women through occupational categories in the 2001 Census compared with 1980 is much more like the distribution of employed men through occupation groups. By 2005, the position is likely to show even more equality. In this sense gender differences in occupational status have narrowed considerably over this 25 year period. What the WES allowed us to do, largely for the first time, was examine the moving picture behind these snapshot statistics. This turned out to be vital to gaining a better understanding of where problems can arise and for formulating more appropriate policy responses.

At the time the WES was collected in 1980, Britain had passed sex discrimination legislation (see Appendix Table 2A.1 for further details) in 1975, outlawing discrimination against women in employment on grounds of their sex or marital status. We had also introduced statutory maternity leave from 1975, offering those qualifying the right to return to work after childbirth to the same job and same employer, and offering some maternity pay. But clearly the eligibility conditions of having worked for six months with the same employer before pregnancy meant that many women were either ineligible or worked for employers who were not covered by the legislation. Relatively few of the women in the WES would have benefited from these new laws and entitlements by 1980.

In the past 25 years, further legislation has been passed to strengthen the sex discrimination legislation and extend women's rights. These include successive extensions of the maternity leave period, with a widening of its coverage to more and more women; successive increases in the paid maternity leave entitlement; the introduction of parental leave and paid paternity leave to allow fathers to have rights related to childbirth and parenting; and the Part-time Work Directive. This demanded employees working part-time be given the same rights as full-timers.

In this chapter, we set out to examine how women's occupational status and mobility have changed over the years since 1980. Women's and men's occupational mobility over their lifetime are important elements of their labour market position and rewards. It contributes to the determinants of how equal or unequal men and women are in the labour market. Women and men can be unequal by entering different occupations, or by entering the same occupations but moving up, down or staying the same at different rates. Of course they can also be unequal in their pay by being paid directly at different rates for doing the same job. This chapter is mainly concerned with vertical occupational mobility, which tracks occupations over time, using a hierarchy of occupations. The WES was useful in documenting and quantifying the extent of women's downward occupational mobility over the first childbirth and across their whole lifetime up to 1980. However, it only covered women. Twenty-five years later, we are able to draw some comparisons between women's data from 1980 to take the story forward about how women's occupational mobility has been changing in the light of better rights and entitlements. In addition, we have the more recent data about men's occupational changes, but no earlier cohort data with which to compare it.

PLAN OF THIS CHAPTER

In the rest of this chapter we present a picture of change in women's occupations and occupational mobility between occupational categories since 1980 and compare this briefly with men's occupational mobility from a more recent cohort. To some extent illustrating the changes for women had to be pieced together from the various data sets that are available, whilst also manoeuvring carefully around the intervening changes to the occupational classifications and categories (Blackwell 2001). The version of this chapter presented here only goes part way to completing the picture, since it does not yet include data from the most recent birth cohorts and it does not consider within occupational career mobility or wage mobility over the life course.

A summary of the data sources used is presented in the next section followed by a discussion of how we intend to operationalise the measurement of vertical occupational mobility in this chapter. From there, we go on to present, first, cross-sectional occupation distributions to cover the period, showing the overall change in the picture of women's employment. Following this we compare the WES findings with other more recent data on women's occupational mobility, both at the point of childbirth, and up to age 42. The chapter documents changes in the timing of women's return to (paid) work after first childbirth and the extent of occupational change for women across their life course and across childbirth. The chapter will also document changes in the timing of women's return to employment, after first childbirth and the nature of the jobs to which they return. It also examines whether the likelihood of downward mobility has changed over time for women in different positions in the labour market.

EARLIER STUDIES

Occupational mobility has been studied in a number of social science disciplines including sociology, management studies and economics. Within each discipline, there are further distinctions in the approaches adopted and the focus of interest. In sociology, studies have examined the determinants of individuals' occupational attainment (for example, Blau and Duncan 1967), the extent of intergenerational social mobility (for example, Goldthorpe et al. 1987), careers and occupations as organisational or occupational careers, and occupational progression in particular professional occupations. Economists have tended to focus on hourly wage rates and the determinants of individuals' wage growth mobility, focusing sometimes on highly qualified groups of men and women graduates in order to have more closely matched population groups for the comparisons (see Dolton and Silles 2001). The labour market segmentation theories also considered occupational immobility with internal labour markets or organisational careers being offered to the workers in the primary segment where the best high paid jobs were located compared to high job mobility in the secondary segment where the worst and low-paid high turnover jobs without career prospects were located. While having a heyday in the 1970s such theories declined in visibility but are still being debated (see recent review article by Leontaridi 1998; Stewart and Swaffield 1999; Theodossiou 1995).

The literature covering occupational mobility is, therefore, substantial and far too wide-ranging to include a thorough review in this chapter. Both sociological and economic studies focused originally on men's occupational mobility. But increasingly papers have covered women's occupational mobility as well; for example sociological studies of social mobility (see, for example, Payne and Abbotts 1990), economists' analyses of wage growth (Booth and Francesconi 1999), and labour market segmentation theories (Sousa-Poza 2004).

Longitudinal data-sets, of which the WES was one, provided the opportunity to analyse occupational mobility. Moving up the occupational scale was shown to be linked to childlessness, and downward moves to taking up part-time jobs (Dex 1987; Elias and Main 1982; Joshi 1984; Joshi and Newell 1987; Martin and Roberts 1984; Stewart and Greenhalgh 1984). Jacobs (1999), using the SCELI data and the Cambridge scale analysed occupational mobility continuously over the lifetime of men and women, similar to Rosenfeld in the USA (1979). Jacobs showed that there is considerable occupational mobility over men's lifetime, as measured by the Cambridge scale. The other findings were broadly the same as the earlier studies where being a childless woman or a man as well as being highly qualified helped achieve upward occupational mobility, whereas being employed part-time did not. Gender segregation has also been shown to be associated with the lack of upward progress of women and this is also related to working part time for women (Jacobs 1999; Marshall et al. 1988). Men have gained advantages in occupational mobility over women by working in female-dominated occupations and, in at least one study, have the same chances of advantage, even when the occupation is male dominated (Heitmueller 2004).

DATA SOURCES

Starting with the position of women in 1980 from the Women and Employment Survey and 1981 Census, this chapter charts the change in occupations and occupational mobility of women by 2001. Several data sources are used to construct this account.

The Women and Employment Survey was a cross-sectional representative sample of all women aged 16–59 in Great Britain. As well as the main cross-sectional interview, it asked women about their past employment history since leaving school and this contained retrospective records for 5320 women of their occupation and fertility histories up to 1980. The National Child Development Study (NCDS), based on a census of babies born in a certain week of 1958 in Great Britain, contains information from up to six main interview waves up to 2000, plus retrospective histories of employment and fertility about the women's and men's occupations; 5732 women's records and 5617 men's records were available for analysis from the wave 6 data. It was possible to recode the occupation categories in these two data-sets to the same set of codes as the ones used in the 1980 Women and Employment Survey, described in more detail below.

The extent of occupational mobility will be examined using the 1980 WES data broken down into quasi cohorts as produced in Dex and Shaw (1986), and the 1958 birth cohort of women as far as its most recent contact at wave 6 (1999–2000).

The WES cohorts analysed in Dex and Shaw (1986) were aged 44–58 and 26–36, which in 1980 translates into years of birth of 1922–36 and 1943–53 a gap, on average, of 21 years. These can be compared with the 1958 cohort of women born on average nearly nine years later than the more recent of these WES cohorts.

OCCUPATIONAL CATEGORIES AND RECODING

The WES constructed its own set of 12 occupational categories for coding women's occupations (Box 2.1). At the time, the official Office of Population Censuses and Surveys (OPCS) Socio-Economic Group-based social class classification placed women's jobs into a rather small number of categories of occupations. The WES extended these to 12 in order to allow for an examination of more distinctions between women's jobs. Details of the contents of WES categories are presented in Appendix Box 2A.2.

The WES scheme was applied to the NCDS occupational codes to enable comparisons. As a check on the recoding, we compared the first ever occupation distributions of NCDS employed women and men with women aged approximately 22 in the WES data (born in 1958). We can only carry out this comparison in an approximate way using Martin and Roberts's (1984) table 10.13 (see Appendix Table 2A.1). There is much

---

BOX 2.1   WOMEN AND EMPLOYMENT SURVEY
           OCCUPATIONAL CODES

1.   Professional occupations
2.   Teachers
3.   Nursing, medical and social occupations
4.   Other intermediate non-manual occupations
5.   Clerical occupations
6.   Shop assistant and related sales occupations
7.   Skilled occupations
8.   Childcare occupations
9.   Semi-skilled factory work
10. Semi-skilled domestic work
11. Other semi-skilled occupations
12. Unskilled occupations

---

reassuring correspondence between these occupational distributions. However, it is possible that the recoding of NCDS occupations has classified slightly too many in the WES 'skilled' group and slightly too few in the 'semi-skilled factory' group.

VERTICAL OCCUPATIONAL MOBILITY

Clearly there is an approximate hierarchy in these WES occupation groups in Table 2.1. Dex (1987) examined the occupational profiles over women's lifetimes and ranked the occupations using the substitutability among some of these women's occupations. This led to grouping some of the lower levels of this list together since women clearly moved between shop assistant, semi-skilled domestic and other semi-skilled and child care occupations in a way that demonstrated they were substitute jobs for people with few if any qualifications or skills.

In this chapter, we adopt the Dex rankings which collapse the 12 categories into eight and rank them in a clear order. This is mainly because we wish to draw some comparisons with Dex's earlier WES analyses of occupational mobility. The ranking on which we measure vertical occupational mobility is then as follows:

1.   Professional
2.   Teaching

3.   Nursing
4.   Intermediate non-manual work
5.   Clerical
6.   Skilled
7.   Semi-skilled factory work
8.   All other semi-skilled, shop assistant, childcare and unskilled.

The unskilled category was combined with the other semi-skilled groups because of its small sample size. Note that one 'non-manual' group, sales, is ranked below two 'manual' groups, 'skilled' and 'semi-skilled factory work'. Joshi (1984) examined the hourly pay of each of these occupations and found, from the ranking of the 12 WES occupations, using hourly pay overlaps with Dex's eight groupings and their order with one exception. Ranking by hourly pay places childcare at the bottom, below other semi-skilled and unskilled categories. In this chapter, also due to its small sample size, childcare is combined with the other semi-skilled and unskilled jobs.

There is one other issue which arises in analysing vertical occupational mobility across cohorts. If occupational mobility occurs, and we know it does, one can get different impressions of individuals' occupational progress by comparing them at different ages. So controlling for the ages or life stages will be important to the analysis. Our comparisons of what happens to women across childbirth controls for life stage, but not for age. Similarly, our comparisons of most recent jobs occur for NCDS women at age 42 (the most recent interview). For the WES cohorts whose data stop in 1980, those born from 1922 to 36 have most recent job information in 1980 at ages 44 to 58, and for those born 1943–53 most recent jobs apply to them at ages 27 to 37. We need to consider these differences in drawing conclusions from our analyses. Where histories were truncated at younger ages of the woman or of the youngest child, they may in principle contain censored observations, that is, mothers who have not yet made any return to the job market, than those observed in their late forties. In practice these are very small differences.

OCCUPATIONAL DISTRIBUTIONS

An approximate comparison of the Census (1981) and General Household Survey (1980) distributions of employed women and the Census (2001) results for employed women and men in 2001 is displayed in Table 2.1. The large shift up the occupational hierarchy by women is evident in these figures. The proportion of managers among employed women more than

Table 2.1   Occupational distributions of the employed

Occupation categories	1981 Women 16–59 (Census) %	1980 Women* (GHS) %	1980 Men* (GHS) %	2001 Women 16–74 (England & Wales Census) %	2001 Men 16–74 (England & Wales Census) %
Managerial	5.3	4.0	13.0	11.1	18.5
Professional & associate professional	17.2	16.0	19.0	24.2	25.6
Administrative and secretarial	30.2	33.0	6.0	22.7	5.4
Skilled trades	2.7	3.0	26.0	2.4	19.5
Personal service	20.6	23.0	3.0	12.7	2.0
Sales and customer service	8.7	9.0	4.0	11.9	4.1
Process plant & machinery; elementary trades	6.3	11.0	25.0	15.0	24.9
Miscellaneous & others	4.7	1.0	3.0	—	—
Total	95.7[a]	100.0	100.0	100.0	100.0
Number	987 888	3354	8024	10 836 000	12 791 000

Note: [a] In this column a category of 'Inadequately described occupations=4.3%' has not been included in the table.

Source: Martin and Roberts (1984: 23; table 3.1).

doubled from between 4 and 5.3 per cent in 1980–81 to 11.1 per cent in 2001. While women's representation was below that of men in managerial jobs at both times, the gap had narrowed substantially by 2001. Employed women also had a much larger percentage in professional and associate professional jobs by 2001, increasing from 16–17 per cent in 1980–81 to 24.2 per cent in 2001, very close to the same percentage of men in such jobs in 2001 (25.6 per cent).

In the 1980 WES data, only a minority of women were classified as professional. One per cent of women in the 1981 Census were called professionals except that another 6 per cent were in teaching and 7 per cent in nursing or medical jobs which overlapped with the 'professional and associate professional' categories in the Census, making 14 per cent in total. The same figure across all professional and associate professional jobs for employed women in the NCDS at wave 6 was 19 per cent.

OCCUPATIONAL MOBILITY

A selection of ways of looking at occupational mobility are considered in this chapter by varying the origin and destination points that are compared. We follow Dex's earlier focus on the occupations either side of the first childbirth. But we also consider mobility over the whole of the recorded occupational histories. The examination of a variety of lifespans of occupational mobility here is largely because we have some data on men's occupational mobility in the NCDS which provides additional interest. However, it does not make sense to examine men's mobility across fatherhood since men do not usually change their jobs at this point in time. We examine first the childbirth span for women. In addition we examine the gaps out of employment mothers take around childbirth and the types of jobs they take on returning, both of which have also changed considerably in a way that is related to the occupational mobility that occurs at this life stage.

EITHER SIDE OF CHILDBIRTH

Dex's earlier analyses of women's occupational mobility across childbirth showed that there were large proportions of downward occupational mobility at this point in women's employment histories. However, the extent varied by the origin occupation, measured as the last job before childbirth. Women in professional and teaching occupations (as a combined group because of the small number of professionals) all had significantly lower likelihood of downward occupational mobility than those whose pre-birth occupations were lower down the occupational hierarchy. The group with the largest chance of downward mobility were those in intermediate non-manual occupations prior to childbirth. Joshi and Newell (1987) found a similar pattern among the mothers and daughters of the 1946 cohort and suggested that those whose pre-birth job was one of the intermediate office jobs, such as for the government or banks, would have 'firm'-specific skills that were less transferable to other employers than those with more portable professional credentials.

In Table 2.2 we present comparisons between 3 birth cohorts using the WES and the NCDS cohort of women who have been through childbirth by their pre-birth origin occupation. On the whole, downward mobility is

Table 2.2 *Women's last job before and first job after childbirth*

Occupational categories	Born 1922–36					Born 1943–53					Born 1958				
	%↑	Same	%↓	Total (%)	N	%↑	Same	%↓	Total (%)	N	%↑	Same	%↓	Total (%)	N
Professional	(100)	—	—	100	1	—	(80)	(20)	100	5	—	69	31	100	132
Teachers	—	(87)	(13)	100	39	—	83	19	100	40	3	84	13	100	169
Nursing, medical and social	6	53	41	100	51	2	72	26	100	57	1	77	22	100	366
Other intermediate non-manual	(6)	(31)	(63)	100	16	(8)	(48)	(42)	100	23	7	65	28	100	424
Clerical	6	49	45	100	377	5	49	46	100	288	8	56	36	100	1522
Skilled	16	36	48	100	106	9	50	41	100	76	14	43	43	100	517
Semi-skilled factory work	8	50	42	100	357	5	51	44	100	173	31	34	35	100	325
Other semi-skilled	26	61	13	100	302	30	58	12	100	176	28	59	13	100	860
Unskilled	(63)	(37)	—	100	27	33	(67)	—	100	6	44	56	—	100	100
Total	13.2	51.9	34.9	100	1276	10.5	54.7	34.8	100	844	14.0	57.5	28.5	100	4415

Sources: 1922–36 cohort from WES data in Dex and Shaw (1986) regrouped.
1943–53 cohort from WES data in Dex and Shaw (1986) regrouped.
1958 cohort based on our analysis from NCDS data.

less likely for those born in 1958 (28.5 per cent) compared to those born between 1943–53 (34.8 per cent) and 1922–36 (34.9 per cent). The figures for each cohort suggest that higher level occupations tend to have more stability across job transitions than occupations further down the hierarchy. Upward moves are more plentiful from the lower level occupations than they are from the higher ones although its extent is not usually as great as the extent of downward mobility.

Looking across these three cohorts at the top of the occupational hierarchy suggests that downward occupational mobility has declined over more recent cohorts at this life stage. For example, 19 per cent of teachers were downwardly mobile across childbirth when born in 1943–53 compared with 13 per cent of the 1958 cohort of mothers. Women who had pre-birth jobs in nursing, medical or social occupations experienced downward occupational mobility in 41 per cent of cases if born in 1922–36, 26 per cent if born in 1943–53 and 22 per cent if born in 1958. The same trends over time can be seen across these three cohorts for mothers whose pre-birth jobs were intermediate non-manual (although based on very small numbers in the WES cohorts), skilled and other semi-skilled occupations. There were also declines in downward occupational mobility visible for women with pre-birth jobs in clerical and semi-skilled factory jobs by the time of the 1958 birth cohort, although not necessarily between the two earlier WES quasi birth cohorts.

The changes in downward occupational mobility (Table 2.3) could arise in two ways; either by the proportions staying in the same occupation across childbirth increasing, or by upward occupational mobility increasing at this point. On the whole, the reductions of downward occupational mobility across childbirth in the experiences of the 1958 cohort were predominantly improvements in the 'no change' percentages for pre-birth nursing, medical and social, intermediate non-manual, clerical and other semi-skilled occupations. For teachers, skilled and semi-skilled factory, the improvement arose from increases in upward occupational mobility, even to the extent of causing a decline in the percentages of women who stayed in the same occupation across childbirth.

These results suggest that there has been considerable change occurring over successive birth cohorts in the extent of women's occupational mobility across childbirth. Some of the change is consistent with the increased availability of maternity leave, giving women entitlements to return to the same job and occupation after childbirth. Also in some cases employers have introduced conscious policies to retain women with family responsibilities, such as career break schemes, flexible working and job sharing, whose efficacy interacts with shorter breaks. The increased upward occupational mobility at this life stage for some groups of women is probably due to an expansion of labour market opportunities for women that they faced on returning to work after childbirth.

DURATIONS OF TIME OUT OF WORK FOR CHILDBIRTH

Over time the gap that women spend out of work giving birth to their first child has shortened considerably. This was evident in Martin and Roberts's (1984) analysis of WES women's work histories. Fourteen per cent of WES women who had given birth and returned to work did so within six months. This proportion was lowest at 9 per cent in those who gave birth earliest from 1945 to 1949, and progressively increased as the age groups advanced to reach 17 per cent among those who gave birth from 1975 to 1979. The highest educated women were those who returned to work fastest after childbirth, but the differences by level of qualification were quite small in the WES, ranging from 14 to 17 per cent returning within six months of the first birth.

The same trend of a declining gap from employment can be seen in successive birth cohorts of women (Figure 2.1). Of mothers born in 1946, 50

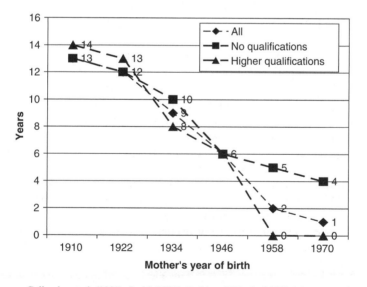

Sources: Callender et al. (1997); Joshi (1985); Joshi and Hinde (1993); Macran et al. (1996); Martin and Roberts (1984).

Figure 2.1   Years between first birth and next job at the median

per cent of them had returned to work when their first child was 6 years old. Of mothers born in 1958, 50 per cent had returned by two years after the birth and of those born in 1970, 50 per cent had returned by one year after the birth. These figures varied in each cohort according to the level of qualification mothers held, especially since the 1958 cohort of mothers; more highly qualified mothers have made faster returns than those with lower levels of qualifications or no qualifications (Callender et al.1997; Joshi 1985; Joshi and Hinde 1993; Macran et al. 1996; Martin and Roberts 1984).

HOURS OF RETURN JOBS

The majority of first returns to employment after childbirth in the WES were to part-time jobs, 68 per cent compared to 53 per cent of first returns in the NCDS. This is one of the things better maternity leave provision has had a large impact on. More new mothers have been returning to full-time employment with the same employer after childbirth, as they have taken up maternity leave entitlements as shown in McRae's (1991; 1996) two surveys of mothers on maternity leave.

LIKELIHOOD OF DOWNWARD OCCUPATIONAL MOBILITY ACROSS FIRST CHILDBIRTH

Following Dex's (1986; 1987) earlier examination of the probabilities of downward occupational mobility of women in the WES data, we can examine how these probabilities have changed by the time NCDS mothers experienced their first childbirth (Table 2.3). We follow the earlier logistic model estimated on WES data reasonably closely in order to provide points of comparison. However the occupation groups are much larger in size in NCDS data and capable of being estimated separately rather than grouped together. The results show a large measure of overlap in the determinants of downward occupational mobility for first time mothers in the WES and the NCDS. Returning to a part-time job after childbirth and spending longer out of employment both significantly increased the likelihood of downward occupational mobility occurring at this life stage. Being in a teaching or nursing, medical and social occupation before childbirth decreased the likelihood of experiencing downward occupational mobility compared with someone in a semi-skilled factory occupation. An increased likelihood of downward occupational mobility was associated with a pre-birth occupation in intermediate non-manual work, clerical or skilled work.

Table 2.3   Correlates of women's downward occupational mobility

Independent variables		WES 2 cohorts Logit[a]	NCDS Women with birth model one[b]	NCDS Women with birth model two[b]
Returns part-time		0.306 (6.1)	2.11 (0.09)	1.47 (0.10)
Duration	Years	0.028 (4.9)	0.11 (0.01)	—
to return	0 to 4 months	—	—	Reference[c]
	5 to 12 months	—	—	1.71 (0.16)
	13 to 24 months	—	—	1.70 (0.16)
	25 to 60 months	—	—	1.91 (0.14)
	61+ months	—	—	2.11 (0.14)
Pre-birth occupations	Professional + teacher	−0.263 (2.5)	—	—
	Professional	—	0.48 (0.24)	0.56 (0.26)
	Teacher	—	−0.79 (0.28)	−0.85 (0.28)
	Nursing	−0.128 (1.5)	−0.37 (0.18)	−0.39 (0.19)
	Intermediate non-manual	0.043 (0.4)	0.28 (0.17)	0.40 (0.18)
	Clerical	0.030 (0.6)	0.18 (0.13)	0.14 (0.13)
	Skilled	0.013 (0.2)	0.64 (0.15)	0.59 (0.16)
	Other semi-skilled	Reference[c]	Reference[c]	Reference[c]
	All others	—	−1.89 (0.17)	−1.91 (0.17)
Constant		0.143 (3.2)	−2.47 (0.13)	−3.14 (0.15)
N		679	4357	4357
Pseudo R^2		0.130	0.248	0.279
Log likelihood		−459.45	−1969.371	−1889.102

Notes:
[a]   t statistics in parenthesis.
[b]   Standard errors in parenthesis.
[c]   This is omitted category from a set of dummy variables.

The sizes of selected estimates of the effects on the probabilities of downward occupational mobility are displayed in Figures 2.2, 2.3 and 2.4. This shows that the probability of downward occupational mobility has changed over time in a number of ways. All occupations have a reduced likelihood of downward mobility after childbirth in the 1958 cohort than in the WES data, by a relatively small amount, after controlling for other things (Figure 2.2). In the case of skilled workers, the reduction is much smaller than for other occupations.

The likelihood of downward occupational mobility after childbirth has declined over time from the WES cohorts to the NCDS cohort if the

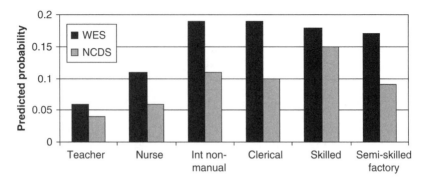

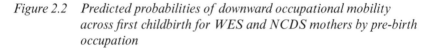

Notes: Based on a standard individual working full-time, one year out of the labour market and model one for NCDS. Mothers who did not return were excluded from the calculations, although relatively few (<10 per cent for WES and <5 per cent for NCDS) never returned to work.

Figure 2.2   Predicted probabilities of downward occupational mobility across first childbirth for WES and NCDS mothers by pre-birth occupation

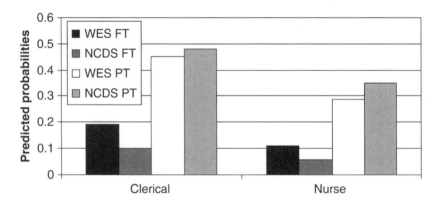

Notes: Based on a standard individual, one year out of the labour market and model one for NCDS. Mothers who did not return were excluded from the calculations, although relatively few (<10 per cent for WES and <5 per cent for NCDS) never returned to work.

Figure 2.3   Predicted probabilities of downward occupational mobility across first childbirth for WES and NCDS mothers, whether the first return was a full-or part-time job

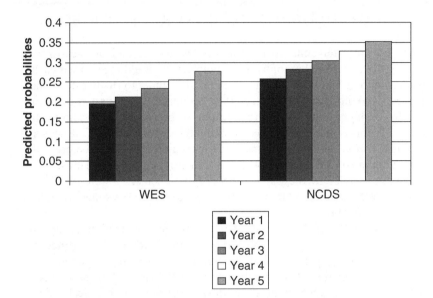

Notes: Based on standard individual working part-time and a teacher before first birth and model one for NCDS. Mothers who did not return were excluded from the calculations, although relatively few (<10 per cent for WES and <5 per cent for NCDS) never returned to work.

Figure 2.4   *Predicted probabilities of downward occupational mobility across first childbirth for WES and NCDS, teachers by years before first return to work*

mother returned to work full-time (Figure 2.3). However, returning to work part-time after childbirth is associated with a considerably higher chance of being downwardly mobile in the NCDS compared with the WES. The career penalty associated with working part-time after childbirth appears to have increased over time, although, as reported earlier, there were fewer first returns to part-time employment among NCDS than among WES women. The penalty of increased downward occupational mobility associated with taking longer breaks from work over childbirth also increased, year on year, in the NCDS compared with the WES (Figure 2.4).

While there has been some improvement in women's prospects, therefore, these improvements appear to be associated with behaviour that is more like those of men, having short or no breaks from employment across childbirth and returning to work full-time as soon as possible. If women have longer breaks or return after childbirth to a part-time job, in the more traditional ways, the occupational penalties appear to have increased.

BEFORE CHILDBIRTH TO MOST RECENT JOBS

The first job after childbirth is not necessarily the end of the story of women's occupational mobility. In principle, they could regain their earlier status where it had been lost. They could also undergo further downward moves. Even those who maintained their occupational status across the first childbirth might find it harder to maintain if they go on to have more children. We have made a further preliminary examination of downward mobility across the same three cohorts by comparing last job before childbirth with most recent job (Table 2.4). As mentioned above, the most recent occupations refer to the older WES cohort when they were 44–58, the younger WES cohort when they were 27–37, and NCDS women when they were 42 years old.

The NCDS cohort experienced a far greater proportion of upward moves by their most recent job at age 42 than either of the other two groups. This is consistent with opportunities for women growing in extent and nature over the 1980s and 1990s in Great Britain. However, it is no longer the case in these figures that downward mobility has declined systematically over time across these three cohorts. For example, in nursing, medical and social occupations, there is a lower percentage of downward occupational mobility in the cohort born in 1943–53 (23 per cent) than in the 1958 birth cohort (30 per cent). Also, for some origin occupations, including nursing, medical, social, intermediate non-manual, skilled and semi-skilled factory, there are greater proportions of downward mobility in the most recent occupations than was visible in the first return jobs after childbirth (see Tables 2.4 and 2.5 for the NCDS). As mentioned above, a range of experiences can lie in wait for women after they return to work after their first childbirth, potentially with different effects on their vertical occupational mobility. We are currently not able to unpick from these figures which of the various explanations and changes that underpin them. This will have to wait for future analysis. Clearly it is not a story of mothers' onward and upward mobility or of unequivocally regaining lost occupational status after the first return to work after childbirth.

FIRST JOB EVER COMPARED WITH MOST RECENT JOB

The summary of occupational mobility from the first job ever to the most recent job for WES and NCDS women and NCDS men is displayed in Table 2.6. Among NCDS women with a child, 35 per cent had a higher occupation in their most recent job compared with 14 per cent of WES

Table 2.4   Occupation of last job before childbirth to most recent job

Occupational categories	Born 1922–1936					Born 1943–1953					Born 1958				
	%↑	Same	%↓	Total (%)	N	%↑	Same	%↓	Total (%)	N	%↑	Same	%↓	Total (%)	N
Professional occupations	—	(100)	—	100	1	—	(80)	(20)	100	51	—	58	42	100	134
Teachers	—	(80)	(20)	100	39	—	(85)	(15)	100	40	4	78	18	100	171
Nursing, medical and social occupations	8	55	37	100	51	2	75	23	100	57	3	67	30	100	372
Other intermediate non-manual occupations	(25)	(19)	56	100	16	(4)	(48)	(48)	100	23	12	51	37	100	425
Clerical occupations	13	51	36	100	377	7	53	40	100	289	19	46	35	100	1537
Skilled occupations	26	19	55	100	106	14	36	50	100	76	27	27	46	100	416
Semi-skilled factory work	17	31	52	100	357	17	32	51	100	173	28	22	50	100	330
Other semi-skilled occupations	39	46	15	100	302	30	49	21	100	176	43	49	8	100	875
Unskilled	(64)	(36)	—	100	28	(100)	—	—	100	6	74	26	—	100	100
Total	22	42	36	100	1277	14	50	36	100	891	27	41	32	100	4360

Sources: 1922–36 cohort from WES data in Dex and Shaw (1986) regrouped.
1943–53 cohort from WES data in Dex and Shaw (1986) regrouped.
1958 cohort based on our analysis from NCDS data.

71

Table 2.5   *Occupation level of most recent job compared with first*
             occupation in working life

Most recent job compared to first job is:	WES with children*	WES without children**	NCDS all women	NCDS with child	NCDS without child	NCDS men
Higher	14	24	35	35	34	38
Same	49	60	35	32	45	42
Lower	37	16	30	33	21	20
Total	100	100	100	100	100	100
N	3019	1316	6708	5004	1704	7000

Sources: *(Martins and Roberts (1984: table 10.16); ** Martins and Roberts (1984: table 10.14).

women with a child; 32 per cent of NCDS women were in the same occupations compared with 49 per cent of the WES sample and 33 per cent of NCDS women with a child were in lower occupations than they started out in compared with 37 per cent of WES women. Over the life course up to age 42, NCDS women who had children had experienced more occupational progression compared with the earlier WES sample of mixed ages.

For women without children in these two surveys the same findings are evident with 34 per cent of NCDS childless women being in a higher occupation in their last recent job compared with their first ever job, compared with 24 per cent of WES childless women. These figures confirm that over time women have been improving their rates of upward career mobility. However, this improvement has to be viewed against the greater downward mobility of women who have had children compared to the childless in the WES and the NCDS. Also NCDS men's overall upward mobility by age 40 (38 per cent) is larger than NCDS women's (35 per cent), even childless women's upward mobility.

ALL OCCUPATIONAL TRANSITIONS BY GENDER

We can now investigate whether women's occupational transitions vary from those of men in the NCDS data. We consider all occupational transitions made by both men and women up to age 42 using the extended range of WES occupations in order to have more variation across men's jobs (Table 2.6).

When all transitions are included, the most stable occupation-to-occupation transitions are those between skilled jobs for men and teacher jobs

Table 2.6   All occupational transitions (NCDS)

Occupation category	ALL NCDS women up to 42 yrs old					ALL NCDS men up to 42 yrs old					All Childless women in NCDS up to 42 yrs old				
	% ↑	Same	% ↓	Row %	Total	% ↑	Same	% ↓	Row %	Total	% ↑	Same	% ↓	Row %	Total
Professional	—	53	47	100	770	—	48	52	100	1615	—	55	45	100	213
Teachers	2	73	22	100	865	4	56	40	100	257	5	67	28	100	195
Nursing, medical and social	3	65	32	100	2483	8	49	43	100	301	4	64	33	100	428
Other intermediate non-manual	10	42	48	100	2812	8	59	33	100	4735	13	48	39	100	709
Clerical	15	61	24	100	9281	26	48	26	100	2431	20	62	18	100	1791
Skilled	23	41	36	100	2994	11	67	22	100	12393	31	38	31	100	460
Semi-skilled factory work	30	31	29	100	1722	46	25	29	100	2131	43	29	28	100	216
Shop assistant and related sales	44	35	21	100	3564	54	31	15	100	1527	53	31	16	100	510
Semi-skilled domestic work	52	33	15	100	2088	56	19	25	100	611	65	25	10	100	252
Other semi-skilled	66	23	11	100	1604	57	32	11	100	2928	68	26	6	100	237
Unskilled	67	27	6	100	1301	81	21	—	100	2938	72	23	5	100	117
Childcare	72	28	—	100	988	97	3	—	100	118	79	21	—	100	205
All	27	47	26	100	30 472	27	50	23	100	31 985	29	48	23	100	5333

Source: All occupational transitions including those who only ever had one occupation.

for women, although nursing and clerical occupations also have high rates of transition to the same occupation. On the whole, men are much less likely than women to move to the same occupation when they change jobs. The gender differences in some occupational transitions are particularly large at the high end of the occupational spectrum.

In the top three occupations it is notable that men have greater percentages of downward occupational mobility than women, although similarly small percentages of upward occupational mobility. At the bottom of the occupational hierarchy, men are more likely to have higher rates of upward mobility than women from many occupations (semi-skilled factory, sales, semi-skilled domestic, unskilled and even childcare) while men's extent of downward mobility is more equal to that of women's from the same origin occupations. One exception is skilled work where men are less likely to have downward and upward mobility than women, because men have such high rates of transitions to the same occupation. However, we need to remember at this point, as mentioned earlier, that the skilled category may have suffered from over-coding of semi-skilled factory jobs into the higher 'skilled' category which would lead to a small overestimate of stability and a balancing small underestimate of downward occupational mobility.

There is slightly less downward occupational mobility from many origin occupations for childless as compared with all women (intermediate non-manual, clerical, skilled, sales and the semi-skilled categories), but the top occupation groups have either similar amounts of downward mobility for childless and all women or greater amounts for the childless. The experiences of childless women appear much more like those of all women in the NCDS than they appear similar to men's experiences of occupational mobility.

These results are fairly surprising and run counter to many expectations on gender differences although they were also evident in Jacobs's research on men's employment histories. There is considerable occupational mobility in both women's and men's employment histories, more than would probably be expected. The overall picture gained from these comparisons of men's and women's occupational transitions over their life course is that men in the 1958 cohort are not unequivocally doing better than women in all respects after they enter one of the higher-level occupations. However, we have been dealing with very broad occupational categories in this chapter, and it is still possible that men have more advantages over women within each broad occupational group, and in terms of their earnings within occupations. However, as far as our data reveal and circumscribed by suitable caveats, women born in 1958 are achieving a certain measure of broadly defined equality with men in their occupational transitions up to age 42. Also, in terms of occupational mobility, childless women are more similar to women with children than they are to men. This is because there is occupational segregation of women into certain occupations (for example, clerical) with low mobility profiles, irrespective of motherhood status, and these occupations accounted for a high proportion of women's jobs. These transitions give a picture of a very fluid labour market, and not one that is rigidly segmented, but one that has patterns of occupational mobility associated not only with the occupation but with the predominant gender of that occupation.

The NCDS men and women have lived through a long period of UK labour market restructuring, from 1974 to 1998, as well as an expansion of opportunities for women. Our findings suggest that these things have made a substantial contribution to their occupational mobility, but also to redefining the labour market structuring, functioning and gendering.

CONCLUSIONS

Dex's analysis of the 1980 WES occupation data was used to suggest a modification to the segmented labour market theories current at the time. This chapter reviews where we have got to 25 years later, on women's place in the labour market and the workings of the labour market in general.

The Women and Employment Survey was a major landmark in showing that by 1980, women were successfully combining motherhood with employment. It came as something of a surprise to learn from the employment histories that as many as 90 per cent of mothers eventually returned to the labour market after a gap for childbirth. It was also evident, even then, that successive (quasi) cohorts were bringing forward this return and closing the gap.

These changes were seen in 1980, shortly after the UK had embraced statutory provisions for mothers' employment rights for maternity and legislation about discrimination. The WES data suggested that women's behaviour had been changing even in advance of the statutory framework.

It was less surprising to find that women suffered downward occupational mobility at this life stage of giving birth, although some managed to regain their earlier status. This downward occupational mobility varied by occupation but was at higher rates with longer durations out of employment for childbirth and with returning to a part-time job. This was an aspect of women's employment where the new right to return to the same job had not had time to affect many lives.

The intervening 25 years show much continuity with these earlier trends. Women have continued to return to work after childbirth at faster rates. More of them have returned after childbirth to the same jobs, the same employers and the same full-time hours of work. These changes have undoubtedly been assisted by the embedding and enhancement over

25 years of statutory maternity leave arrangements, and the realisation that human resource management could be relevant for women, particularly the new cohorts of qualified womanpower.

In this chapter we have been able to follow women's progress up to 2000 through the experiences of women born in 1958. Through this lens we have seen that downward occupational mobility over first childbirth has declined compared with earlier generations in the WES. However, there is still additional downward occupational mobility following the first return after first childbirth to most recent jobs for some of these women. We were unable to identify its causes at this point.

The 1958 cohort of women also demonstrates that the penalties to their occupational status of taking a part-time job on returning to work after (first) childbirth, or spending a few years out of employment, have increased compared with the WES generations. One other important finding from the analysis of NCDS men's occupational mobility is that men, too, experience at least as much downward occupational mobility as women over their careers up to age 40, although they do not on the whole drop into part-time jobs. Also this is unlikely to be concentrated around the arrival of children. Where women worked in the less gender-segregated parts of the British labour market of the 1980s and 1990s, and maintained employment profiles hitherto characteristic of men, they were able to maintain occupational status and progression and keep pace with the men. Where they wanted to deviate and spend more time being mothers, the penalties appear to have been greater. Clearly this examination of mobility between occupational categories is only part of the story. There is within-occupation progression and wage rate mobility which should be linked with occupational category changes.

In addition, this clearly is not the end of the story. We have more recent cohorts to examine, some of whom have been having their children under the more recent legislation requiring equal treatment for part-time employees and offering rights for parents to request flexibility from employers. These recent developments may help to break the link between downward occupational mobility and part-time jobs. We will have to see.

REFERENCES

Blackwell, L. (2001), 'Women's work in UK official statistics and in the 1980 reclassification of occupations', *Journal of Royal Statistical Society*, **164**, 2, 307–25.

Blau, P.M. and O.D. Duncan (1967), *The American Occupational Structure*, New York: Wiley and Sons.

Booth, A. and M. Francesconi (1999), 'Job mobility in 1990s Britain: does gender matter?', *Research in Labor Economics*, **19**, 173–89.

Callender, C., N. Millward, S. Lissenburgh and J. Forth (1997), *Maternity Rights and Benefits in Britain*, Social Security Research Report 67, London: The Stationery Office.

Dex, S. (1987), *Women's Occupational Mobility*, Basingstoke: Macmillan.

Dex, S. and L.B. Shaw (1986), *American and British Women at Work*, Basingstoke: Macmillan.

Dolton, P. and M. Silles (2001), 'Over-education in the graduate labour market: some evidence from alumni data', Centre for the Economics of Education Discussion Paper 9, London School of Economics.

Elias, P. and B. Main (1982), *Women's Working Lives: Evidence from the National Training Survey*, Coventry: Institute for Employment Research, University of Warwick.

Goldthorpe, J. (1987), *Social Mobility and Class Structure in Modern Britain*, Oxford: Clarendon Press.

Heitmueller, A. (2004), 'Job mobility in Britain: are the Scots different? Evidence from the BHPS', *Scottish Journal of Political Economy*, **51**(3), 329–58.

Jacobs, S. (1999), 'Trends in women's career patterns and in gender occupational mobility in Britain, *Gender Work and Organization*, **6**(1), 32–46.

Joshi, H. (1984), *Women's Participation in Paid Work: Further Analysis of the Women and Employment Survey*, Department for Employment, Research Paper, No. 45, London: HMSO.

Joshi, H.E. (1985), 'Motherhood and employment: change and continuity in post war Britain', in *Measuring Socio-Demographic Change*, Occasional Paper No. 34, London: OPCS.

Joshi, H. and P. Hinde (1993), 'Employment after childbearing: cohort study evidence', *European Sociological Review*, **9**, 203–27.

Joshi, H. and M.L. Newell (1987), 'Job downgrading after childbirth', in M. Uncles, (ed.), *London Papers in Regional Science 18. Longitudinal Data Analysis: Methods and Applications*, London: Pion. pp. 89–102.

Leontaridi, M.R. (1998), 'Segmented labour markets: Theory and evidence', *Journal of Economic Surveys*, **12**, 63–101.

Macran, S., H.E. Joshi and S. Dex, (1996), 'Employment after childbearing: a survival analysis', *Work Employment and Society*, **10**(2), 273–96.

Marshall, G., H. Newby, D. Rose and C. Vogler (1988), *Social Class in Modern Britain*, London: Hutchinson.

Martin, J. and C. Roberts (1984), *Women and Employment: A Lifetime Perspective*, London: Department of Employment and OPCS.

McRae, S. (1991), *Maternity Rights in Britain*, London: Policy Studies Institute.

McRae, S. (1996), *Maternity Rights in Britain*, London: Policy Studies Institute.

Payne, G. and P. Abbott (eds) (1990), *The Social Mobility of Women*, London: Falmer.

Rosenfeld, R.A. (1979), 'Women's occupational careers, individual and structural explanations', *Sociology, Work and Occupation*, **6**(3), 283–311.

Sousa-Poza, A. (2004), 'Is the Swiss labor market segmented?', *Labour*, **18**(1), 131–61.

Stewart, M. and C. Greenhalgh (1984), 'Work history patterns and the occupational attainment of women', *Economic Journal*, **94**(375), 493–519.

Stewart, M.B. and J.K. Swaffield (1999), 'Low pay dynamics and transition probabilities', *Economica*, **66**, 23–42.

Theodossiou, I. (1995), 'Wage determination for career and non-career workers in the UK: is there labour market segmentation?', *Economica*, **62**, 195–211.

APPENDIX

BOX 2A.1   SEX DISCRIMINATION LEGISLATION IN BRITAIN

Sex Discrimination Act 1975
The Sex Discrimination Act 1975 makes sex discrimination unlawful in employment, vocational training and education. This legislation prohibits any direct or indirect discrimination, victimisation and harassment on the grounds of sex and has been updated to also prohibit any discrimination on the grounds of pregnancy or maternity leave.

In employment and vocational training, this legislation also prohibits any discrimination against a person due to their marital or partnership status (updated from December 2005 to include a civil partner).

Equal Pay Act 1970
The Equal Pay Act 1970 was passed to prohibit employers to discriminate between men and women who are doing the same work or similar/equivalent work which is of equal value. This covers the salary and other terms and conditions such as bonus payments, holidays and sick leave.

BOX 2A.2   WOMEN'S EMPLOYMENT SURVEY OCCUPATIONAL CATEGORIES

1. *Professional occupations*
    Barristers, solicitors, chartered and certified accountants, university teachers, doctors, dentists, physicists, chemists, social scientists, pharmacists, dispensing opticians, qualified engineers, architects, town planners, civil servants – Assistant Secretary level and above.
2. *Teachers*
    Primary and secondary school teachers, teachers in further and higher education (not universities), head teachers, nursery teachers, vocational and industrial trainers.
3. *Nursing, medical and social occupations*
    SRN, SEN, nursing auxiliary, midwife, health visitor, children's

nurse, matron/superintendent, dental nurse, dietician, radiographer, physiotherapist, chiropodist, dispenser, medical technician, houseparent, welfare occupations (including social workers), occupational therapist.

4. *Other intermediate non-manual occupations*
Civil Servants – Executive Officer to Senior Principal level and equivalent in central and local government, computer programmer, systems analyst, O & M analyst, librarian, surveyor, personnel officer, managers, self-employed farmers, shopkeepers, publicans, hoteliers, buyers, company secretary, author, writer, journalist, artist, designer, window dresser, entertainer, musician, actress.

5. *Clerical occupations*
Typist, secretary, shorthand writer, clerk, receptionist, personal assistant, cashier (not retail), telephonist receptionist, office machine operator, computer operator, punch card operator, data processor, draughtswoman, tracer, market research interviewer, debt collector.

6. *Shop assistant and related sales occupations*
People selling goods in wholesale or retail establishments, cashiers, in retail shops, check out and cash and wrap operators, petrol pump attendant, sales representative, demonstrator, theatre/cinema usherette, programme seller, insurance agent.

7. *Skilled occupations*
Hairdresser, manicurist, beautician, make-up artist, cook, domestic and institution housekeeper, nursery nurse, travel stewardess, ambulance woman, van driver and deliveries, baker, weaver, knitter, mender, darner, tailoress and dressmaker (whole garment), clothing cutter, milliner, upholsterer, bookbinder, precision instrument maker and repairer, instrument assemblers, laboratory assistant, driving instructor, policewoman.

8. *Childcare occupations*
Childminder, school meals and playgroup supervisor or leader, nanny, au pair, people doing housework in addition to childcare (NB exclude nursing and teaching).

9. *Semi-skilled factory work*
Assembler, packer, labeller, grader, sorter, inspector, machinist, machine operator, paper wrapping, filling or sealing containers, spinner, doubler, twister, winder, reeler.

10. *Semi-skilled domestic work*
   Waitress, barmaid, canteen assistant, people serving food at tables or counters, serving school meals, home help, care attendant, ward orderly, housemaid, domestic worker.
11. *Other semi-skilled occupations*
   Agricultural worker, groom, kennel maid, shelf filler, bus conductress, ticket collector, post woman, mail sorter, laundress, dry cleaner, presser, mail order and catalogue agent, market and street trader, collector saleswoman, traffic warden, telephone operator, photographer.
12. *Unskilled occupations*
   Cleaner, charwoman, kitchen hand, labourer, messenger.

Table 2A.1   First occupations (percentages)

Occupation categories	WES 20–24	WES 25–29	NCDS women	NCDS men
Professional occupations	—	2	1.7	4.8
Teacher	2	6	2.8	1.0
Nursing, medical and social occupations	4	5	5.7	0.5
Other intermediate non-manual occupations	2	3	5.1	9.3
Clerical occupations	39	39	38.9	9.5
Skilled occupations	10	9	12.3	43.4
Shop assistant and related sales occupations	17	16	14.1	5.1
Childcare occupations	1	1	2.4	0.2
Semi-skilled factory work	15	15	6.1	7.3
Semi-skilled domestic	4	2	4.2	1.8
Other semi-skilled	4	2	4.8	10.1
Unskilled	2	0	1.9	6.9
Total	100	100	100	100
N	560	679	6708	7000

Source: Dex and Shaw (1986).

3. Ethnic differences in women's labour market activity

Angela Dale, Joanne Lindley, Shirley Dex and Anthony Rafferty

INTRODUCTION

This chapter provides an overview of ethnic differences among women in the labour market. Much research on ethnic differences in employment has shown not just the extent of inequalities but also the variation between ethnic groups (Berthoud 2000; Blackaby et al. 2002). Research on women's employment has demonstrated greater differentials between ethnic groups than for men, with economic activity highest for Black Caribbean women and lowest for Pakistani and Bangladeshi women in the 1990s and early 2000s. Unemployment was higher for all minority ethnic groups than for white women over this period – except for Chinese women who have rates very similar to white women (Lindley et al. 2004).

However, there has been little systematic analysis of employment differences in relation to key life stages – despite the fact that, for white women, there are very large life-stage differences. Extensive work on (white) women's employment has shown that it is strongly influenced by both life stage and cohort – and both are mediated by level of qualifications (Dex and Joshi 1996; Dex et al. 1998; Elliott et al. 2001; Macran et al. 1996). Theories that explain women's labour market behaviour have been developed around norms and assumptions that apply to white women. So, for example, much research on women's employment is concerned with the effects of domestic responsibilities and childcare on the employment of mothers. Whether these factors impact in a similar way on women from minority ethnic groups is an open question. In this chapter we compare ethnic differences in levels of economic activity for women at different life stages. Qualifications are recognised as playing an important explanatory role in the rise in women's labour market participation in recent decades, particularly amongst women with young children. Qualifications also protect against unemployment. However, we do not know the extent to which this holds true across different ethnic groups.

THE BACKGROUND CONTEXT

The marked differences in the labour market activity of women from different ethnic groups need to be understood in the context of the reasons for, and timing of, migration to the UK. Thus Black Caribbean people came to Britain as economic migrants, mainly in the 1950s and early 1960s in response to a demand for labour in the UK post-war economy. Many women were recruited to the newly formed National Health Service.

By contrast, the Pakistani and Bangladeshi groups are more recent migrants, many coming from poor rural areas and bringing to the UK few economic or educational resources. Migration was male led, with settlement often in areas of declining industry. Women tended to come to Britain as dependents, from a culture where men were expected to be the breadwinners. First-generation migrants, women in particular, generally had few qualifications and spoke little English. However, a growing generation of young people are UK born; over 60 per cent of 19–25-year-old Pakistani and nearly 30 per cent of 19–25-year-old Bangladeshi people are UK born (Lindley et al. 2004) and have therefore gained UK qualifications. Nor do they face the language barriers experienced by their parents. We may expect that traditional assumptions over gender roles will be rather less for second-generation young people than for their parents.

The Indian group are more diverse with significant differences in timing of migration between the key groups. The role of the British in India, dating from the seventeenth century, resulted not only in close trading links but also in the English language being widely spoken in urban India. The most recent migrants are the East African Indians, many expelled from Uganda in the 1960s, who often brought to Britain considerable business experience and educational assets – although deploying them in Britain was not always easy. Over 70 per cent of 19–25-year-old Indian people are UK born (Lindley et al. 2004).

Chinese migration to Britain has a long history. A major influx of Chinese from Hong Kong after the Second World War provided restaurants and catering businesses across Britain. Later migrants, in the 1960s and 1970s, came from other parts of South East Asia, often with professional qualifications. Settlement patterns for the Chinese are much more dispersed than for other groups. For all groups, timing of settlement influences the extent of exposure to the UK educational system and associated culture. Individuals who have grown up in the UK will have gained qualifications that are recognised by employers, will be fluent in English and will have familiarity with dominant cultural norms related to education and employment.

RESEARCH QUESTIONS AND CHAPTER PLAN

Table 3.1 shows headline figures for level of economic activity and unemployment for key ethnic groups at two time points: 1992–6 and 2001–5.[1] Although there has, for most groups, been an increase in economic activity and a decline in unemployment over this decade the differences between ethnic groups remain largely unchanged. However, as explained in the first section, we know little about how life stage and qualification interact to influence women's labour market behaviour. These major influences on women's levels of economic activity need to be included in multivariate analyses before we can distinguish whether differences in levels of economic activity shown in Table 3.1 are simply due to different characteristics of women in different ethnic groups, or whether we need to look for other explanations. We therefore begin by examining the relationship between economic activity and life stage and level of qualifications.

We then examine further the components of economic activity, particularly the differences in levels of unemployment shown in Table 3.1 and ask, again, how far these can be explained by individual characteristics and the extent to which qualifications protect against unemployment.

Finally, we explore the concept of under-employment for those women who are in paid work. Here we focus particularly on women with degree level qualifications and examine ethnic differences in the extent to which women with degree-level qualifications are occupying graduate occupations.

DATA SOURCES AND CONCEPTS

The Data Source: The Quarterly Labour Force Survey

The Quarterly Labour Force Survey (QLFS) is conducted by the Office for National Statistics and available for academic use through the Economic and Social Data Service (ONS, 2003). Since 1992 the QLFS has conducted repeat interviews at each sampled address at three-monthly intervals with the fifth interview taking place a year after the first. Each quarter, interviews are achieved at about 59 000 addresses with about 138 000 respondents. A response rate of about 77 per cent was achieved for the first wave of the survey in 2002. All first interviews (with the exception of a very small sample located north of the Caledonian Canal) are carried out by face-to-face interview. Subsequent interviews are carried out by telephone. We use data for England, Wales and Scotland for sweep 1 of each quarter. The Office for National Statistics (ONS) calculates weights for the QLFS which are designed to produce population estimates in line with the latest census. All

Table 3.1 Economic activity by ethnic group for 1992–96 and 2001–05

Ethnic group	(1) % economically active, aged 19–60	(2) Of those active: % unemployed	(3) Total N in sample, aged 19–60	(4) % FT student aged 19–29	(5) Total N age 19–29
1992–96					
White	73.5	06.4	163 602	09.2	41 692
Black Caribbean	74.6	15.8	1 682	13.8	465
Black African	68.1	26.7	729	26.3	255
Black Other	73.4	17.1	307	17.1	142
Indian	66.4	11.1	2 778	16.4	748
Pakistani	25.4	22.7	1 390	09.0	525
Bangladeshi	18.8	28.6	423	10.1	170
Chinese	65.9	07.2	460	43.9	94
Other	63.3	14.6	1 601	26.5	455
2001–05					
White	76.5	03.4	127 835	14.8	23 706
Black Caribbean	77.5	07.9	1 353	29.1	208
Black African	66.1	12.2	1 181	35.7	282
Black Other	77.1	13.3	482	24.0	167
Indian	69.9	05.7	2 465	24.5	545
Pakistani	31.1	14.8	1 549	18.7	513
Bangladeshi	20.8	15.6	560	09.7	236
Chinese	68.8	05.3	479	55.8	103
Other	76.5	08.7	2 272	28.4	557

Note: Columns 1 and 2 omit full-time (FT) students.

Source: Quarterly Labour Force Survey (QLFS), England, Wales and Scotland, weighted.

tables showing percentages and means have been weighted, but the number of cases shown in margins refer to the unweighted data. Multivariate models which do not seek to provide descriptive population estimates have used unweighted data.

The QLFS collects family and demographic information on each member of the household. This allows us to identify information about a woman's partner and her children. The QLFS also asks extensive information on employment and qualifications that are consistent each year. In addition, questions on ethnicity, country of birth and year of arrival in the UK are asked.

Ethnic Group in the QLFS

By using the QLFS we are restricted to the definitions of ethnicity used in that study and changes that have occurred to the categories over time. Creating consistent categories for ethnic groups over the survey cross-sections involved grouping the two mixed race categories 'White and Caribbean' and 'White and African' into 'Black Other', and also grouping 'White and Asian' and 'other mixed' into a single 'other non-White' composite group. A fuller discussion of this process is available in Lindley et al. (2004). In this chapter we have provided details of nine ethnic groups where numbers permit but, for more detailed analyses, have focussed on Black Caribbean, Indian, the combined Pakistani and Bangladeshi group and the Chinese. The QLFS sampling design and large sample size means that reliable estimates can be obtained for ethnic minorities by combining data for several years.

DEMOGRAPHIC DIFFERENCES BETWEEN ETHNIC GROUPS AND CHANGE OVER TIME

Operationalising a Quasi Life-stage Approach

The lack of any longitudinal data that can represent minority ethnic groups in the UK means that we cannot follow individuals through their life course. Instead we have had to use repeat cross-sectional data to identify the current stage of the life course for the sample members. We cannot, therefore, assume that women will necessarily move through the life course in any predictable way and we cannot disentangle age, cohort and generation. However, we have used information on whether women were born or brought up in the UK as a way of distinguishing first and second generation immigrants. Women who arrived in the UK at 16 or older are classified as 'not UK born or bought up' and thus distinguished from women who arrived at a younger age or who were born in the UK and who may be expected to have experienced UK schooling.

In Table 3.2, we present seven quasi life-course stages which summarise demographic and partnership information. Partnership is based on the respondent's self-description and includes either being married or cohabiting. A woman who reported herself as married (but not separated) but had no partner in the household was classified as married. This is particularly important for South Asian groups where a partner may be temporarily overseas but is likely to be supporting his wife financially and where norms associated with marriage still prevail.

A child is defined as under 16 and living in the same household as its mother. For women without dependent children at home we distinguish between those who are at a pre-family formation stage and those whose children may now be 16 or over. Women who are under 35 without children are assumed to be at a pre-family stage. The vast majority of women in life stages 6 and 7 either have older children still at home or will have had children who have left home. We expect that the past influence of these children will still be reflected in these women's labour market behaviour. Our life stage variable identifies lone mothers with a child under 16 from mothers living in a household with a partner and children, based on whether the youngest child is under 5, or 5–15.

Ethnic Differences in Life Stages

Before moving on to examine how women's economic activity varies with life stage and qualifications, we first examine ethnic differences in both. Differences will be explained in part by the different age distributions of the ethnic groups, but also by differences in preferences over partnership and child-bearing.

Table 3.2 shows the proportions of QLFS respondents in each life stage by ethnicity for the years 1992–96 and 2001–05 respectively. One of the key differences is the greater propensity for Black women to be unpartnered by comparison with other ethnic groups – evident in columns 1 and 2. Lone motherhood – column 2 – also increases over time for all groups (except the 'other' category). However, further analysis shows that Pakistani and Bangladeshi lone mothers tend to be separated, divorced or widowed rather than single, whilst over three-quarters of Black Caribbean and 'Black Other' mothers are single.

There is also a marked contrast between Black women and South Asian women in the percentage who are partnered with children (columns 4 and 5). In 2001–05, 53 per cent of Pakistani women and 64 per cent of

Table 3.2   Life stage by ethnic group for 1992–96 and 2001–05

	(1) No partner, ndc & age <35	(2) No partner, has children <16	(3) Partner ndc & age <35	(4) Partner, youngest child 0–4	(5) Partner, youngest child 5–15	(6) No partner, ndc & age >=35	(7) Partner ndc & age >=35	Total %	Total N
1992–1996									
White	11.3	7.8	8.7	15.2	18.0	9.2	29.8	100	163 602
Black Carbn	18.7	27.4	4.4	9.5	9.2	16.6	14.3	100	1682
Black Afcan	18.1	27.2	7.7	20.9	10.6	8.9	6.6	100	729
Black Other	23.0	28.7	10.1	13.0	11.7	7.1	6.4	100	307
Indian	10.1	3.2	9.0	23.5	26.6	6.4	21.2	100	2778
Pakistani	7.7	6.9	8.5	38.0	24.8	3.6	10.5	100	1390
Bangladeshi	8.3	6.2	4.8	45.3	24.4	3.4	7.6	100	423
Chinese	11.2	3.1	10.9	19.2	26.9	8.8	19.8	100	460
Other	13.4	11.4	9.6	22.4	19.5	8.6	15.3	100	1601
2001–2005									
White	9.8	9.8	7.9	13.2	18.0	11.3	30.1	100	127 835
Black Carbn	10.3	32.5	3.5	10.2	10.9	20.1	12.5	100	1353
Black Afcan	14.0	27.2	5.4	18.4	12.9	14.6	7.5	100	1181
Black Other	15.9	34.8	7.5	12.5	9.4	12.1	7.8	100	482
Indian	12.9	4.2	8.9	18.5	23.1	7.7	24.7	100	2465
Pakistani	11.1	10.8	9.00	30.9	21.7	4.3	12.4	100	1549
Bangladeshi	8.9	9.8	5.6	42.8	21.0	4.5	7.4	100	560
Chinese	13.0	6.0	12.8	17.0	18.5	7.3	25.4	100	479
Other	11.9	9.3	12.1	21.0	17.0	11.1	17.6	100	2272

Notes:

Females aged between 19 and 60.

Partner = married/cohabiting. ndc = no dependent children.

Source: QLFS Spring Quarters for GB. Data are weighted.

Bangladeshi women aged 19–60 were partnered with a child under 16, compared with 21 per cent of Black Caribbean women, 22 per cent of Black Other women and 31 per cent of White women. However, for the South Asian groups the proportion of partnered women with children was considerably lower in 2001–05 than in 1992–96, suggesting a reduction in family size took place over time.

Amongst the two older life stages, women of 35 and over without children under 16, the South Asian groups are much less likely to be unpartnered (column 6) than other groups whilst the Black Caribbean group, in particular, is overrepresented in this life stage – possibly because their children are now 16 and over.

In summary, White women are more likely than other ethnic groups to be without any children aged under 16: in total, 41 per cent in 2001–05 had no children under 16 compared with 33 per cent for Black Caribbean, 28 per cent for Pakistani and 21 per cent for Bangladeshi women. Pakistani and Bangladeshi women are the groups most likely to be married with dependent children while Black Caribbean, Black Other and Black African women are most likely to be raising a child without a partner.

ETHNIC DIFFERENCES IN QUALIFICATIONS

We have used the detailed information on qualifications in the QLFS to develop a five-point classification (Table 3.3) that is consistent across time.

Table 3.3   Classification of qualifications

Degree and higher qualification NVQ and key skills 4 and 5	Higher degrees, first degrees, teaching qualifications, nursing, HNC/HND, BTEC higher, NVQ levels 4 and 5
A level NVQ and key skills 3	A levels typically gained at age 18; required for university entrance; Scottish Highers, advanced craft certificates, NVQ level 3
O level NVQ and key skills 2	O levels, GCSE grades A–C, typically gained at age 16 at the end of compulsory schooling, NVQ level 2, GNVQ intermediate
Other qualification Key skills level 1 and entry level	CSE below grade 1, NVQ 1, GNVQ/GSVQ foundation level Other qualifications incl. overseas qualifications
No qualifications	No qualification reported, including don't know and no answer

Overseas qualifications are recorded in the 'Other' category – consistent with evidence that such qualifications have little positive impact on levels of economic activity for ethnic minorities in the UK (Dale et al. 2001).

Table 3.4 shows the difference between ethnic groups in the level of qualifications and how this has changed over the two time periods. At both time points, Pakistani and Bangladeshi women were the least likely to hold degree-level qualifications and the most likely to have no qualifications and Chinese women were the best qualified (39 per cent of Chinese women had degree-level qualifications by 2001–05 compared with 12 per cent for Pakistani and 8 per cent for Bangladeshi women). For all groups, the proportions with some qualifications increased over the time period, with a particularly marked increased in those with degree-level qualifications: 18.1 per cent in 1992–96 compared with 25.9 per cent in 2001–05 and this trend was apparent for women from all ethnic groups. At both time points White women were less likely to have degree level qualification than the three

Table 3.4   Highest qualification by ethnic group, 1992–96 and 2001–05

Ethnic group	Degree	A level	O/GCSE	Other	None
1992–1996					
White	18.16	13.88	23.77	14.25	29.94
Black Caribbean	18.77	14.30	22.32	15.80	28.81
Black African	21.55	11.38	13.82	30.46	22.80
Black other	22.23	14.01	27.30	17.95	18.51
Indian	15.92	8.73	12.19	23.93	39.23
Pakistani	6.16	5.31	9.05	19.24	60.24
Bangladeshi	2.80	2.94	7.04	21.24	65.99
Chinese	27.77	7.50	6.50	21.81	36.42
Other	21.36	11.01	12.52	30.67	24.43
2001–2005					
White	25.87	15.97	26.63	13.21	18.33
Black Caribbean	28.26	15.36	27.83	16.23	12.32
Black African	31.61	9.91	10.96	29.54	17.98
Black other	27.26	17.00	25.70	14.28	15.76
Indian	28.60	10.41	13.26	25.05	22.68
Pakistani	12.01	8.11	15.22	22.01	42.66
Bangladeshi	7.63	6.14	13.51	18.87	53.85
Chinese	39.06	7.70	7.72	23.87	21.64
Other	29.29	8.44	9.90	34.40	17.97

Note: Women aged 19–60 excluding FT students.

Source: QLFS, weighted.

groups of Black women, Chinese women and the 'Other' category. By 2001–05 Indian women were also more likely to have higher qualifications than White women. Table 3.1, showing the percentage of full-time students for women aged 19–29, is consistent with these figures and suggests that, over time, Pakistani women may increase their levels of qualification to overtake White women. However, these figures hide potential differences in the grade of degrees . For example, Connor et al. (2004) found that fewer minority students gained first or upper second class degrees compared with White students.

THE RELATIONSHIP BETWEEN ECONOMIC ACTIVITY, LIFE STAGE AND QUALIFICATIONS

Life stage (age, children and partnership) and qualifications all have big impacts on women's economic activity and, from the above tables, it is clear that multivariate analysis is needed to control for the differences between ethnic groups and thus establish the *relative* influence of each element. For example, the relationship between children and economic activity can be compared across ethnic groups in a way that controls for differences in the likelihood of having a child.

We have estimated logistic models to predict the propensity of being economically active for women in each ethnic group. We include all women aged 19–60 (except full-time students[2]) from the QLFS for 1992–2005. Separate models are used for each ethnic group because we want to establish the different way in which these factors impact on each ethnic group. The response variable is dichotomous, indicating whether or not a woman is economically active. Economic activity includes those who are either employed or unemployed using ILO definitions of unemployment.[3] A set of explanatory variables comprise stage of life-course (described in Table 3.2), qualification level (described in Table 3.3), whether born or brought up in the UK and variables to represent the year of the survey (from 1992 to 2005). As we want to make comparisons between ethnic groups we have extracted predicted probabilities of economic activity, based on these models, for each of our key ethnic groups. Table 3.5 reports these probabilities by position in the life stage and by qualification.

Amongst young women aged 19–34 with neither child nor partner, probabilities of being economically active are very similar in each ethnic group – between 94 and 97 per cent for women with degree-level qualifications. This belies the widely accepted generalisation of low rates of labour market participation for Pakistani and Bangladeshi women (for example, as shown in Table 3.1). However, amongst women with no qualifications in this life

Table 3.5 *Predicted probabilities of being economically active*

Life stage	White Level of qualification					Black Caribbean					Indian					Pakistani/ Bangladeshi					Chinese				
	1	2	3	4	5	1	2	3	4	5	1	2	3	4	5	1	2	3	4	5	1	2	3	4	5
(1) Single 19–<35, no partner, no child	97	94	94	92	84	95	92	91	87	78	97	95	94	89	81	94	91	84	73	47	97	94	93	88	85
(2) Partner, 19–<35, no children	98	96	96	94	88	96	93	92	87	79	92	89	86	74	62	87	82	70	47	25	92	83	80	71	65
(3) Partner, youngest child under 5	76	64	63	56	36	83	74	71	61	44	77	71	66	49	32	54	44	29	14	05	74	55	49	37	30
(4) Partner, youngest child 5–15	91	85	84	80	64	94	91	90	84	73	91	88	85	74	59	70	62	48	27	11	88	78	74	63	55
(5) Single, child less than 16	75	63	61	55	34	82	73	71	61	43	81	74	70	54	36	61	52	37	20	07	71	50	44	32	26
(6) 35–60, single, no children <16	87	79	78	72	54	89	82	80	72	56	81	75	71	55	38	70	64	42	26	11	93	86	81	73	67
(7) 35–60, partner, no children <16	89	82	80	75	58	93	88	87	80	67	85	80	76	61	44	66	57	49	25	11	86	72	68	58	49

Note: Key to level of qualification: 1 = degree level; 2 = A level; 3 = O level; 4 = other; 5 = no qualification.

Source: Quarterly Labour Force Survey, England, Wales and Scotland, QLFS, 1992–2003, unweighted, excludes FT students.

stage, economic activity rates are below 50 per cent for Pakistani and Bangladeshi women but over 80 per cent for all other ethnic groups. Amongst the comparable group of young women (19–34) with no children but *with* a partner (row 2) there is a clear distinction between White and Black Caribbean women, on the one hand and South Asian and Chinese women, on the other. For the former, economic activity is higher at all levels of qualification for women with a partner (row 2) than without (row 1), but lower for the latter groups and particularly so for Pakistani and Bangladeshi women. This different relationship between economic activity and partnership for White and Black Caribbean women and South Asian and Chinese women is probably linked to different cultural expectations concerning gender roles.

The additional effect of a young child (under 5) can be seen by comparing rows 2 and 3 – women aged 19–34 with a partner but no children and women with a partner and a child under 5. As expected, economic activity rates are generally lower in the latter group and show a steep gradient with level of qualifications. Such rates are higher, and the gradient with qualifications least, for Black women. For Pakistani and Bangladeshi women, rates of activity are much lower than for other ethnic groups across all qualification levels (only 5 per cent for those with no qualifications) with a range of nearly 50 percentage points between the highest and lowest qualification groups.

Where the youngest child is of school-age (row 4) rates of activity are higher and differentials by level of qualification are less than for women with a pre-school child – except for Pakistani and Bangladeshi women where activity for degree-level women is 70 per cent by comparison with only 11 per cent for women in this group with no qualifications.

Single Black women with children (row 5) have considerably higher rates of economic activity than other ethnic groups and, again, levels of economic activity are lowest for Pakistani and Bangladeshi women.

Older women (35–60) without children under 16 generally have levels of activity which are similar to women with a partner and children aged 5–15, across levels of education and across ethnic groups. Most of this group will have had children, and, for some, older children will still be at home.

In summary, Black women have higher rates of economic activity across the life course than White women; they are more likely to remain economically active when they have children than White women. Black single mothers have higher rates of economic activity than White single mothers. These results are consistent with Black women having a much looser association between having children, and being in a partnership whereby single Black women may be seen as taking the role of both bread-winner and care provider (Duncan and Irwin 2004; Duncan et al. 2003; Reynolds 2005). In a culture where paid work is the 'norm' we see only limited reduction in activity for Black mothers with the presence of children and across levels of qualification.

Although Indian women's patterns of family formation show a much more traditional link between marriage and childbearing, their rates of economic activity within the life stage and qualification categories resemble those of White women. Thus, whilst Indian women's economic activity is more responsive to partnership and children than for Black Caribbean women, nonetheless Indian women have much higher rates of economic activity than Pakistani and Bangladeshi women.

Pakistani and Bangladeshi women are distinctive in the strength of the relationship they exhibit between the rate of economic activity, qualifications, partnership and the presence of children, resulting in a much greater variation in rates of economic activity than for other ethnic groups. Whilst most commentators assume that there is little generational change in these women's rates of employment, we show that women at a pre-family formation stage (single, 19–34 and with no partner) with higher levels of qualification, are as likely to be economically active as women in other ethnic groups. However, rates of economic activity are much lower for women with few or no qualifications. This is consistent with a tradition of strongly gendered roles and a male breadwinner model. The findings provide strong support for the ideal of children and maternal care of children among Pakistani and Bangladeshi mothers. However, amongst younger, more highly qualified women, there are indications that things are changing, with a delay in marriage and childbearing. In more traditional Pakistani and Bangladeshi families, unmarried daughters may face considerable family resistance to taking a paid job outside the home, although women with degree-level qualifications have more power within the family, both in terms of decisions over employment and also in selecting a marriage partner (Dale et al. 2002). This helps to explain the marked difference in economic activity rates by level of qualification shown in Table 3.5. These results also confirm that the ethnic differences shown in Table 3.1 are not simply the result of ethnic differences in family formation, qualifications or generation.

In this analysis it is clear that the range and complexity of employment patterns across the life course for different ethnic groups is not captured by any single theory of the family. Whilst economic theories of the family (Becker 1981) may appear to explain the traditional, gender segregated, family organisation of Pakistani and Bangladeshis in Britain, it does not, as Blossfeld and Drobnic (2001) point out, explain the increase in young women obtaining higher qualifications. Qualitative research on Pakistani and Bangladeshi women, however, shows that education for daughters is often seen to enhance family status and improve a daughter's marriage prospects. For young women themselves, education may provide an opportunity for personal development, independence and self-fulfilment (Dale et al. 2002).

UNEMPLOYMENT

The section above has indicated the strong relationship between economic activity and qualifications and how this is mediated by life stage. However, economic activity includes both unemployment and employment and, in this section, we consider the relationship between unemployment and qualifications for women in different ethnic groups.

A great deal of research has analysed unemployment differences between ethnic groups in the UK (Blackaby et al. 1997; 1999; 2002; Leslie et al. 1998). Studies have examined the relationships between male unemployment and the local labour market (Fieldhouse and Gould 1998), the role of qualifications and the penalty associated with being foreign born (Heath and Yu 2005). Yeandle et al. (2006) have focused specifically on women in the local labour market and have identified some of the barriers that militate against getting employment. These include a lack of confidence, difficulties in accessing information, a lack of social and support networks as well as unpaid caring responsibilities.

We have based our consideration of unemployment on the International Labor Office (ILO) definition as used by the QLFS. This requires a person to have not worked more than one hour in the survey reference week, to be able to start work, and to have been actively seeking work in the four weeks before the date of the interview. However, formal definitions of unemployment do not correspond well to women's own perception of whether or not they are unemployed (Cragg and Dawson 1984; Dex 1985). For example, the ILO definition excludes women working a very small number of hours each week and also women who plan to arrange childcare after they have received a job offer and therefore may not be 'able to start a job'. For these reasons levels of unemployment may be underestimated for women.

Table 3.1 showed that, at both the earlier and later time points, the percentages of minority ethnic women who are unemployed are consistently higher than for White women. Despite the fact that overall levels of unemployment for women were, in 2001–05, almost half the level in 1992–96, the disparity between White and minority groups remained almost the same.

Table 3.6 shows variation in levels of unemployment by qualification. Levels of unemployment are about three times as high for women without any qualifications as for those with degree-level qualifications. However,

Table 3.6   *Level of unemployment by highest qualification and ethnic group, 1992–2005*

Ethnic group	Degree	A level	O/GCSE	Other	None
White	2.3	4.2	4.8	6.3	7.5
Black Caribbean	4.9	11.9	14.4	14.9	14.8
Black African	9.5	20.5	21.5	20.7	28.7
Black other	7.6	8.7	21.2	18.3	30.0
Indian	4.4	8.3	7.6	10.3	11.0
Pakistani	8.1	11.1	18.9	29.1	22.3
Bangladeshi	12.2	17.3	18.1	35.5	32.9
Chinese	6.1	3.7	5.7	8.8	4.8
Other	6.7	11.9	12.3	12.6	13.9

Note: Women aged 19–60, excludes FT students.

Source: QLFS, weighted.

this is not the case for Chinese women, for whom unemployment is, on average, only slightly higher than for White women (Table 3.1) but also there is no gradient with level of qualifications.

Differences in the likelihood of being unemployed have been estimated using two logit models – one for the period 1992–96 and a second for the period 2001–05 (Table 3.7). This allows us to estimate the marginal effect of being in a minority ethnic group by comparison with the White group, holding constant other variables such as age and level of education. Table 3.7 shows that, in 1992–96 and 2001–05, all ethnic groups except the Chinese were significantly more likely to be unemployed than White women. In 1992–96 Black Caribbean women had levels of unemployment that were almost 3 percentage points higher than White women, whilst for Black African women and Pakistani and Bangladeshi women unemployment was estimated at about 8 percentage points higher. In 2001–05 a very similar pattern is found, although levels of unemployment are generally lower for all groups.

Figure 3.1 uses predicted probabilities based on these two models. It charts the predicted level of unemployment for each ethnic group taking into account qualifications, age, regional level of unemployment, year, whether UK born or brought up and family situation. Column 1 uses exactly the same models as reported in Table 3.7 and produces predicted levels of unemployment very similar to the raw figures shown in Table 3.1. Column 2 omits ethnic group from the models. It is, therefore, predicting expected levels of unemployment, based on the individual's characteristics, but ignoring any effect due to ethnicity. For all minority groups except the

Table 3.7   Marginal effects (%) for unemployment from logit model: employed; unemployed

	1992–96		2001–05	
	%M. effect	St. error	%M. effect	St. error
Age in years	**−0.43**	0.07	**−0.36**	0.05
Age squared	**0.00**	0.00	**0.00**	0.00
Degree level	**−5.35**	0.18	**−3.51**	0.17
A level	**−2.99**	0.18	**−2.34**	0.15
O level	**−3.10**	0.15	**−1.57**	0.14
Other qualification	**−1.51**	0.24	**−0.44**	0.14
Not UK born/ brought up	**0.87**	0.26	**0.82**	0.30
Black Caribbean	**2.98**	0.91	**1.76**	0.26
Black Other	**4.88**	1.57	**4.29**	1.04
Black African	**8.01**	0.90	**3.90**	0.85
Indian	**2.25**	0.68	**1.58**	0.50
Pakistani and Bangladeshi	**7.75**	1.18	**5.76**	1.22
Chinese	**−0.00**	1.48	1.31	1.01
Other ethnic group	**4.96**	0.76	**3.10**	0.72
Regional unemployment	**0.28**	0.04	**0.32**	0.04
Year	**−0.20**	0.08	−0.07	0.07
Partner working	**−7.34**	0.23	**−3.73**	0.16
Partner not working	0.58	0.30	**−0.40**	0.17
Child less than 5	**8.66**	0.40	**3.46**	0.29
Child age 5–15	**3.83**	0.27	**2.38**	0.18
N cases	128 842		103 851	
Pseudo R-squared	9.23		8.99	
Mean unemployment	6.83		3.74	

Notes: Calculated at the mean for each ethnic group; significant effects (at 5% level) in bold.

Source: Quarterly Labour Force Survey, 1992–2005, unweighted, women aged 19–60, excludes FT students.

Chinese the predicted levels of unemployment fall, indicating that 'ethnicity' plays a role in explaining the levels of unemployment for minority groups. The 'ethnic penalty' is highest for Bangladeshi, followed by Pakistani and Black African women and shows little change, proportionately, between the earlier and the later period. For Chinese women, the level of unemployment is slightly higher in 1992–96 when ethnicity is ignored – that is, they have a negative penalty – and they are, therefore, less likely to be actually unemployed than would be predicted by their educational level and other characteristics.

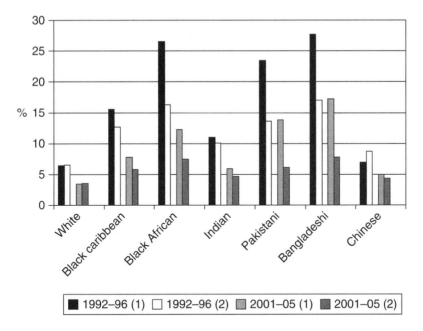

Figure 3.1   *Predicted levels of unemployment for 1992–96 and 2001–05*
(1) including ethnicity, (2) ignoring ethnicity, based on models
in Table 3.7

Table 3.8 takes this analysis a step further by reporting the marginal
effects from a logit model run separately for each ethnic group. As in Table
3.7, the marginal effects represent the increase in the level of unemployment
(in percentage points) for a unit increase in each of the characteristics in the
table. For example, for White women, a degree level qualification reduces the
likelihood of being unemployed by 4 percentage points, by comparison with
a White women with no qualifications. The analysis shows that qualifications play an important role in reducing unemployment for all women
except the Chinese – thus confirming the results in Table 3.6. The protective
effect of qualifications is highest for Pakistani and Bangladeshi women for
whom a degree-level qualification reduces the likelihood of unemployment
by over 13 percentage points. Not being born or brought up in the UK
increases the chances of unemployment for all minority ethnic groups
except Indian, with the greatest effect for the Pakistani and Bangladeshi
women. For the Chinese this is the only variable which is significant. For all
groups (except the Chinese) a working partner reduces the likelihood of
unemployment, whilst a child under 5 increases it – except for Pakistani and
Bangladeshi women. The absence of relationship between a young child and

Table 3.8   Marginal effects (%) for unemployment from logit model: employed; unemployed

	White		Black Caribbean		Indian		Pakistani/Bangladeshi		Chinese	
	%M.eff	St. error	%M.eff	St. error	%M.eff	St. error	%M.eff	St. error	%M.eff	St. error
Age in years	**-0.38**	0.04	**-2.09**	0.40	**-0.91**	0.37	-1.22	0.82	0.30	0.70
Age squared	**0.00**	0.00	**0.02**	0.01	**0.01**	0.00	0.011	0.01	-0.01	0.01
Degree level	**-4.28**	0.09	**-9.15**	1.07	**-6.49**	0.92	**-13.43**	2.78	-0.04	2.19
A level	**-2.60**	0.11	**-3.69**	1.58	**-3.48**	0.81	**-10.55**	2.67	-1.46	3.25
O level	**-2.35**	0.09	**-3.59**	1.41	**-3.38**	1.02	-3.81	2.76	2.07	5.21
Other qual	**-1.16**	0.13	-1.67	1.41	-0.35	0.94	4.05	3.23	1.36	2.52
Not UK born/brought up	**1.08**	0.18	**4.17**	1.48	1.13	1.20	**10.45**	3.18	**3.27**	1.36
Regional unemployment	**0.25**	0.03	0.46	0.33	0.14	0.20	0.72	0.61	0.52	0.35
Year	**-0.16**	0.02	-0.11	0.22	-0.34	0.21	0.23	0.42	0.12	0.18
Partner working	**-5.41**	0.11	**-12.28**	1.39	**-6.69**	1.36	**-14.62**	2.70	-3.95	2.25
Partner not working	0.12	0.15	**-3.23**	1.15	0.88	1.22	-4.61	3.25	1.53	3.04
Child less than 5	**6.47**	0.24	**7.78**	1.78	**5.93**	1.45	-0.37	3.08	-1.09	2.53
Child age 5–15	**3.38**	0.15	**6.48**	1.26	1.84	1.30	1.56	3.41	-2.89	1.92
N cases	303 035		3184		4879		1439		873	
Pseudo R-squared	9.3		12.5		6.2		10.3		5.6	
Mean unemployment	4.8		11.5		8.3		18.8		6.0	

Notes:
Separate models have been run for each ethnic group.
Calculated at the mean for each ethnic group; significant effects (at 5% level) in bold.

Source: Quarterly Labour Force Survey, 1992–2005, unweighted, women aged 19–60, excludes FT students.

unemployment for Pakistani and Bangladeshi women may be explained by their very low levels of economic activity when children are young (Table 3.5).

These results suggest that we need a much better understanding of the disadvantage experienced by Black women and Pakistani and Bangladeshi women by comparison with Indian and Chinese women. Whilst levels of unemployment are generally much higher for women from minority groups than for White groups, we need to avoid making blanket generalisations about ethnic minorities as a whole and about the role of particular characteristics such as qualifications. These differences raise further questions that cannot be answered here. For example, what role do unmeasured characteristics play, including cultural and family expectations about employment; the acceptability in their community of women holding particular kinds of jobs; whether job search is confined to the locality in which the woman lives – which may have a high level of unemployment; the role of local and social networks in finding employment; and the attitudes and stereotypes of potential employers.

UNDEREMPLOYMENT AND OVER-EDUCATION

Underemployment is conceptualised in many different ways and may include those not in work who would like to be working, those working part-time or shorter hours than they would like and also those working below their potential. In the latter category research often focuses on establishing the extent to which individuals are in jobs which match their educational qualifications, experience and skills and the extent to which they are over or under-educated (Chevalier 2003; Chevalier and Lindley 2006; Dex and Lindley 2007). Over- or under-education is usually measured by comparing the level of education required for a specific job with the level of education held, or, if this information is not available, using the average level of education for each occupation and comparing this with particular population sub-groups. Whilst there is considerable variation in the extent of over-education depending on the methods and the data source, levels of about 30 per cent or more are widely reported in UK studies.

Generally studies find that levels of over-education exceed those of under-education, for ethnic minorities as well as the general population. Battu and Sloane (2004) found that only Indians, African Asians and the Chinese men and women were more likely to be over-educated than the White group, whilst Bangladeshi men and women were much less likely to be over-educated. Among women, Dex and Lindley (2007) found that Black African and Chinese women had much higher rates of over-education than

White women but that Bangladeshi women were less likely to be over-educated than White women.

A number of studies based on graduates also find high levels of over-education. For example, Dolton and Vignoles (2000) found that 38 per cent of UK graduates leaving higher education in 1980 were over-educated in their first job and 30 per cent were still over-educated six years later. Chevalier and Lindley (2006) using a cohort of 1995 graduates found about 35 per cent were not in 'graduate' jobs.

In this chapter we have focused on the role of degree-level qualifications in promoting economic activity and protecting against unemployment and, in this section, we retain this focus on women with degree level qualifications and explore the extent to which they are in graduate level jobs. These qualifications are much less ambiguous than many other types of qualification and many minority ethnic women with this level of qualification will have been educated in the UK and will therefore have fluent English.[4] In addition, an increasing portion of the population are obtaining degree-level qualifications. In 2005–06 the Higher Education Initial Participation Rate (HEIPR) for 17–30-year-olds was 43 per cent (DFES 2007) and, as we saw in Table 3.4, ethnic minority women are generally increasing their highest qualification faster than White women. As described in Table 3.3, degree-level qualifications include: higher degrees, first degrees, teaching qualifications, nursing, HNC/HND, BTEC higher and NVQ levels 4 and 5.

We therefore focus on women who are in employment and for whom occupational information was recorded in the QLFS. We have used a classification of graduate occupations designed by Elias and Purcell (2004) which allocates occupations coded to the Standard Classification of Occupations (SOC) to one of five different categories, 'traditional', 'modern', 'new', 'niche' and 'non-graduate' occupations, as defined in Box 3.1.

This classification provides a clear gradient in terms of the requirement for a graduate qualification. For example, amongst our QLFS respondents in 2001–05, 91 per cent of those in traditional graduate occupations held a degree-level qualification compared with only 44 per cent in niche graduate occupations. We expect there to be ethnic differences in the distribution of women across these categories which may be based on preferences for particular kinds of occupations (for example, solicitors, doctors versus management accountants or nurses). However, we expect that niche occupations (for example, personal assistant, office manager) may be taken by those who are finding it hardest to obtain graduate-level work.

Table 3.9 shows the occupational distribution of women with degree-level qualifications, using the four groups of graduate occupations and

BOX 3.1   A CLASSIFICATION OF GRADUATE OCCUPATIONS

Traditional graduate occupations – for which a degree is usually a standard entry qualification (for example, solicitors, doctors, scientists, lecturers, secondary school teachers)

Modern graduate occupations – these are represented by the newer occupations that have typically been filled by graduates since the 1960s expansion of higher education, for example, senior managers in large organisations, IT professions

New graduate occupations which often require a degree, for example, occupational therapists, quantity surveyors, medical radiographers, public relations officers and management accountants

Niche graduate occupations are those which form a boundary between graduate and non-graduate. The majority of those employed in these occupations do not have degrees and most of the jobs do not normally require a degree. However, many are judged to provide opportunities for degree-level skills, for example, planning and quality control engineers, hotel and accommodation managers and nurses.

Non-graduate occupations. These are all the rest not covered by the other categories

Source: Elias and Purcell (2004: table 1).

also non-graduate occupations. The sample is further restricted to women with a job. Because of the small number of women with degree-level qualifications we have combined data for 1992–2005. Indian, Pakistani and Bangladeshi women with degree-level qualifications are all more likely to be represented in the 'traditional' graduate occupations than their White counterparts, whilst Black Caribbean women are much less likely to be in this category. Inspection of the occupations in this category (not reported here) shows that for Indian, Pakistani and Bangladeshi women in traditional graduate occupations, medical practitioners and pharmacists account for about 40 per cent of women, whilst for Chinese women in such occupations, the most popular occupations are medical practitioner, followed by dentistry and teaching in higher education. By contrast, Black Caribbean women in traditional graduate occupations are mainly found in further and secondary education. Secondary teaching is

Table 3.9   Occupational distribution of women with degree-level qualification by ethnic group

Ethnic group (row %)	Traditional graduate occupations	Modern graduate occupations	New graduate occupations	Niche graduate occupations	Non-graduate occupations	Total %	Total N unweighted
White	17.5	19.9	11.7	26.7	24.1	100	74 459
Black Caribbean	10.4	15.6	9.3	39.3	25.4	100	822
Indian	22.0	15.5	10.4	23.4	28.8	100	1 270
Pakistani/Bangladeshi	23.1	15.8	11.0	14.2	35.9	100	306
Chinese	18.0	7.9	17.8	32.0	24.4	100	348

Note: Women aged 19–60 with degree level qualifications and in paid work, excludes FT students.

Source: QLFS pooled annual surveys 1992–2005, weighted.

also important for Pakistani and Bangladeshi women with degree-level qualifications.

Amongst those in 'modern graduate' occupations, primary and nursery school teaching predominate for White women but these have much less dominance for minority ethnic groups. Black Caribbean women with higher qualifications in modern graduate jobs are prominently in social work and related occupations, whilst software development is important for Chinese women in these occupations and, to a lesser extent, for Indian women.

In the 'new' graduate occupations, Black Caribbean women in such occupations often hold jobs as housing and welfare officers. By contrast, 44 per cent of Chinese women and a quarter of Indian women in such occupations are chartered or management accountants.

Degree-level Black Caribbean women are over-represented in the 'niche' graduate occupations – explained by the fact that well over 50 per cent of these women in such occupations are in nursing or midwifery. By contrast, fewer than 20 per cent of Pakistani and Bangladeshi women in niche graduate occupations are in nursing – which contributes to the over-representation of the former and the under-representation of the latter in niche occupations.

Overall, nearly a quarter of women with degree-level qualifications are not in graduate level occupations. However, this is significantly higher for Pakistani and Bangladeshi women (36 per cent) and Indian women (29 per cent) than for other groups, with little difference between the percentages for White, Black Caribbean and Chinese women with degree-level qualifications. There is, however, considerable similarity in the type of non-graduate occupations held by women. Clerical jobs in the civil service, local government, accounts and wages, and general office work account for 25 per cent of White and Black Caribbean women who are in non-graduate occupations. Comparable figures for Indian and Pakistani/ Bangladeshi women are 35 per cent and 44 per cent for Chinese women. Over a quarter of Chinese women with degree level qualification who are working in non-graduate occupations are wages and accounting clerks.

One of the noteworthy contrasts in Table 3.9 is the low percentage of Pakistani and Bangladeshi women with degree-level qualifications who are in niche graduate occupations and the much higher level in non-graduate occupations (36 per cent), by comparison with other ethnic groups. This is particularly surprising because the non-graduate jobs identified above are all found in the 'niche' category at higher levels. So, for example, executive-level civil service posts and financial and accounting technicians are both found in the 'niche' graduate category. An unanswered question is why degree-level Pakistani and Bangladeshi women are not accessing these higher-level graduate jobs. Qualitative interviews with Pakistani and

Bangladeshi women with degrees (Ahmed and Dale 2008) suggest that they may take clerical work in order to gain experience or get a foothold on the career ladder if they have had difficulty getting 'graduate' occupations. They may also be constrained by the availability of graduate jobs in local labour markets and by discrimination in the labour market.

DISCUSSION AND CONCLUSIONS

This chapter has highlighted very considerable ethnic differences in women's patterns of labour market behaviour. We can see how historical and cultural factors influence current labour market outcomes. This is most apparent in the very different relationship between economic activity, partnership and children for Black Caribbean women compared with Pakistani and Bangladeshi women. It is also evident that qualifications play a very important role for all ethnic groups in promoting economic activity and, for all but Chinese women, in protecting against unemployment. Apart from the Chinese group, rates of unemployment, taking into account differences in levels of qualifications and other personal characteristics, are much higher for minority ethnic women than for White women – although we have to remember that our measures of qualification ignore distinctions and quality differences within each qualification level. The fact that there appears to be no ethnic penalty on unemployment for Chinese women suggests the need for further work to identify whether the Chinese differ in unmeasured personal characteristics or whether they face fewer barriers in the labour market than other minority groups. Our classification of graduate jobs helps to reveal some of the occupational segregation amongst women from different ethnic groups, but also suggests that Pakistani and Bangladeshi women with degree-level qualifications are finding it harder than other groups to gain graduate occupations that are appropriate to their level of qualification.

NOTES

1. Section 4 provides details of the data sources and definitions used.
2. Students' employment status is likely to be secondary to their studies and based on a different set of decisions than for non-students.
3. The International Labour Office (ILO) definition of unemployment used in the LFS refers to those people who have not worked more than one hour during the week before the interview, but who are available for work and have actively looked for week in the four weeks before the interview.
4. In our sample, just over two-thirds of Pakistani and Bangladeshi women with degrees were either born in the UK or arrived before the age of 16. However, for the Chinese this was only 30 per cent.

REFERENCES

Ahmed, S. and A. Dale (2008), 'Pakistani and Bangladeshi women's labour market participation', CCSR Working Paper 2008–01, University of Manchester, Manchester.

Battu, H. and P. Sloane (2004), 'Over-education and ethnic minorities in Britain', *The Manchester School*, **72**(4), 535–59.

Becker, G.S. (1981), *A Treatise on the Family*, Cambridge, MA: Harvard University Press.

Berthoud, R. (2000), 'Ethnic employment penalties in Britain', *Journal of Ethnic and Migration Studies*, **26**(3), 389–416.

Blackaby, D., S. Drinkwater, D. Leslie and P. Murphy (1997), 'A picture of male and female unemployment among Britain's ethnic minorities', *Scottish Journal of Political Economy*, **44**(2), 182–97.

Blackaby, D., D. Leslie, P. Murphy and N.C. O'Leary (1999), 'Unemployment among Britain's ethnic minorities', *The Manchester School*, **67**(1), 1–20.

Blackaby, D.H., D.G. Leslie, P.D. Murphy and N.C. O'Leary (2002), 'White/ethnic minority earnings and employment differentials in Britain: evidence from the LFS', *Oxford Economic Papers*, **54**, 270–97.

Blossfeld, H.-P. and S. Drobnic (2001), *Careers of Couples in Contemporary Society*, Oxford: Oxford University Press.

Chevalier, A. (2003), 'Measuring over education', *Economica*, **70**(3), 509–31.

Chevalier, A. and J. Lindley (2006), 'Over-education and the skills of UK graduates', mimeo, paper presented European Association of Labour Economists Annual Conference, Prague.

Connor, H., C. Tyers, T. Modood and J. Hillage (2004), *Why the difference? A Closer Look at Higher Education Minority Ethnic Students and Graduates*, Research Report RR552, London: DfES.

Cragg, A. and T. Dawson (1984), Unemployed Women: A Study of Attitudes and Experiences, Research Paper 47, London: Department for Employment.

Dale, A., N. Shaheen, V. Kalra and E. Fieldhouse (2001), 'Labour market prospects for Pakistani and Bangladeshi women', *Work, Employment and Society*, **16**(1), 5–26.

Dale, A., N. Shaheen, V. Kalra and E. Fieldhouse (2002), 'Routes into education and employment for young Pakistani and Bangladeshi women in the UK', *Ethnic and Racial Studies*, **25**(6), 942–68.

Department for Education and Skills (DfES) (2007), www.dfes.gov.uk/rsgateway/ (accessed 18 April 2007).

Dex, S. (1985), *The Sexual Division of Work*, Brighton: Harvester Press.

Dex, S. and H. Joshi (1996), 'A widening gulf among Britain's mothers', *Oxford Review of Economic Policy*, **12**(1), 65–75.

Dex, S. and J. Lindley (2007), 'Labour market job matching for UK minority ethnic groups', Working Paper, No. 2007003, University of Sheffield, Economics Department.

Dex, S., H. Joshi, S. Macran and A. McCulloch (1998), 'Women's employment transitions around childbearing', *Oxford Bulletin of Economics and Statistics*, **60**(1), 97–115.

Dolton, P.J. and A. Vignoles (2000), 'The incidence and effects of over education in the graduate labour market', *Economics of Education Review*, **19**(2), 179–98.

Duncan, S. and S. Irwin (2004), 'The social patterning of values and rationalities: mothers' choices in combining caring and employment', *Social Policy and Society*, **3**(4), 391–9.

Duncan, S., R. Edwards, T. Reynolds and P. Alldred (2003), 'Mothering, paid work and partnering', *Work, Employment and Society*, **17**(2), 309–30.

Elias, P. and K. Purcell (2004), 'Report – SOC(HE): A classification of occupations for studying the graduate labour market', research paper no. 6, Employment Studies Research Unit, University of West of England and Institute for Employment Research, University of Warwick.

Elliott, J., A. Dale and M. Egerton (2001), 'The influence of qualifications on women's work histories, employment status and earnings at age 33', *European Sociological Review*, **17**(2), 145–68.

Fieldhouse, E. and M.I. Gould (1998), 'Ethnic minority unemployment and local labour market conditions in Great Britain', *Environment & Planning* A, **30**(5), 833–53.

Heath, A. and S. Yu (2005), *Understanding Social Change*, Oxford: Oxford University Press.

Leslie, D., S. Drinkwater and N. O'Leary (1998), 'Unemployment and earnings among Britain's ethnic minorities: some signs for optimism', *Journal of Ethnic and Migration Studies*, **24**, 489–507.

Lindley, J., A. Dale and S. Dex (2004), 'Ethnic differences in women's demographic and family characteristics and economic activity profiles 1992–2002', *Labour Market Trends*, **112**(4), 153–65.

Macran, S., H. Joshi and S. Dex (1996), 'Employment after childbearing: a survival analysis', *Work, Employment and Society*, **10**(2), 273–96.

Office for National Statistics (ONS) (2003), *Labour Force Survey User Guide – Volume 1, Background and Methodology* www.statistics.gov.uk/downloads/theme_labour/LFSGU_Vol1_2003.pdf, accessed on 10 January 2008.

Reynolds, T. (2005), Caribbean Mothers: Identity and Experience in the UK, London: Tufnell Press.

Yeandle, S., B. Stiell and L. Buckner (2006), *Ethnic Minority Women and Access to the Labour Market: Synthesis Report*, Sheffield: Sheffield Hallam University.

PART II

Dynamics of Employment and Family across
the Life Course

4. Putting women on the research agenda: the 1980 Women and Employment Survey[1]

Jean Martin and Ceridwen Roberts

INTRODUCTION

From a distance of over 25 years it is hard to remember how 'revolutionary' or 'radical' major programmes of social science enquiry into the life circumstances of women were in late 1970s Britain. The Women and Employment Survey (WES) which was conducted in 1980 and published in 1984 (Martin and Roberts 1984a; 1984b) holds a seminal role in social science research on women and contributed to informing practice and policy throughout the 1980s. Its several methodological innovations also made a major contribution to social science, particularly the development of event or life history data collection techniques and analysis. This chapter reviews the origins, scope and key findings of the study against the background of women's changing roles and the legislative context of the late 1970s as well the development of the social science function in central government.

WOMEN'S CHANGING ROLES AND LABOUR MARKET POSITION

The 1970s were a period of considerable change for women, both in their economic and social roles and more particularly in the public recognition of this which major legislative change embodied. There was an explosion of interest in women's situation explored by numerous academic studies and popular writings generated frequently from the growth of feminism and the emerging and very active women's movement and pressure for equality from women in trade unions. At the same time rising divorce rates and growing numbers of lone-parent families, as much as women's increased labour market participation and a concern to achieve equal pay and improved treatment both at work and more generally, all contributed to making women the centre of much political, social and intellectual attention from a range of different perspectives. The development of interest in the position of women in the labour market that occurred within the Department of Employment (DE) during the 1970s must be seen against this general background.

There had been a steady increase in the levels of women's labour market participation during the 1960s and a large increase in levels of part-time employment. Indeed, most growth in employment during the mid-1960s to mid-1970s had been in part-time jobs: over 1 500 000 new jobs were created during the period. These jobs were predominantly filled by married women (Robertson and Briggs 1979). By 1979, 18 per cent of all employees worked part-time and of these 94 per cent were women (OPCS 1982). The greater availability of part-time work both facilitated and was encouraged by married women's return to employment after a period out of the labour market for childrearing (Beechey and Perkins 1985) and the periods of absence were becoming shorter as part-time jobs enabled women to combine paid work with their unpaid domestic and caring work.

There is no doubt that the increased need to encourage women into the labour market which had characterised employment policy thinking in the 1960s coupled with agitation to introduce equal pay and conditions were crucial factors in changing the position of women workers. Audrey Hunt's 1965 national survey (Hunt 1968) commissioned at a time of comparative labour shortage looked at the experiences and attitudes of women workers in order to enable employers and society generally to understand their needs better. As levels of women's labour market participation rose, the political demand for legislation to improve their pay and conditions increased. The demand for equal pay was a long-established one; it had first been passed as a Trades Union Congress (TUC) resolution in 1888 but it was not until the mid-1960s that the pressure for political action combined with the existence of a Labour government was strong enough to lead to legislation (Snell et al. 1981).

The Equal Pay Act, enacted by a Labour government in 1970 and fully implemented from 1975, coupled with anti-inflationary incomes policies with flat rate rises had an immediate effect on women's pay. Earnings began to rise: non-manual women's earnings saw an increase from an average 49.7 per cent of men's in 1970 to 60.5 per cent in 1975, while manual women's earnings rose from 50.0 per cent in 1970 to 61.2 per cent of men's by 1978. These changes unleashed a momentum for wider change as legislation against sex discrimination more generally was seen as an essential complement to the Equal Pay Act. So the Sex Discrimination Act 1975 was passed and, for the first time, protection and pay were given to qualifying pregnant women as statutory maternity pay and job reinstatement rights were enacted in the Employment Protection Act 1975.

Legislative and labour market change and the championing of women's issues by senior politicians like Barbara Castle was accompanied by a considerable amount of research both within government and outside to document women's disadvantaged position (DE 1974a; 1974b; 1975a; 1975b; Hakim 1979; Hunt 1975) and explain the inequalities between men and women. The main focus of both academic and more campaigning studies was on the relationship between home and work and how women's position in society and the labour market was influenced by and shaped their reproductive role and the domestic division of labour (Barker and Allen 1976a; 1976b; Comer 1972). However, many of the studies were small scale and unrepresentative of women as a whole.

As a result of all these changes it is understandable that there was enormous political and policy interest in the Department of Employment in the whole area of equal pay and opportunities, and therefore a growing sense that we needed to know more about women's labour market behaviour and attitudes. A major academic research study had been commissioned from the London School of Economics to examine the implementation of the equality legislation (Snell et al. 1981). This was indicative of the increasing interest in and use of social science research and statistics within government, which the establishment of the Central Statistical Office (CSO) publication *Social Trends* in 1970 illustrated. The setting up of a Social Science Branch within the department from the mid-1970s staffed mainly by industrial sociologists and industrial relations specialists consolidated this in the DE.

A programme of social science research on women in the labour market started to grow from 1978 when a social scientist was charged with developing a programme of research on women to meet the policy information needs and challenge some of the limitations of official statistics developed on the basis of men's employment status and behaviour. In total 11 major projects on different aspects of women's employment were commissioned between 1979 and 1983 (Roberts 1985) of which the WES was the cornerstone.

THE DEVELOPMENT OF A CASE FOR A NATIONAL SURVEY OF WOMEN

National surveys are very expensive and time-consuming activities and require a good case to be made for this use of resources. It had been 15 years since the previous government survey of women (Hunt 1968) and there was recognition that there had been many changes since that date; thus there were both general and specific factors encouraging a survey. In general it was felt that there had been an increase in the range of information available about women's labour market activity, particularly from official sources.

However, none focused on women directly or covered the wide range of issues that might help to understand why and when women take paid work, and with what consequences. Nor did they consider how this related to the wider issue of men's and women's roles in the family. But more specifically, the trigger factor was increasing concern about the level of female unemployment. This was particularly raised by the Advisory Committee on Women's Employment, which represented a wide range of women's interests across both sides of industry and more broadly. This met regularly with Department of Employment ministers and senior officials to review women's employment issues and was key in pressing Labour ministers and, subsequently, Conservative ministers after the 1979 election, to find out more about the extent and consequences of rising unemployment among women.

By the late 1970s Britain had moved into a deep recession with rising levels of unemployment; women's registered unemployment was increasing faster than men's. It rose from a very low base of 1.2 per cent in the early 1970s to 5.2 per cent by 1980. But it was thought that registered unemployment, already known as a less than comprehensive count of actual unemployment for men, was much less likely to be an adequate indicator of real levels of unemployment for women. So there was little information about the real extent of unemployment among women and its consequences for them and their families. In addition, the 1970s had seen major changes in the family. Fertility had been falling, women were starting families at increasingly older ages and divorce and lone motherhood were increasing, all of which could be expected to have an impact on or be related to employment trends.

A research strategy started to emerge around these concerns. It needed to deal with definitional problems which made measuring the incidence of unemployment complex, together with the wish to look at both current and longer-term consequences of experiencing unemployment. It meant that any study needed to be representative of all women of working age. Therefore, this required a new national survey so that it would be possible to compare 'unemployed' women with both women who were employed and those who were economically inactive.

More generally, the survey aimed to establish how important a paid job was for women and how much of their adult lives they spent in employment. Thus the overall focus was on the place of employment in women's lives, the importance of paid work to women and their job priorities. Underlying these aims was the question of how far the situation of women was different from that of men. The survey also aimed to test the assumptions that were prevalent at the time. These included the idea that work was less important for women than for men. There had not been any systematic examination of this and other assumptions about the place of employment in women's lives. The WES aimed to explore these issues. There was the need to look at women's current situation in the context of their whole lives, that is, both their educational and employment histories, as well as their relationship and family formation history. This policy and research need was to lead to a major research innovation – the collection of work and family histories.

SURVEY DESIGN AND CONTENT

The survey interviewed a nationally representative survey of 5588 women of working age (16–59) in Great Britain in 1980 and also a sub-sample of 799 of the husbands of the married women. The response rates for the two samples were 83 per cent and 81 per cent respectively.

Information was collected by interviewers from the Office for Population Censuses and Surveys (OPCS, now the Office for National Statistics) using face-to-face structured interviews. The interview schedules had been designed following extensive qualitative work and pilot interviews. The interviews collected an enormous amount of material and some of the interviews were very long. They covered both information about the current situation and detailed retrospective work and family histories so could, potentially, cover 45 years for a woman who had left school at 14 and was aged 59 at the time of the survey in 1980.

The potential scope of the survey was enormous. Essentially, we wanted to get as comprehensive a picture as possible of women as paid workers. We wanted to identify the factors which took them in and out of the labour market and jobs, and the conditions under which they worked, both at their place of work and in terms of the interplay with any caring or domestic work they undertook. We wanted to know about their priorities and attitudes to working or not, as well as their general views about the sexual division of labour. In retrospect it is clear that a highly significant factor shaping this survey was the fact that all the wider research team were either industrial sociologists, psychologists or social survey analysts with a particular interest in women. Thus, unlike on many surveys and much government social research now, the team was drawing directly on substantive knowledge of the current debates in the sociology and psychology of work and wanted to test out these ideas on a large nationally representative sample. Moreover, the team consulted widely with the academic and policy community inside and outside government in the design stages. From the start the study was seen as a resource for the whole community. Therefore, although policy driven this survey was not policy dictated.

COMPLEMENTARY QUALITATIVE STUDIES

As was standard practice at the time at OPCS, qualitative exploratory interviews were carried out to provide a basis for the design of the structured questionnaire. Some of the qualitative work was carried out by OPCS and some by a commercial market research agency. In addition, a qualitative study of non-working women was commissioned to explore their situation in more detail and, in particular, their perceptions of whether they were 'unemployed'. We wanted to understand the meaning women gave to being 'out of a job' and how this tallied with the official definition of unemployment which at that period was associated with being in receipt of unemployment benefit. The results showed a complex pattern of movement in and out of economic activity with spells started for one reason, such as losing a job so that a woman fitted the classic definition of unemployed, changing their status as women stayed out of work for other types of reasons and vice versa. Consequently, we decided not to attempt to distinguish between periods of unemployment and periods of being economically inactive in the retrospective work histories since most women's experiences showed a lack of a clear and consistent distinction between the two. Although recognised at this juncture, it appears to have got lost since as articles on unemployment and inactivity in *Labour Market Trends* since 2000 have been making this point as if new (Weir 2003).

METHODOLOGICAL INNOVATIONS AND KEY FINDINGS

It is worth recalling how much has changed in the survey world since 1980. In the 1980s far fewer surveys were being carried out than today and most were quite small in terms of sample size. The WES was the largest ad hoc government survey of its day; only the major continuous and regularly repeated surveys were larger.

As well as the attention the survey attracted for its actual findings, within the social research community it was seen as extremely important in breaking new methodological ground. These innovations were essential to answer key research and policy questions. Chief of these were the retrospective work histories, the occupational classification developed to better measure women's occupations and a new measure of workplace occupational segregation.

The survey also included a large number of different attitude questions most of which were designed to produce scales rather than just being analysed individually, although we did that as well. Many of these have been used in subsequent surveys, particularly the British Social Attitudes Surveys, to track attitude change over time.

WORK AND LIFE HISTORIES

In 1979 collecting work histories was a very rare activity especially in large-scale surveys. In deciding to attempt this we were influenced by the substantive knowledge that understanding women's lifetime patterns of employment was essential background to understanding both their attachment to work and also to their 'success' or not in the labour market. Very importantly we were influenced by two other surveys. The Family Formation Survey (Dunnell 1979) had asked a survey of women about their fertility and family formation history, and the National Training Survey (NTS) conducted for the Manpower Services Commission had asked men and women about their training. The NTS had been very large and ambitious and though mainly about training histories did collect work information as well (Elias and Main 1982; Greenhalgh and Stewart 1981).

However, the NTS remained relatively under-analysed as there were severe technical problems handling the data with limited software. Aware of this, we still embarked on collecting retrospective detailed life and work histories on a large scale designed for quantitative analysis and, most importantly, working out how to analyse the data so as to avoid the problems of the NTS. The methods developed to collect them have been major influences on the subsequent collection of work and event histories on surveys such as the British Household Panel Survey, most prominently, but also the Social Change and Economic Life Initiative (SCELI) studies in the late 1980s, the Family and Working Lives survey (1994) and Employment in Britain (Gallie et al. 1998).

The retrospective work histories provided longitudinal data that allowed us to look at women and employment from a lifetime perspective that had not been possible before. Today, with far more rich and varied data at our disposal, it is difficult to remember that there were all sorts of questions that could not be answered with the data available before the WES was carried out, particularly those requiring longitudinal data. From the outset we realised that this would be a very rich and complex data set and that any work the DE/OPCS did in-house should be complemented by simultaneous secondary analysis so that as much analysis could be released as early as possible. Therefore, two academic economists, Shirley Dex and Heather Joshi, with specific interests in women's issues and the technical and analytical skills to manage complex data-sets, particularly hierarchical and longitudinal data, were commissioned to work on different aspects[2] alongside us (Dex 1984; 1987; 1988; Joshi 1984).

The life and work histories were an important part of the interviews, particularly for older women who had had many jobs over a period of more than 40 years. We first collected details of major life events: the respondent's date of birth, date of leaving school, dates of marriages, and ends of marriages and of the births of children. Family transitions are well remembered by women so there were unlikely to be problems with recall errors. These dates served as anchors for the work histories. We then asked about dates of finishing full-time education and starting and stopping work as well as changing between full- and part-time work. Having established the skeleton of the life and work history, we went back and asked more detailed questions about reasons for changes in employment status, the jobs women were doing and what they were doing when they were not working. However, we did not try to separate periods of unemployment from economic inactivity during periods of not working since, for the reasons described above.

After the data were collected and captured electronically the life events and work history data were interleaved into a chronologically sequenced event history file so that the order and timing of any type of event and the duration of any kind of state could be determined. This allowed us, for example, to find out how long after a birth a woman had returned to work, whether she worked between two consecutive births, and how many job changes she had had. This rich source of data allowed us to look at how employment changes as women pass through different life stages and to compare women born at different points in time.

Before the survey there were various 'myths' about women and employment but little evidence to actually support or disprove them. So although we knew from cross-sectional surveys that the outline employment profile looked bimodal for women of different ages, we did not have longitudinal data to tell us about patterns of movement in and out of work and from full- to part-time work as domestic responsibilities and other factors changed over the life course. We also did not know about the extent to which different groups of women had different labour market careers.

Figure 4.1 shows how women's economic activity in 1980 (excluding full-time students) varied by age and could have been generated from contemporary cross-sectional data available from other surveys such as the Labour Force Survey or the General Household Survey. It shows the high proportions of women working in the younger age groups falling as

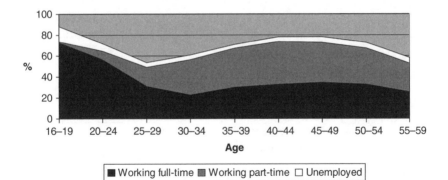

Figure 4.1 *Women's economic activity in 1980, by age (except full-time students)*

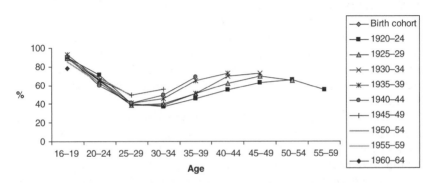

Figure 4.2 *Proportion of women working at different ages, by cohort*

women enter the childbearing years, rising as children get older, and falling again as the state retirement age approaches: the classic bimodal picture. But here we are not looking at how the economic activity of the same women changes over time: women of different ages in 1980 were born at different points in time and had different work patterns when they were younger. We were able to explore these patterns using the retrospective histories.

Figure 4.2 uses the longitudinal histories to show for different birth cohorts the proportions of women working at different ages. Here we are looking at how the work behaviour of birth cohorts of the same women change as they age. The point at which the lines stop reflects the ages of the different birth cohorts at the time of the 1980 survey. Among women in the WES the behaviour at younger ages was very similar for all cohorts, but differences opened out from the late twenties with each successive cohort

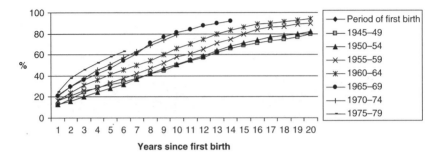

Figure 4.3   Proportion of women returning to work by varying intervals since first birth, by period of first birth

having higher rates of working than the one before, chiefly because they returned to work earlier in the lives of their children.

The work histories also allowed us to establish whether women returned to work between successive births or waited until all their children were older and what age their youngest child was when they returned to work, again showing how women's employment patterns were changing across the generations.

In Figure 4.3 we see how the timing of returning to work after the first birth changed for women whose first births occurred at different points in time. Even among the women with children born in the 1940s (most of whom were born in the 1920s), a large majority returned to work eventually: 80 per cent had done so by the time their oldest child was aged 20, and 87 per cent had returned at some time since their first birth. There was a clear trend, with women with more recent births returning to work much sooner than those whose first birth was in the 1940s. This was a striking finding which effectively destroyed a myth still prevalent in 1980 that older generations of women had stopped work permanently once they had children, with only a minority returning, and that only more recently had this changed: the results showed that even most of the oldest respondents covered by the survey returned to paid work eventually.

While the WES showed that women did not leave the labour market permanently when they had children, it provided evidence that having children nevertheless modified women's lifetime earnings dramatically. Joshi (1990) modelled the relationship between earnings observed in the survey and patterns of full- and part-time work, showing how a typical mother of two would have about half the lifetime earnings that she could have expected had she remained childless. This and other work on women's lifetime earnings have informed the development of policy in a number of areas, from childcare and equal opportunities to the treatment of pensions both in cases of divorce and for women more generally.

Occupational Segregation

The Equal Pay Act stipulated that men and women doing the same work at the same place of work should be paid at the same rate. So there was interest in the extent to which men and women were working side by side in the same jobs. However, most of the research on occupational segregation at the time had used measures based on the proportions of men and women found in different occupational categories using national survey data. The innovation in the WES was to look at occupational segregation at the workplace level from the perspective of women themselves. We asked women whether at their place of work any men were doing the same sort of work as them or only other women. We also asked an analogous question of the sample of husbands.

The results were striking: 57 per cent of women said they worked in jobs which were only done by other women (34 per cent said both men and women were doing their kind of work; the remaining 9 per cent either worked alone or were the only people doing that kind of work). Occupational segregation was much higher for part-time workers at 70 per cent compared with 58 per cent for the full-time workers. But even more surprisingly 81 per cent of the husbands of the married women said that they worked in jobs done only by other men. These findings were very important because the legislation on equal pay could only operate if men and women were doing the same kind of work at a specific place of work, which we showed was not usually the case. This measure of occupational segregation has since been used on other surveys including the National Child Development Survey (NCDS) fifth sweep in 1991, the SCELI studies of six local labour markets (MacEwen Scott 1994) and, more recently, the graduate survey by Purcell and Elias in this volume so enabling us to see how workplace occupational segregation has changed over time.

Classifying Women's Occupations

It was well known that the standard occupational classifications available at the time, such as Registrar General's (RG) Social Class and Socio-Economic Group (SEG), did not discriminate very well for women: large proportions of women's occupations fell into a small number of categories. As we wanted to use the WES work histories' job details to study movement between different kinds of jobs we needed a more subtle classification of

Table 4.1   Registrar General's social class and WES occupational classification compared

RG class			WES classification
	%	%	
I	1	1	Professional
		6	Teaching
II	19	7	Nursing, medical, social
		6	Other intermediate non-manual
III non-manual	39	30	Clerical
		9	Sales
III manual	7	7	Skilled manual
		10	Semi-skilled factory
IV	25	11	Semi-skilled domestic
		4	Other semi-skilled
V	9	9	Unskilled

occupations that would be suitable for women's occupations. Because we were particularly interested in studying occupational mobility we wanted an ordered classification so the RG classification was a better basis to start with than SEG (which is not an ordinal classification). However, as 86 per cent of women fell into three of the six RG categories, we decided to develop our own classification with more detailed categorisation of common women's occupations, but based on RG class, to allow comparison with other sources (Table 4.1). The WES classification subdivided RG classes II, III non-manual and IV but, even so, 30 per cent of women were in the clerical occupations category which could not easily be further divided as the occupations in it were fairly homogeneous. We also ordered the WES groups and assumed that the classification was roughly hierarchical and so were able to use it to study occupational mobility, particularly in relation to the impact of childbearing. Secondary analysis by Heather Joshi that looked at hourly pay by WES occupations found it was hierarchical except that childcare occupations should be at the bottom and shop work should be below or bracketed with skilled factory work (Joshi 1984).

Occupational Mobility

Before the WES we knew from cross-sectional data that women with dependent children who were working tended to be in lower level occupations than those without children. However, cross-section data did not allow us to determine to what extent this was due to differential returns to work

Table 4.2   *Occupational level of first job since first birth compared with last job before first birth*

	First job since first birth was:		All who worked before and since first birth
	Full-time	Part-time	
Level of first job since first birth compared with last job before first birth:	%	%	%
Higher	17	13	14
Same	64	42	49
Lower	19	45	37
	100	100	100

following childbirth or to movements between different types of work: we did not know whether those in higher-level occupations were less likely than those in lower-level occupations to go back to work when their children were young or whether women changed job levels when they returned to work, moving to lower-level jobs. Longitudinal data were needed to answer this question.[3]

Using the work history data we could compare the last job a woman was in before the birth of her first child with the first job she returned to subsequently in terms of job level and whether she returned to full- or part-time work. We also knew how long it was since the first birth before she returned to work. In all, 51 per cent of women who had returned to work since their first birth had returned to a different job. As Table 4.2 shows, 37 per cent of women experienced downward mobility on returning to work after the birth of their first child. However, this was much higher for those returning to work part-time than full-time: 45 per cent compared with 19 per cent respectively.

We found that it was also the case that the longer a women was out of the labour market, the more likely she was to experience downward occupational mobility. However, when we looked at both together, it was clear that the move to part-time work had a stronger effect than time out of the labour market, a fact that had not previously been recognised.

How Women Combine Paid and Unpaid Work

A dominant research theme reflecting one of the key intellectual and political debates was the need to explore the interaction between women's paid and unpaid work over the course of their lifetime. This encapsulated both their caring work for young children and frail elderly or sick family members as much as their domestic work. The key question was how far women were essentially the primary carer and secondary earner in their family. This involved comparing their situation with that of their husband: a first step was to get a clear picture of when in the day and week women worked, so a seven-day 24-hour grid was developed and women's actual times when they were in paid worked or travelling to and from work were charted.

Although it was assumed women worked when their children were at school the survey showed how most women's hours of work were shaped by their domestic commitments and the age of their youngest child in particular. For example, mothers of school-age children were back at home when school finished, while women working the twilight shift were disproportionately mothers of pre-school children who worked while their husbands cared for the children. Women working fewer hours spent less time travelling to work than those working full-time as for women time away from the house was crucial in terms of childcare arrangements.

What was clear too was the way in which family members supported mothers' employment by sharing childcare. In 1980 formal childcare was rare, so few of the working mothers reported using it. Fathers, followed by grandmothers, were the most frequent sources of care, with child-minders and then other relatives the next most common. The tendency for mothers and fathers to practise shift parenting which has become more pronounced now (La Valle et al. 2002) was already emerging. Not surprisingly, expenditure on childcare costs was low, at an average weekly sum of £8.70p.

Other caring work such as looking after a sick or elderly person was undertaken by about a fifth of women over 40 but affected their employment less, although for small numbers it had either prevented them from working at all or reduced the number of hours they worked.

Women as Employees

Because a significant proportion of women worked part-time, some for only a few hours a week, it was clear that many women were operating in the labour market on a different basis from men. We wanted to see to what extent their actual position at work reflected this status and to what extent some women had access to a good 'remuneration package' and opportunities for advancement by being in primary sector jobs while others were more clearly in the secondary labour market. Detailed information was collected on their pay, holidays, sick leave, training and promotion opportunities, and whether or not there was a trade union they could join at their place of work. Analysis by occupational status, the level of workplace occupational segregation, and whether a job was full or part-time showed the heterogeneity of women's situations. Women who were full-time workers in white-collar jobs which were also done by men enjoyed much better pay and conditions; they were clearly working in the primary sector. These women not only had better pay but were more likely to have training and promotion opportunities. But the majority of women were in secondary sector jobs with poor pay and no pensions, few opportunities for training or promotion and often little trade union representation.

One of the 'myths' about women employees the study examined was whether or not they were 'always leaving jobs for domestic reasons'. This was something employers frequently gave as a reason for not employing women at all or, at least, not in senior jobs. From the work histories we could look not only at the numbers of jobs women had, but also at their reasons for leaving them. Therefore, we could see whether they were changing jobs or leaving employment and whether they chose to leave or were forced to go through redundancy. On average women worked for four or five employers over their working life and more women (about 60 per cent) left employers to change jobs rather than for domestic reasons, contrary to employers' beliefs. But the reason for leaving the labour market might not remain the reason for staying out: it was not uncommon, for example, for women to leave a job for a job-related reason but then to stay out for domestic reasons, or vice versa.

It was also clear that re-entering the labour market was often not clear-cut. Not all women who got a job had looked for one – some were offered one directly. Domestic returners were often 'pulled back' into part-time work in this way. In our qualitative studies they gave graphic accounts of the process, describing, for example, a classic situation where they 'had not been looking for a job' as such but their former employer asked them to 'come back temporarily to help out' and when they found they 'could manage and liked being back at work' they stayed. While financial reasons for working were paramount, domestic returners were particularly likely to mention the sociability of work as a reason for returning.

Working women were asked about their attitudes to working in general, using attitude statements measuring three dimensions:

- financial dependence on work (for example, 'I couldn't manage unless I was earning')
- intrinsic attractions of work (for example, 'Working makes me feel I'm doing something useful')
- coping with home and work (for example, 'I have less time than I would like to spend with my friends and family').

Working women also rated the importance of different aspects of their current job and how satisfied they felt with each of these and how satisfied they were with their job overall. Both working and non-working women also answered questions forming measures of perceived psychological stress and of financial stress.

We were able to use these measures to debunk some myths about the lack of importance of work to women, particularly to married women. One was the 'pin money' myth: that married women were working only for 'pin money' and did not really need to work. We showed that most families were highly dependent on the wife's earnings and that there were higher levels of financial stress among families with children where the wife did not work than where she did. Dex (1987) carried out multivariate analysis of women's orientations to work and compared them with men's

We also showed that most women enjoyed work and were satisfied with their jobs, but hours of work, particularly for the part-timers, and the people they worked with were greater sources of satisfaction than pay and prospects.

But we found that the young childless women were less satisfied than older women. However, since it is not possible to collect attitude data retrospectively we could not tell whether those who were less satisfied were subsequently less likely to work when they had young children than those who were more satisfied, or whether their financial circumstances would prove to be more important. Prospective attitude measures such as those included on the British Household Panel Survey are needed to answer that question.

Who was Unemployed?

Identifying the prevalence of unemployment among women was a key objective of the study. It was recognised that many married women did not register as unemployed (and therefore did not figure in the official unemployment statistics) because their eligibility for unemployment benefit was very limited; the reforms of 1978 had made little change to their position. It was important to disentangle the variations in status and intent among the one-third of women who were not in paid work at the time of interview. One simple question was not sufficient to do this. Rather, several questions were used to generate a scale of attachment to the labour market and, as a result, five groups of 'non-working' women were identified along a continuum. Almost none never intended to work or look for work again and, of these, most were older women nearing retirement age. For most women this period of not working was deemed temporary. But it was clear that the official definition of unemployed, based then on being registered as such had little meaning for women, as those registered as unemployed were scattered across the continuum and some 'unemployed' women were clearly happily economically inactive while some women not registered as unemployed clearly were actively looking for work and thus clearly unemployed.

Women who were not working were asked about their feelings about not having a job (for example, 'I often get depressed about not having a job') and their financial need to work (for example, 'I wish I was earning some money'). Their answers were strongly related to their position on the attachment to work continuum with those clearly unemployed and looking for work, indicating their discontent with their situation and high levels of financial stress.

Attitudes to Gender Roles

As well as questions about women's attitudes to their current situation, we also developed more general measures of attitudes to gender roles that were asked of everyone on the survey, including the sample of the partners of the married women. These covered:

- traditional attitudes to home and work (for example, 'A husband's job is to earn the money; a wife's job is to look after the home and family')
- benefits of work to women and family (for example, 'A woman and her family will all be happier if she goes out to work')
- attitudes to whether women with children of different ages (under school age, with children who are all at school, with children who have all left school) should work compared with married women and single women with no children.

The married women were asked questions about what they thought their own husbands' attitudes were to their working, while the husbands were asked for their views so we could compare the two; this generally revealed that husbands were somewhat less positive about their wives' working than wives believed them to be. It was a novel feature in a large survey to ask both separately and then compare the responses.

In 1980 attitudes tended to be quite traditional, particularly among the older women and among the husbands, although few supported the traditional view that 'a woman's place is in the home' and most accepted that working is beneficial for women. Despite the positive attitudes to work, we found that for most women paid work was secondary to domestic responsibilities and that husbands endorsed this view. The latter were not generally particularly enthusiastic about their wives working even when their family would suffer financial hardship if their wife did not work. However, younger women and women with higher levels of qualifications held less traditional views and strongly endorsed the benefits of women working even when they had young children.

A series of questions to young childless women about their views of their future working lives showed that most expected to return to work after having children and over a quarter expected to take only the short statutory maternity leave. Of course, since the WES we have seen a significant rise in the proportions of women working who have pre-school children and, by 2000, the proportion of women taking a short period of maternity leave had roughly doubled.

TECHNOLOGICAL CHALLENGES

In a chapter looking back some 25 years we thought it worth reminding particularly younger researchers what it was like carrying out large-scale quantitative research in 1980 from a practical point of view. In 1980 we had very primitive tools at our disposal: this was before the days of personal computers (PCs) let alone computer-assisted interviewing. Interviewers recorded answers on paper questionnaires which had to be coded and keyed into electronic form and then edited before being ready for analysis. This took considerable time and effort, particularly checking and editing the work histories to deal with errors, gaps and inconsistencies.

Computing arrangements in general and data analysis software in particular were still in their infancy. One could not sit at one's desk and run analyses with results instantly available to print on a nearby printer. Analyses generally had to be specified in advance to be run on a mainframe computer by a programmer who brought back the results (piles of printout) a few days later. Even when improved tools meant that we could carry out our own analyses, we had to write the programs specifying the analysis, submit the job and then wait for it to run and be printed before going to collect the output some hours or even days later.

It was a real challenge to structure the complex data to carry out analysis particularly of the work histories. The skilled OPCS staff who undertook this made the analysis very much easier both for the authors and subsequent secondary analysts. It was also difficult to do sophisticated multivariate analysis. There were various software packages and programs available, not all of which were particularly easy to use. For example, at that time it was not possible to do log linear analysis in SPSS. Handling longitudinal work history records containing details of multiple spells often had to be done by writing software programmes. The analyses took place before the now common discussion and use of random and fixed effects models and corrections for unobserved heterogeneity. However, these days with the advent of easier multivariate analysis, it is possible to forget that a considerable amount of valuable analysis can be done with only cross-tabulations to control for different variables if one has a reasonably large sample. This is how a large amount of the analysis in the WES report was carried out.

Even writing the report was a technical challenge. There were no facilities to extract results from printouts electronically so all results for publication had to be transcribed from the printout and needed careful checking to avoid transcription errors. Although we did not have PCs, word processors had just arrived but only for use by clerical staff, not researchers. As authors we used an electric typewriter or wrote by hand. We would send a draft chapter off for typing and wait several days for it to come back for us to check and return with corrections. We did a huge amount of cutting and pasting (with scissors and glue, not a word processor). All of this goes to explain why a survey whose fieldwork took place in 1980 did not have its full report published until four years later, although we did publish preliminary findings along the way.

THE PLACE OF THE WES IN SOCIAL AND POLICY RESEARCH

The WES was the most comprehensive and path-breaking survey of women and employment at the time it was done. When it was published in 1984 it attracted a mass of publicity. It was covered in all the newspapers, popular and broadsheet, with leaders in several, including *The Times*. There was also radio interest, which in 1984, was much less common than it is now. Civil servants on the *Jimmy Young Show* were something government press officers were clearly unused to!

But did all this popular interest mean anything in terms of policy and practice? Who used the survey most and has it had enduring effect? There is no doubt that both in 1984 and certainly over time the WES has been more used by the research community than by policy-makers, pressure groups and practitioners. But is this a failure of the study or a consequence of a change of circumstances?

Even by 1984, when the study was published, the Conservative government was much more concerned about youth than women's unemployment as the large cohort of 16-year-olds entering the labour market in the early 1980s failed to find jobs. Indeed, the Department of Employment social research post on women included youth issues, and managing youth research, including evaluations of the growing number of employment initiatives, was a much more important part of the job by 1984. Women had slipped down the order of priorities with a Conservative government that was less interested in intervening to promote equality. Consequently, by 1984 within the Department of Employment no further research was commissioned for several years once the programme of women's research was completed.

The greatest policy impact the study had was 'it gave birth to the phrase "women returners" as it scotched once and for all the idea that only a minority of women returned to employment after having children' (Ballard, personal communication). So for the next few years policy, and therefore research, interest focused on issues around the operation of maternity leave legislation and the increasing numbers of mothers making earlier returns to employment (Daniel 1980; 1981; McRae 1991). Women were integrated more into the standard employment studies but there was little investigation of their particular situation and studies tended to be gender blind. In the latter part of the 1980s as the debates about primary and secondary labour markets developed, for example, little was made of the different position women and men held in these segmented and 'flexible' labour markets.

No doubt this was partly a result of the changing approach to the role of social science based research in government or at least in the then Department of Employment. Increasingly, emphasis was being put on evaluation research and less on understanding the wider context of labour market behaviour. Therefore, the focus became more the technical one of conducting policy focused social research rather than developing the substantive knowledge of the structural and attitudinal factors which underlay and shaped men's and women's employment. The competencies and interests of the changing cadre of the professional staff also reflected and reinforced this.

Government's priorities received little effective challenge. The trade unions which had been active in supporting legislative change for equality and championing women as workers had few friends at court and bigger problems to deal with as they handled declining jobs, membership and popular support. The Equal Opportunities Commission, never a particularly strong organisation or independent of government, was not in a position to use the research findings to push for change in this new climate although they did pay for further analysis (Dex and Shaw 1986; Hunt 1988). Of course, in this climate, feminist groups and more general women's pressure groups were not strong enough to push equality issues. The major exceptions to this were some spectacularly successful challenges to unequal pay and instances of sex discrimination throughout the 1980s and 1990s organised by women workers, usually through their trade union. But these were very much a minority activity although they set crucially important precedents for others.

The WES was received much more successfully in the social science community both by researchers and teachers. There were several reasons for this. There is no doubt that it helped that it was in an area in which academics were still very interested as academically funded work by Ermisch and Wright on lone mothers and on the gender pay gap illustrated (Ermisch and Wright 1989a; 1989b). There were also several detailed, accessible reports which not only gave people numerous findings but also quickly alerted people to the potentialities of the dataset. This coupled with its quick lodging at the Data Archive and the cleanness of the data meant it was attractive to use. There is no doubt, too, that involving academics in simultaneous analysis and report writing helped to get the study into academic circles very quickly. So the WES rapidly became one of the most used datasets at the archive. The growth of women's studies and gender studies during the 1980s and 1990s also meant that it became a very useful teaching text. Much of this is also attributable to the exemplary way in which the data-set was prepared for archiving and subsequent secondary analysis by the OPCS.

During the 1990s, interest in women's labour market behaviour and the challenge they had faced in managing domestic and paid work has generally been seen and studied in the context of the growth of interest in reconciling family and working life. There is a logic to this. It both allows men's and women's situations as parents/carers and workers to be compared and it also more closely fits with the dominant policy agenda both in Europe since the 1980s and in the UK since the mid-1990s. Therefore, under this theme there has been development of many of the ideas which the WES explored and good summaries published of some of these findings (Dex 1999; 2003). However, what seems lost is a focus on the issue of women as workers and the inequalities both between them and men and also, very importantly, amongst women which the WES showed so clearly. But, as much as anything this may be because of a considerable weakening of interest in classic industrial sociology as well as equality issues over this period. It is salutary that, 25 years after the WES, the first national programme of research on gender funded by the Economic and Social Research Council (ESRC) has been set up which aims to take theoretically informed empirical work on the situation of men and women further (www.genet.ac.uk).

CONCLUSIONS

On a personal level both of us found the experience of designing and executing the Women and Employment Survey an exciting challenge. It proved a showcase for collaborative working between different disciplines and skills within the social sciences and across different government departments as well as the academic/non-academic divide. It also showed the usefulness of the design, analysis and report-writing being done by the same team. This enabled a comprehensive standalone report aimed at a general lay public to be created. The subsequent practice of separating these activities seems to have weakened the overall value and general usefulness of many government surveys. Few non-academics read journal articles.

However, the WES was predicated on taking for granted the capacity of a major survey organisation to handle successfully (for the time) a very large survey, make major methodological innovations, developing complex research instruments and difficult technical analysis as part of the delivery of a survey. Arguably things have not moved uniformly forward in this respect, as the experience on some subsequent surveys has shown.

Most of all, though, the WES showed that research initiated for policy and political reasons can also have a wider salience and utility and be widely used outside policy corridors. This should raise questions as to why these partnerships are not more widespread today. We feel both government research and policy-making and social scientific endeavour would greatly benefit.

NOTES

1. An earlier version of this article was originally published in the 21st Century Society *Journal of the Academy of Social Sciences*, 1(2), 129–148, November 2006, www.informaworld.com/smpp/title~content=t724921265~db=all.
2. Joshi mostly worked on cross-sectional data apart from using work histories to build a model of pay. It is thought that the original motivation of the Department of Employment was to see if we could improve the method used to make official labour force projections.
3. The ranking of occupations used in Martin and Roberts to calculate the extent of downward occupational mobility was slightly different was slightly different to the one used in Dex (1987) further analysis and used in the chapter by Dex et al. in this volume.

REFERENCES

Barker, D.L. and S. Allen (eds) (1976a), *Sexual Divisions and Society: Process and Change*, London, Tavistock Publications.
Barker, D.L. and S. Allen (eds) (1976b), *Dependence and Exploitation in Work and Marriage*, London: Longman.
Beechey, V. and T. Perkins (1985), 'Conceptualising part-time work', in B. Roberts, R. Finnegan and D. Gallie (eds), *New Approaches to Economic Life*, Manchester: Manchester University Press, pp. 246–63.
Comer, L. (1972), *Wedlocked Women*, London: Feminist Books.

Daniel, W.W. (1980), *Maternity Rights: The Experience of Women*, PSI No. 588, London: Policy Studies Institute.

Daniel, W.W. (1981), *Maternity Rights: The Experience of Employers*, PSI No. 596, London: Policy Studies Institute.

Department of Employment (DE) (1974a), *Women and Work: A Statistical Survey*, Manpower Paper No. 9, London: HMSO.

Department of Employment (DE) (1974b), *Women and Work: Sex Differences and Society*, Manpower Paper No. 10, London: HMSO.

Department of Employment (DE) (1975a), *Women and Work: A Review*, Manpower Paper No. 11, London: HMSO.

Department of Employment (DE) (1975b), *Women and Work: Overseas Practice*, Manpower Paper No. 12, London: HMSO.

Dex, S. (1984), *Women's Work Histories: An Analysis of the Women and Employment Survey*, Department of Employment Research Paper No. 46, London: Department of Employment.

Dex, S. (1987), *Women's Occupational Mobility*, Basingstoke: Macmillan.

Dex, S. (1988), *Women's Attitudes towards Work*, Basingstoke: Macmillan.

Dex, S. (ed.) (1999), *Families and the Labour Market: Trends, Pressures and Policies*, London: Family Policy Studies Centre/Joseph Rowntree Foundation.

Dex, S. (2003), *Families and Work in the Twenty-first Century*, York: Joseph Rowntree Foundation/Policy Press.

Dex, S. and L. Shaw (1986), *British and American Women at Work: Do Equal Opportunities Policies Matter?*, London: Macmillan.

Dunnell, K. (1979), *Family Formation 1976*, London: HMSO.

Elias, P. and B. Main (1982), *Women's Working Lives: Evidence from the National Training Survey*, Institute for Employment Research, University of Warwick.

Ermisch, J.F. and R.E. Wright (1989a), 'Employment dynamics among British lone mothers', CEPR Discussion Paper 302, Centre for Economic Policy Research, London.

Ermisch J.F. and R.E. Wright (1989b), 'The dynamics of lone parenthood in Britain', CEPR Discussion Paper 303, Centre for Economic Policy Research, London.

Gallie, D., M. White, Y. Cheng and M. Tomlinson (1988), *Restructuring the Employment Relationship*, Oxford: Oxford University Press.

Greenhalgh, C. and M. Stewart (1981), *The Effects and Determinants of Training*, Warwicks Economics Research Papers Series 213.

Hakim, C. (1979), *Occupational Segregation*, Department of Employment Research Paper No. 9, London: Department of Employment.

Hunt, A. (1968), *A Survey of Women's Employment*, London: HMSO.

Hunt, A. (1975), *Management Attitudes and Practices towards Women at Work*, London: HMSO.

Hunt, A. (ed.) (1988), *Women and Paid Work*, Basingstoke: Macmillan.

Joshi, H. (1984), *Women's Participation in Paid Work: Further Analysis of the Women and Employment Survey*, Department of Employment Research Paper No. 45, London: Department of Employment.

Joshi, H. (1990), 'The cash opportunity costs of childbearing: an approach to estimation using British data', *Population Series* **44**(1), 41–60.

La Valle, I., S. Arthur, C. Millward, J. Scott, with M. Clayden (2002), *Happy Families? Atypical Work and Its Influence on Family Life*, Bristol: Policy Press.

MacEwen Scott, A. (ed.) (1994), *Gender Segregation and Social Change*, Oxford: Oxford University Press.

Martin, J. and C. Roberts (1984a), *Women and Employment: A Lifetime Perspective*, London: HMSO.

Martin, J. and C. Roberts (1984b), *Women and Employment: Technical Report*, London: HMSO.

McRae, S. (1991), *Maternity Rights in Britain: The Experience of Women and Employers*, London: Policy Studies Institute.

Offic for Population Censuses and Surveys (OPCS) (1982), *Labour Force Survey 1979*, London: HMSO.

Roberts, C. (1985), 'Research on women in the labour market: the context and scope of the Women and Employment Survey', in B.R. Roberts, R. Finnegan and D. Gallie (eds), *New Approaches to Economic Life*, Manchester: Manchester University Press, pp. 232–45.

Robertson, J.A.S. and J.M. Briggs (1979), 'Part-time working in Great Britain', *Employment Gazette*, July, 671–75.

Snell, M.W., P. Glucklich and M. Povell (1981), *Equal Pay and Opportunities*, Department of Employment Research Paper No. 20, London: Department of Employment.

Weir, G. (2003), 'A detailed analysis of voluntary and involuntary job separations', *Labour Market Trends*, **111**(3), 121–32.

5. The new dynamics of family formation and the explosion of childbearing outside marriage

John Ermisch

5.1 INTRODUCTION

In 1979, just before the Women and Employment Survey (WES) started interviewing its respondents, couples living together outside legal marriage – cohabiting unions – were relatively rare, as were births outside marriage. Among never married women in 1979, 8 per cent of those aged 20–24 and 18 per cent of those aged 25–29 reported themselves as living in cohabiting unions (Brown and Kiernan 1981). The corresponding percentages from the 2003 British Household Panel Survey were 24 per cent and 41 per cent (weighted data). Even more striking is the rise in childbearing outside marriage: 11 per cent of births were outside marriage in 1979 compared with 41 per cent in 2003. After 1975, when the contraceptive pill became freely available to all women, childbearing outside marriage began to increase rapidly after decades of relative stability (see Figure 5.1).

The WES provided comprehensive birth and marriage histories for a nationally representative sample of women, and it also collected retrospective employment histories. Together the histories provide dates of childbirth and start and end dates for marriages, employment (distinguishing and full- and part-time) and non-employment spells. This permitted for the first time the analysis of the dynamics of marriage and childbearing in relation to employment. No cohabiting union dates were collected, probably reflecting the relative novelty of the phenomenon at the time and perhaps contemporary stigma associated with 'living together', which discouraged asking questions about it.

Using these data, Ermisch (1991) studied pre-marital childbearing among women who reached their sixteenth birthday between 1960 and 1976 (that is, women born from 1944 to 1960), which approximates the period when the availability of the contraceptive pill was limited to married women. He found, for example, that being in employment was associated

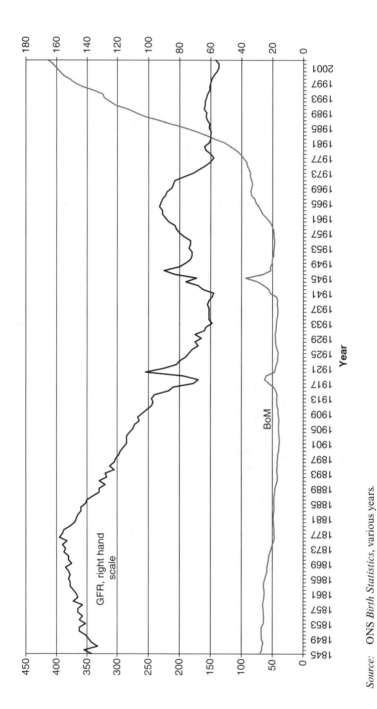

Source: ONS *Birth Statistics,* various years.

Figure 5.1   Births outside marriage (per 1000 births) and general fertility rate (per 1000 women aged 15–44)

with a lower risk of a pre-marital birth, but, given employment status, leaving school before the age of 16 nearly doubled the risk. This chapter uses similar history data from the British Household Panel Survey (BHPS) to shed light on the reasons for the explosion of pre-marital childbearing after 1975. Importantly for the story, the BHPS also collected histories of cohabiting unions.[1]

The second section shows that the increase in the percentage of births outside marriage between 1975 and 2003 is mainly accounted for by a large fall in the proportion of women aged 20–34 who are married. This is in turn associated with a dramatic rise in cohabiting unions. As these unions are short-lived before either dissolving or being converted into marriage, non-marital childbearing appears, therefore, to be associated with modern courtship. Section 3 presents a theory of marriage market search (courtship) in which out-of-wedlock childbearing may be a rational choice, and Section 4 explains how it can become widespread when a woman's welfare as an unmarried mother is influenced by the prevalence of unmarried mothers in the population and why the sharp rise in unemployment in the first half of the 1980s may have been a catalyst for the increase. Section 5 presents evidence that socio-economic differences in the chances of having a child before marriage widened as childbearing outside marriage becomes more common. Section 6 discusses the diffusion of cohabiting unions from the better educated to the rest of the population, which may provide an alternative or complementary explanation for the explosion of non-marital childbearing, and the final section presents conclusions.

5.2   DEMOGRAPHIC ACCOUNTING, 1938–2003

Figure 5.2 shows the age-specific fertility rates outside marriage, a direct measure of the propensity to have a birth outside marriage relative to the 'population at risk'. After the Second World War 'spike', these non-marital fertility rates did not drop back as far as their 1938 levels, and from the mid-1950s they increased dramatically for all age groups, peaking in 1964 (for those aged 20–34) and then declining until the mid-1970s. As comparison with Figure 5.3 indicates, marital fertility rates showed a similar 'baby boom and bust' pattern, but rose and fell proportionately less around their much higher levels. The following analysis is confined to women aged under 35.[2]

The number of births outside marriage among women in the j-th age group in year t (BOM_{tj}) is by definition equal to the product of four variables: the female population aged 15–34 in year t (Pop_t), the proportion of the population aged 15–34 in the j-th age group (a_{tj}), the proportion of the female population in the j-th age group who are not married ($1 - m_{tj}$) and

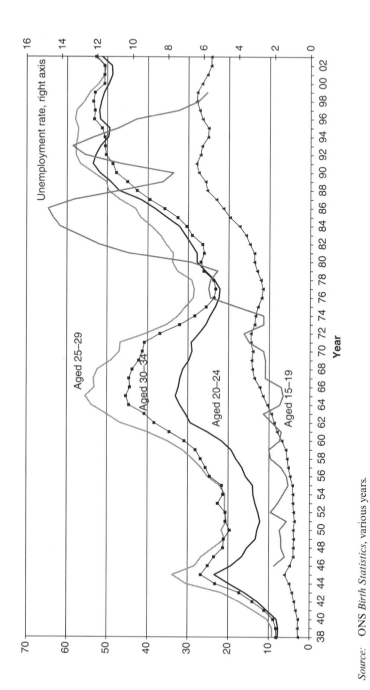

Source: ONS *Birth Statistics*, various years.

Figure 5.2 Birth rate outside marriage, per 1000 unmarried women

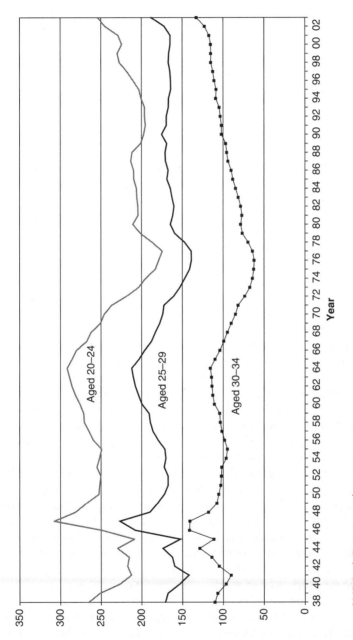

Source: ONS *Birth Statistics*, various years.

Figure 5.3   Birth rate within marriage, per 1000 married women

the fertility rate of the unmarried women in the j-th age group (fom_{tj}); that is, $BOM_{tj} \equiv (Pop_t) \cdot (a_{tj}) \cdot (1 - m_{tj}) \cdot (fom_{tj})$. The number of births inside marriage for women in the j-th age group is defined analogously: $BIM_{tj} \equiv (Pop_t) \cdot (a_{tj}) \cdot (m_{tj}) \cdot (fim_{tj})$, where fim_{tj} is defined as the fertility rate of married women in the j-th age group.

Then the *proportion* of births to women aged 15–34 outside marriage, defined to be bom_t, is given by the following equation:

$$bom_t \equiv (\Sigma_j BOM_{tj}) / (\Sigma_j BIM_{tj} + \Sigma_j BOM_{tj}) \qquad (5.1)$$

where Σ_j indicates summation over the four five-year age groups between ages 15 and 34. We can unpack the contribution to changes between any two years of the various elements underlying the proportion of births outside marriage (bom_t) by hypothetically fixing, in turn, each of the various components of BOM_{tj} and BIM_{tj} (age structure, marital structure and fertility rates) at their base year values.

First consider the period 1938–64. Among women aged 15–34, 4.4 per cent of births were outside marriage in 1938, and at the peak of the baby boom this percentage was 7.4 per cent.[3] Figure 5.4 shows the large declines in the proportion of women *not* married among those aged 20–34. The unpacking exercise, or decomposition, indicates that the percentage of births outside marriage to women aged 15–34 would have increased from 4.4 per cent in 1938 to 17.2 per cent in 1964, rather than the actual value of 7.4 per cent in 1964, if the proportions married in each age group had remained at their 1938 values while the age structure and fertility rates of unmarried and married women changed as they actually did. Thus, large rises between 1938 and 1964 in the proportion of women in each five-year age group who are married is mainly responsible for moderating the increase in the proportion of births outside marriage (bom_t) in the face of the large increase in non-marital fertility rates (fom_{tj}).

Changes in the proportion of women married also played a large role in accounting for changes in the proportion of births outside marriage (bom_t) during the period 1975–2003. Figure 5.2 shows that the age-specific fertility rates of unmarried women increased from the mid-1970s to the early 1990s and then were relatively constant after that, at levels higher than at the 1964 peak. Age-specific fertility rates of married women aged 20–34 exhibited a moderate upward trend (Figure 5.3). The big change is the large rise in the proportion of women who are not married during the post-1975 period, as shown in Figure 5.4. The examination of components of change for the 1975–2003 period indicates that if the proportions married in each age group had remained at their 1975 values while the age structure and fertility rates of unmarried and married women changed as they

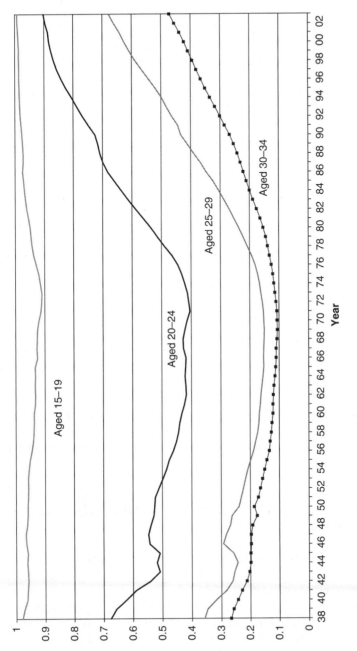

Source: ONS *Birth Statistics*, various years.

Figure 5.4 Proportion of women not married

actually did, the proportion of births outside marriage to women aged 15–34 would have increased from 9.1 per cent in 1975 to only 11.6 per cent in 2003, rather than the actual value of 44.2 per cent in 2003.[4] Thus, less than one-tenth of the 1975–2003 increase in the proportion of births outside marriage can be accounted for by simultaneous changes in non-marital and marital birth rates in each age group and in age structure. A similar picture emerges if we consider what would have happened if age-specific non-marital and marital fertility rates were held constant at their 1975 level and the proportions married and age structure changed. This exercise indicates that percentage of births outside marriage among women aged 15–34 would have risen to 40 per cent, very close to the observed 44 per cent. Changes in the proportions married also played an important role in the large increase in the percentage of births outside marriage in the USA (Gray et al. 2006).

The shift from legal marriage to cohabiting unions as the common mode of first partnership mainly accounts for the delay of first marriage in Britain and the rise in the proportion of women not married (Ermisch and Francesconi 2000). Among women born in the 1950s, about one-quarter cohabited in their first live-in partnership. This proportion increased to three-fifths among women born in the 1960s and to 85 per cent among women born in the 1970s.[5] But there has also been a delay in the age of first partnership: comparing women born in the 1950s, 1960s and 1970s, the median age at first partnership has risen from 22 to 24 to 25, respectively. The penultimate section discusses possible reasons for the diffusion of cohabiting unions.

The hypothetical assumptions made to attribute change to its various components (that is, asking, what if only one element changed?) are only an accounting exercise. Changes in non-marital fertility rates and the changes in proportions married are likely to be interdependent and to change alongside each other.

5.3 THE DECISION TO HAVE A CHILD OUTSIDE MARRIAGE

Throughout the 1950s and early 1960s, *unmarried* women continued to have no recognised legal right of access to contraception. The absence of reliable contraception produced many unplanned pregnancies, and the risks of and taboos against illegal abortion made the outcome of premarital pregnancies relatively clear – have the child, with or without a husband, perhaps putting the child up for adoption. The contraceptive pill changed all that. It was introduced in 1961 to family doctors (general practitioners – GPs), and in 1962 the Family Planning Association (FPA) started offering it to married women, provided they had permission from their GP. It became available from the National Health Service (NHS) from December 1961, but only to married women whose health would be endangered by further pregnancy. In 1966, the NHS allowed GPs to charge for pill prescriptions not given for medical reasons – pill sales rose sharply from then on, helped by a fall in its price during the 1960s. In 1968, the FPA gave branches permission to provide contraceptives to unmarried women, and from 1970 they were required to make provision. Contraception became free to all women from 1975. These developments were associated with a relatively rapid diffusion of pill use. Abortion became legal in 1969.

The free availability of contraception and abortion after 1975 is likely to have played an important role in the postponement of marriage illustrated in Figure 5.4. Before the pill and legal abortion, there were considerable costs from delaying marriage – sexual abstinence or pregnancy risk. By reducing these costs, the pill encouraged all women and men to delay marriage to a time when their tastes, character and economic position were better formed. In particular, widespread unmarried cohabitation is probably inconceivable without the pill (with safe legal abortion as a backup).

After 1975, 'accidents' were no longer a convincing reason why a large percentage of women had a birth outside marriage. Of the components that account for the rise in non-marital childbearing, discussed above, the decrease in the proportion of young women who are married was found to play a large role. This would be on the assumption that non-marital birth rates stayed constant. But non-marital birth rates would have been predicted to fall over this same period as single women then had access to contraception that would help them avoid unmarried pregnancies. A better understanding of the increase in non-marital childbearing requires a behavioural model of the decision to have a birth outside marriage that takes into account the reliability of modern fertility control and the interdependency between marriage and childbearing decisions.

Marriage markets are subject to frictions. It takes time to meet potentially suitable members of the opposite sex and gather information about them.[6] These market frictions affect who marries whom and also open the possibility of childbearing outside marriage as a rational choice, even when a woman can control her fertility perfectly.[7] When a man and woman are in a relationship, the man can choose whether to marry the woman or not, if she will have him. While a woman faces the same choice when she meets a man, she can also choose to have a child by the man and then raise it without the father. Depending on state benefits available to single parents and whether the father is willing to contribute resources, a woman's welfare when raising a child by herself may be greater than what she obtains when single and childless. But there are also costs in terms of future marriage market prospects associated with raising a child alone. A single woman with a child may find it more difficult to meet potential husbands while looking after a child. A woman who has a relationship with a man she does not wish to marry, or who will not marry her, would choose to have a child by the man if the gain exceeds any perceived long-term costs in terms of her marriage prospects.

Cohabiting unions can be viewed as a way to learn about the suitability of one's partner for marriage (Sahib and Gu 2002), that is, part of the modern courtship process rather than a permanent alternative to formal marriage. A large proportion of these unions dissolve because the match turns out to be unsuitable for either the man or the woman. An important implication of the model above is that couples who find each other to be mutually acceptable marriage partners wait to have children within marriage, while a woman may have a child outside marriage if this is not the case. This suggests that sexual relationships that produce a child outside marriage should be much less likely to lead to marriage than those that do not. In general it is difficult to observe the outcomes of relationships, but we can observe the outcome of cohabiting unions. The evidence indicates that cohabiting unions that produce children are much less likely to be converted into marriage and more likely to break up than childless ones (Ermisch and Francesconi 2000). Thus, women having a child in a cohabiting union experience a high risk of being a single mother in the near future. According to the model, this is because such women are disproportionately selected from more fragile unions.

Those women who expect to obtain a significant increase in welfare when they marry suffer a greater long-term cost by having a child outside marriage than women whose marriage prospects are such that they expect to gain little from marriage. Thus, women with poorer marriage prospects, in terms of the type of spouse that they can attract, are more likely to have children outside marriage. If, for example, marriage market prospects are worse for poorer women (for example, those with low educational attainments), because they can only marry poorer men, we would expect that poorer women would be more likely to have children before marriage, a prediction which is repeatedly confirmed (for example Del Bono 2004; Ermisch 2001).

Conditions of higher unemployment tend to reduce men's incomes, particularly those men whom women with poorer marriage market attributes might have a chance of marrying. Thus, the value of waiting childless for the right man to marry relative to having a child outside marriage, either in or outside a cohabiting union, is reduced in labour markets in which the unemployment rate is higher. Provided that state benefits to lone mothers (or the father's resource contributions) are sufficient, poor employment opportunities also reduce a woman's opportunity cost of having a child outside marriage. Thus, we may expect that a higher unemployment rate increases childbearing outside marriage. Analysis of a large cohort of women born in 1970 (Del Bono 2004), who were making childbearing and partnership decisions in the late 1980s and 1990s, indeed indicates that women living in countries with higher male unemployment were more likely to become a mother outside a live-in partnership and less likely to enter a partnership (compared with remaining single and childless).

A woman's welfare as an unmarried mother (and possibly the amount by which being an unmarried mother reduces her subsequent marriage prospects) is affected by any 'social stigma' attached to being an unmarried mother. Throughout the 1950s and early 1960s, illegitimacy continued to carry great stigma (Szreter 1996: 577). Among women who object to abortion, this stigma increases the chances that she marries if she becomes pregnant and reduces the odds of a birth outside marriage. If such stigma declines, then more women would decide to have a child with a man whom she rejects as a husband (or who rejects her as a wife), and among women who object to abortion, fewer would marry in response to a pregnancy. The next section presents a social interaction model that can produce rapid erosion of such stigma, which would both increase childbearing outside marriage directly and increase the unmarried population.

5.4   SOCIAL INFLUENCE AND INTERACTION

Suppose that the well-being associated with being an unmarried mother relative to that associated with remaining childless is larger when more women in her reference group (for example, defined by nationality, religious or ethnic group) become mothers outside marriage; this may be because social stigma is less. Then the probability that a woman becomes an unmarried mother when she and her partner do not agree to marry increases with the *expected* proportion of women in a woman's reference group who have their first birth outside marriage in this situation.[8] This is what we shall call a *social interaction effect*.

A *social equilibrium* occurs when women's expectations are consistent with the average proportion in the reference group who become a mother when a couple does not marry, that is, when the actual proportion in the reference group is equal to the expected proportion. If the social interaction effect is large enough, there can be more than one social equilibrium: one in which unmarried mothers are rare and another in which they are common. When they are rare, social stigma discourages unmarried motherhood;

when they are common, social stigma disappears and it is socially acceptable to become one.

Initial expectations can, therefore, be important in determining the proportion who becomes unmarried mothers when people respond sufficiently to what others are doing. In this sense, 'history matters' for the selection of the 'rare' or 'common' equilibrium. Furthermore, *temporary* changes in the socio-economic environment that alter non-marital childbearing behaviour and/or expectations can produce dramatic changes in the proportion who become single mothers, by causing a move from a 'rare non-marital childbearing' to a 'common non-marital childbearing' equilibrium. For example, some temporary development that led women to expect that the proportion becoming unmarried mothers would be sufficiently high would encourage a *permanent* dramatic increase in the proportion.

The relevance of this model for recent British history is the following. It is difficult to believe that the fundamental determinants of the decision to become an unmarried mother have changed by an order of magnitude sufficient to raise the percentage of births outside marriage from 9 per cent in 1975 to 42 per cent in 2004. The large observed changes in the percentage of births that are non-marital may reflect temporary changes in these determinants, the effects of which are magnified by the social interaction effect. One possible driver of these changes is the steep rise in unemployment during the late 1970s and early 1980s, which may have reduced the pool of men that poorer women would find acceptable to marry, or who find themselves in the position to offer marriage, thereby discouraging women from waiting to begin childbearing until they were married. Figure 5.2 shows that the timing of the increase in unemployment roughly coincides with the large increase in non-marital birth rates. Even though unemployment subsequently fell, the rise may have been sufficient to increase the actual proportion becoming unmarried mothers sufficiently to alter expectations for subsequent cohorts. The new equilibrium to which Britain is moving may be one like the 'common' one, and we may be observing the dynamics that takes it there during recent years.

More generally, we are looking for catalysts that initiated the dynamics driven by the social interaction effect. Comparison across countries of changes in the non-marital birth percentage may shed some light on what these might be. Figure 5.5 shows acceleration in its increase around 1980 in a number of European countries. The similarity between France and England and Wales is particularly striking, but there were also rapid rises in the Netherlands, Ireland, Spain and Portugal, starting about 1980. Other European countries have also seen large increases in more recent years: Germany since the mid-1990s (reaching 29 per cent in 2004) and Italy since

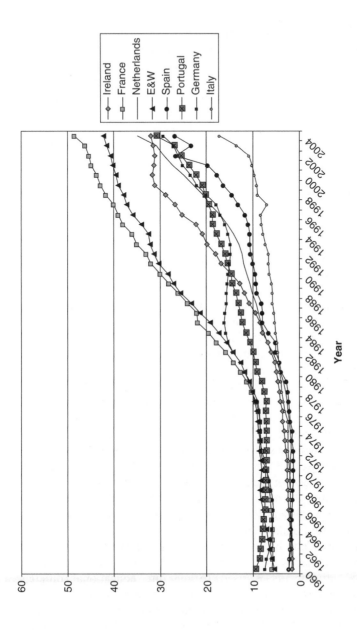

Source: Eurostat statistics.

Figure 5.5 Percentage of births outside marriage, Western Europe

the late 1990s (reaching 17 per cent in 2004). Whatever the catalysts might be, it appears that they are not specific to one country.

Unemployment increased substantially during the first half of the 1980s in all of these countries (for example, see Nickell et al. 2005), and so it is a candidate for such a catalyst. Figure 5.6 provides a 'scatter plot' between the change in the percentage of births outside marriage (*BoM*) between 1979 and 2004 and the increase in the average unemployment rate (*UR*) between 1973–79 and 1980–87 for a number of European countries and the USA. A longer period has been used for the change in *BoM* to allow for social interaction effects. Spain is an outlier on the far right of Figure 5.6, and France experienced a large change in *BoM* with relatively small increase in *UR*, but the broad tendency is for the rise in extra-marital child-bearing to be larger for countries experiencing a larger increase in unemployment in the 1980s.[9]

5.5   EDUCATIONAL DIFFERENCES IN PRE-MARITAL BIRTH RATES – CHANGES BY BIRTH COHORT

It was argued in section 5.3 that women with poorer economic prospects are more likely to become an unmarried mother. To be more concrete, it seems likely that women with lower educational attainments have poorer prospects in marriage and labour markets. Also, assume that a person's reference group consists of those with a similar level of education. Suppose that there is a temporary change in the environment (say, higher unemployment) that increases the actual proportion of women in the lower education group who become single mothers sufficiently, while the higher educated group is affected less, if at all, and remains at the 'rare' equilibrium. Then the dynamics of social interaction would drive women in the lower education group to the 'common' equilibrium. In this new equilibrium, the difference between the education groups in their proportion becoming unmarried mothers would be much greater than before.

The data for analysing the validity of this prediction come from the British Household Panel Survey retrospective histories of cohabiting unions, marriages and births, which have been updated with information during the panel, 1993–2003.[10] For simplicity, a dichotomous indicator of educational attainments is used to measure educational differences among women. It is whether or not a woman's highest qualifications exceed 'O levels (later, General Certificate of Secondary Education), which are usually obtained by the time a person is 16 years old. Three sets of cohorts are distinguished: those born in the 1950s, in the 1960s and the 1970s, who

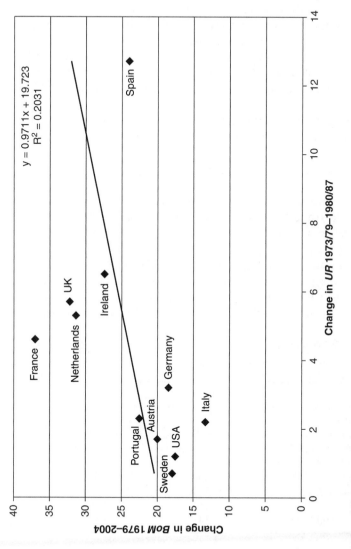

Source: OECD and Eurostat statistics.

Figure 5.6 Change in BoM, *1979–2004 and change in average* UR, *1973/79–1980/87*

reach the primary ages for having births before marriage about 20 years later. The dependent variable of interest is the 'hazard rate' of a pre-marital first birth for woman j at age t, denoted h_{jt}. Women are assumed to be at risk for such a birth from the age of 14, and they drop out of the population at risk when they marry or when they have a first birth. Women who remained childless and never-married from age 14 to the time of the last survey in which they are present remain in the population at risk until the time of their last interview. Thus, there are two groups who are 'censored' (that is, go out of observation without having a non-marital birth): those who marry childless and those who neither marry, nor have a child before the time they are interviewed last.

In order to have a simple parameter to compare across birth cohorts, a 'proportional hazard' model is estimated for each cohort; it takes the form

$$h_{jt} = g(t)\exp(\beta E_j) \qquad (5.2)$$

where $E_j = 1$ denotes a woman leaving education with 'low qualifications' (O-level or less) and $E_j = 0$ denotes a woman with higher qualifications. The function $g(t)$ is an unspecified function of age. This provides an estimate of the ratio of the pre-marital birth hazard of a woman with 'low education' to that of a woman with 'high education' which can be read off in Table 5.1 as $\exp(\beta)$, the parameter β being estimated by Cox's partial likelihood method . The estimates of this ratio increase across cohorts. The hazard for the less educated is 3.05 times that of the more educated among women

Table 5.1   First birth rate before marriage: differences by educational group

Birth cohort	1950–60	1960–70	1970–80
Ratio of birth rates of	3.05	3.95	4.41
Low to High level	(0.60)	(0.45)	(0.44)
education = $\exp(\beta)$*			
Standard Error			
N-high education	468	852	1374
N-low education	794	987	1062
N	1262	1839	2436
N of pre-marital births	148	419	516

Notes:
* Cox proportional hazard model of a pre-marital first birth.
'Low' level education is O level or below; 'High' is above O level.

Source: author's estimates from BHPS data.

born in the 1950s and 4.41 among women born in the 1970s. This is consistent with the emergence of a 'common non-marital childbearing' equilibrium for less educated women.

Table 5.2 breaks down non-marital first births between those before the first live-in partnership and those in the first cohabiting union. Panel A follows women who have not had a child until their first cohabitation or

Table 5.2　First birth rate before marriage: differences by educational group before and during first cohabiting union

A. Before first live-in partnership

Birth cohort:	1950–60	1960–70	1970–80
Ratio of birth rates of Low to High level education = exp(β)* Standard Error	2.17 (0.51)	3.91 (0.48)	4.82 (0.67)
N-high education	514	890	1329
N-low education	871	1077	1067
N	1385	1967	2396
N of pre-partnership births	183	359	276

Notes:
* Cox proportional hazard model of first birth before the first partnership.
'Low' level education is O level or below; 'High' is above O level.

Source:　Author's estimates from BHPS data.

B. Within first cohabiting union

Birth cohort	1950–60	1960–70	1970–80
Ratio of birth rates of Low to High level education = exp(β)* Standard Error	1.81 (0.64)	2.50 (0.48)	2.80 (0.43)
N-high education	147	412	450
N-low education	154	371	428
N	301	783	878
N of within first cohab.union births	37	124	198

Notes:
* Cox proportional hazard model of first birth within the first cohabiting union.
'Low' level education is O level or below; 'High' is above O level.

Source:　Author's estimates from BHPS data.

later. Panel B follows childless women who enter a cohabiting union from its start until their marriage, first birth or interview, whichever comes sooner. In each case the ratio of the hazard between less and more educated women is higher for women born in the 1960s than for women born in the 1950s, and higher again for women born in the 1970s, particularly for births outside of a live-in partnership.

5.6   THE DIFFUSION OF COHABITING UNIONS

An alternative, but also possibly complementary, explanation is that the large rise in the proportion of women who cohabit in their first partnership (rather than marry) is responsible for the dramatic increase in non-marital childbearing in the last quarter century. This may be the case even if none of the growth in cohabitation was a permanent alternative to marriage. The reason follows from examining the dynamics of cohabiting unions. Analysis of the BHPS data indicates that the time spent living together in cohabiting unions before either marrying each other or the union dissolving is usually very short – the median duration was about 2 years for women born in the 1950s and 1960s, rising to 3.5 years for those born in the 1970s. There has been an upward trend in the proportion of women's first cohabiting unions that dissolve rather than turn into marriage: 30 per cent, 37 per cent and 50 per cent for women born in the 1950s, 1960s and 1970s, respectively. Most of those who re-partner after their first cohabiting union dissolved also start their next partnership by cohabiting. It takes about two years for one-half to have formed a new partnership, which is again subject to the high risk of dissolution. Thus, the time spent cohabiting, the relatively high risk that the union dissolves and the time it takes to cohabit again all contribute to a longer time before any marriage takes place and, therefore, more time at risk to have a birth outside marriage. Adding to this time at risk is the delay in first partnerships (cohabiting or marital) for more recent cohorts discussed earlier. At *fixed* average age-specific fertility rates for women outside of a live-in partnership or in cohabiting unions, the increase in the exposure time to these non-marital birth rates would have increased childbearing outside marriage. Ermisch (2005) estimates that about 70 per cent of the rise in the percentage of first births outside marriage between women born during 1950–62 and women born during 1963–76 can be *accounted for* by the increase in women's propensity to cohabit in their first partnership and the delay in first partnership.

But why did the average fertility rates of women in cohabiting unions not fall when more women cohabited? Women had the means (contraception and legal abortion) to avoid non-marital childbearing if they wanted to do so, and so the substitution of cohabiting unions for marriages need not have raised non-marital fertility. This consideration leads us back to the explanations suggested by the models in sections 5.3 and 5.4: purposeful decisions to have a child outside marriage and erosion of the stigma against doing so. Also, the exposure time argument begs the question: why did cohabiting unions become the common type of first partnership, and why was first partnership delayed? If there was initially social stigma operating against cohabitation, its dramatic increase may be due to a social interaction model like that outlined in section 5.5, applied to cohabiting unions. It could also be the case that cohabiting unions and partnership delay were only attractive when the stigma associated with childbearing outside marriage was less important.

In addition to the contraceptive pill and legal abortion, another possible driving force for change in patterns of first partnership may have been important changes in young people's education. For instance, one-third of 18-year-olds were in full-time education in 1992, compared with 15 per cent in 1979. Bagnoli and Bergstrom (1993) argue that young men who expect to prosper in later life will postpone marriage until their success becomes evident to potential marriage partners. Those who do not expect their economic status to advance much will seek to marry at a relatively young age. The careers of those who obtain university degrees take longer to develop and their earnings peak later in their life. Thus, as more young men go on to higher education, the proportion of young men who might think it is worth waiting to signal their better economic status is likely to increase. The same may now apply to women, and women who are university graduates may prefer to marry graduate men.

Beyond a certain age, young people may nevertheless prefer to have a live-in partner, particularly in an era of reliable contraception, and cohabiting unions cater for this preference while allowing them to postpone making a long-term commitment. Thus, higher educational achievement would both encourage young people to enter live-in partnerships later and to cohabit when they do. The short spells of cohabitation that are observed are consistent with the argument that it is used while waiting to signal economic success and as a learning experience before stronger commitments are made. The social interaction model outlined above could explain why cohabitation spread so rapidly in response to these stronger incentives to cohabit before marriage, even if the incentives were confined to those with higher educational attainments.

Table 5.3 presents evidence from the BHPS on the timing of first live-in partnership and the odds of cohabiting in this partnership. Panel A presents the estimates of a proportional hazard model like equation (5.2) for the 'hazard' of a first union. It indicates that there is little change between the

Table 5.3   First union: differences by educational group

A. Age at first union

Birth cohort:	1950–60	1960–70	1970–80
Ratio of birth rates of	1.30	1.29	1.46
Low to High level	(0.08)	(0.07)	(0.08)
education = exp(β)*			
Standard Error			
N-high education	516	905	1332
N-low education	876	1086	1072
N	1392	1991	2404
N of first unions	1100	1576	1237

Notes:
* Cox proportional hazard model of first partnership formation.
'Low' level education is O level or below; 'High' is above O level.

Source: Author's estimates from BHPS data.

B. Odds of cohabiting union relative to marriage

Birth cohort	1950–60	1960–70	1970–80
Logit coefficient for	−0.69	−0.38	0.13
Low level education*	(0.14)	(0.10)	(0.15)
Standard Error			
N-high education	395	691	595
N-low education	705	885	642
N	1100	1576	1237
N of cohab.unions	297	955	1034

Notes:
* Logistic model of odds of cohabiting in first partnership.
'Low' level education is O level or below; 'High' (omitted category) is above O level.

Source: Author's estimates from BHPS data.

1950s and 1960s birth cohorts in the educational difference in the timing of
first union – the hazard rate for 'low educated' (as defined earlier) women is
about 30 per cent higher – but the difference in union formation rates widens
for the 1970s cohort – that is, the higher educated wait even longer to start
their first partnership. Panel B presents estimates of a logit model for the
odds of cohabiting relative to marrying in a woman's first union. As the arguments above predict, low-educated women born in the 1950s and 1960s were
much less likely to cohabit in their first partnership, but as cohabiting in one's
first partnership became almost universal (85 per cent), arguably through

social interaction effects, this is no longer true for the 1970s cohort.[11] The results are consistent with social interaction effects spreading cohabitation widely from better educated women, who always had an incentive to cohabit before marrying, to a large proportion of the population.

Through its link to the widespread substitution of cohabiting unions for direct marriage, the increase in non-marital childbearing may, therefore, be due in part to the expansion of higher education acting in conjunction with social interaction effects. For this argument to be correct it is not necessary to show that university graduates were themselves having children in cohabiting unions to a significant degree (they were not). They were the pioneers of cohabiting unions, but social interaction effects spread them widely through society, to people who would have stronger incentives to have children within such unions (see section 5.4).

5.7 CONCLUSIONS

After 1975, when the contraceptive pill became freely available to all women, childbearing outside marriage began to increase rapidly after decades of relative stability, reaching 42 per cent in 2004. This was partly driven by a steep increase in age-specific non-marital births rates among women aged 20–34 from the mid-1970s to the early 1990s, after which they stabilised at a high level. At *fixed* average non-marital and marital age-specific birth rates, this increase in the proportion of births outside marriage can be mainly *accounted for* by a large fall in the proportion of women aged 20–34 who are married, which is in turn associated with a dramatic rise in cohabiting unions. These unions are short-lived before either dissolving or being converted into marriage. But this begs the question: why did average non-marital fertility rates not fall when more women cohabited? Women had the means (reliable contraception and legal abortion) to avoid non-marital childbearing if they wanted to do so, and so the substitution of cohabiting unions for marriages need not have raised non-marital fertility.

A theory of marriage market search (courtship) in which out-of-wedlock childbearing is an option suggests why it may be a rational choice, even when fertility can be controlled. A woman's well-being as an unmarried mother is likely to be influenced by the prevalence of unmarried mothers in the population. When their prevalence is low, non-marital childbearing is discouraged, because of social stigma against them. A temporary change in the determinants of non-marital childbearing that raises it, like the large rise in unemployment in the in the first half of the 1980s, can produce rapid erosion of the stigma and a self-reinforcing rise in childbearing outside marriage. This dynamic is likely to be concentrated among a segment of the population who already have stronger incentives to have a child before marriage, such as women with low levels of education. The evidence indeed indicates that the chances of having a child before marriage increased by much more among women with low levels of education. An alternative, or complementary, explanation stresses the role of the rise in cohabiting unions and delay in partnership. These generated an increase in non-marital births by increasing the unmarried population. This view also points to the operation of a social influence model in explaining the dramatic rise in cohabitation, and the chapter provides evidence consistent with a diffusion of cohabiting unions from the better educated to the less educated population.

NOTES

1. Information on cohabitation is elicited by the following question: 'As you know some couples live together without actually getting married. Have you ever lived with someone as a *couple* for three months or more?' If yes, the dates at which they started and stopped living together were collected for each union.
2. Over the period 1938–64, women aged 15–34 produced about 85 per cent of all births and 90 per cent of all births outside marriage. During 1964–2003, women aged 15–34 produced about 90 per cent of all births and 93 per cent of all births outside marriage.
3. The corresponding percentages for births to women of all ages were 4.3 per cent and 7.2 per cent.
4. The corresponding percentages for births to women of all ages were 9.1 per cent and 41.4 per cent.
5. These estimates come from the partnership histories in the British Household Panel Study, used later in the chapter to examine social differentials.
6. The tendency to consider as potential spouses mainly people in one's 'social group' (for example, defined by education or social class) is also a reflection of imperfect information – they are more likely to be suitable long-term partners than persons outside it.
7. What follows is a brief description of the matching model presented in Burdett and Ermisch (2002) and Ermisch (2003: ch. 7).
8. See Ermisch (2003: ch. 11) for details of the model, Nechyba (2001) for a similar model and Schelling (1978) for social interaction models more generally.
9. From left to right (that is, in order of unemployment change), the countries are Sweden, the USA, Austria, Italy, Portugal, Germany, France, Netherlands, UK, Ireland and Spain. For what it is worth, when Spain is omitted, the regression line is $y = 2.9751x + 13.835$, with an R^2 of 0.612.
10. I am grateful to Chiara Pronzato for constructing the demographic history files combining retrospective and prospective panel information.
11. The impact (standard error) of having *a higher educational attainment* (that is, above A level qualifications, usually obtained by 18, or nursing qualifications) on the log odds of cohabiting in one's first partnership is: 0.64 (0.13), 0.54 (0.12) and −0.38 (0.17) for women born in the 1950s, 1960s and 1970s, respectively. But note that those who have formed a union in 1970s cohort under-samples women who have a higher educational attainment, both because they have not had a union and because some of them have not had time to complete a higher educational attainment.

REFERENCES

Bagnoli, M. and T. Bergstrom (1993), 'Courtship as a waiting game', *Journal of Political Economy*, **101**, 185–202.

Brown, A. and K. Kiernan (1981), 'Cohabitation in Great Britain: evidence from the General Household Survey', *Population Trends*, **25**, 1–10.

Burdett, K. and J.F. Ermisch (2002), 'Single mothers', Institute for Social and Economic Research Working Paper 2002-30, Colchester: University of Essex.

Del Bono, E. (2004), 'Pre-marital fertility and labour market opportunities: evidence from the 1970 British Cohort Study', IZA Discussion Paper No. 1320, Bonn.

Ermisch, J.F. (1991a), *Lone Parenthood: An Economic Analysis*, Cambridge: Cambridge University Press.

Ermisch, J.F. (2001), 'Cohabitation and childbearing outside marriage in Britain', in L. Wu and B. Wolfe (eds), *Out of Wedlock*, New York: Russell Sage Foundation, pp. 109–42.

Ermisch, J.F. (2003), *An Economic Analysis of the Family*, Princeton, NJ: Princeton University Press.

Ermisch, J.F. (2005), 'The puzzling rise in childbearing outside marriage', in A. Heath, J. Ermisch and D. Gallie (eds), Understanding Social Change, Oxford: Oxford University Press.pp. 23–53.

Ermisch, J.F. and M. Francesconi (2000), 'Cohabitation in Great Britain: not for long, but here to stay', *Journal of the Royal Statistical Society, Series A*, **163**, 153–71.

Gray, J., J. Stockard and J. Stone (2006), 'The rising share of nonmarital births: fertility choice or marriage behavior?', *Demography*, **43**, 241–54.

Nechyba, T.J. (2001), 'Social approval, values, and AFDC: a reexamination of the illegitimacy debate', *Journal of Political Economy*, **109**, 637–72.

Nickell, S., L. Nunziata and W. Ochel (2005), 'Unemployment in the OECD since the 1960s. What do we know?', *The Economic Journal*, **115**, 1–27.

Sahib, P.R. and X. Gu (2002), ' "Living in sin" and marriage: a matching model'. *Journal of Population Economics*, **15**, 261–82.

Schelling, T.C. (1978), *Micromotives and Macrobehavior*, New York: W.W. Norton.

Szreter, S. (1996), *Fertility, Class and Gender in Britain, 1860–1940*, Cambridge: Cambridge University Press.

6.   Changing gender role attitudes[1]

Jacqueline Scott

In their introduction to the 1980 Women and Employment Survey, Martin and Roberts (1984) state that the previous 20 years had seen an explosion of interest in, and writings about, the changing roles of women. The changes are well known. Throughout the 1960s and 1970s there had been a significant rise in the level of economic activity among women. Most of the rise was accounted for by increasing proportions of mothers returning to work after having children, and having less time out of the labour market. In Britain many mothers throughout the latter part of the twentieth century have worked part-time, although whether part-time work was a matter of choice, or a matter of constraint, or some mixture of the two is disputed.

Writing at the start of the 1990s, Witherspoon and Prior (1991) suggest that there is clear evidence that women are the key advocates for change in the gender division of labour. It seems hardly surprising that there is a sex divide in terms of whether or not people favour a traditional gender division of labour. It clearly works in men's favour if women are both contributing to the household income and maintaining their primary role for care of the home and children. Yet, although the main focus of Witherspoon and Prior is the attitudes of working-age women, they conclude that, without changes in men's attitudes to care work, occupational segregation based on gender is likely to continue.

There is no denying, however, that the male breadwinner system has been in decline for at least half a century, not just in Britain but throughout Europe. Between 1960 and 2003 women's activity rates, relative to men's activity rates, increased from 44 to 79 per cent in the then 15 member countries of the European Union (EU) (McInnes 2006) whereas, as we illustrate below, in Britain, between 1961 and 2001, the comparable increase is even larger 43 to 84 per cent. The shift from male breadwinner and female carer model to double-income and single-parent households has transformed the established ways of distributing work between men and women. In policy terms at least, women are no longer seen as being solely responsible for family work and care. The expectation on the part of policy-makers today is increasingly that women will be fully 'individualised', in the sense of economically autonomous, although policies are often ambiguous on this score (see Lewis, this volume). Social reality is more mixed; women are still disproportionately in part-time work and still do the bulk of unpaid care. Yet by the start of the twenty-first century the notion of work–life balance (WLB) is firmly established in policy rhetoric. Why might this be?

One possible explanation lies in the recent acceleration of attitudinal changes regarding gender roles and the related shifts in the domestic division of labour. A second explanation may lie in the concern that increased employment participation of women may further negatively affect fertility rates in Europe where the population is rapidly ageing. There are also concerns that the welfare of children themselves may suffer if mothers, like fathers, spend increasing amounts of time at work. These practical concerns play out against a strong ethos of gender equality, as represented in equal opportunities legislation and practical progress in provision of parental leave (including paternal leave) and childcare.

In this chapter I examine 25 years of attitudinal change in gender roles. We know from previous research that attitudes have become steadily more supportive of women's dual work and family roles (Scott 1990; Scott et al. 1996). However, there is suggestion of a more recent backlash (for example, Scott 1999). This might be triggered by rising unemployment, as in Germany in the wake of reunification (Braun et al. 1994), but it is also conceivable that opinions may shift as the shine of the 'super-mum' syndrome wears off, and the idea of women juggling high-powered careers while also baking cookies and reading bedtime stories is increasingly seen to be unrealisable by ordinary mortals.

In Britain and cross-nationally there are time-series studies of representative population samples that allow us to examine attitude trends at the aggregate level. Unfortunately, the interpretation of such trend data is problematic because it is impossible empirically to disentangle whether change is due to what are called 'period' effects, or to the ageing process, or to cohort effects (Alwin and Scott 1996). However, strong theoretical considerations can guide interpretation. Cohort effects can change the overall structure of attitudes as older generations, whose views were formed in a different era, die off and are replaced by younger ones with perhaps more 'modern' (egalitarian) attitudes. At the population level there have been significant changes over the past 25 years in employment behaviour and in education, and both are likely to have a profound effect on attitudinal shifts across time.

The notion of a 'rising tide' of support for gender equality was coined by Ingelhart and Norris (2003) who claim that the move towards greater equality between men and women is part of a much broader dimension of cultural change. However they also suggest that tides can ebb and flow, and that government policies need the support of public opinion if they are not to prove transient or even provoke a backlash. To what extent do people in Britain and Europe support gender equality? Are there continuing concerns about the impact of mother's employment on the well-being of children and family? Examining how Britain compares with other countries in Europe, where policy initiatives for supporting motherhood and employment vary greatly, helps us identify in what ways Britain is distinctive.

CHANGES IN LABOUR FORCE PARTICIPATION AND FAMILY LIFE

Just over half a century ago the 1949 Royal Commission on Population report was concerned that the then existing employment bars against married women working were harmful all round, to women, the family and the community. True, the Commission was hardly giving a ringing endorsement to working mothers. For example it observes that 'there is often a real conflict between motherhood and a whole-time career' (ibid.: 160). Nevertheless it went on to acknowledge that, at least in part, the conflict is due to artificial barriers that restrict the contribution that women can make to the cultural and economic life of the nation. The report urged that a 'deliberate effort should be made to devise adjustments that would render it easier for women to combine motherhood and the care of a home with outside activities' (ibid.: 160).

Some 50 years later the BBC documentary series *Panorama* broadcast a programme called 'Back to the Kitchen' (Powell 2000). Using analysis based on data from the British Household Panel Study, a longitudinal study that follows over 5000 households across time, the report stated that, within just two years, one-third of women who had gone back to work full-time following the birth of their first child, had given up their full-time jobs, with 17 per cent switching to part-time work and 19 per cent giving up work altogether. The report concludes with the assertion that British women feel somewhat disillusioned and the promises to make work and motherhood reconcilable have not materialised.

A premise that is shared by both the Royal Commission and the BBC report is that there are distinctive sex- or gender-roles. In this chapter we use the term gender-roles to acknowledge that existing norms concerning male and female division of labour has as much or more to do with socio-cultural influences, as biological differences. The traditional gender-role divide is for the husband to be the breadwinner while the wife's role is to look after the home and children. This traditional gendered division of labour was temporarily suspended during the Second World War when there were large-scale efforts to make the mobilisation of married women for the war effort practicable on a national scale. War factories were moved into areas where labour reserves were available; day nurseries were set up and canteen services were organised; the provision of part-time jobs was encouraged; the marriage bar for women in non-industrial occupations including the civil service, the teaching profession, the police and the London County Council was removed. The removal of the marriage bar was enormously influential in opening up working opportunities for women. But after the war many married women returned home, in part due to the widespread sentiment that jobs ought to be 'kept for the boys' as things got 'back to normal' (Myrdal and Kline 1956).

At the start of the new millennium, there was an understandable tendency to focus on change. Duncan Gallie (2000), writing on labour force change, notes that, while the overall labour force participation rate has been remarkably stable across the twentieth century, this is because the declining trend of men's participation has been balanced by the increasing participation rates for women – especially married women. Here we update Gallie's table of labour force participation rates (in which figures are adjusted to take account of the changes in mandatory school leaving age) to include data from the 2001 Census (see Figure 6.1).

It can be seen that men's participation rates have declined from 94 per cent in 1911 through to 76 per cent in 2001. In contrast, women's participation rates are continuing to rise. In 1911 just over a third of women (35 per cent) were in the labour force; by 2001 this had risen to 64 per cent.

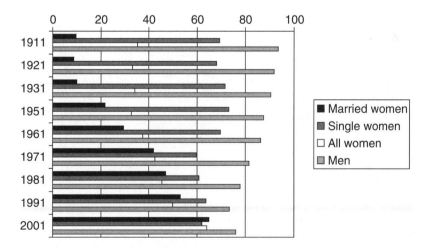

Figure 6.1   Labour force participation rates in Great Britain, 1911–2001 (percentage)

Whereas at the beginning of the century there was a 58 per cent difference in the participation rates for men and women, by 2001 the difference is only 12 per cent.

The huge increase in women's participation in the labour market is largely reflected in the changes in the activity of married women. It can be seen that participation rates for single women have been consistently high over the twentieth century. In 1911, 69 per cent of all single women over compulsory school age were economically active, whereas by 2001 this was the case for 62 per cent. In contrast, there has been a striking growth in the participation rates of married women. The 10 per cent jump between 1931 and 1951 is likely to reflect the war-time impact referred to above that legitimated a role for women in employment. Facilitated by the collapse of the marriage bar, the trend moved steadily upwards. Whereas in 1951 less than a quarter of married women were in the work force, by 1991 this was the case for half of all married women, and the proportion continued to rise in 2001 to 65 per cent, with the participation rate of married women surpassing the rate for single women. As Martin and Roberts (1984) noted about the early 1980s, marital status serves, in part, as a proxy for motherhood, and the presence and age of children were crucial determinants of whether or not women were employed.

Not surprisingly, the labour force participation of mothers varies greatly with country, where policies differ markedly in their support of working mothers. Figure 6.2 shows the trends in labour force participation rates of mother with children under 18 for Britain, West Germany, and the USA (Alwin et al. 1996, updated). Britain is now very close to the USA in

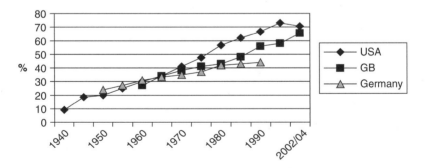

Source: The US data are from the US Department of Labor; the German data are from Statistisches Bundesamt; the British figures come from ONS Social Trends, updated in 2004 using data from the British Household Panel Study.

Figure 6.2   Labour force participation rates of mothers with children under 18, by country, 1940–2004

participation rates, albeit with much higher rates of part-time work. West Germany, prior to reunification, had a strong male-breadwinner culture that is now coming under question, with increasing concerns that the popularity of marriage and motherhood are being eroded.

There is a close association between the remarkable changes in labour force participation and the dramatic changes in family life. In Britain, in just one generation, the numbers marrying have halved, the numbers divorcing have trebled and the proportion of children born outside marriage has quadrupled (Pullinger and Summerfield 1997). People are marrying later and having fewer children than was the case in previous generations. The average number of children in a family has declined from 2.0 in 1971 to 1.8 in 2004. In 2004 one in four dependent children lived with a lone parent; whereas in 1972 it was only one child in 14. The rapid increase in unmarried cohabitation is one of the most spectacular ways in which traditional family life is changing in Britain (see Ermisch, this volume). Living together before marriage is now the norm. Among women, the proportion of those who cohabited with their future spouse prior to marriage has risen from less than 4 per cent of those whose first marriage was in 1966 to 68 per cent of those who were married in 1993. By the 1990, the vast majority of newly formed partnerships (over 70 per cent) were cohabiting rather than legally married, although many of those in partnerships do go on to marry.

These changes in partnerships are likely to reflect and reinforce a fundamental shift in family values. It is not only perspectives on marriage and the desirability of parenthood that have shifted but also attitudes concerning appropriate gender-roles. While second-wave feminism has undoubtedly influenced both male and female conceptions of gender equality, the timing is wrong for the 1970s feminist movement to be credited with the marked changes in women's roles at work and in the home. As we saw in Figure 6.1, women's move into employment pre-dates second-wave feminism. Women's marked increase in labour force participation throughout the second part of the twentieth century is not unique to Britain. Throughout most industrial nations of the West, there has been a huge rise in demand for labour, especially in service sectors where women have traditionally been concentrated. As we saw, in the 1960s most men and a very substantial proportion of single women were already employed. Thus increased labour market demands associated with expanding economies helped draw married women, including those with dependent children into the labour force.

The economic pressures on married women and mothers to be in paid work have, if anything, increased. In Lisbon in March 2000 the heads of government of the European Union subscribed to the very ambitious goal of raising the employment rate of both men and women by almost 10 percentage points in less than 10 years. Across Europe as a whole, this goal can only be achieved by the greater participation of women, with a target set for 60 per cent participation by 2010 (Boeri et al. 2005). However, there is also some concern that the increased labour force participation of women may further reduce fertility rates in a continent where the population is rapidly ageing (Esping-Andersen 2005). More children are needed to ensure there are sufficient workers to underwrite the growing welfare provision required for older people. There is also concern about the welfare of children, and worries about whether public childcare provision can substitute adequately for parental (primarily maternal) care.

The UK has already surpassed the Lisbon target for a female labour force participation rate of 60 per cent by 2010. However, there is little to be complacent about. In Britain women's participation in full-time employment has risen quite slowly. In 1951, 30 per cent of women aged 20–59 were in full-time employment (Joshi 1989); 40 years later in 1991 this figure has risen only slightly to 34 per cent. In the same period part-time work has quintupled (from 5 per cent in 1951 to 26 per cent in 1991). In 2002, 70 per cent of working age women were economically active with 42 per cent of those in employment working part-time (WEU 2004). Whether women chose to work part-time in order to juggle family and work roles, or whether lack of childcare alternatives and a traditional gender-role division of labour within the home leaves them no choice, is something that is far from clear. What is clear is that part-time work still has disadvantages in pay and promotion trajectories. How much impact the part-time work imperatives that have attempted to reduce inequities in pay and conditions will have remains to be seen but, as the Women and Work Commission Report (2006) emphasised and the Equal Opportunities Commission survey on sex and power (2007) highlights, there is little indication that, given current rates of progress, gender inequalities in either pay or in representation in top management positions will be eradicated in our lifetime.

TWENTY-FIVE YEARS OF ATTITUDINAL CHANGE

In this section I look at three aspects of gender-role change. First, I examine the direction and extent of attitudinal change within the UK and I examine whether there is any indication of a backlash. Second, I compare what is known about attitudinal trends cross-nationally, in order to identify what is distinctive about Britain and whether there has been a convergence towards greater egalitarianism in attitudes across Europe and the USA. Third, I explore how far the different theoretical explanations of social change in attitudes towards gender egalitarianism are or are not supported, in Great Britain, West Germany, and the USA.

On each of these issues, there is a considerable amount of previous research that informs our understanding about gender role change. However, what is new in this chapter is, first, that I extend the information about attitudinal change in the UK through into the new millennium. Second, new data from the International Social Survey Programme (ISSP) on gender-role changes allow us to compare the speed and direction of attitudinal change across time for seven different countries (West Germany, Great Britain, the USA, the Netherlands, Italy, Ireland and Spain). Third, the ISSP data provides a sufficient time span (14 years, with surveys in 1988, 1994 and 2002) for the systematic investigation of the underlying causes of attitudinal change.

Attitudinal Changes in Great Britain

Trend data from Britain are available from the early 1980s. In 1980, the Women and Employment Survey asked a series of questions about women's roles and some items have been replicated later in the British Social Attitudes Surveys through to 2002. Table 6.1 shows the percentage of men and women taking an egalitarian stance on each of several questions which are grouped together as concerning various nurturant or instrumental roles for women. These labels come from the influential book of Parsons and Bales (1955), where they suggested that the differentiation of sex-roles within the family along the instrumental-expressive lines embodies the social, as distinct from the purely reproductive, differentiation of sex-roles. Here I am mainly concerned to trace how far there remains support for the notion of a distinctive gender division of labour whereby women are seen as mainly responsible for family care and men for the breadwinning role. The use of the term 'egalitarian' signifies support for the feminist position that favours women's economic independence.

Nurturant items include measures that raise the issue of whether maternal employment is harmful to children or families. These consist of four items asking for people's views about whether a woman and her family will be happier if she goes out to work; whether family life suffers if the woman works full-time; whether a pre-school child is likely to suffer if his or her mother works; and whether a working mother can establish as warm and secure a relationship with her children, as a mother who does not work. Instrumental items tap agreement with traditional gender-role ideology and attitudes about women's jobs, and ask about whether a job is all right, but what most women really want is a home and children; whether a husband's job is to earn the money and a wife's job is to take care of the children; whether having a job is the best way for a woman to be an independent

Table 6.1   Percentage egalitarian responses to gender-role attitude questions in Britain, WES and BSA Surveys, 1980–2002

	WOMEN								MEN							
	1980	1984	1987	1988/9	1991	1994	1998	2002	1980	1984	1987	1988/9	1991	1994	1998	2002
Nurturant roles – sample N in brackets																
Woman & family happier if she goes out to work[1]	29.2 (5213)		12.9 (651)	22.9 (676)	14.1 (604)	14.2 (483)					14.5 (586)	14.7 (547)	15.9 (548)	15.7 (466)		
Pre-school child likely to suffer if mother works[2]				40.5 (691)	35.6 (624)	48.1 (493)		49.7 (1060)				29.4 (555)	27.5 (560)	38.1 (474)		37.3 (865)
Working mother can establish as warm and secure relationship[1]				65.0 (686)		69.8 (501)		70.9 (1064)				51.8 (558)		50.0 (473)		60.4 (864)
Family life suffers if woman works full-time[2]				43.4 (694)	49.2 (626)	50.7 (493)	51.0 (449)	46.5 (1052)				37.6 (561)	40.1 (561)	51.8 (477)	45.9 (318)	42.2 (874)
Instrumental roles – sample N in brackets																
Job all right but what most women want is home and children[2]	33.7 (5222)		48.7 (651)	52.4 (686)	55.0 (620)	53.7 (497)		54.0 (1042)			34.3 (584)	42.3 (545)	45.6 (553)	53.7 (497)		43.6 (848)

Table 6.1 (continued)

	WOMEN								MEN							
	1980	1984	1987	1988/9	1991	1994	1998	2002	1980	1984	1987	1988/9	1991	1994	1998	2002
Husband's job to earn income; wife's to take care of children[2]	31.5 (5221)	40.8 (823)	37.0 (651)	58.0 (699)	48.3 (636)	61.1 (499)		68.9 (1064)		34.5 (708)	28.3 (586)	47.1 (562)	41.8 (567)	57.2 (481)		58.9 (880)
Job is best way for woman to be independent[1]	67.0 (5215)	69.4 (798)	62.5 (651)	65.7 (698)	64.3 (622)	60.8 (497)		54.9 (1057)		69.5 (820)	62.8 (676)	60.3 (553)	56.7 (557)	60.6 (479)		54.1 (859)
Both husband & wife should contribute to house income[1]				57.0 (690)		59.2 (498)		59.2 (1059)				51.3 (552)		64.4 (482)		62.0 (867)

Notes:
Blank cells for years where question not asked.
1   Agree with question statement.
2   Disagree with question statement.

person; and whether both the husband and wife should contribute to the household income.

We can see from the top half of Table 6.1, which shows the items concerned with women's nurturant role, that there is very low support for the notion that a woman and family will all be happier if she goes out to work. However, this item is clearly ambiguous and the respondent has no adequate response option if they feel that women and family interests may be different. Regarding whether pre-school children suffer if mothers work, there is a quite pronounced gender difference with the time trend showing more people rejecting this through to the mid-1990s and then little or no change. A similar pattern holds true for views as to whether family life suffers if women go out to work, with the same slowing down or even reversal of egalitarian positions. The view that working mothers can achieve as good a relationship with children as mums who are not employed is endorsed more by women than men (71 per cent v. 60 per cent in 2002), with both male and female views moving in a more egalitarian direction, over time.

Regarding instrumental roles, the notion that what women really want is a home and children is rejected more by women than men. While only a third of women rejected this view in 1980 this rose to almost half the population taking the egalitarian stance by the end of the 1980s and attitudes remained quite stable through the 1990s. Women are also more likely to reject the notion there should be a gender-role divide and there has been a clear increase in both men and women's egalitarianism over time. The notion that a job is a best way to achieve independence shows very little gender difference, and both men and women's agreement with this view has declined over time. Support for dual-earners started out with women more in favour than men but, since the mid-1990s, men are as likely or even more likely to support two-earner households as are women.

It is not an exciting story. We find that the British, in the early 1980s are fairly conservative. There is one exception – the quite high proportion who believed that a job is the best way for a woman to be independent. There has been some shift towards greater egalitarianism on both nurturant and instrumental roles. However, there is also some evidence of a retreat with mounting concerns about whether family life suffers and increasing doubts about whether jobs allow women to be independent. It is only a small minority who are sanguine about whether women and families are happier if the woman has a job. As expected, we find that women tend to be more egalitarian than men on most items, with the one exception being support for dual-earners where men are marginally more in favour than women. The change over two decades has been much slower and more uneven than those who represent the story as one of revolutionary change followed by backlash would like us to believe. Of course, there may have been a marked change in gender-role attitudes before 1980. Nevertheless attitudinal change on most items over the past two decades has been surprisingly modest. In the next section we examine how far Britain is distinctive in this respect, in comparison other Western industrial countries.

Attitudinal Change across Nations and Time

Seven of the eight attitudinal items shown in Table 6.1 have also been carried in the International Social Survey Programme modules on family and gender-role change that took place in 1988 (or 1989 in Great Britain), 1994 and 2002. The ambiguous question about women and families all being happier was dropped. In Table 6.2 we can see the attitudinal changes across time in seven countries: West Germany, Great Britain, the USA,[2] Italy, Ireland, the Netherlands and Spain. Unfortunately, in both Italy and Spain survey participation was only for two of the three waves, with Italy not participating in 2002 and Spain not participating in 1988. The percentages reflect the combined attitudes of men and women, although separate analysis (not shown) shows that in all countries women tend to be somewhat more egalitarian than men on most items.

Regarding people's views about whether pre-school children suffer if their mother works, it can be seen that Ireland is the most egalitarian of these countries, with Great Britain next. Opinion in the USA is becoming more concerned about the negative consequences that women's work may have on the children. By contrast, the relatively positive views about the warmth of the working mother's maternal relationship have levelled off in both Ireland and the Netherlands, whereas in Great Britain and the USA attitudes have become more positive over time. However, there is some evidence of a retreat from egalitarianism in terms of rising concern that family life suffers if the woman has a full-time job, in both the USA and Great Britain. In views concerning the instrumental role of women, the West Germans are now the most egalitarian of these countries in rejecting the notion that what women really want is a home and job. However, there has been some reversal of sentiment in the USA, Great Britain and the Netherlands. On the item that taps support for traditional gender-role ideology, it is only in the USA that there is any indication of a fall in support for gender egalitarianism. West Germany is moving in a markedly more egalitarian direction across time, with shifts towards greater egalitarianism in both Ireland and Spain. It is interesting that two predominantly Catholic countries are among the least traditional of these seven countries on this measure. There is a very substantial cross-national difference in attitudes regarding whether both men and women should contribute to the household income with Spain being the most in favour of dual-earner households and the Netherlands the least.

So what does this cross-national comparison reveal? Gender-role attitudes differ considerably, depending on the issue, but the notion that there has been a steady increase in favour of women's instrumental roles and a move away from positions that endorse women's primary nurturant responsibilities is a myth. Particularly on those issues that best tap mounting concerns about work–family balance there is clear indication that women's changing role is viewed as having costs both for the woman and for family.

Nevertheless there is little evidence to support those who talk of gender-role backlash. Although, it could be argued that countries are at a different point in a cycle of attitudinal change. For most countries, attitudes were more conservative in the 1980s than in the subsequent decades. However, it may be that the shift from a conservative to a more egalitarian position reaches a peak followed by a retreat. The USA may be more advanced in the cycle than other countries, in showing retreat or greater awareness of potential conflicts between women's labour force participation and family life. By contrast, West Germany shows an increase in egalitarianism on most items, albeit starting from a rather traditional stance. In Great Britain, change over time has been relatively modest on most items.

The different trajectories and speed of change in the different countries begs for further analysis of the underlying drivers of social change. There has been a wealth of theoretical and empirical work, particularly in the USA, which has highlighted potential factors that influence social change in this area, including generational or birth cohort effects, educational advances, changes in women's labour force participation, changes in partnership formation, different religious traditions, and increasing secularisation (for example, Bumpass 1990; Mason and Lu 1988; Thornton et al. 1983). In the next section we put some of the competing explanations of social change in gender role attitudes to the test, by analysing the predictors of such change in Great Britain, the USA and West Germany.

What are the Drivers of Attitudinal Change?

By comparing the drivers of attitudinal change in Great Britain, West Germany and the USA, we can see whether the underlying factors of change are similar or very different in these three nations. In order to examine gender-role change, we use a summary measure of gender role attitudes. The summary item adds together the three nurturant measures shown in Table 6.2, together with three of the instrumental measures. Thus this summary measure adds six binary scores, giving a range of zero through six, with higher scores indicating greater egalitarian consistency.

Table 6.2   *Percentage egalitarian responses to gender role attitudes questions across countries and time (ISSP)*

		WG	GB	USA	Italy	IRL	NL	Spain
Nurturant roles								
Pre-school child likely to suffer if mother works[2]	1988	16.2	35.6	44.2	19.1	39.4	25.8	—
	1994	18.2	43.2	46.2	18.2	42.4	34.6	36.3
	2002	30.1	44.2	36.8	—	51.1	35.4	36.8
Working mother can establish as warm and secure a relationship[1]	1988	70.1	59.1	65.6	59.4	54.7	57.3	—
	1994	75.3	64.6	70.9	62.2	62.1	71.5	56.2
	2002	79.8	66.3	73.4	—	61.4	68.4	63.2
Family life suffers if woman works full-time[2]	1988	26.1	40.8	49.8	22.5	37.4	33.8	—
	1994	23.9	51.2	51.2	21.2	39.0	37.4	30.6
	2002	37.2	44.6	37.6	—	48.6	33.8	33.4
Instrumental roles								
Job is alright but what most women want is a home and children[2]	1988	36.6	47.9	38.9	34.9	30.4	41.5	—
	1994	48.1	50.4	43.5	35.8	33.5	43.3	39.6
	2002	62.4	49.4	31.1	—	45.6	39.6	43.9
Husband's job to earn income; wife's to take care of children[2]	1988	35.9	53.1	51.5	46.2	45.6	55.2	—
	1994	47.7	59.2	59.4	48.3	53.3	63.9	53.5
	2002	61.1	64.5	52.5	—	69.3	67.5	66.4
Job is best way for women to be independent[1]	1988	68.4	63.3	44.4	69.2	58.5	45.4	—
	1994	75.8	60.6	45.4	72.8	67.9	50.8	74.9
	2002	77.7	54.5	52.7	—	58.8	56.7	80.5
Both husband and wife should contribute to household income[1]	1988	50.4	54.5	49.7	73.0	65.2	24.0	—
	1994	67.0	61.7	57.6	81.1	77.3	28.5	84.4
	2002	66.1	60.5	58.3	—	69.6	40.1	87.9

Notes:
1   Agree with question statement.
2   Disagree with question statement.

The item concerning a job being the best way for a woman to be independent is dropped in order to improve the internal reliability of the new summary measure, in all three nations. The chronbach alphas are .70 for Great Britain, .71 for West Germany and .72 for the USA. In our analysis we drop the small number of cases where there are missing data on more than three of the items.

The predictor variables are cohort, year of survey, highest education; employment status of the female respondent or male respondent's female partner/wife; marital status; religion; and church attendance. A form of dummy regression, multiple classification analysis (MCA), is used to show the deviations of each category from the grand mean adjusted for the effects of the other variables included in the model. As Table 6.3 shows clear patterns emerge regarding gender role change in the three countries. First, it is worth noting that women have more egalitarian sympathies than do men in all three countries; respective grand means are 2.66 (female) versus 2.44 (males) in West Germany; 3.32 (females) versus 2.89 (males) in Great Britain, and 3.24 (females) versus 2.71 (males) in the USA. Thus Great Britain is marginally the most egalitarian country on this measure and West Germany the least. The most important predictor of gender-role attitudes in all three countries is cohort (etas, a correlation ratio, shows the strength of relationship) although for men in Great Britain having a partner who works (full-time or part-time), rather than a home-maker is also a strong predictor.

Figure 6.3 shows the adjusted mean scores by cohort on gender role attitudes for men and women in the three nations. Women from Great Britain and the USA tend to be the most egalitarian. The adjusted mean scores associated with the year of survey differ quite substantially between countries, as Figure 6.4 makes clear. In West Germany attitudes have become increasingly egalitarian over time, for both men and women, albeit from a lower base point than the other two countries. In Great Britain, there has been little shift in attitudes over the 14 years, although women's attitudes in 2002 are, if anything, less egalitarian than in 1988 on this summary measure. In the USA there is evidence that egalitarianism had peaked by the end of the 1980s and recent years have seen a retreat, with both men and women's attitudes becoming markedly less egalitarian in the new millennium.

In Table 6.3 it can be seen that education is a significant predictor of gender-role attitudes, except for British men. In addition, women's work status is particularly influential for women's attitudes in all countries. Without panel data that follows the same individuals across time, it is not possible to disentangle whether women with more egalitarian views are more likely to obtain employment, whether employment experience encourages more egalitarian attitudes, or whether both are true.

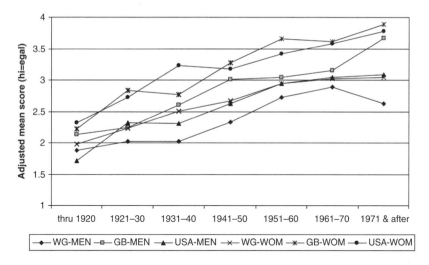

Figure 6.3   Cohort effects on gender-role attitudes, by country and gender

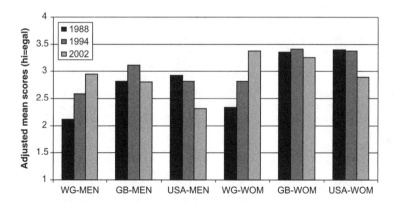

Figure 6.4   Year effects on gender-role attitudes, by country and gender

However, we are able to estimate how far cohort effects can be 'explained' by differences in education and work status. In analysis (not shown) we ran three MCA models, the first estimating the effect of cohort and year alone; a second that included cohort, year, education and work status; and a third model, with the additional variables of marital status, religion and church attendance corresponding to Table 6.3. Interestingly, cohort effects are not reduced or 'explained' by the introduction of controls for education and labour force participation. Perhaps this is not surprising as, by 1988, the rapid rise of women's education and labour force participation had already

Table 6.3   Predictors of gender-role attitudinal change: WG, GB and USA

		Women			Men		
		WG	GB	USA	WG	GB	USA
Deviation from mean (adj)							
Cohort	Through 1920	−0.68	−1.1	−0.92	−0.56	−0.76	−1
	1921–30	−0.43	−0.49	−0.51	−0.42	−0.65	−0.39
	1931–40	−0.15	−0.55	−0.01	−0.42	−0.29	−0.4
	1941–50	0.01	−0.05	−0.06	−0.11	0.12	−0.08
	1951–60	0.29	0.34	0.18	0.28	0.15	0.24
	1961–70	0.36	0.3	0.34	0.45	0.26	0.33
	1971& after	0.38	0.57	0.54	0.19	0.78	0.38
	Eta	0.41***	0.31***	0.29***	0.35***	0.27***	0.24***
Year	1988	−0.32	0.03	0.16	−0.32	−0.07	0.22
	1994	0.16	0.09	0.14	0.15	0.22	0.11
	2002	0.72	−0.06	−0.35	0.51	−0.08	−0.4
	Eta	0.25***	0.08ns	0.09***	0.17***	0.12**	0.09***
Education	Below 2ndry	−0.28	−0.13	−0.38	−0.25	−0.06	−0.22
	2ndry complete	−0.09	0.05	−0.11	−0.03	0.14	−0.13
	High sch dip	0.25	0.03	0.06	−0.12	0.07	0.04
	College	0.64	0.27	0.3	0.42	−0.05	0.23
	Eta	0.24***	0.19***	0.2***	0.16***	0.12ns	0.13**
Women's work	Workg (ft/pt)	0.442	0.28	0.29	0.53	0.4	0.14
	Home-maker	−0.39	−0.83	−0.66	−0.32	−0.89	−0.73
	Other/no wife	0.04	0.012	−0.06	−0.09	0.05	0.14
	Eta	0.38***	0.3***	0.31***	0.29***	0.29***	0.19***
Marital status	Married	−0.03	−0.04	−0.14	−0.06	0.1	0.08
	Prev married	−0.05	0.19	0.07	−0.09	−0.19	−0.18
	Never married	0.15	−0.06	0.25	0.16	−0.26	−0.04
	Eta	0.26*	0.11bs	0.17***	0.20**	0.09*	0.13ns
Religion	Cath	−0.05	0	0.08	−0.06	0.26	0.01
	Prots	0.05	−0.08	0.02	0.04	−0.11	−0.03
	Other	−0.31	−0.24	−0.14	−0.67	−0.35	−0.04
	None	0.11	0.14	−0.22	0.24	0.09	0.09
	Eta	0.16***	0.15*	0.07ns	0.17***	0.16***	0.08ns
Church attend	Weekly	−0.26	−0.11	−0.22	−0.26	−0.34	−0.22
	Sev month	−0.04	−0.02	0.19	−0.06	−0.11	0.11
	Less freq	0.14	0.16	0.19	−0.01	−0.13	0.16
	Never	0.23	0.02	0.21	0.24	0.09	0.07
	Eta	0.27***	0.1ns	0.15***	0.21***	0.14*	0.11**
Grand mean		2.66	3.32	3.24	2.44	2.89	2.71
N		3216	2257	2290	2876	1919	1670
R square		0.29	0.18	0.18	0.22	0.16	0.12

Notes:
* p<.05; ** p<.01; *** p<.001.
ns = not significant; bs = borderline significant p<.10.

occurred. Controlling for other factors (marital status, religion and church attendance) also does not change the basic finding that most of the variation that we can explain is attributable to cohort effects and the amount of such cohort variation that is due to different patterns of education and work or religiosity across cohorts is negligible. Nevertheless, in all countries and for both genders the explained variance does increase as education, marital status and religion are introduced into the models. As Table 6.3 shows, the total variance explained in the summary measure of gender role attitudes is highest in West Germany (22 per cent for men and 29 per cent for women) and markedly lower in both Great Britain and the USA (16 per cent GB men, 12 per cent US men, and 18 per cent for women in both countries). Thus the model works best in West Germany, where attitudinal shifts have been catching up with the egalitarianism that seems to have peaked earlier in other countries.

SUMMARY AND DISCUSSION

In this chapter we have looked at three aspects of gender role change. First we investigated the extent of attitudinal change within Great Britain and considered whether or not there is evidence of a backlash. Second we compared what is known about attitudinal change cross-nationally to find out what is distinctive about Britain and whether there has been any convergence of attitudes in Europe and the USA. Finally, we explored empirically various explanations of social attitudinal change, in particular we wanted to find out to what extent generational differences are the main drivers of attitudinal change and, if so, whether such differences are reduced once education and labour force participation are taken into account.

We found that gender-role attitudinal change in Britain does not support a story of revolutionary change and backlash. Interestingly, however, we do find that gender attitudes seem to follow a cyclical period of change, showing a move towards greater egalitarianism followed by retreat. Of course, the fact that people's attitudes have changed relatively slowly and inconsistently does not provide any direct evidence about behaviour. However, attitudes do matter and women (and particularly mothers) can experience considerable strain when attitudes reinforce the notion that employment and family interests conflict. There is considerable commitment to the traditional gender-role divide and there remains concern that maternal employment may compromise family and child well-being. (For similar observations regarding trends in USA, see Thornton and De Marco 2001.)

In terms of our cross-national comparison of gender-role change, we found attitudes differ considerably depending on the issue. However, the idea that there is near universal support for egalitarianism is clearly a myth. Interestingly, there is evidence of mounting concern about work–family balance on items which tap the conflicts that employment and family care raise for women. There is also clear evidence that countries differ markedly in terms of their trajectories and speed of change in a way that begs additional analysis to improve our understanding of what is driving attitudinal change.

In this chapter we limited out exploration of the drivers of attitudinal change to three countries: West Germany, Great Britain and the USA. We found that the dominant predictor of gender-role attitudes is generation or birth cohort. Moreover, the importance of generation remains, even when controlling for differences in education, women's labour force participation and religion. For the most part our societies are moving towards an epoch of equalisation in terms of opportunities and constraints on men and women. However, in gender-role attitudes there is some evidence of egalitarianism reaching a peak and retreat, particularly in the USA. Moreover, there is still a pronounced generational lag in support for more egalitarian gender roles. It is perhaps not surprising that 'old-fashioned' notions of gender difference are proving surprisingly resilient, given that new gender equalities have imposed a double burden on women, whose employment status does little to ease their burden of family care.

Is the new millennium going to bring further progress or retreat in gender-role egalitarianism? To answer this question we need to do a better job in monitoring gender-role attitudinal change than is currently the case. The existing questions are relatively crude indicators for preferences concerning the complex ways men and women can divide up paid and unpaid labour (see Braun 2007). Existing surveys contain little information about men's roles outside of paid work. We need to explore the disjuncture between practice and expectations concerning work and family life, which have challenged both men and women over the last few decades. Are people concerned about the potential negative effects of maternal employment, because caring is seen as predominantly woman's work, or is it because there are no practical alternatives to the woman being the primary carer? Is it primarily men who must change in their contribution to unpaid care or will greater egalitarianism be achieved more readily by the increasing commodification of care? Existing measures are designed to tap support or rejection of the traditional gender-role divide. But the interesting issues are now about how men and women can best work together to achieve a work–family balance that meets the needs of different generations, at different stages of the life course. To make progress in devising egalitarian interventions that the public would support, we need to know more about what gender-roles people view as practical, as possible, and as fair.

NOTES

1. I gratefully acknowledge support for this research from a grant by the Economic and Social Research Council (RES-225-25-1001).
2. The 2002 data for the USA are not strictly comparable with early time-points because the response categories changed.

REFERENCES

Alwin, D. and J. Scott (1996), 'Attitude change – its measurement and interpretation using longitudinal surveys', in B. Taylor and B. Thomson (eds), *A Decade of Change in Social Values*, Aldershot: Dartmouth, pp. 75–106.

Alwin, D., J. Scott. and M. Braun (1996), 'Sex-role attitudes change in the United States: national trends and cross-national comparisons', Working Paper, University of Michigan, Ann Arbor.

Boeri, T., D. Del Boca and C. Pissarides (2005), *Women at Work: An Economic Perspective*, Oxford: Oxford University Press.

Braun, M. (2007), 'Using egalitarian items to measure men's and women's family roles', Working Paper, ZUMA, Mannheim.

Braun, M., J. Scott and D. Alwin (1994), 'Economic necessity or self-actualization? Attitudes towards women's labour force participation in East and West Germany', *European Sociological Review*, **10**(1), 29–47.

Bumpass, L. (1990), 'What's happening to the family? Interaction between demographic and institutional change', *Demography*, **27**, 483–98.

Equal Opportunities Commission (2005), *Sex and power: who runs Britain?*', www.eqgualityhumanrights.com/Documents/EOC/PDF/Policy/who_runs_britain.pdf (accessed 7 January 2008).

Esping-Andersen, G. (2005), 'A jobless and childless Europe?' in T. Boeri, D. Del Boca and C. Pissarides (eds), *Women at Work: An Economic Perspective*, Oxford: Oxford University Press, pp. 268–74.

Gallie, D. (2000), 'Labour force change', in A. Halsey, with J. Webb (eds), *British Social Trends 3rd Edition*, Houndsmill: Macmillan, pp. 281–323.

Ingelhart, R. and P. Norris (2003), *Rising Tide: Gender Equality and Cultural Change around the World*, Cambridge: Cambridge University Press.

Joshi, H. (1989), 'The changing form of women's economic dependency', in H. Joshi (ed.), *The Changing Population of Britain*, Oxford: Basil Blackwell, pp. 157–76.

Martin, J. and C. Roberts (1984), *Women and Employment: A Lifetime Perspective*, London: OPCS.

Mason, K. and Y.-H. Lu (1988), 'Attitudes toward women's familial roles: changes in the United States 1977–1985', *Gender and Society*, **2**, 39–57.

McInnes, J. (2006), 'Work–life balance in Europe: a response to the baby bust or reward for the baby boomers?', *European Societies*, **8**(2), 223–50.

Myrdal, A. and V. Kline (1956), *Women's Two Roles: Home and Work*, London: Routledge and Kegan Paul.

Parsons, T. and R. Bales (1955), *Family, Socialization and the Interaction Process*, Glencoe, IL: Free Press.

Powell, S. (2000), 'Back to the Kitchen Sink', *Panorama*, BBC News, http://news.bbc.co.uk/1/hi/programmes/panorama/archive/613615.stm (accessed 7 January 2008).

Pullinger, J. and C. Summerfield (eds) (1997), *Social Focus on Families*, London: ONS.

Royal Commission on Population (1949), *Report*, London: HMSO.

Scott, J. (1990), 'Women and the family: changing attitudes and cross-national comparisons', in R. Jowell, S. Witherspoon, and L. Brook (eds), *British Social Attitudes the 7th Report*, Aldershot: Gower, pp. 51–71.

Scott, J. (1999), 'Family change: revolution or backlash in attitudes', in S. McRae (ed.), *Changing Britain: Families and Households in the 1990s*, Oxford: Oxford University Press, pp. 68–99.

Scott, J., D. Alwin, and M. Braun (1996), 'Generational change in gender-role attitudes: Britain in a cross-national perspective', *Sociology*, **30**, 471–92.

Thornton, A. and L. De-Marco (2001), 'Four decades of attitudes towards family issues in the United States: the 1960s through to the 1990s', *Journal of Marriage and Family*, **63**, 1009–37.

Thornton, A., D. Alwin and D. Camburn (1983), 'Causes and consequences of sex-role attitudes and attitude change', *American Sociological Review*, **48** 211–27.

Women and Equality Unit (WEU) (2004), 'Women and men in the workplace', www.womenandequalityunit.gov.uk/research/gender_briefing_nov04.doc (accessed7 January 2008).

Women and Work Commission (2006), *Shaping a Fairer Future*, London: DTI, www.womenandequalityunit.gov.uk/publications/wwc_shaping_fairer_future06.pdf(accessed, January 2008).

Witherspoon, S. and G. Prior (1991), 'Working mothers free to choose?', in R. Jowell, L. Brook and B. Taylor (eds), *British Social Attitudes, the 8th Report*, Aldershot, Dartmouth, pp. 131–54.

PART III

Work–Life Balance

7. Working full-time after motherhood

Susan McRae

INTRODUCTION

This chapter explores the experiences and characteristics of women who work full-time after having children. The findings are drawn from three surveys which tracked women from the time they gave birth in late 1987/early 1988 until 1999, when the child was between 11 and 12 years old. The pattern of increasing labour force activity among women with dependent children is well known. In Britain in 1966, 11 per cent of women with dependent children were economically active; some four decades later in 2004, this had risen to 67 per cent of women with dependent children. Over half of mothers with pre-school children have jobs, rising to almost 80 per cent of those whose youngest child is aged 11 or older (Summerfield and Babb 2004). It is also well known that the majority of women work part-time after becoming mothers. Surveys of new mothers examining the provision and take up of maternity rights and benefits from 1979 onwards have shown a steady rise in mothers' part-time employment, from 19 per cent of all new mothers in 1979 to 54 per cent in 2002. There was over these years a rise also in full-time employment among new mothers, but to a substantially lower level. Full-time employment among new mothers stood at 5 per cent in 1979 and reached 24 per cent in 1996, only to fall back to 18 per cent in 2002 (Callender et al. 1997; Daniel 1980; Hudson et al. 2004; McRae 1991).

Despite the substantial rise in the labour force participation of women in Britain, men's and women's roles in the family remain much as they were 30 years ago. British mothers continue to do most of the domestic work and childcare, even when they hold full-time jobs. British fathers continue to work very long hours, even when their partners work full-time. The gender gap in time spent on household work has fallen over time, but largely because some women are doing less housework and not because men are doing more (Crompton et al.2005; Harkness 2003).

Moreover, British women have not yet achieved parity with men in the labour market and despite 30 years of increasing participation, tend still to earn less, hold fewer top jobs, work largely in gender-segregated workplaces, and enjoy fewer job-related benefits (Burchell et al. 1997). Women employed part-time, who comprise almost half of the female workforce, fare particularly badly in comparison with men – and with women employed full-time.

The gender gap in pay has proved particularly intransigent for part-timers, although it has declined between men and women employed full-time. In 1970, full-time employed women employees earned 63 per cent of men's full-time hourly pay; rising to 77 per cent in 1990 and to 82 per cent in 2000 (Joshi 2005: 161; Olsen and Walby 2004). The pay of women employed full-time vis-à-vis men has improved, according to Joshi, largely because of an equalisation in human capital (qualifications, training, and job experience) between men and women.[1] By 2006, women employed full-time had narrowed the gap to earn on average 17 per cent less than men full-time employees (Women and Work Commission 2006).

Full-time employment during the period of family formation is, however, undertaken by only the minority of women in Britain, particularly on a continuous basis. Elsewhere I have argued that, contrary to the predictions of preference theory (Hakim 2000), women who might choose to work full-time after motherhood are constrained by other circumstances in their lives; that although women cannot be sharply distinguished in terms of their preferences for particular lifestyles, they do differ in terms of their abilities to act on those preferences (McRae 2003a; 2003b). This chapter sets aside the question of differing preferences among women after childbirth and examines the incidence of continuous full-time employment 12 years after a first childbirth, the factors influencing continuous full-time employment and the extent to which full-time employment (whether continuous or not) may lead to labour market benefits for women with children.

THE COMBINED DATA-SET (CDS)

The chapter draws on longitudinal survey research with a sample of women who became mothers during a six-week period between November 1987 and January 1988[2] and who were surveyed at three points in time – eight to nine months after the birth, when the child was 5 years old, and again six years later when the child was between 11 and 12 years of age. Personal interviews were also carried out with smaller sub-sets of respondents in 1992 and 2003, but these are not discussed here. Data collected from mothers who responded to all of the three surveys carried out in 1988, 1993 and 1999 were merged to create a combined data-set which includes 1516 mothers, of whom 988 had had their first child in 1988 (see the appendix to this chapter for survey details). The analyses presented here focus on first-time mothers, in order to maximise the representativeness of the data.

The first survey in 1988 was drawn from Department of Health and Social Security (DHSS) child benefit records and was based on a nationally representative sample of women with new babies (McRae 1991). For the two follow-up surveys, the target base was mothers who had been economically active during their 1987 pregnancy. This decision slanted the follow-up surveys towards first-time mothers, as the majority of women with previous children were not employed during their 1987 pregnancy. Three-quarters of the women who became first-time mothers in 1988 had been employed during pregnancy, compared with just over one-third of women who had had their second or subsequent child at that time. Although a focus on first-time mothers ameliorates much of the sample bias introduced by this decision, very young mothers (who were either in education or unemployed) and non-working lone mothers[3] remain under-represented in the combined dataset as they were less likely to be in paid employment during their first pregnancy.

The representativeness of married or cohabiting mothers in the combined data-set, in terms of economic activity and occupational level 12 years after their first birth, is reasonably good, however. In 1999, 27 per cent of married/cohabiting mothers in the combined data-set were employed full-time, 52 per cent were employed part-time, and 21 per cent were inactive. This compares reasonably well with national data for partnered women with a youngest child aged 5 to 10 years, of whom 25 per cent were employed full-time, 50 per cent were employed part-time, and 25 per cent were inactive in 1999 (Matheson and Summerfield 2000). A comparison across broad occupational groups between first-time mothers in the combined data-set and Social Trends data for women whose youngest child was aged 5–10 shows a similar level of congruence, with a slight bias in the combined data-set towards higher level occupations and a concomitant bias away from sales and operative jobs; but generally, the occupational distribution in 1999 of the combined data-set is not out of line with the national picture (Matheson and Summerfield 2000).

DEFINING CONTINUOUS FULL-TIME EMPLOYMENT

Because the data used in the analyses presented below were collected through postal surveys, it was not possible to collect detailed life and work histories. Therefore, to analyse employment continuity (and subsequently occupational mobility), it was necessary to define continuity on the basis of the information available, rather than employ life-history techniques. It was also decided, in defining continuous employment, to make allowance for periods of maternity leave, which in this study are counted as periods of

Table 7.1   Defining continuous employment

Continuous employment 1988–1993 and 1988–1999
Returned to work within 12 months of first birth; and
In work 90 per cent of time since first birth; and

1999 only, the above plus:
Self-defined as 'always worked since having children, except for periods of
  maternity leave'; or
Self-defined as 'worked most of the time except for short breaks (with or without
  maternity leave) to care for my children'

---

employment whether or not formally recognised as such by an employer. Table 7.1 summarises the information from the surveys used to create two continuous employment variables for the periods 1988 to1993 and 1988 to 1999. In order to be counted as having been continuously employed since the birth of their first child, mothers must have returned to work within the first year of their first birth and have been in the labour force 90 per cent or more of the time since that birth.[4] In 1999 mothers had the opportunity to self-define their working history and these responses were added to the definition of continuous employment for 1988 to 1999. Information about full-time or part-time status was was also based on mothers' self-reports.

This definition provides a 'broad brush' estimation of employment continuity. Moreover, each element within the definition can be challenged. While it is unlikely that anyone would insist upon 100 per cent of time being spent in the labour force as the basis for calculating mothers' continuity of employment, arguments could be made for durations higher or lower than 90 per cent of time in employment. Our view is that this cut-off allows a reasonable amount of time out of the labour market for the birth of other children or for brief periods of unemployment as a result of job changes, while preserving the essence of a continuous labour force attachment.

WORK HISTORIES AFTER A FIRST BIRTH

Defining continuity of employment in this way allowed examination of mothers' work histories up to the time their first-born child was aged about 5 and again when that child was aged between 11 and 12 years (1988 to 1999). This approach provides a more detailed view of mothers' labour force participation than that provided by 'snapshots' of labour force participation rates derived from individual surveys. These patterns are shown in Figure 7.1.

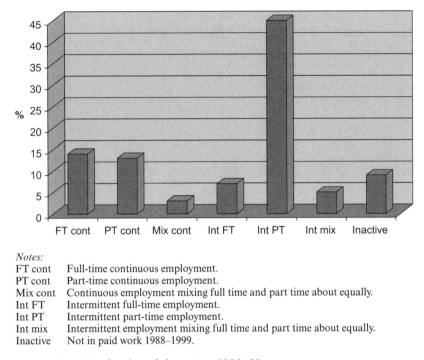

Notes:

FT cont	Full-time continuous employment.
PT cont	Part-time continuous employment.
Mix cont	Continuous employment mixing full time and part time about equally.
Int FT	Intermittent full-time employment.
Int PT	Intermittent part-time employment.
Int mix	Intermittent employment mixing full time and part time about equally.
Inactive	Not in paid work 1988–1999.

Figure 7.1   Mothers' work histories, 1988–99

By 1999, mothers who followed the traditional pattern of intermittent part time employment were the largest single group (45 per cent). However, a substantial proportion of mothers had periods of full-time employment during the 11 to 12 years following their first birth. Thirty per cent of mothers had held full-time employment to some extent by 1999, either continuously (14 per cent) or combined with part-time employment whether continuous or not (9 per cent) or intermittent and combined with spells out of the labour market (7 per cent). The analyses which follow identify significant influences on mothers' continuous full-time employment after a first childbirth for the period 1988 to 1999, and the benefits that are associated with it.

FACTORS WHICH INFLUENCE FULL-TIME CONTINUOUS EMPLOYMENT

Table 7.2 summarises the results of logistic regression analyses, expressed as odds ratios or the greater or lesser chances mothers with certain

Table 7.2   Factors associated with continuous full-time (FT) among first-time mothers, 1988 to 1999 (main effects model)

	Continuous FT odds ratios
Occupation (ref: manual/sales)	
Management	4.48**
Professional	3.72*
Associate professional	4.78**
Clerical/secretarial	2.28
Personal and protective	2.18
Woman's % contribution to joint income (1999)	1.02***
Childcare problems *never* affected job opportunities	3.60**
Childcare problems affected job opps in 1993 or 1999 (ref: childcare affected job opportunities in *both* 1993 and 1999)	1.50
Used paid childcare	3.27***
Used unpaid childcare (ref: did not use childcare)	.92
Not true that husband prefers her job to fits with family life (ref: true or partly true)	2.15**
Not true that husband thinks caring for family is her main job (ref: true or partly true)	2.58***
Always disagrees that man's job to earn; woman's job to care for family	1.78*
Always disagrees that women want job with no worries or responsibilities	2.17**
Has only one child	3.51**
Has two children (ref: three or more children)	2.60**
Constant	.001***
N	649
Nagelkerke R Square	.434

Notes:
Occupations classified using Standard Occupational Classification (SOC).
* $p < .05$; ** $p < .01$; *** $p < .001$.

characteristics have of working full-time continuously after having their first baby. As might be expected, occupational level is statistically significantly associated with mothers' behaviour patterns, with mothers in higher level jobs between four and five times more likely to have stayed in the labour market full-time continuously than mothers in other jobs. The number of children mothers have is also highly significant in terms of their employment careers. The more children mothers have, the less likely they are to remain continuously in full-time employment; put another way, mothers who stay in the labour market full-time are more likely than other mothers to stop at one child.

The use of paid childcare is an obvious facilitator of full-time continuous employment during family formation. Its importance is reflected in the model: compared with mothers who did not use childcare and mothers who used unpaid care, those who paid for childcare were significantly more likely to work continuously on a full-time basis. Among other key influences identified, one of the most important is problems with childcare arrangements that hinder mothers' job opportunities. Mothers who reported in both 1993 and 1999 *not* having had such difficulties were more than three times more likely to work full-time continuously than mothers who reported childcare difficulties in both 1993 and 1999.[5] Table 7.2 also indicates that the more mothers contribute to their family income, the more likely they are to remain in full-time continuous employment.[6]

Attitudes to Mothers' Employment

In 1993, mothers were asked about their husband's or partner's views about their employment, either actual if the woman was in work or potential if she was out of the labour market.[7] Two aspects appeared to affect whether or not a woman would stay in the labour market full time after becoming a mother: whether her partner thinks that her main job is to look after the family; and whether her partner is only happy for her to work if it fits with family life. Mothers who reported that these views were 'untrue' (that is, her husband did not think this way or hold that view) were more than twice as likely to stay in the labour market continuously on a full-time basis than mothers who reported this position to be 'true' or 'partly true' (cf. Werbel 1998).

Questions about mothers' own attitudes to employment were asked in both 1993 and 1999. Two aspects appeared statistically significant when mothers expressed consistent disagreement; mothers who *disagreed in both 1993 and 1999* with the view that 'most working women with families want jobs with no worries or responsibilities' or that 'a man's job is to earn money; a woman's job is to care for the family' were twice as likely to have worked continuously on a full-time basis over the 12 years since becoming a mother than women who either agreed with this view in both 1993 and 1999 or agreed in one survey and disagreed in the other.

DOWNWARD OCCUPATIONAL MOBILITY

For many years now, studies have shown that childbirth is the biggest single cause of vertical downward occupational mobility for women. Perhaps the most important early British study, the Women and Employment Survey, indicated that 45 per cent of women who returned to work part-time and 19 per cent of women who returned full-time after a break for childbirth experienced downward occupational mobility (Dex 1987; Martin and Roberts 1984: 88). Smeaton (2005) utilising a comparison between first-time mothers in the 1958 National Child Development Study (NCDS) cohort and the 1970 Birth Cohort Study (BCS) cohort demonstrates that although downward mobility has declined over time, it nonetheless remains a salient factor in women's employment careers.

Table 7.3 indicates the proportion of mothers who were working at occupational levels below the level of the job they had held in 1987 (*before* their first birth), at two points in time – after six years (1993) and after 12 years (1999). A limited comparison with Smeaton (2005) suggests that the proportions experiencing downward mobility in this research compare

Table 7.3   *Percentage experiencing downward mobility from pre-first birth occupational level at (1) first return in 1988 and (2) between 1987 and 1993 and (3) between 1987 and 1999*

Pre-birth job level 1987	Management	Professional	Asst Prof.	Sec/ Clerical	Personal and protective	(N)
Work history (1) 1988 return to:						
Full-time	52	18	7	20	7	178
Part-time	65	46	9	21	10	254
(2) 1993						
Cont FT	50	11	0	11	11	121
Cont PT	75	44	6	0	22	113
Int PT	79	44	41	41	32	390
(3) 1999						
Cont FT	55	5	4	5	9	130
Cont PT	92	31	25	8	33	126
Int PT	81	35	32	44	24	349

Notes:
All relationships significant at p = < 000.
Work history (continuous v. non continuous) 1993 measures continuity from returning to work in 1988 to the 1993 survey; for 1999, it measures continuity from returning to work in 1988 to the 1999 survey. For the definition of continuous employment see text and Table 7.1.

Cont FT   Mothers employed full-time continuously after a first birth in 1988.
Cont PT   Mothers employed part-time continuously after a first birth in 1988.
Int PT   Mothers intermittently employed part-time after a first birth in 1988.

reasonably well with other data-sets.[8] Table 7.3 demonstrates at least three key results. First, as in the early 1980s, returning full-time is almost always better than returning part-time, in terms of 'holding on' to one's occupational level; second, motherhood is not a good option for women in managerial jobs, even if they work continuously; and third, in some occupations, continuity of employment helps part timers to maintain their pre-motherhood occupational level. The advantage conferred by full-time employment is clear: mothers whose first return to work in 1988 was to a full-time job and those who maintained full-time employment over time were substantially less likely to experience downward occupational mobility from their pre-birth jobs. By 1999 – but excluding mothers who had been in managerial roles in 1987 – fewer than 10 per cent in all other occupational groups were working below the level they had held before the birth of their first baby.

Women in managerial jobs before motherhood, however, experienced high and increasing rates of vertical downward mobility after motherhood. Even when continuously employed on a full-time basis, fewer than half maintained their pre-birth occupational level; while among those employed part-time, upwards of 80 per cent experienced downward mobility. Moreover, continuity of employment did not help part-timers avoid downward mobility. These general patterns describe well-known characteristics of women's employment. Women remain the minority in most management posts: in 2004, they comprised 12 per cent of local authority chief executives, 17 per cent of trade union general secretaries, 24 per cent of civil service top management, and 33 per cent of private sector managers (EOC 2005). Despite various government initiatives, family-friendly working practices for women in private sector management are not widespread and women managers who wish to work after motherhood tend to take jobs elsewhere.

As noted above, a key outcome of the 1980 Women and Employment Survey was to demonstrate the penalty attached to part-time returns to the labour market after childbirth. Table 7.3 points to the enduring validity of this result, but at the same time suggests that maintaining a continuous attachment to employment can, in some occupational groups at least, overcome the part-time penalty. This seems to be particularly the case in the typically female occupational groups associate professional and clerical/secretarial. Thus, while by 1993 41 per cent of women who had been employed in secretarial/clerical occupations prior to motherhood experienced downward mobility if they subsequently followed an intermittent part-time career, none of their counterparts who had been continuously employed part time were downwardly mobile. By 1999 the proportions downwardly mobile from this occupational group were 8 per cent for continuously employed part-timers and 44 per cent for those employed intermittently. A similar gap between continuously and intermittently employed part-timers in associate professional occupations was found in 1993; but this gap had narrowed substantially by 1999, when one-quarter of continuously employed part-timers in associate professional jobs before motherhood had moved into lower level jobs compared with one third of intermittently employed part-timers.

PROMOTION CHANCES

Achieving promotion in work can depend on a range of factors including the type of job held, access to training, job seniority, working part-time or full-time, as well as innumerable other workplace aspects and individual characteristics. An analysis of British Household Panel Study (BHPS) data from 1991 to 1995 suggests that there are no significant gender differences in promotion opportunities (Booth et al. 1999). However, work by Gallie and his colleagues at about the same time posits a 'fault line' between women part-timers and full-time employees, whether male or female, in terms of skills required for the job performed, the use of skills in employment, training opportunities, and opportunities for self-improvement (Gallie et al. 1998). In light of this, it seemed worthwhile to ask if full-time (continuous) employment improves mothers' chances of promotion and to identify any other significant influences on mothers' opportunities for advancement. In the event, it proved difficult to identify many important influences, particularly in the early stages of mothers' return to work.

In both 1993 and 1999, 20 per cent of employed mothers in the combined data-set reported that promotion was not applicable to the type of job that they held. By 1993, 18 per cent had been promoted at some point in the previous five years; by 1999, the proportion promoted had increased to 25 per cent (on a larger base of mothers in work). For the majority, promotion entailed movement into a higher grade job. Only a small proportion entered management with promotion: 4 per cent in 1993 and 6 per cent in 1999.[9]

Table 7.4 indicates the factors influencing the odds of achieving promotion within six years of a first childbirth and during the subsequent six years. For the period 1988 to 1993, continuity of employment when combined with full-time employment was the strongest influence on mothers' chances of promotion, and increased the odds (in comparison with mothers employed part time intermittently) fivefold. Indeed, full-time employment status was a key influence on promotion, whether continuous, intermittent or combined with part-time employment. Formal training, particularly in a mother's own workplace, also increased the chances of

Table 7.4   Factors influencing job promotions

	Promoted between 1988 and 1993 (odds ratios)	Promoted between 1993 and 1999 (odds ratios)
Occupation (ref: manual/sales)		
Management	.575	7.23***
Professional	.650	3.09**
Associate Professional	.663	4.13***
Clerical/secretarial	.638	3.86***
Personal & Protective	.899	1.15
Promoted between 1988 and 1993		2.90***
Work history (ref: intermittent part-time)		
Continuous full-time	5.30***	1.82*
Continuous part-time	1.37	.86
Mixed FT & PT continuous	7.13***	1.06
Intermittent full-time	3.45**	1.34
Mixed FT & PT non-continuous	4.03***	2.77**
Mother's % contribution to household income	.996	1.01**
Mother's weekly pay	1.004**	.979
Had formal training course at workplace	4.14***	n.a.
Had formal training course away from workplace	2.07**	n.a.
Uses paid childcare (1993)	1.68	
Uses paid childcare (1999) (ref: does not use childcare)		
Uses unpaid childcare		1.51
Uses paid childcare		1.98**
Holds traditional views	.616	.572**
Constant	.025***	.046***
Nagelkerke R squared	.360	.282
N	756	732

Notes:
* p = < .05; ** p = < .01; *** p = < .001.
n.a. = question not asked.
Occupational level based on Standard Occupational Classification (SOC).

promotion; while the higher her earnings, the more likely she was to have been promoted.[10] While it seems likely that the significance of hourly pay is linked to the job held, occupation did not exert a significant influence on the likelihood of promotion between 1988 and 1993.

During the subsequent period, 1993 to 1999, occupational level made an enormous difference to mothers' promotion chances. Mothers employed in each of the intermediate white-collar and higher broad occupational groups were substantially more likely to have been promoted between 1993 and 1999 than mothers in lower-level sales or manual occupations – a result no doubt due in part at least to the bureaucratic structures of white-collar and higher-level occupations, and concomitant opportunities for promotion. Having previously achieved promotion doubled the odds of promotion, as did using paid childcare. Not surprisingly, holding traditional views exerted the opposite effect.

Full-time status remained a significant aid to promotion when linked to continuity of employment, and nearly doubled the chances of promotion among mothers employed continuously full-time. Surprisingly, women who combined full-time and part-time employment over the course of an intermittent work history also enjoyed significantly higher chances of promotion than the reference group, that is, mothers employed intermittently on a part-time basis. While the full explanation for this result remains uncertain, it is likely that differing occupational profiles accounts for at least some of the differences between these two groups. In particular, mothers combining full- and part-time employment within an intermittent work history were twice as likely to work in managerial and professional jobs than were intermittent part-timers.

PAY

As with opportunities for skill development and promotion, a key influence on pay levels for mothers is whether employment is undertaken full time or part time. The pay penalty for working part-time has actually increased over the years; while the gender gap between men's and women's full-time pay has decreased (Joshi 2005). Table 7.5 presents differences in average hourly net pay in 1999 by occupational level and provides an expected hierarchy. Professionals earn more than mothers in management ($p > 000$), while the pay difference between management occupations and associate professionals is not significant, although the latter earn significantly more per hour than clerical and secretarial workers. There is no statistically significant difference in the hourly pay of the broad groups encompassing manual, sales and personal and protective occupations, probably because of fundamental similarities in the labour markets represented by these two occupational groups.

Table 7.6 presents net hourly pay differences in 1999 by work history and demonstrates the benefit of full-time employment continuity. Mothers who

Table 7.5 Net hourly pay by occupational level (all women in work 1999)

	N	Mean	Std. dev.	Std. error	95% confidence interval for mean		Minimum	Maximum
					Lower	Upper		
Professional	88	9.8340	4.55389	.48271	8.8747	10.7933	1.50	29.46
Management	89	7.4563	3.69970	.39439	6.6724	8.2402	1.19	23.08
Assoc. Prof.	110	7.3660	2.54778	.24292	6.8845	7.8475	1.25	19.00
Clerical/Sec	197	5.5001	1.66551	.11866	5.2660	5.7341	1.69	15.00
P&P	131	4.3750	1.47072	.12850	4.1208	4.6292	1.43	9.23
Manual/Sales	137	4.2383	1.70566	.14572	3.9501	4.5265	1.15	19.45
Total	752	6.0890	3.15139	.11492	5.8634	6.3146	1.15	29.46

Note: Occupations classified according to Standard Occupational Classification (SOC).

Table 7.6   Net hourly pay by work history (all women in work 1999)

	N	Mean	Std. dev.	Std. error	95% confidence interval for mean		Minimum	Maximum
					Lower	Upper		
FT cont	134	7.6903	3.93283	.33975	7.0183	8.3623	2.42	29.46
PT cont	128	6.7876	3.42799	.30299	6.1880	7.3872	1.92	23.08
Mixed cont	31	6.2191	2.38466	.42830	5.3444	7.0938	3.33	15.00
Int FT	48	5.8342	2.29157	.33076	5.1688	6.4996	1.67	11.54
Int PT	349	5.3951	2.71442	.14530	5.1094	5.6809	1.15	20.51
Int Mix	42	5.2936	2.29569	.35423	4.5782	6.0090	1.19	11.10
All	732	6.1166	3.17110	.11721	5.8865	6.3467	1.15	29.46

Notes:
FT cont   Full-time continuous employment.
PT cont   Part-time continuous employment.
Mix cont   Continuous employment mixing full-time and part-time about equally.
Int FT   Intermittent full-time employment.
Int PT   Intermittent part-time employment.
Int mix   Intermittent employment mixing full-time and part-time about equally.

remained in continuous full-time employment come at the top of the earnings hierarchy and earn statistically significantly more per hour than continuous part-timers who are the next highest paid. This reflects, in part at least, the greater preponderance of the full-timers in management and professional occupations and of the part-timers in clerical and sales jobs. Hourly pay differences are not significant between continuously employed part-timers and mothers working continuously but with spells of both part- and full-time employment; again because of occupational differences, with mothers with mixed work histories less likely to hold managerial jobs in 1999 and more likely to be in manual, sales or personal and protective occupations. For mothers employed part-time, however, continuity makes a difference and mothers with this work history earned in 1999 almost £1.50 per hour more than mothers with intermittent part-timer work histories.[11]

CONCLUSIONS AND DISCUSSION

Maintaining a presence in the labour market has become the norm among British women after they become mothers. The majority mix paid employment with spells out of the labour market in order to take primary responsibility for family life while also taking opportunities to contribute financially to the household, retain their occupational skills or professional contacts, mix with other adults, and so on. Continuous employment during the period of family formation is undertaken by the minority only, especially if that employment is full-time. The research reported here indicates that just over one-quarter of mothers worked continuously during the 11 years following the birth of their first child in 1988: 14 per cent full-time, 13 per cent part-time and 3 per cent who mixed these two about equally. The remaining mothers followed more traditional mothers' careers, mixing spells of employment, including some full-time, with periods out of the labour market to care for their families.

The Advantages of Full-time Continuous Employment

Women who remain in *full-time* continuous employment after becoming mothers are significantly more likely to retain their pre-birth occupational level in all occupational groups. Even when the loss of pre-birth occupational level is at its highest – among mothers who held management positions before motherhood – working continuously full-time makes a difference. Mothers employed continuously on a *part-time* basis are also able to maintain their job level in comparison with those who work more intermittently, but with some exceptions – most notably in management and professional occupations. For mothers employed during pregnancy in associate professional occupations or, most notably, in clerical and secretarial occupations, the benefits of continuity are high for both full-timers and part-timers.

Increased promotion chances are associated with continuous employment but only for full-timers and, in any event, less strongly than avoidance of downward mobility. In the first five years after returning to work, any full-time status enhances mothers' chances of promotion, while over the longer term employment in higher level and intermediate occupations dominate. Higher levels of hourly pay are also associated with employment continuity, to the benefit of both continuous full-time and continuous part-time workers.

Continuous Full-time Employment and Family Life

Do mothers who work continuously on a full-time basis after becoming mothers sacrifice a happy family life to do so? The stereotypes might suggest that they do; the findings of this research are much less certain. Continuous full-time employment is associated with a higher incidence of relationship breakdown (spells of lone motherhood) than continuous part-time employment – but at levels no higher than that experienced by mothers following the traditional pattern of intermittent part-time employment.

Between 1993 and 1999, 18 per cent of full-timers employed continuously and 18 per cent of part-timers employed intermittently had at least one spell of lone motherhood; 14 per cent of each group were lone mothers at the time of the 1999 interview. The comparable proportions for continuously employed part timers are 11 per cent (a spell of lone motherhood) and 10 per cent (lone mother in 1999).[12] Mothers employed continuously full-time were also substantially less likely than continuous part-timers to be legally married (77 per cent v. 87 per cent) and to still be living with the father of their first child (84 per cent v. 97 per cent) but again fewer percentage points separate continuous full-timers and intermittent part-timers (80 per cent legally married, 88 per cent living with father of first child).

One significant difference exists between continuous full-timers and mothers working part-time, whether continuous or not, in relation to the number of additional children these mothers had during the decade after the birth of their first child. Mothers employed continuously full-time were the most likely to have only one child and the least likely to have three or more children. One-third of continuous full-timers had one child and only 14 per cent had three or more, compared with 20 per cent and 27 per cent of continuous part-timers and 13 per cent (one child) and 31 per cent (three or more) of intermittent part-timers.[13] Logistic regression analysis also showed that increasing numbers of children decreased the odds mothers will work continuously on a full-time basis (Table 7.2).

Childcare, of course, figures prominently in the calculations mothers make about holding paid employment. To work full-time, and to do so continuously throughout the period of family formation, childcare needs to be arranged in ways that break down as seldom as possible. *Not* having childcare problems in fact characterises the continuously employed full-timers included in this research: 71 per cent reported in both 1993 and 1999 that childcare problems had never affected their job opportunities. Further, the odds of working continuously full-time were three times greater for these mothers when compared with mothers who reported childcare problems in both years (Table 7.2). The way that mothers working continuously full-time have largely avoided such problems is by paying for childcare – 66 per cent used paid childcare in 1993, falling to 54 per cent in 1999.[14] And, of course, by having fewer children.

However, avoiding childcare problems is probably not the only reason why mothers employed continuously full-time have fewer children. Two-thirds of such mothers hold higher-level managerial, professional or associate professional jobs. Often such jobs are synonymous with long working hours (Harkness 2003) and other pressures on family life. To combine this type of employment with motherhood is likely to mean that a trade-off between working hours and numbers of children will be made: longer hours and fewer children; fewer hours and more children. It is also the case that nearly half (48 per cent) of mothers continuously employed full-time reported that their husbands/partners were only happy for them to work if their employment fitted in with family life. None of this, of course, provides a definitive answer to the question posed above about family life and working full-time continuously, although it seems highly likely that the labour market benefits gained from maintaining continuity of employment on a full-time basis after motherhood can carry a high price tag.

NOTES

1. Joshi also refers to other factors that helped to improve the relative position of women employed full-time including the weakening of men's labour market position during the 1980s as trade union power declined and unemployment rose; and the tendency towards wage equality as a result of labour market deregulation (Joshi 2005: 156).
2. For ease of presentation, the year of birth is subsequently referred to as 1988 and the pregnancy or pre-birth period as 1987.
3. Lone mothers in the combined dataset, of whom there were 147 in 1999 (15 per cent), were more likely to be economically active than is the case nationally. Thirty-five per cent of lone mothers in the combined dataset were in full-time employment in 1999, compared with 19 per cent of all lone mothers with children aged between 5 and 10; while about equal proportions were in part-time employment (29 per cent and 30 per cent). Overall, only just over one-third of lone mothers in the combined dataset were inactive, compared with half of all lone mothers with children aged between 5 and 10 years.
4. In both surveys, information about duration in the labour market was obtained by asking respondents to fill in the number of boxes corresponding to their work history on a strip that ranged from 0 to 100 per cent. An example of what was wanted was provided.
5. Respondents were asked: 'Have difficulties with childcare arrangements ever affected your job opportunities?' Those responding positively were asked to describe these difficulties.
6. The result presented in Table 7.2 is based on mothers' income as a percentage of mothers' and partners' combined income in 1999. Logistic regression analysis examining employment continuity for the period 1988 to 1993 also identified women's contribution to income as statistically significant, based on mothers' income as a percentage of mothers' and partners' combined income in 1993.
7. Although it would have been ideal to ask these attitudinal questions in 1988, the sponsors funding the research were not interested in the issue.
8. Smeaton compared job during pregnancy with first job after, regardless of how much time had lapsed before the mother's return to the labour market, and included both part-time and full-time returns. The data from the mothers' surveys (CDS) includes only returns within eight to nine months after a first birth. BCS = Birth Cohort Study; NCDS = National Child Development Study.

	CDS 1988–99 (%)	BCS 1970 (%)	NCDS 1958 (%)
Management	60–71	41	40
Professional	25–28	13	18
Associate Prof.	19	14	23
Clerical/secretarial	10–30	22	44
Personal and protective	14–26	13	22

9. Respondents were asked: 'Have you had any job promotions at any time since returning to work after the birth of your 5 year old child (1993) in the past six years (1999)? If yes, they were asked to indicate if the promotion was into a management position/job, a supervisory position/job, a higher grade job, a job with more responsibility, or some other promotion (asked to give details). Follow-up questions explored if the respondent had wanted promotion, to what level or why not, what they thought might stop them from achieving promotion and if they were interested in further promotions.

10. Of course, mothers who were promoted would be likely to earn more than mothers who had not achieved promotion, at least within the same broad occupational grouping.

11. The level of hourly pay averaged across the whole sample of mothers appears low in comparison with women's average hourly pay for Britain in 1999 (£6.12 v. £8.22). This is due in part to the fact that the combined dataset asked for information about *net* pay, but also in part to the relatively younger ages of the mothers included in the data-set and the predominance of part-time employment, given their stage in the family formation cycle.

12. Continuous full-timers and intermittent part-timers were also more likely to be lone mothers eight to nine months after their first birth (9 per cent of the former; 8 per cent of the latter) than continuous part-timers (4 per cent).

13. Cf. Houston and Marks (2000) who reported that 40 per cent of mothers intending to have more children planned to reduce their working hours or to stop working due to anticipated practical problems and childcare costs. The mothers interviewed by Houston and Marks found it difficult to combine work with the care of one child and could not imagine having to do so with more than one child.

14. The comparable proportions using paid childcare among continuously employed part-timers are 47 per cent in 1993 and 36 per cent in 1999. For intermittently employed part-timers the figures are 15 per cent in 1993 and 20 per cent in 1999.

REFERENCES

Babb, P. H. Butcher, J. Church and L. Zealey (eds) (2006), *Social Trends*, No. 36, Office of National Statistics, Basingstoke: Palgrave Macmillan.

Booth, A., M. Francesconi and J. Frank (1999), *Glass Ceilings and Sticky Floors*, Institute for Labour Research Discussion Paper, Colchester: University of Essex.

Burchell, B., A. Dale and H. Joshi (1997), 'Part-time work among British Women', in H.-P. Blossfeld and C. Hakim (eds), *Between Equalization and Marginalization: Women Working Part-time in Europe and the United States of America*, Oxford: Oxford University Press, pp. 210–45.

Callender, C., N. Millward, S. Lissenburgh and J. Forth (1997), *Maternity Rights and Benefits in Britain 1996*, London: The Stationery Office.

Crompton, R., M. Brockmann and C. Lyonette (2005), 'Attitudes, women's employment and the domestic division of labour: a cross-national analysis in two waves', *Work, Employment and Society*, **19**(2), 213–33.

Daniel, W.W. (1980), Maternity Rights: The Experience of Women, PSI Report No. 588.

Dex, S. (1987), *Women's Occupational Mobility: A Lifetime Perspective*, London: Macmillan Press.

Equal Opportunities Commission (EOC) (2005), *Facts about Men and Women in Britain*, Manchester: EOC.

Gallie, D., M. White, Y. Cheng and M. Tomlinson (1998), *Restructuring the Employment Relationship*, Oxford: Clarendon Press.

Hakim, C. (2000), *Work-Lifestyle Choices in the 21st Century: Preference Theory*, Oxford: Oxford University Press.

Harkness, S. (2003), 'The household division of labour: changes in families' allocation of paid and unpaid work, 1992–2002', in R. Dickens, P. Gregg and J. Wadsworth (eds), *The Labour Market Under New Labour: The State of Working Britain* Oxford: Oxford University Press, pp. 150–69.

Houston, D. and G. Marks (2000), 'Employment choices for mothers of pre-school children: a psychological perspective', Economic and Social Research Council (ESRC) End of Award Report, grant number L212252019.

Hudson, M., S. Lissenburgh and M. Sahin-Dikmen (2004), Maternity and Paternity Rights in Britain 2002: Survey of Parents, Department of Work and Pensions In-house Report No. 131.

Joshi, H. (2005), 'Gender and pay: some more equal than others', in A. Heath, J. Ermisch and D. Gallie (eds), *Understanding Social Change*, Oxford: Oxford University Press, pp. 153–85.

Martin, J. and C. Roberts (1984), *Women and Employment: A Lifetime Perspective*, London: HMSO.

Matheson, J. and C. Summerfield (2000), *Social Trends 30*, London: The Stationery Office.

McRae, S. (1991), *Maternity Rights in Britain: The Experience of Women and Employers*, London: Policy Studies Institute.

McRae, S. (2003a), 'Constraints and choices in mothers' employment careers: a consideration of Hakim's preference Theory', *British Journal of Sociology*, **54**(3), 317–38.

McRae, S. (2003b), 'Choice and constraints in mothers' employment careers: McRae replies to Hakim', *British Journal of Sociology*, **54**(4), 585–92.

Olsen, W. and S. Walby (2004), *Modelling Gender Pay Gaps*, Manchester Equal: Opportunities Commission.

Smeaton, D. (2005), 'Developments in employment outcomes and working time regimes post-childbirth', Economic and Social Research Council (ESRC) End of Award Report', grant number RES-000-22-0488.

Summerfield, C. and P. Babb (eds) (2004), *Social Trends 34*, London: TSO.

Werbel, J. (1998), 'Intent and choice regarding maternal employment following childbirth', *Journal of Vocational Behavior*, 53, 372–85.

Women and Work Commission (2006), *Shaping a fairer future*, London: Department of Trade and Industry.

APPENDIX

The combined data-set (CDS) is derived from responses to the following three surveys:

1988 Maternity Rights Survey   The 1988 survey was a nationally (GB) representative survey of mothers of new babies. A random sample of 7704 women who had had babies during a period of six weeks in December 1987 and January 1988 was generated by the Department of Social Security (DSS) from their child benefit records. Following checks on the sample by DSS, 7680 questionnaires were mailed to mothers in September 1988, some 9 to 10 months after the birth. Of these, 123 were unable to be delivered. Of the remainder, 4991 usable questionnaires were returned (66 per cent).

1993 Survey   The 1993 survey had for its base women from the 1988 Maternity Rights Survey who were employed during that pregnancy (whether or not they had returned to work after the birth) and women who were not in the labour market during that pregnancy but who were looking for work after the birth. Access to these women was maintained by the DSS. The potential number available in these categories from the 1988 survey was 2910. Of these, 107 were removed by the DSS for a variety of reasons, leaving 2803 possible respondents. With 2011 actual respondents, the 1993 survey achieved a 72 per cent response rate.

1999 Survey   The base for the 1999 survey began, as in 1993, with 2910 potential respondents. Adjustments by the DSS resulted in 2604 questionnaires being posted, of which a further 10 were inappropriate (death of child or mother) or unable to be delivered. By the end of fieldwork, 1904 responses had been received (73 per cent). Of these, 1516 proved to be respondents to both 1993 and 1999 surveys and thus comprise the 'combined data-set'.

8. Class differences in mothers' work schedules and assessments of their 'work–life balance' in dual-earner couples in Britain

Colette Fagan, Linda McDowell, Diane Perrons, Kathryn Ray and Kevin Ward[1]

INTRODUCTION

Since the Women and Employment Survey was conducted in 1980 (Martin and Roberts 1984), mothers' labour force participation has continued to rise. In 2005, 56 per cent of mothers with a child aged under 5 years were in employment and more than 70 per cent once the youngest child is school age (National Statistics 2006). However, only a minority of mothers resume full-time employment directly after maternity leave (McRae, this volume) and part-time work continues to play a pivotal role in the work histories of mothers. In this chapter we focus on the working-time patterns of mothers' in dual-earner couples whose children are pre-school or in primary school. Drawing on rich qualitative interviews we analyse mothers' work schedules and their reflections on their 'work–life balance', exploring the lived experience of occupational class differences among mothers in full-time and part-time employment.

WORKING-TIME SCHEDULES AND 'WORK–LIFE BALANCE' IN BRITAIN

While it is common to distinguish between 'part-timers' and 'full-timers' within these categories there is wide variation in work schedules. This diversity is structured by occupational class and the type of workplace. Full-timers are more likely to work long hours if they are men, but for both sexes this is most prevalent for managers and professionals, particularly those at senior levels. Overall, long hours are most common in the private sector and in non-unionised workplaces (Cully et al. 1999: table 7.6), and the incidence is higher in Britain than most other European countries (Fagan 2004).

Manual employees who work long hours are the most likely to say they do so for financial reasons, while managers and professionals usually emphasise their job commitment (although financial rewards may come later via promotion or bonuses). Those with the highest degree of autonomy over how they organise their work are the most likely to attribute long working hours to their job commitment, even after taking into account their occupational level (Cully et al. 1999). This indicates the double-edged nature of autonomy: flexibility and discretion can go hand-in-hand with a sense of obligation to work long hours when required to cover variable or persistently heavy workloads. Working long hours may also become a key element in competition for promotion in flatter and more individualised organisational structures (Crompton and Brockmann 2006).

Part-time employment is dominated by women and exists in 83 per cent of British workplaces (Kersley et al. 2006). It is disproportionately concentrated in low-paid service and manual jobs, often with very short hours (Women and Work Commission 2006). However, some part-timers hold higher-level and better-paid jobs: one-fifth of female part-timers are in professional and associated positions, although part-time working remains rare for women who enter management or male-dominated professions.

A growing proportion of establishments offer flexible working options (such as flexitime, working from home, job shares) in Britain, but the availability and take-up varies (Bell and Bryson 2005; Cully et al. 1999; Dex 2003; Kersley et al. 2006). Broadly speaking, managers and professionals have the most scope to vary when they work – because their hours are not directly monitored or because they have formal flexitime arrangements – and they are also more likely to be able to do some of their work from home. Flexitime is common for clerical workers, particularly in the public sector and the financial sector. Conversely, routine and manual workers are more likely to have their hours fixed by their employers, and shiftwork and part-time work feature more often in their schedules (see also Warren 2003). There are no occupational differences in the incidence of compressed weeks, jobshares or term-time working (Kersley et al. 2006: table 6.24). Flexible working options are more common generally in the public sector, in large workplaces, where a union is recognised or where more than half of the workforce is female.

A 'satisfactory work–life balance' is a common aspiration for employees according to the British Social Attitudes Survey, although it is not ranked as the most important priority as often as having job security or interesting work (Bell and Bryson 2005). The survey also shows that substantial proportions of employees experience problems balancing work and home life, and that, in themselves, flexible working options do not substantially alleviate the pressures (Bell and Bryson 2005: 50). A good work–life balance depends on a number of workplace and domestic factors, but long working hours have been shown to exert a significant and dominant negative effect and working-time autonomy offers only limited compensation (Fagan and Burchell 2002; OECD 2004). Mothers' perceptions of whether their work and family lives are 'in balance' will also depend on what work patterns they consider to be compatible with being a 'good mother', which is shaped by the interplay of their experiences, resources and the web of social relationships they are situated in (McDowell et al. 2005b). By way of example, women in management and professional positions are the most likely to report that their jobs are interesting and are more than just a means to earn a living and are more likely to favour maternal employment when children are young than are women in routine and manual jobs (Crompton 2006).

In the rest of this chapter we explore these occupational differences in mothers' work schedules and sense of work–life balance in more detail through our analysis of in-depth qualitative interviews. Next, therefore, we provide some background to our study (further details of the sample and methodology can be found in McDowell et al. 2005a; 2005b).

THE STUDY

Our research draws on interview data collected in 2002 and 2003 as part of an ESRC-funded study of two-parent households in urban settings where at least one parent was employed.[2] We focus on the 74 interviews obtained with mothers from dual-earner households in which the man is employed full-time and the children are either pre-school or in primary school.[3] In 36 of these households the mother was employed part-time.

The interview focus was designed in the tradition of previous studies of 'household work strategies' (Pahl 1984; Wallace 2002): detailed information was collected on the employment and working-time schedules of all household members, the gender division of responsibilities for domestic tasks and childcare, and informal exchanges of help with family and friends in other households. We also collected information about patterns of daily life, and explored how mothers felt about their current working-time arrangements, their 'work–life balance' and their work plans for the future.

The mothers were employed at a range of occupational levels which we grouped into managers and professionals; intermediate-level administrators and clerical workers; and routine service and manual positions. The majority of the mothers in managerial/professional positions lived with men that were also employed at this broad occupational level. Where the mother was employed at lower occupational levels the man was much more likely to be in manual work, either skilled (for example, craft-related jobs such as construction trades or engineering) or lower-paid jobs (for example, warehouse distribution, assembly production, or transport). Both the full-time and part-time employed mothers used various combinations of informal and formal childcare arrangements. The main difference was that full-timers spent more on childcare. The mothers in high-income households were also more likely to pay for a cleaner or domestic services, reflecting the general picture whereby the amount of time women spend on domestic tasks and caring is proportionately less for employed mothers in high income couples compared with manual households (Warren 2003).

WORKING-TIME SCHEDULES OF MOTHERS IN DUAL-EARNER HOUSEHOLDS

The mothers' descriptions of their working days revealed qualitative insights into the detail of their working-time arrangements and the types of flexibility they have access to. Their accounts illustrate pronounced differences based on occupational position, particularly between mothers employed at managerial and professional levels and those in manual jobs. This can be seen in the number of hours they worked; the type of work schedule and flexibility they had; and adjustments from full-time to part-time hours.

The Number of Hours Worked by Mothers

The majority of full-time employed mothers worked 35–38 hours a week, whether employed in manual, intermediate or professional and managerial positions. If professionals or managers, they were mostly employed in the public sector in areas such as education, social services and middle-management.

The full-timers who worked in excess of 40 or even 50 hours per week fell in two class locations. Long hours were common for some managers and professionals, typically senior and well-paid private sector positions in functions such as finance or marketing, though there were also examples from senior public sector positions. These mothers explained that long hours were a requirement of their job and that if they negotiated shorter hours they would be heavily penalised. Typical examples of penalties were demotion from team leader, loss of bonuses or, as one participant plainly put it, 'career suicide'. In workplaces where long full-time hours are the norm, someone who works shorter full-time hours may be judged as 'part-time'. For example, Caitlyn had secured a 40-hour contract as a television director but explained that she was widely considered to be 'part-time' by the people she worked with since the usual full-time arrangement was at least 45 hours and her career had reached an insecure plateau as a consequence.

There were also mothers working long full-time hours in low-paid manual jobs. Their husbands' earnings were also modest, making most of these households eligible for the Working Families Tax Credit. Examples include Shamara, who worked 40-plus hours a week running a corner shop with her husband, and Nickie who worked 44 hours a week as a childminder plus 4 hours on a Saturday as a health assistant, while her husband was a low-paid shift worker.

Among part-timers, longer hours were worked in managerial or professional positions than at lower occupational levels. Typically professionals and managers, in both the public and private sector, worked around 25 hours or more per week and many worked 30–34 hours. Arrangements of 20 hours or less per week were common for other occupations, particularly manual jobs, including some mothers in poorly paid manual jobs who were juggling two short part-time jobs or who worked extra hours when their employer made them available. What counts as 'part-time' work, therefore, is situation specific and significant conceptual blurring occurs when hours begin to creep beyond 30 hours a week.

Work Schedules and Day-to-day Flexibility

About half of the mothers employed full-time and one in three of those employed part-time were able to vary when they worked via flexitime or informal systems (31 of the 74 mothers interviewed). Nearly one in three of the mothers did some of their work from home.

The mothers who worked long full-time hours in managerial or professional positions generally had some scope to manage their time. They tried to start later or finish earlier than the norm at their workplace to provide some basic fit with their children's morning and evening routines. They caught up by working through lunch and taking work home in the evening or at weekends. For example, Rosemary, a financial director, works Monday–Friday starting between 8.30 a.m. and 9.30 a.m., depending on whether she was taking her children to school, and then working through until 7 p.m. She brings work home at least one night a week, doing another five hours after the children have gone to bed, in addition to several hours over the weekend. This pattern of adjusting work schedules around children's routines and maintaining long hours by working in the evening or at weekends was common in a number of occupations where at least part of the job could be done remotely. Formal permission was rarely needed to make these adjustments, in part because of the self-directed organisation of their work, but also because they were usually only making modest changes of an hour or so to when they arrived or left their workplace. However, all were acutely aware that they could not be seen to leave work 'too early' regardless of how many hours they did at home and that their planned schedules could be disrupted by workplace demands such as meetings scheduled late in the day or clients calling. In other words, they had to be visibly present and respond flexibly to the demands of their job in order to demonstrate their adherence to the 'long hours' organisational culture in which they were embedded.

Many of the mothers who worked shorter full-time hours in managerial or professional jobs also had some autonomy to vary their hours, as did most of those employed in administrative and clerical positions. Flexitime systems were common, particularly for the latter occupational group, but also for some public sector professionals and middle managers in certain functions such as housing or social services. Typically they used flexitime so they could drop or fetch their children from school or childcare; some compressed their hours so that they worked a shorter day once a week or fortnight. Among those without flexitime the mothers in professional/managerial jobs had more informal flexibility than the administrators and clerical employees whose modest discretion usually meant they could vary their start or finish times by about 30 minutes provided they 'made up the time'.

Some managers and professionals working shorter full-time hours did part of their work from home; a few did a regular half or full day a week from home and others did so occasionally. But it was unusual for them to take a large amount of work home to do in the evening or at weekends, with the exception of teachers during term time. Working from home was rare for the mothers we interviewed in the intermediate-level administrative or clerical positions and most emphasised that they never worked evenings or weekends either at home or the office.

However, not all of the managers and professionals had personal flexibility. This applied for 'front-line' service delivery roles in which the very nature of their job required their physical presence during specified periods for large parts of their working day. School teachers are 'locked in' to the school day; although there is flexibility in when and where they do their class preparation and marking. Many health professionals also have fixed schedules of attendance, such as nurses, where the flexibility available depends on the scope to switch shifts and is limited on a day-to-day basis.

Mothers working full-time in manual jobs had much less discretion in their working day than those at higher occupational levels. Typically their working hours were fixed by their employer. A few had some modest leeway provided they made the time up later, such as Janette, a full-time retail stock controller, who could vary her start or finish time by up to 15 minutes. The limited scope these mothers had to control their start and finish times came from finding jobs which offered specific times which were convenient to them, or shifts which could be swapped with co-workers.

Occupational differences were also evident in the schedules of part-timers. While many part-time jobs are organised to provide some fit with school hours, some mothers were employed part-time in the evening, at night or weekends when the father or another relative can provide child-care. This was revealed in the Women and Employment Survey (Martin and Roberts 1984) and has persisted for more recent cohorts of mothers (Fagan 2001). The mothers in this study who were employed part-time in manage-rial, professional or administrative positions usually worked three or four 'full days' during the week, or three to five shorter days organised in rela-tion to school hours. Regular evening or weekend work is rare for part-timers at these occupational levels; except for some health professionals working shifts. Vanessa was a nurse who exemplifies this process; she switched to a part-time night shift when she had children so that she could arrange childcare between herself, her husband and her father. In contrast, it was quite common for mothers in manual jobs to have their jobs organ-ised into shorter work periods or 'scattered hours' (Breedveld 1998) cover-ing lunchtimes, evenings or weekends, such as Katherine who was a school dinner lady and after-school care worker, and Sharon who worked night and early morning shifts of four-hour blocks as a transport customer service attendant.

If hours are varied by the employer at short notice, this may conflict with domestic schedules. In our sample, this practice was less common than arrangements which gave mothers some formal or informal personal flexibility, but it still figured in the lives of one in six of the mothers, both full-time and part-time, and was found at all occupational levels. Term time is a rarer but more predictable form of variation, mainly found in educa-tion and reflecting the operating hours in this sector (Kersley et al. 2006). The mothers in this study whose hours varied on a term-time basis worked in education at a range of occupational levels: teachers and teaching assis-tants, administrators and cooks.

Transitions from Full-time to Part-time Hours

Mirroring the work history patterns exposed in survey analysis (Dex, this volume) the mothers in managerial and professional positions had higher qualification levels and had mostly pursued a continuous employment history, resuming their job immediately after maternity leave. Some of those currently employed full-time in managerial/professional positions had previously worked reduced hours for a short period following maternity leave, and this was more common for those employed in the public sector than in private firms. Moreover, if they worked in the public sector, they tended to have taken longer maternity leave, had better maternity leave benefits and reported fewer difficulties in taking maternity leave or in reducing their hours if they had made such a request. Conversely, the mothers employed full-time in professional/managerial positions in the private sector reported more workplace difficulties in their efforts to adjust their working hours. A few had forgone some of their maternity leave because they felt under pressure to return quickly; some had continued working full-time hours because their request for part-time hours had been refused; others had only been able to secure reduced hours by moving to another employer or through demotion.

Most of the mothers who were currently employed part-time in managerial/professional positions had previously worked full-time hours in their current or a similar job, and had negotiated reduced hours on their return from maternity leave. These negotiations had mostly preceded the introduction in 2003 of the statutory right for parents with young children to request reduced or flexible hours. But, in any case, the ability to use formal options for reduced working hours is heavily contingent on the attitudes of line managers and colleagues (Lewis 1997). As was the case with full-timers, those working in the public sector appeared to have been more able to secure 'family-friendly' arrangements than those in the private sector; they rarely reported problems with taking maternity leave or negotiating adjustments to their working hours. However, reduced hours incurred some career costs. By way of example, one of our participants, a teacher, had been able to move between full-time and 80 per cent hours several times across the period of raising her three children. While emphasising how supportive the head teacher had been when she made these requests, each time she reduced her hours she was demoted from her specialist duties as a team leader and lost the additional premium and professional standing until she resumed full-time work.

In contrast, more of the lower-qualified mothers, and particularly those who were employed part-time at the time of the interview, had had periods out of employment. Many of the mothers who had exited employment explained they had wanted to do this to be at home when their children were young because they saw this as an important part of 'good mothering' (Duncan 2006). This was also the reason mothers in professional or managerial positions gave for switching from full-time to part-time arrangements. However, labour market constraints also featured to a much greater degree in the accounts of mothers in manual jobs. Some had been forced to leave their job because they did not qualify for maternity leave or because their line manager had 'made it difficult' for them to stay, which offers insight into the bigger picture of pregnancy discrimination in Britain (Adams et al. 2005). Others were unable to continue in employment because their employer would not let them adjust their hours, or they did not have access to suitable childcare (either affordable formal services or informal arrangements with family or friends), and they had been unsuccessful in their search for an alternative job with shorter hours or closer to home. For some it was the poor economic situation in their workplace that was the main reason their employment had been interrupted. These types of problems were also faced by some of the highly qualified mothers; but the difference was that the lower-qualified mothers were more likely to have dropped out of employment as a result and subsequently faced a more precarious route to obtaining part-time work.

MOTHERS' PERCEPTIONS OF THE QUALITY OF THEIR 'WORK–LIFE BALANCE'

Finally, we also asked our participants how they felt about the balance between their employment and home life, and whether there were any changes they would like to make in either sphere to improve their quality of life. Responses typically focused on time pressures and the types of working-time adjustments they would like to make, but answers also revealed differences that were connected to class position and hours of work.

Many of the mothers explained that they felt rushed or short of time in the effort to co-ordinate the demands of their jobs and the changing needs of their children: 'it's a constant effort to keep it in balance' (Dawn, public sector middle management). This problem was compounded when daily routines were disrupted by job pressures or changes in their children's lives as they switched out-of-school activities, became ill, went through difficult periods at school, and so forth. This was particularly evident in the accounts given by mothers working full-time hours, although part-timers also talked about the pressures involved in co-ordinating their work day with childcare and other tensions. Some full-time employed mothers did not want to reduce their hours, but still felt pressures and stress in managing the different parts of their lives. As Rosemary, a mother working long hours in a well-paid managerial/professional job, said: '[But] there just aren't enough hours in the week . . . I feel like I short-change everything, I short-change my job, I short-change my children, but it's sort of the best optimum compromise.' Carole has shorter full-time hours and is lower paid than Rosemary and her assessment of the balance between her work and family is 'quite good' and manageable. Nevertheless, she feels things are still hectic with no time left for herself: 'I've sort of got my family life and my work life sorted out but I just need to sort out my social life.'

Most of the full-time employed mothers in managerial or professional positions wanted to reduce their hours or gain more flexibility in how they organised their hours. A four-day week was often mentioned as the ideal. They talked about how their job was interesting and satisfying. Typically they wanted to stay in 'a demanding job but for a smaller amount of time' (Nasrin, works 44 hours). Many of those who would like to reduce to part-time arrangements had, however, decided not to act to secure this change. The main rationale they gave for sticking with their current full-time arrangement were their assessments that shorter hours were not feasible in their job or workplace. Financial pressures – usually large mortgages or school fees – were mentioned less often; and when raised it came as a secondary or additional consideration to their primary concern about the feasibility of performing their job. Some had resigned because they had not been able to negotiate reduced hours or the arrangement that was agreed was not sustainable. Ruth, an advertising executive, had been able to negotiate her hours down to a four-day week but found the compromise unworkable and so had just resigned and was planning a break of one year before looking for another job:

> I think that actually four days is too much, I mean I work in an industry where we are expected to work long hours, and we're in a recession at the moment and it's very tough, and it's just not helping the business or me to sort of be in a situation where I can't give them that extra time . . .

The mothers employed full-time in intermediate or manual positions worked shorter hours than some of the mothers in managerial or professional posts, but they too talked about the daily time pressures, and many said that they would like to reduce their hours or get more flexibility. However, there were some notable class differences in their accounts as to why they continued in full-time hours. They were more likely to emphasise the financial pressures they were under, such as housing costs, or being able to afford a holiday. While many said that they liked their job or talked in more general terms about how they liked working or 'couldn't imagine being at home all day' (Janette, working 35 hours), there was a sub-group that were adamant that they would give up work if they could afford to, or that they had planned to but had needed to go back for financial reasons. For example, Tabatha, a teaching assistant, explains that she likes her job but that if her husband earned enough 'I wouldn't work. I would love to stay at home and be there full-time.' Mothers with a preference for this type of homemaking role can be found at all educational levels and occupational positions (Duncan 2006; McDowell et al. 2005b). What this example illustrates is that it may be more difficult for mothers to achieve in low-income households.

The mothers who said that their work–life balance was 'OK', 'about right', 'as good as it can be' or 'reasonably optimal' were mainly working part-time hours or short full-time hours without long commute times. They were employed across a range of managerial, professional and lower occupational levels. For example, Melissa, a nursery worker, who has moved jobs and reduced her hours, said:

> we weren't finishing 'til 5.30 . . . then by the time you got home and you're doing bits . . . you were tired and it was late. But now I finish at three and I've got time to really have a chill and relax, spend time helping them with their homework, cooking, and I don't feel that everything's a rush.

However, part-time employment was not a simple panacea for reconciling the demands of jobs and family life. Mothers in professional/managerial positions who switched to part-time working generally thought that their career was 'on hold' and that promotion prospects and other working conditions had deteriorated as the price for achieving some degree of balance in their lives. Holly, for example, talked about how her three-day week as a market researcher for an advertising company works 'quite well [but] . . . if I wanted to change jobs I don't know whether I could get part-time again, so I'm lucky at the moment but I don't know how long it will last'. Others found that their workload did not reduce proportionately or they missed out on the social side of work, such as networking or training, because they worked so intensively during the time they were actually at work. It was for the first of these reasons that Laura, a youth worker, has recently increased her hours to 30 because 'I'm doing this work anyway so I might as well get paid for it'.

Different issues emerged for the mothers employed part-time in lower intermediate or manual jobs. Here the problems were less to do with career advancement and more about securing enough hours or having to work unsocial schedules. Sarah has a public sector jobshare as a service attendant at a public leisure centre and would like to work another day a week or even full-time but cannot do so because she relies on her mother (who also works part-time) for childcare and could not afford to pay for full-time childcare. Others have resumed employment after a break when their children were young and face limited job options, particularly if they want something close to home to fit with childcare or because they cannot afford travel costs (Ward et al. 2007). Some said the main change they wanted was for their husband to be able to reduce their night shifts or have weekends off; others wanted to change their own work schedules and switch to daytime hours – and hopefully a 'better job' – rather than alter the number of hours they worked. A pertinent example of the difficulties of obtaining so called 'balance' when parents' shifts are out of kilter is Sharon who has worked early morning shifts as a passenger service clerk in transport for over five years. Starting work between 3 a.m. and 5 a.m. for four hours a day six days on/two days off, her husband gets their four children up and takes three of them to school. Then when Sharon comes home she takes the youngest to morning day care while her husband goes off to work. She is asleep on the sofa shortly after he gets in from work.

CONCLUSIONS

The message of this chapter is clear: mothers' work schedules, the options they face and their actions to improve their work–life balance are shaped by occupational class as well as by whether they work full-time or part-time. Mothers in some managerial and professional positions, particularly the better paid and more senior posts, were working very long full-time hours. Mothers at this occupational level generally had some personal autonomy to vary when and where they worked, and often felt their jobs were interesting and satisfying, but they still felt the stresses of being squeezed for time. Some had been unable to negotiate reduced hours at their workplace, or had rejected it as unfeasible and had carried on as they were. Those who had reduced their hours typically paid the price of putting their career on hold or coping with a workload which had not been reduced proportionately.

Full-timers in intermediate administrative or clerical positions worked moderate hours and had some personal flexibility, particularly those with access to a flexitime system, whereas those in manual full-time jobs had very little flexibility. Financial constraints rather than other job rewards were a more dominant part of their explanations for continuing to work full-time and some of them expressed a strong preference to leave employment altogether if their partner were able to earn enough.

While part-timers in managerial or professional positions were faced with the pressures of trying to keep a foothold in a career which they generally enjoyed, the dilemmas faced by part-timers in manual jobs were quite different. Some wanted longer hours; others wanted to find a way for themselves or their partners to escape from working evenings, nights or weekends that had resulted from a combination of childcare constraints, the need for overtime pay and limited employment options.

Improvements over recent years in childcare provision, subsidies for low-income families and the growing proportion of firms which offer flexible options have made work–family co-ordination somewhat easier in Britain.

Other developments, such as growing congestion and a poorly designed, deteriorating public transport system have negative implications for work–life balance given the spatial dispersal of workplaces, housing, child-care and so forth which households contend with (Perrons et al. 2007). But class differences persist in the logistical difficulties which women face and the working-time arrangements which they carve out. For example, while a sizeable proportion of eligible mothers and some fathers have exercised their 'right to request' reduced or flexible hours under the new legislation, few inroads have been made where long full-time hours are the norm (Fagan et al. 2006).

NOTES

1. We would like to thank and acknowledge the ESRC for funding this project ('Living and Labouring in London and Manchester' ESRC project no. R000239470) and the parents we interviewed for giving us their time, energy, thoughtful contributions and hospitality.
2. 'Living and Labouring in London and Manchester', ESRC project no. R000239470.
3. For the focus of this chapter we do not analyse four 'unusual' households where both adults in the couples are employed part-time. No same-sex couples were recruited in this study.

REFERENCES

Adams, L., F. McAndrew and M. Winterbotham (2005), *Pregnancy Discrimination at Work: A Survey of Women*, Working Paper Series no. 24, Manchester: Equal Opportunities Commission.

Bell, A. and C. Bryson (2005), 'Work-life balance – still a "women's issue"?', in A. Park, J. Curtice, K. Thomson, C. Bromley, M. Phillips and M. Johnson (eds), *British Social Atittudes: The 22nd Report – Two Terms of New Labour: The Public's Reaction*, London: Sage, pp. 33–63.

Breedveld, K. (1998), 'The double myth of flexibilization: trends in scattered work hours, and differences in time sovereignty', *Time & Society*, 7(1), 129–43.

Crompton, R. (2006), *Employment and the Family: The Reconfiguration of Work and Family Life in Contemporary Societies*, Cambridge: Cambridge University Press.

Crompton, R. and M. Brockmann (2006), 'Class, gender and work-life articulation', in D. Perrons, C. Fagan, L. McDowell, K. Ray and K. Ward (eds), *Gender Divisions and Working Time in the New Economy – Changing Patterns of Work, Care and Public Policy in Europe and North America*, Aldershot: Edward Elgar, pp. 103–22.

Cully, M., S. Woodland, A. O'Reilly and G. Dix (1999), *Britain at Work – as Depicted by the 1998 Workplace Employee Relations Survey*, London: Routledge.

Dex, S. (2003), *Families and Work in the Twenty-first Century*, York: Joseph Rowntree Foundation/Policy Press.

Duncan, S. (2006), 'Mothers' work–life balance: individualized preferences or cultural construction?', in D. Perrons, C. Fagan, L. McDowell, K. Ray and K. Ward (eds), *Gender Divisions and Working Time in the New Economy – changing patterns of Work, Care and Public Policy in Europe and North America*, London: Edward Elgar, pp. 127–47.

Fagan, C. (2001), 'The temporal re-organisation of employment and household rhythm of work schedules: the implications for gender and class relations', *The American Behavioural Scientist*, **44**(7), 1199–212.

Fagan, C. (2004), 'Gender and working-time in industrialized countries', in J. Messenger (ed.), *Finding the Balance: Working-Time and Workers' Needs and Preferences in Industrialized countries*, London: Routledge, pp. 108–46.

Fagan, C. and B. Burchell, for the European Foundation (2002), *Gender, Jobs and Working Conditions in the European Union*, European Foundation for the Improvement of Living and Working Conditions, Luxembourg: Official Publications of the European Communities, www.eurofound.europa.eu/publications/htmlfiles/ef0249.htm (accessed 25 January 2008).

Fagan, C., A. Hegewisch and J. Pillinger (2006), *Out of Time – Why Britain Needs a New Approach to Working-time Flexibility*, research report for the Trades Union Congress, www.tuc.org.uk/publications/srchResults.cfm (accessed 25 January 2008).

Kersley, B., C. Aplin, J. Forth, A. Bryson, H. Bewley, G. Dix and S. Oxenbridge (2006), *Inside the Workplace. First Findings from the 2004 Workplace Employment Relations Survey*, London: Routledge.

Lewis, S. (1997), 'Family-friendly employment policies: a route to changing organizational culture or playing around at the margins?', *Gender, Work and Organization*, **4**(1), 13–23.

Martin, J. and C. Roberts (1984), *Women and Employment: A Lifetime Perspective*, London: HMSO.

McDowell, L., K. Ray, D. Perrons, C. Fagan and K. Ward (2005b), 'Women's paid work and the moral economies of care', *Social and Cultural Geography*, **6**(2), 219–35.

McDowell, L., D. Perrons, C. Fagan, K. Ray and K. Ward (2005a), 'The contradictions of class and gender in a global city: placing women's lives on the research agenda', *Environment and Planning 'A'*, **37**, 441–61.

National Statistics (2006), 'Work and Family – half of mums of under 5s are in employment', Office for National Statistics website article, published 16 October 2006, www.statistics.gov.uk/cci/nugget.asp?id=1655 (accessed 30 May 2007).

Organisation for Economic Co-operation and Development (OECD) (2004), *Employment Outlook* 2004, Paris: OECD.

Pahl, R. (1984), *Divisions of Labour*, Oxford: Blackwell.

Perrons, D., L. McDowell, C. Fagan, K. Ray and K. Ward (2007), 'Gender, social class and work-life balance in the New Economy', in R. Crompton, S. Lewis and C. Lyonette (eds), *Women, Men, Work and Family in Europe*, London: Palgrave, pp. 133–51.

Wallace, C. (2002), 'Household work strategies: their conceptual relevance and analytical scope in social research', *Sociology*, **36**(2), 275–92.

Ward, K., C. Fagan, L. McDowell, D. Perrons and K. Ray (2007), 'Living and working in urban working class communities', *Geoforum*, **36**(2), 312–25.

Warren, T. (2003), 'Class- and gender-based working time? Time poverty and the domestic division of labour', *Sociology*, **37**(4), 733–42.

Women and Work Commission (2006), *Shaping a Fairer Future*, London: Department of Trade and Industry, www.womenandequalityunit.gov.uk/women_work_commission/ (accessed 25 January 2008).

9. Mothers' employment, work–life conflict, careers and class

Rosemary Crompton and Clare Lyonette

INTRODUCTION

In Britain, women's employment rates increased rapidly during the 1980s. Although still on an upward trend, the rate slowed somewhat during the 1990s, a decade in which 'increasing female participation in the labour market was entirely concentrated among women with children' (Dench et al. 2002: 31). These trends are reflected in the survey data (British Social Attitudes [BSA] data for 1989, 1994, 2002 and 2006) that we draw on in this chapter.[1] In 1989, 62 per cent of the mothers interviewed reported that they had stayed at home when their children were under school age, but by 2006, this percentage had fallen to 47.[2]

However, there are substantial differences by educational background amongst working mothers. Aggregate data shows that among both couple mothers and lone parents educated to degree level, 81 per cent are in employment, whereas, of mothers with no qualifications, only 44 per cent of couple-mothers and 29 per cent of lone parents are in employment (Walling 2005). As Rake et al. (2000: ch. 3) have demonstrated, low- and mid-skilled mothers are more likely to reduce their employment than mothers with higher skills, thus the cost of motherhood (in foregone earnings) is greater among these women. Not surprisingly, these differences are reflected in substantial variation by class in the employment patterns of mothers, and professional and managerial mothers are much more likely to be in paid employment than mothers in the lower occupational categories.

These patterns are reflected in the BSA surveys. A comparison across the four surveys, using the Registrar General's classification, demonstrated that between 1989 and 1994, the proportion of stay-at-home mothers of children under school age in the professional and managerial groupings declined from 50 per cent to 36 per cent, a proportion that has remained remarkably stable since then.[3] Similarly, the decline in stay-at-home mothers among intermediate groupings also occurred between 1989 and 1994 and then

*Table 9.1   Working status when child under school age by class (women
with a child currently under 11 in the household, 2002 and 2006
combined)*

Worked	Prof/managerial	Intermediate	Routine/manual	Total (%)
Full-time	33%	15%	13%	83 (21%)
Part-time	40%	53%	44%	175 (45%)
Stayed home	27%	32%	43%	134 (34%)
Total no. (%)	149 (100%)	99 (100%)	144 (100%)	392 (100%)

Note: Class: professional/managerial women significantly more likely to have worked full-time with a child under school age ($\chi^2 = 25.595$; df = 4; p < 0.001).

stabilised, although this decline is not so extensive (from 67 per cent to 59 per cent). Amongst routine and manual mothers, however, the BSA data suggests that the decline in stay-at-home mothers took place later, and a drop is only evident (from 63 per cent to 58 per cent) between 1994 and 2002, although it has fallen further since then. In Table 9.1, we give evidence on the employment patterns, by class, of mothers of young children drawn from the most recent surveys.[4] Not only are professional and managerial women more likely to be in employment, they are also significantly more likely to work full-time.

These trends in the employment of women are also reflected in changing attitudes to gender roles and mothers' employment, as was demonstrated in a previous analysis of the 1989, 1994 and 2002 data (Crompton et al. 2003a). In 1989, 28 per cent of BSA respondents 'agreed' that 'a man's job is to earn money, a woman's job is to look after the home and family', but by 2006, only 15 per cent agreed with this statement. Similarly, in 1989, fully 64 per cent of respondents agreed that 'women should stay at home when there is a child under school age', but by 2006, this had fallen to 40 per cent. Men are consistently more 'traditional' than women in their answers to these kinds of questions. For example, in 2006, 43 per cent of men thought that mothers of young children should stay at home, compared with 37 per cent of women.

There are also persisting class differences in attitudes to gender roles and mothers' employment, in that managerial and professional men and women are markedly less traditional in their attitudes (although gender differences in attitudinal traditionalism still persist in all classes). For example, by 2006, a mere 7 per cent of professional and managerial women thought that 'a man's job is to earn money, a woman's job is to look after the home and family', whereas 16 per cent of manual women thought this (and 19 per cent of manual men). Nevertheless, attitudes are changing across all class

Table 9.2 '*Women should stay at home when there is a child under school age' by class and sex (1989–2006, all men and women)*

Agree		1989 %	Base	1994 %	Base	2002 %	Base	2006 %	Base
Men	Prof.	61	180	62	151	54	328	40	324
	Intermediate	73	69	69	50	48	88	42	96
	Manual	70	312	57	242	50	421	45	393
	All	67	561	60	443	52	837	43	813
Women	Prof.	53	152	37	138	35	382	32	353
	Intermediate	65	246	51	182	52	353	38	323
	Manual	62	271	59	202	52	343	40	301
	All	61	669	50	522	46	1078	37	977

groupings, and demonstrate a consistent trend. One interesting finding was that attitudinal change in the lower occupational groupings demonstrates a pattern that mirrors the pattern of change in mothers' employment amongst these groups – as we have already mentioned, this increase occurred later than that for professional and managerial women. Thus as Table 9.2 demonstrates, in 1994, 59 per cent of manual women still thought that mothers should stay at home with young children (compared with 37 per cent of women managers and professionals), but by 2006, only 40 per cent of manual women held to this view (compared with 32 per cent of women managers and professionals).

A number of factors, therefore, appear to be shaping attitudes to gender, family and employment. First, changes in the employment of women, particularly mothers. As more and more women remain in paid work when their children are young, so fewer and fewer people hold either traditional gender roles, or to the view that maternal employment is prejudicial for children.[5] Nevertheless, class differences in attitudes – and behaviour as far as mothers' employment is concerned – are persisting, as is men's higher level of gender traditionalism. These class differences in maternal behaviour will, of course, serve to reproduce and deepen class inequalities (Crompton 2006a, b), and as Gregg and Wadsworth (2001) have demonstrated, the patterning of women's employment has contributed to the considerable widening of household inequality.

Nevertheless, despite their very substantial increase in economic activity, women have by no means achieved equality with men in the employment sphere – even when significant factors such as level of education and qualification are controlled for (Wass and McNabb 2006). In some large part this is because women are still held to be largely responsible for caring and domestic work (and, indeed, continue to do most of it), even when in employment. In Britain, this potential conflict between paid work and family life is often resolved (in part) by women switching to part-time work (Table 9.1).

It would be generally recognised that part-time work has a negative impact on career development at all levels, and is yet another reason for women's lack of 'success' in employment. However, the most striking 'class' difference is in respect of full-time employment. About a quarter of professional and managerial women report that they had worked full-time with a child under school age, compared with just over 10 per cent of intermediate and manual women. This means that the level of part-time work is *proportionately* greater among intermediate and manual women, given the very low level of full-time employment among mothers in these groups. These class-differentiated patterns of mothers' employment behaviour, of course, will further deepen class inequalities.

Another feature associated with the increase in mothers' employment is the increasing amount of attention that is being given to the problem of work–life conflict.[6] From BSA data, there are a number of indications that both work and family life are becoming more pressurised (see also, for example, Gershuny 2005). Surveys of work orientations show a steady increase in the proportion of employees – even part-time employees – finding their jobs stressful (Crompton and Lyonette 2007). Individual working hours are probably not increasing (Green 2003). However, the increase in women's employment (and women are working longer hours than they used to), will lead to an increase in the hours of paid work carried out by families (Crompton and Lyonette 2007; Moen 2003).

In the next sections of this chapter, therefore, we examine the interrelationships between class, gender, careers and work–life conflict. We demonstrate that levels of work–life conflict are higher for professional and managerial employees – and for managerial and professional women in particular. This is largely a consequence of the fact that these employees work longer hours. Promotion aspirations, too, are negatively associated with work–life conflict (people who wish to be promoted usually have to work longer hours). Women are less likely to aspire to promotion than men, and such aspirations also vary by class (this might be seen as a realistic adaptation to circumstances, given that promotion opportunities are fewer in lower-level jobs; see Grimshaw et al. 2002). As we shall argue, these very real structures of constraint, by both class and gender, should make us rather sceptical of widespread assertions to the effect that contemporary societies are increasingly characterised by more freedom and 'choice'.

The significance of 'choice' is emphasised by social theorists including Giddens (1991); and Beck and Beck-Gernsheim (2002). They have argued that 'late modern' societies, as compared to previous epochs, are marked by an increase in 'individualisation', where the individual is increasingly 'forced' to choose, as individuals assume responsibility for their own biographies. It would not be sensible to reject such arguments altogether. For example, changes in the occupational structure – in particular, the decline of 'traditional' working-class jobs such as in mining and heavy industry – have made it impossible for sons to follow their fathers into the pit or the steel works. Indeed, the decline of 'good' (that is, well-paid) manual jobs for men has been an important factor in the erosion of the 'male breadwinner' model, as increasingly, two incomes are required to support a family (Crompton 2006b). In respect of women's employment in particular, Hakim (2004) has controversially argued that in countries such as Britain and the USA, where women have secured equal opportunities, and labour markets are flexible and deregulated (as a consequence of neo-liberal economic policies), women are freely able to exercise their 'choices' – particularly in respect of part-time work. As a consequence, Hakim has developed what she describes as 'preference theory', in which the pattern of women's employment reflects the pattern of 'choices' of different 'types' of women, many of whom, she argues, give priority to their homes and families over paid employment.

Again, such arguments should not be rejected out of hand as men and women do indeed make choices in relation to both mothers' employment and family responsibilities more generally. However, choices are always made in the context of the opportunities available to individuals and families. As we shall demonstrate in this chapter, this context remains substantially stratified by both class and by gender, despite the very real changes that have taken place in recent years.

WORK–LIFE 'BALANCE'; GENDERED CAREERS

The question of work–life 'balance' is widely regarded as being 'easier' for professional and managerial women. For example, a recent report from the ESRC Future of Work programme argued that:

> Any sensible approach to work–life policies cannot ignore the . . . phenomenon of occupational class in the amount of access and take-up of work–life balance entitlements. Women in managerial and professional jobs with higher incomes and benefits are in a much better position to achieve a balance than their much lower-paid and insecure counterparts employed, for example, in the retail trade and textiles. (Taylor 2002b: 18)

Table 9.3 *Working hours by class and sex (FT only, no self-employed, 2002 and 2006 combined)*

Sex	Class	N	Mean	S.D.
Male	Professional/managerial	547	46.81	10.99
	Intermediate	93	40.82	6.42
	Routine/manual	455	44.05	9.05
	Total	1095	45.16	10.06
Female	Professional/managerial	439	43.41	9.67
	Intermediate	170	38.02	5.09
	Routine/manual	188	37.29	6.28
	Total	797	40.82	8.63
Total	Professional/managerial	986	45.30	10.55
	Intermediate	263	39.01	5.74
	Routine/manual	643	42.07	8.88
	Total	1892	43.33	9.72

Notes: Class: professional/managerial worked significantly longer hours overall than other occupational groups ($F = 60.922$; $df = 2$; $p < 0.001$).
Sex: men worked significantly longer hours than women ($F = 70.202$; $df = 1$; $p < 0.001$). There was also a significant interaction between class and sex: professional/managerial women worked significantly longer hours than other women and professional/managerial men worked significantly longer hours than other men ($F = 6.715$; $df = 2$; $p < 0.005$). High standard deviations indicate considerable individual variation in working hours in Great Britain (see also Bishop 2004).

It is true that women (and men) in professional and managerial occupations do receive better work–life entitlements from their employers. For example, the 2002 BSA survey found that 64 per cent of managers and professionals, compared with only 38 per cent of routine and manual employees enjoyed 'good' work–family entitlements (Crompton et al. 2003a: 175). However, many women do not feel able to take advantage of these entitlements, particularly if they wish to pursue a career (Crompton et al. 2003b). More particularly, highly educated (managerial and professional) women work longer hours than women in the lower occupational groupings (see Table 9.3). Working hours have been demonstrated to be the major factor associated with levels of work–life pressure (White et al. 2003). Managerial and professional women, even when they work full-time, usually take responsibility for the majority of childcare and domestic work in their households (Harkness 2003).

We developed a measure of work–life conflict[7] using four survey items (respondents were asked to indicate for each item whether this occurred several times a week, several times a month, once or twice, or never. Higher scores indicate higher work–life conflict):

Table 9.4   Work–life conflict by class and sex (FT only, no self-employed, 2002 and 2006 combined)

Sex	Occupational class	N	Mean	S.D.
Male	Professional/managerial	437	7.59	2.18
	Intermediate	66	7.36	2.38
	Manual	354	7.01	2.51
	Total	857	7.33	2.35
Female	Professional/managerial	350	8.13	2.39
	Intermediate	128	7.13	2.25
	Manual	139	7.17	2.24
	Total	617	7.71	2.37
Total (M+F)	Professional/managerial	787	7.83	2.29
	Intermediate	194	7.21	2.29
	Manual	493	7.05	2.44
	Total	1474	7.49	2.37

Note: Class: professional/managerial significantly higher conflict than other classes ($F = 16.307$; $df = 2$; $p < 0.001$).
No significant effects of sex or interactions between sex and class.

I have come home from work too tired to do the chores which need to be done.

It has been difficult for me to fulfil my family responsibilities because of the amount of time I spent on my job.

I have arrived at work too tired to function well because of the household work I had done.

I have found it difficult to concentrate at work because of my family responsibilities.

As Table 9.4 demonstrates, work–life conflict is significantly higher (for both men and women) for those in professional and managerial occupations compared with the other class categories. Although the difference is not statistically significant, levels of work–life conflict would appear to be particularly high for professional and managerial women.

Not only do full-time managerial and professional women work, on average, longer hours than women in the other occupational classes, but they are also more likely to be in partnerships with similar men – a factor that has been recognised as making a contribution to the deepening of class inequalities (Ermisch et al. 2006). In fact, among the BSA respondents, dual full-time households were reported more frequently by both men and women in professional and managerial occupations (Table 9.5).

Table 9.5   *Class by couples' economic activity (partnered respondents only, 2002 and 2006 combined)*

Couples' economic activity	Prof/mgr	Intermediate	Routine/manual	Total
Both FT	431	168	211	810
	(54%)	(41%)	(37%)	(45%)
Man FT/woman PT	228	145	204	577
	(29%)	(35%)	(36%)	(32%)
Man FT/woman not in work	142	97	157	396
	(18%)	(24%)	(27%)	(22%)
Total	801	410	572	1783
	(100%)	(100%)	(100%)	(100%)

Notes: Class: professional/managerial couples significantly more likely to work FT, routine/manual couples significantly less likely to work FT ($\chi^2 = 44.881$; df = 4; p < 0.001). Note that class is based on the respondent's occupational class.

As Table 9.6 demonstrates, for women, levels of work–life conflict are significantly lower in 'man full-time/woman part-time' households – a pattern of household economic activity that may be described as a modified version of the 'male breadwinner' model. As questions on work–life conflict could, logically, only be asked of respondents in paid work, for 'traditional' breadwinner households ('man full-time/woman not in work'), data is only available for men. It is interesting, however, that the presence of a non-employed partner does not appear significantly to reduce levels of work–life conflict for men. It is also of interest that significant class differences in work–life conflict persist at all levels of couples' economic activity.

One way in which women can reduce their levels of work–life conflict, therefore, is to opt for part-time work. However, particularly among professional and managerial women, part-time work is explicitly recognised as having a very negative impact on career development.

As part of the GeNet research project, we have carried out qualitative work–life interviews with men and women at both poles of the occupational hierarchy in finance – qualified accountants, all members of the Institute of Chartered Accountants in England and Wales (ICAEW), and routine employees (often without specific qualifications) in the financial sector.[8] Among qualified mothers, the negative impact of part-time work on promotion opportunities emerged very strongly. As a mother working four days a week put it, your career changes 'very dramatically' even when only working one day less than the 'standard' working week:

Table 9.6 *Work–life conflict by class and couples' economic activity (partnered respondents only, 2002 and 2006 combined)*

Couple's economic activity	Sex of respondent	Class of respondent	N	Mean	S.D.
Both FT	Male	Professional/managerial	156	7.38	2.14
		Intermediate	44	7.14	2.12
		Routine/manual	98	7.02	2.15
		Total	298	7.23	2.14
	Female	Professional/managerial	177	8.14	2.37
		Intermediate	73	7.34	2.64
		Routine/manual	68	7.06	2.04
		Total	318	7.72	2.41
Man FT, woman PT	Male	Professional/managerial	111	7.86	2.23
		Intermediate	42	7.95	2.64
		Routine/manual	57	6.75	2.30
		Total	210	7.58	2.38
	Female	Professional/managerial	86	7.33	2.08
		Intermediate	73	6.81	2.20
		Routine/manual	102	6.70	2.40
		Total	261	6.93	2.26
Man FT, woman not in work	Male only	Professional/managerial	70	7.89	2.05
		Intermediate	47	7.23	2.70
		Routine/manual	67	7.91	2.93
		Total	184	7.73	2.57

Notes: Women only (class): professional/managerial higher work–life conflict than other groups (F = 7.405; df = 2; p < 0.001); (couples' economic activity): women in couples where both partners work FT significantly higher work-life conflict than other groups (F = 7.854; df = 1; p < 0.01). No significant interactions.
Men only: no significant effects.

I mean, the trouble with doing four days a week is, you know, your career profile changes very dramatically when you do that and you just don't get the same opportunities in your career that you do if you're working full time. *Even at four days a week you think?* It shouldn't happen but it does, and that's one of the reasons I chose four days and not three because it's still 80 per cent of a job, and it even used to choke me to describe it as part time, to be honest . . . I know there are at least two jobs during my last eighteen months at (previous firm) that I wasn't considered for, even though I had really good experience, because they wanted definitely five days . . . And this was even me with a good track record of delivering. (A12, F director, business, two children)

Male accountants were equally aware of the problems associated with working less than full-time:

> I mean we've got a girl in, was a Finance Director, and she went off and had a child and has taken a long time to come back, and she's desperately trying to come back two days a week. She's very good, extremely good, but there's nothing, or she'll end up being used because she's very good but it . . . won't be a career role for her; it'll be just a one-off, you know. (A9, M finance executive, business, two children)

Given that professional and managerial women are well aware of the consequences of part-time working, we should not be surprised to find that part-time women are less interested in promotion. Whether this is because less ambitious women 'choose' to work part-time, or whether a lack of interest in promotion is better understood as a realistic adaptation to the reduced opportunities available to part-time women is impossible to say. Certainly, as one of our interviewees put it, many women feel 'torn' about having to make these choices:

> Well, that is where I'm torn (about promotion) because there's a side of me that says no, I'm not content to stay where I am, but there's another side of me that says ah yes, but you actually don't want that level of pressure that would make you feel stressed out all the time and unable to deal with life on a day-to-day basis . . .' (A1, F director, practice, one child)

Attitudinal data from the BSA surveys suggest that both sex and class have an impact on promotion aspirations. Table 9.7 summarises the answers to the question: 'speaking for yourself, how important is it for you to move up the job ladder at work?', and the class and gender differences are quite striking. Men are more likely to express an interest in promotion than women, but there are significant class differences in attitude between men – professional and managerial men are more than 20 per cent more likely to express an interest in promotion than men in the lower occupational groupings. Again, it may be suggested that the lower levels of aspiration amongst men in the lower occupational grouping reflect a realistic appraisal of the promotion opportunities available – as these are much lower in the lower occupational groups. Indeed, it has been argued that with organisational 'downsizing' and 'delayering', promotion opportunities in jobs not requiring formal qualifications are actually in decline (Crompton et al. 2003b; Grimshaw et al. 2002).

A similar 'class gradient' is found among women although, on average, women express themselves as less interested in promotion than men. What is very striking, however, is the difference in attitudes between full- and part-time women employees, particularly professional and managerial

Table 9.7   Promotion aspirations by class and sex (those in employment only, no self-employed, 2002 and 2006 combined)

Sex	Promotion aspirations (how important is it to you to move up the job ladder)	Occupational class			
		Prof/mgr	Intermediate	Manual	Total
Male (FT)	Very/fairly important	64%	44%	43%	546 (54%)
	Not very/not at all important	36%	56%	57%	473 (46%)
	Total no.	513 (100%)	88 (100%)	418 (100%)	1019 (100%)
Female (FT)	Very/fairly important	55%	32%	23%	299 (42%)
	Not very/not at all Important	45%	68%	77%	410 (58%)
	Total no.	389 (100%)	148 (100%)	172 (100%)	709 (100%)
Female (PT)	Very/fairly important	31%	17%	22%	98 (23%)
	Not very/not at all important	69%	83%	78%	326 (77%)
	Total no.	118 (100%)	95 (100%)	211 (100%)	424 (100%)

Note: Class: For FT men only, professional/managerials significantly more likely to have career aspirations ($\chi^2 = 44.610$; df = 2; p < 0.001); the same for FT women ($\chi^2 = 56.806$; df = 2; p < 0.001), but not for PT women, although the trend is still apparent.

women, where the 'aspirations gap' between full- and part-time women is 25 per cent. Intermediate women are less likely to express an interest in promotion than professional and managerial women, although here, again, aspirations drop sharply when women work part-time. This gap is simply not in evidence for routine and manual women, but in any case, only just over a fifth of them would like to 'move up the job ladder'.

Class and sex therefore have a marked impact on promotion aspirations. However, a range of other contextual factors might also affect attitudes to promotion at the individual level. Younger people might be expected to be more ambitious than older people. It is well established that men with young children work longer hours – might their ambitions for their families also make them more interested in promotion? We explored this further by carrying out separate regressions (not reported here) on promotion aspirations for men and women, including (in addition to class and hours of work) age, having a child aged under 11, and spouse's economic activity. For men, we found that having a non-working spouse was significantly predictive of higher promotion aspirations, but having a child under 11 was not significant. As expected, age was significant, as was being a professional/manager. Working hours were not significant.

For working women, as with men, age and class were associated with feeling that 'moving up the job ladder' was important. Longer working hours were significantly predictive of higher promotion aspirations, as were being younger and being a professional/manager. Again, having a child under 11 in the household was not significantly predictive, nor was spouse's economic activity. Both men and women, therefore, are less interested in promotion with age. Interestingly, the mere fact of having a child in the household does not, in itself, affect promotion aspirations.

Besides age, individual level differences in personal ambition will, obviously, affect attitudes to promotion, and these individual differences will be distributed among men, women, and within all occupational classes. Nevertheless, the very marked differences in aspirations for promotion by sex, class, and between full- and part-time women, indicate that substantial normative and structural factors are also shaping these attitudes. Normative pressures that allocate to women the major responsibility for domestic work and caring will make many women acutely conscious of the consequences of having to 'go the extra mile' in order to achieve promotion (although women are no less 'committed' to employment in a general sense than men are. See Crompton and Lyonette 2007). For men and women in the lower occupational groupings, a 'lack of ambition' may be interpreted as reflecting an adaptation to the opportunities available.

Further evidence for these interpretations may be found in the answers to another question as to whether respondents saw their job as part of a 'career'. Over 80 per cent of full-time professional men (and women) saw their jobs as part of a career, compared with 51 per cent of intermediate men and 46 per cent of manual men. For part-time women, the proportions seeing their jobs as part of a career dropped sharply, although even here, class differences were apparent. Over a half (54 per cent) of part-time professional and managerial women saw their jobs as part of a career, compared with only a quarter of manual women.

Taking up part-time work, therefore, is clearly associated with a scaling down of career ambition, particularly for professional and managerial women:

> I won't progress, I don't think, and I know I won't, I had the discussion with my boss two years ago that I didn't want to become a partner because I didn't want to put in the extra time that would be required, so I didn't want to work full time,

I didn't want all the evening commitments that I would have as a partner and all the emotional strain that I'd have as a partner. I could just about manage my life with the role that I have now. I said to him that I'd probably revise that opinion in a few years' time when my children were older, and I will do, but at the moment I don't want any more. (A18, F director, practice, two children)

Building a career, it would seem, means increased levels of work intensity. Indeed, we found that having aspirations for promotion was associated with a significant increase in levels of work–life conflict, particularly for women. Table 9.8 shows that for women, but not for men, wanting to be promoted is significantly associated with higher levels of work–life conflict.

Table 9.8   *Work–life conflict by career aspirations (men and women in employment, no self-employed, 2002 and 2006 combined)*

Important to move up job ladder?	Sex	N	Mean	S.D.
Very/fairly important	Male	433	7.52	2.27
	Female	262	8.05	2.43
	Total	695	7.72	2.34
Not very/not important at all	Male	421	7.13	2.42
	Female	354	7.48	2.31
	Total	775	7.29	2.38
Total	Male	854	7.32	2.35
	Female	616	7.72	2.37
	Total	1470	7.49	2.37

Notes: Sex: women significantly higher work–life conflict than men ($F = 12.456$; df = 1; $p < 0.001$).
Career aspirations: those saying very/fairly important also significantly higher conflict than those not ($F = 14.638$; df = 1; $p < 0.001$).
No significant interactions between sex and career aspirations.

Standard multiple regression analyses with work–life conflict as the dependent variable were then run separately for men and women in employment, entering only those variables which had been shown to be significantly associated in separate tests (above). Table 9.9 shows that for men in employment, age, hours worked and spouse's economic activity were significant predictors of work–life conflict (the significance of class disappeared in the regression given the association between class and hours worked). In other words, being younger, working longer hours and having a non-working spouse led to higher conflict for men. For women, however, the predictors of work–life conflict were rather different. Hours worked, class and having a child under 11 were all significantly predictive: that is, working longer hours, being a professional/managerial and having a young

Table 9.9 Regressions on work–life conflict (men and women in employment, no self-employed, 2002 and 2006 combined)

Independent variables entered	Men only		Women only	
	Beta (standardized)	t-value	Beta (standardized)	t-value
Constant		9.566***		12.885***
Age	−.131	−2.881**	−.021	−.591
Hours worked	.166	3.750***	.306	6.303***
Intermediate class[1]	.010	.249	−.071	−2.018*
Manual class[1]	−.079	−1.898	−.097	−2.604**
Child under 11	.069	1.583	.131	3.774***
Promotion aspirations	.012	.273	.015	.420
Works full-time	−.021	−.479	−.070	−1.492
Spouse working PT[2]	.036	.828	—	—
Spouse not in work[2]	.117	2.579**	—	—
No.	615		910	

Notes: *p < .05; ** p < .01; *** p < .001.
[1]   Reference category for class = professional/managerial
[2]   Reference category for spouse's economic activity = full-time (not included in the regression for women, as not significant in an ANOVA)
Men only: $r = .281$; $r^2 = .079$; adjusted $r^2 = .065$. R for regression was significant: $F_{(9, 605)} = 5.756$, $p < .001$.
Women only: $r = .323$; $r^2 = .104$; adjusted $r^2 = .097$. R for regression was significant: $F_{(7, 902)} = 15.011$; $p < .001$.

child in the household led to higher conflict. Whereas the presence of a young child increased conflict for working women, it did not do so for men – a reflection, we would suggest, of the greater responsibility for child-care assumed by women.

CLASS AND 'CHOICE'

As noted in the first section of this chapter, compared with professional and managerial employees, routine and manual respondents would appear to be relatively more 'traditional' in their attitudes to gender roles, and to place a relatively greater emphasis on the importance of family life. While we would not wish to suggest that family affection and commitment is any less prevalent among managers and professionals, it is not particularly difficult to construct a 'causal narrative' as to why people in routine and manual occupations might place a greater degree of emphasis on their family lives and obligations. Professional and managerial jobs are more rewarding than routine and manual jobs, not only in a material sense, but also in respect of social recognition and self-esteem. A wide range of quantitative and qualitative evidence has documented class differences in attitudes to and experiences of employment. For example, the Working in Britain survey (Taylor 2002a) found that whereas only 21 per cent of higher professional and managerial employees thought of their job as 'just a means to earn a living', this was true of 58 per cent of skilled manual, and 54 per cent of semi-skilled and unskilled manual employees (Taylor 2000a: 14). Classic texts such as Sennett and Cobb's *The Hidden Injuries of Class* (1973) describe how manual workers suffering from 'injured dignity' turn to their families as a way of recovering lost pride. It should be emphasised that this pattern is not peculiar to manual employees, as middle-class men who feel unsuccessful in their careers may also seek solace in their family lives. It is not being argued here that a tendency to place a greater emphasis on the family is necessarily class-specific, but rather, that the characteristics of working class jobs are more likely, in aggregate, to result in people in such jobs putting a greater emphasis on their families than people in more rewarding jobs.

These class-related differences in attitudes to the family are, as we have already demonstrated in Table 9.2, reflected in class differences in attitudes to mothers' employment – in 2006, 32 per cent of managerial and professional women of all ages thought that a woman should stay at home with a child under school age, compared with 40 per cent of routine and manual women. To explore this issue further, we developed a scale to measure attitudes to women's employment (AWE) from five items:

A working mother can establish just as warm a relationship with her children as a mother who does not work.
A pre-school child is likely to suffer if his or her mother works.
All in all, family life suffers when the woman has a full-time job.
Do you think that women should work outside the home full-time, part-time or not at all when there is a child under school age.
Do you think that women should work full-time, part-time or not at all after the youngest child starts school.[9]

Using the combined 2002 and 2006 data set, the average AWE score confirmed the class differences that we had already established using the single variable. For professional and managerial women with a child under 11 in the household the score was 11.08, for intermediate women 12.35, and for routine/manual women 12.10 (significant effect of class $F = 4.391$, df = 2; $p < 0.05$). As we have seen, these differences in attitude are reflected in the differing patterns of mothers' employment among the different occupational classes, which themselves contribute to the reproduction of class inequalities.

However, within all class groupings, mothers who stayed at home when their children were young had more 'traditional' attitudes to mothers' employment.[10] Indeed, for mothers with a child under 11 in 2002/2006, professional and managerial women who had stayed at home when their child was under school age were even more conventional in their attitudes to the employment of mothers of young children (AWE = 14.40) than were routine and manual women who had stayed at home (AWE = 13.21). For these women, attitudes were highly congruent with behaviour and these professional and managerial mothers could be described as exercising their 'choices' in respect of employment when their children were young. For professional and managerial women with a child under 11, there was a 5.43 difference in the AWE scale, as between mothers who had worked full-time and mothers who had not worked.

Within the professional and managerial category, therefore, in the BSA sample about a quarter of mothers with a child under 11 expressed a strong preference for maternal care, and had themselves stayed at home when their children were young. However, qualitative research (Duncan 2005; Irwin 2003) has suggested that even among stay-at-home mothers, professional and managerial women hold (realistic) aspirations for themselves as workers and careerists. As we have seen in the discussion of our survey data, professional and managerial women, whether they have children or not, are significantly more likely to see their jobs as part of a career, and to have aspirations for promotion.

In all class groupings, mothers who had worked when their children were young had lower AWE scores. However, employment appeared to have a much less significant impact on AWE scores as far as intermediate, and routine and manual, mothers were concerned. As we have already noted, there was an over five-point gap in AWE scores between full-time and stay-at-home professional and managerial mothers, but the difference for intermediate mothers was only 2.74, and for manual mothers, 2.28. In short, among intermediate and routine and manual women, a relatively high level of traditionalism is found even among working mothers. This finding, we would suggest, indicates that in the lower occupational class categories, there is a higher proportion of mothers who would in fact prefer to reduce their levels of employment.

Moreover, women who earn good salaries (and who are likely to be in partnerships with similar men) have the capacity to choose a lower level of work intensity without necessarily facing economic hardship:

> I could do reasonable hours, not get stressed, come home and the only downside was that I'm probably earning about 20% less than I could earn, but I'm still earning a very, very good salary and not having stress and I'm thinking well, if

I move a step up, and my work keeps trying to persuade me to go for different jobs, I keep saying no, I'm just happy here because I'll double my stress for a 20% pay rise and it's just not worth it. (A3, F director, business, one child and pregnant)

In contrast, women in less well remunerated jobs are more likely to be working because of economic need:

And have you always worked full time throughout? Yes, afraid so . . . I'd still like to go part time now; if I could afford to go part time today, I would . . . I'd really like to think that I could do that (*reduce hours*), because I'd like to think if we got ourselves into a financial situation where my husband was doing well, and confident his earnings were coming in, and he was confident and happy with what he was doing, because I think it would make my family life better. (F6, F human resources officer, two children)

CONCLUSIONS

The BSA survey data confirms what has already been identified in aggregate trends. That is, there have been extensive changes in both mothers' employment as well as in attitudes to gender roles and the impact of maternal employment on children. Nevertheless, there remain significant class differences in the extent of maternal employment, as well as in attitudes to domestic and gender roles and mothers' employment. There are also persisting differences by sex, in that men (in all class groupings) tend to be more traditional in their attitudes than women. It might be argued that although women's claims to equality in civil society and employment have been largely accepted, men in aggregate still benefit from what Connell (1995) has described as a 'patriarchal dividend' as a consequence of the gendered division of labour. That is, as Lewis and Giullari (2005) have argued, the customary allocation of care and domestic work to women in practice restricts their 'agency freedom' and is a major source of gender inequality. The rather more traditional gender-role preferences of men, therefore, might be an expression of a reluctance to relinquish the advantages that men in aggregate derive from a traditionally gendered division of labour.[11] To put the argument another way, the more traditional gender-role attitudes and preferences expressed by men might be an expression of an underlying gender conflict of interests.

Despite claims as to the increasing significance of individualism and choice, both class and gender persist as major structural constraints shaping the decisions men and women make and the opportunities they have available, as was demonstrated in our analysis of both work–life conflict and aspirations for promotion and career development. Work–life conflict is higher among managers and professionals, particularly managerial and professional women, than in the other occupational class categories. This is largely because of the longer hours worked by professional and managerial employees. For women in employment, the presence of young children is associated with higher levels of work–life conflict, but not for men.

Promotion aspirations vary systematically by both sex and class. Women are less likely to want to 'move up the job ladder' than men, and managerial and professional employees of both sexes are much more likely to aspire to promotion than employees in the other occupational classes. In the case of women, we would suggest that their lower levels of aspiration compared with men reflect, in aggregate, women's adaptation to prevailing gender norms that hold them primarily responsible for caring and domestic work – responsibilities that are incompatible with the efforts required to develop a career. In the case of intermediate and manual employees – particularly manual employees – we would argue that the lower aspirations in these groups reflect the realities of the relatively restricted opportunities available.

Women who work part-time report significantly lower levels of work–life conflict, but part-time work is associated with a significant drop in promotion aspirations, particularly for professional and managerial women. Indeed, for these women, aspirations for promotion are significantly associated with higher levels of work–life conflict. Women, therefore, face an extremely difficult 'choice'. If they wish to develop a career, they are likely to find that the incompatibility between employment and family life will become even greater. 'Scaling back' career development, as many women do in practice (Blair-Loy 2003), means that women 'fail' to realise their full potential. This might be represented as a reflection of the 'choices' made by women and families, but as Lewis and Giullari have argued (and has been argued in this chapter), the normative assignment of caring and domestic work to women means that women do not have the same capacity to 'choose' between care and paid employment as men do, and thus their 'agency freedom' is restricted.

Nevertheless, men and women do make choices. However, our comparative analysis of attitudes, and maternal employment behaviour, within the different occupational classes suggests that the capacity to make these choices varies systematically by class. Managerial and professional women with strong views on the importance of maternal care are highly concentrated among stay-at-home mothers, whereas in the other occupational class groupings, attitudinal traditionalism is more evenly distributed among full-time, part-time and stay-at-home mothers. This suggests – and indeed, was confirmed by our interview data – that better-qualified women in higher-level employment can make these choices without suffering too great a material loss (although their careers will suffer), whereas women in the lower occupational groupings are more likely to feel constrained to work for material reasons.

We find that, although there have been very substantial changes in the distribution of paid work between men and women in recent years, nevertheless the underlying pattern of gender relations, and the division of labour between men and women, has been reconfigured, rather than transformed. As Williams (2000) has put it, despite the acceptance of women's equal status with that of men, the 'ideology of domesticity'(for women) did not die in the twentieth century; it mutated. New problems of work–life conflict, and increasing material inequalities between households, have emerged, and it is likely that these issues will become even more pressing in the future.

NOTES

1. We would like to acknowledge the following grants: ESRC R000239727 and ESRC GeNet Research Network, which funded extra questions on the 2002 survey and made possible the 2006 survey.
2. As these figures include mothers of all ages, they will overestimate non-employed mothers and do not give an accurate picture of the current behaviour of working mothers. See note 4 below.
3. In Britain, the national social class classification was revised for the 2001 census, and the Office of National Statistics Socio-Economic Classification (ONS-SEC) replaced the Registrar General's (RG) classification. The ONS-SEC is available for the 2002 and 2006 surveys, but not for the previous years. 'Class' comparisons over all four surveys, therefore, are based on the RG classification, as estimates of RG were available for 2002 and 2006. Our 'class' analysis of the 2002 and 2006 surveys, however, uses the ONS-SEC classification, as this is argued to be a superior measure (Rose and Pevalin 2002).
4. Although the same question on mother's employment when a child was under school age was asked in all of the surveys, data on the age of children is not available for all surveys. We therefore present the most recent data on the working patterns of mothers of children under secondary school age.
5. A further demonstration of attitudinal following on behavioural change in this area is given in Himmelweit and Sigala (2003).
6. This topic is more usually described as work–life 'balance'. We have described elsewhere (Crompton and Lyonette 2006) our lack of satisfaction with this term, and prefer to use the concept of work–life 'articulation'.
7. Cronbach's alpha 0.73; factor analysis showed one factor with an Eigen value of 2.2, explaining 56 per cent of variance. Questions on work–life 'balance', and attitudes to promotion, were only asked in the 2002 and 2006 surveys. Our analysis, therefore, is confined to this recent data, and we are not able to report on trends.
8. Eighty work–life interviews are being conducted. This analysis is based on the data already collected from qualified accountants and people working in finance (10 men and 10 women in each sector), all in employment, and all with at least one child aged under 14. Our interview guide covered a very wide range of topics, from past career inspirations to the current practicalities of childcare. In terms of occupational class classifications, qualified accountants would be in the managerial and professional

grouping, and more routine employees in finance would be in the intermediate category.

9. Scores ranged from 1 to 5, with a maximum of 21 (most traditional). Factor analysis showed one factor with an Eigen value of 2.632, explaining 53 per cent of the variance. A reliability analysis recorded a Cronbach's alpha of 0.77.

10. Analyses showed that whether the respondents worked was highly significant of attitudes: $F = 33.184$; $df = 2$; $p < 0.001$, but class was also significant: $F = 3.30$; $df = 2$; $p < 0.05$.

11. Support for this argument may be found in the finding that women, but not men, with more liberal gender role attitudes and involved in a less traditional division of domestic labour report a higher level of personal and family happiness than women in more 'traditional' circumstances (Crompton and Lyonette 2005).

REFERENCES

Beck, U. and E. Beck-Gernsheim (2002), *Individualization*, London: Sage.

Bishop, K. (2004), 'Working time patterns in the UK, France, Denmark and Sweden', *Labour Market Trends*, March, 113–22.

Blair-Loy, M. (2003), *Competing Devotions: Career and Family among Women Executives*, Cambridge, MA, and London: Harvard University Press.

Connell, R.W. (1995), *Masculinities*, Cambridge: Polity.

Crompton, R. (2006a), 'Class and family', *Sociological Review*, November, 658–76.

Crompton, R. (2006b), *Employment and the Family*, Cambridge: Cambridge University Press.

Crompton, R. and C. Lyonette (2005), 'The new gender essentialism: domestic and family "choices" and their relation to attitudes', *British Journal of Sociology*, **56**(4), 601–20.

Crompton, R. and C. Lyonette (2006), 'Work–life "balance" in Europe', *Acta Sociologica*, **49**(4), 379–93.

Crompton, R. and C. Lyonette (2007), 'Are we all working too hard? Women, men, and changing attitudes to employment', in A. Park, J. Curtice, K. Thomson, M. Phillips and M. Johnson (eds), *British Social Attitudes 23rd Report*, London: Sage, pp. 55–70.

Crompton, R., M. Brockmann and D. Wiggins (2003a), ' A woman's place . . . employment and family life for men and women', in A. Park, J. Curtice, K. Thomson, L. Jarvis and C. Bromley (eds), *British Social Attitudes, the 20th Report*, London: Sage, pp. 160–87.

Crompton, R., J. Dennett and A. Wigfield (2003b), *Organisations, Careers and Caring*, Bristol: Policy Press.

Dench, S., J. Aston, C. Evans, N. Meager, M. Williams and R. Willison (2002), *Key Indicators of Women's Position in Britain*, London: Department of Trade and Industry.

Duncan, S. (2005), 'Mothering, class and rationality', *Sociological Review*, **53**(2), pp. 50–76.

Ermisch, J., M. Francesconi and T. Seidler (2006), 'Intergenerational mobility and marital sorting', *Economic Journal*, **116**(573), July, 659–79.

Gershuny, J. (2005), 'Busyness as the badge of honour for the new superordinate working class', *Working Paper of the Institute for Social and Economic Research, Paper 2005–9*, Colchester: University of Essex.

Giddens, A. (1991), *Modernity and Self Identity*, Cambridge: Polity.

Green, F. (2003), 'The demands of work', in R. Dickens, P. Gregg, and J. Wadsworth (eds), *The Labour Market under New Labour*, Basingstoke: Palgrave Macmillan, pp. 137–49.

Gregg, P. and J. Wadsworth (2001), 'Everything you ever wanted to know about measuring worklessness and polarization at the household level but were afraid to ask', *Oxford Bulletin of Economics and Statistics*, **63**, 777–806.

Grimshaw, D., H. Beynon, J. Rubery and K. Ward (2002), 'The restructuring of career paths in large service sector organisations: "delayering", upskilling and polarisation', *Sociological Review*, **50**(1), 89–115.

Hakim, C. (2004), *Key Issues in Women's Work*, London: GlassHouse Press.

Harkness, S. (2003), 'The household division of labour: changes in families' allocation of paid and unpaid work, 1992–2002', in R. Dickens, P. Gregg and J. Wadsworth (eds), *The Labour Market under New Labour: The State of Working Britain*, Basingstoke: Palgrave Macmillan.

Himmelweit, S. and M. Sigala (2003), 'Internal and external constraints on mothers' employment', Working Paper No. 27, ESRC Future of Work Programme.

Irwin, S. (2003), 'The changing shape of values, care and commitments', paper prepared for ESPAnet conference, Danish National Institute of Social Research, Copenhagen, 13–15 November.

Lewis, J. and S. Giullari (2005), 'The adult worker model family, gender equality and care: the search for new policy principles and the possibilities and problems of a capabilities approach', *Economy and Society*, **34**(1), 76–104.

Moen, P. (2003), *It's about Time: Couples and Careers*', Ithaca, NY, and London: ILR/Cornell University Press.

Rake, K., H. Davies, H. Joshi and R. Alami (2000), *Women's Incomes over the Lifetime*, London: The Stationery Office.

Rose, D. and D. Pevalin (2002), *A Researcher's Guide to the National Statistics Socio-Economic Classification*, London: Sage.

Sennett, R. and J. Cobb (1973), *The Hidden Injuries of Class*, New York: Vintage Books.

Taylor, R. (2002a), *Britain's World of Work: Myths and Realities*, Economic and Social Research Council, Future of Work Programme, University of Leeds.

Taylor, R. (2002b), *The Future of Work–Life Balance*, Economic and Social Research Council, Future of Work Programme, University of Leeds.

Walling, A. (2005), 'Families and work', *Labour Market Trends*, July, 275–83.

Wass, V. and R. McNabb (2006), 'Pay, promotion and parenthood', *Work, Employment and Society*, **20**(2), 289–308.

White, M., S. Hill, P. McGovern, C. Mills and D. Smeaton (2003), '"High-Performance" management practices, working hours and work–life balance', *British Journal of Industrial Relations*, **41**(2), 175–95.

Williams, J. (2000), *Unbending Gender*, New York: Oxford University Press.

10. The household division of labour: changes in families' allocation of paid and unpaid work

Susan Harkness

INTRODUCTION

Historically much of economic policy has been based on the premise that households, and in particular those with children, specialise in their division of labour, with men concentrating their efforts on market work and women in household production. Recent decades have, however, seen a rapid decline in the male breadwinner model of employment as the numbers of dual-earner and single-adult households have grown. Women's position in the labour market has improved enormously over recent decades, both in terms of employment and relative earnings. The rise in employment among women of working age has been well documented, growing by 10 percentage points since 1979, to 70 per cent by 2006.[1] This rise has been particularly marked among mothers and, especially since 1997, among those with pre-school children and single parents. While these changes might be expected to have important implications for the ways in which families organise work, both inside and outside the home, male employment patterns underwent little change in the 1990s and in particular there was little evidence of a significant reduction in the number of hours being worked by men. In 2002, the Organisation for Economic Co-operation and Development (OECD) reported that men full-timers in Britain worked some of the longest hours in Europe, while press reports suggest that the 'macho' long-hours culture in Britain is leading to an increasingly stressed workforce, having an adverse effect on family relationships, and contributing towards the relatively poor status of women in the labour market.[2] The net effect of the rising female employment has been a large rise in the number of hours of market work within families. There is evidence too that workers would increasingly be happy to forgo pay for a reduced working week. Analysis of the British Household Panel Survey (BHPS) suggests that around 40 per cent of all full-time workers would be happy to work fewer hours even if it meant foregoing pay, and this figure rises to almost one-half of all full-time working women with children aged under 5.

The increase in the number of market hours that families are working clearly has implications for the time available for other activities, including work within the home and leisure. As gender roles change, an important question is whether, in response to increasing gender equality in the labour market, the division of labour within the household has also become more egalitarian? Or is it the case that as women enter into the labour market they increasingly face a 'double-burden' of household and market work? Alternatively, have the number of hours spent on household production fallen with households substituting away-from-home production, either by investing in labour-saving devices (such as dishwashers and ready made meals) or purchasing services (such as cleaning) previously provided at home?

Several theories have been put forward which may help explain the observed allocation of spouses' time to both market and household work. First, unitary models of household production (Becker 1991) suggest households maximise a single utility function, with utility depending both on the consumption of both purchased goods and those produced in the home. Utility is maximised by specialisation, and so the spouse with the greatest comparative advantage in market work (household production) will work the greatest number of market hours (contribute most to home production). In Becker's specialisation model it is therefore the amount of time devoted to paid work that determines the division of household tasks within the home. Unitary models of household production have been criticised for their assumption that families optimise a single utility function. Alternative models remove the altruistic assumption implicit in Becker's model, and instead assume that individuals are self-interested. Bargaining models suggest a game theory framework for analysing the division of household tasks (see Pollak 2007 for a recent review) with the outcomes of these models relying on threat points, either divorce or non-cooperation within marriage. The utility of individuals at these threat points is dependent on spouses' outside options, which depend on a wide range of factors including efficiency in household production, earnings potential, and access to non-labour income. Bargaining theories therefore suggest that the division of household labour will be less dependent upon the availability of time (or hours of work) than on (potential) relative wages. Both theories, however, lead us to predict that recent labour market changes should have led to a reduction in the amount of housework carried out by women within the home. Moreover these changes could be expected to have a cumulative impact, with the pay gap falling further as women devote less effort to housework, as Hersch and Stratton conclude:

> The allocation decisions that result in women doing more housework than men
> set up a vicious cycle . . . Only the evidence indicating that younger women are
> spending less time on housework and more time in the labour market suggest
> that the gender difference in work histories and housework time may be dimin-
> ishing. Such changes will further decrease the gender wage gap, leading to still
> greater equity in the allocation of housework. (Hersch and Stratton 1994: 124)

However, these predicted changes have not fully materialised; a range of studies show that in spite of rising female hours of employment women retain primary responsibility for household tasks and childcare. Alternative theories suggest reasons for predicting a less optimistic scenario. Recent economic theory has emphasised the role of gender identity in determining the allocation of household work. Akerlof and Kranton (2000) suggest that notions of identity play a strong role in the division of household labour. They argue that identity is an important explanation of individual actions and that women may gain utility from doing housework, or lose utility from working outside the home. Identity models of the household predict an asymmetric division of labour between men and women. Thus while comparative advantage theories suggest that those working more outside the home will do less within it; identity theories can explain why real-world data show that when a wife works more hours outside the home she still undertakes a larger share of the housework. Moreover, where women earn more than their partners, men suffer a loss in utility because of the reversal of gender roles. In order to restore equality between men and women, women respond by taking on an even greater share of housework. Gender identity theories therefore support the notion that improvements in women's labour market position may result in a 'double burden' of paid and domestic work. Game theoretic models, where women have a different taste for home production could lead to similar conclusions.

In the remainder of this chapter I look at empirical evidence on family employment, earnings and household work in Britain examining changes over the period 1992–2004. The key questions addressed are: (1) How has increased employment affected patterns of household employment? (2) How have total hours of paid work changed within households? (3) How have total hours of household work responded to these changes? (4) How have these changes been reflected in the division of household tasks?

DATA

Throughout the chapter data from the BHPS is used to chart changes in work. The BHPS has been collected since 1991 with an original sample of around 5500 households from England, Scotland and Wales. The BHPS collects a wide range of socio-economic data on individuals and households. Here we restrict our sample to prime-age working women, aged between 25 and 49. This age group allows a better comparison between mothers and childless women (by excluding older women whose children may have left home). Women are defined as living in a couple if they live with their partner, regardless of marital status. Similarly single women are defined as all those women who do not live with a partner. For couples we exclude from our data those women with partners older than retirement age (over 64). Full-time students are also dropped from our sample. The analysis is based on two cross-sections of individual level data and does not follow individuals longitudinally.

DEFINITIONS

Hours of Paid Work

Throughout total hours of work are defined as the number of hours respondents are normally expected to work each week *plus* usual hours of paid and unpaid overtime *and* usual hours worked per week in a second job. This differs from actual hours of work largely because respondents have reported being ill or having taken holiday (annual leave or Bank Holidays) over the past week and so actual hours are not a good reflection of the typical working week. Full-time workers are defined as those working 30 hours or more a week, including paid and unpaid overtime, in their main job only.

Unpaid Work

Data on housework is defined in the BHPS by the question: 'About how many hours do you spend on housework in an average week, such as time spent cooking, cleaning and doing the laundry?' There has been debate about the value of this type of self-recorded question versus data recorded in time use questionnaires, which is burdensome to collect and in existing studies includes much less detailed information on employment and demographic characteristics of other household members. The BHPS panel data also has the advantage of allowing comparisons to be made over time. Several studies have contrasted data recorded from time use studies with self-reported questionnaire data on time use. Gershuny et al. (2005: 664) concluded that 'the less burdensome questionnaire based "stylized" time-use instruments, although less accurate, are not substantially or systematically biased when compared to diary-based estimates – they are simply "noisy" '. Some studies have suggested that women tend to report their housework hours more accurately than men suggesting that the gender gap in housework participation will be if anything underestimated (ibid.). Others suggest no tendency to over-reporting in surveys and no or little gender difference (Bonke 2005; Kitterød and Lyngstad 2005).

PAID WORK WITHIN HOUSEHOLDS

Change in Household Employment Structures

The past decade has seen a rapid growth in female employment, particularly among mothers with young children. Figure 10.1 plots employment rates for prime-aged working women (aged 25–49) between 1992 and 2004. While employment rates for childless women have always been high, since 1992 there has been a substantial rise in employment among mothers, with increases being particularly large for those with children under 5 and for lone mothers. While women are working more there is no evidence of a compensating decline in employment among men in these households. These changes are reflected in household employment patterns. Harkness et al. (1997) showed that there had been a decline in the 'male breadwinner' model of household employment between 1979 and 1992. Since 1992 these changes have continued apace, with the growth in 'dual-earner' families being particularly marked for those with young children. Data on changes in household patterns of employment are reported in Table 10.1 for both couples and single women. Since the early 1990s the share of partnered women living in dual-earner households rose by 6 percentage points with the majority of this increase occurring among 'dual-career' couples with both partners working full-time. Much of this change occurred within families with children: among couples with children the share of dual-earner families grew by 6 percentage points with almost all this rise being in full-time employment. Since 1997 there has also been an even more substantial rise in employment for those with pre-school children; for this group the number of dual-earner households rose by 10 percentage points since 1993–94, with much of this rise occurred post-1997 subsequent to a series of government initiatives including increased support for childcare and improved maternity leave provision. For those with older children employment gains were much smaller, although there was a very large switch from part- to full-time employment for those with children aged 11–16.

The second panel in Table 10.1 shows employment among single women families. Again substantial changes are seen for those with children, particularly since 1998 when a series of policy reforms were introduced with the objective of raising lone parent employment. Employment has risen by 24 percentage points since 1993–94 for single mothers with children under 5, 13 percentage points for those with a youngest child aged 5–11 and 4 per cent for those whose oldest child is aged over 11. Most of this increase has been in part-time work, with full-time employment rates showing a fall among lone parents with older children. These changes, at least in part, reflect the strong effect of the introduction of Working Families Tax Credits (WFTC), and Child Tax Credits (CTC) on incentives to work a minimum of 16 hours each week.

Change in Household Hours of Paid and Unpaid Work

How have these changes in employment patterns affected hours of paid and unpaid work within households? Changes in household hours of paid and unpaid work are reported in Table 10.2. and, over more points in time for couples only, in Figure 10.2. Housework hours (defined in 'unpaid work' section above) include time spent on household tasks such as cooking, cleaning and doing the laundry, but do not include time spent caring for children. Between 1993–94 and 2003–04 average hours of paid work among women with partners rose by an average of two hours per week. As with employment, changes in hours are greatest among those with children and particularly large for those who have children under 5; average hours of paid work for all partnered women with pre-school children rose by five hours per week, to 18 hours in 2003–04. This increase in paid hours reflected two changes; first overall rises in women's employment and second an increase in the number of hours worked by those in employment. For men there was little change in average hours of work.

As paid employment rises we may expect to see some decline in the total number of hours spent on unpaid work within the home. This is indeed the case here, with average total household hours spent on unpaid work declining by five hours per week, and by eight hours for those with children under 5. This decline is a consequence of a fall in unpaid work hours among women; there is no evidence of a rise in the number of hours of unpaid work carried out by men to compensate for the greater engagement of their partners in the labour market. It is notable, too, that the decline in unpaid hours among wives is greater than the rise in hours of paid work and this may reflect improvements in women's bargaining position within the household. Nonetheless, in 2003–04 male and female patterns of work remained strongly gendered, with women undertaking 75 per cent of housework hours within the family but 38 per cent of hours of paid work.

The second panel of Table 10.2 shows hours of work for single women with and without children. A similar picture is observed here, with rising

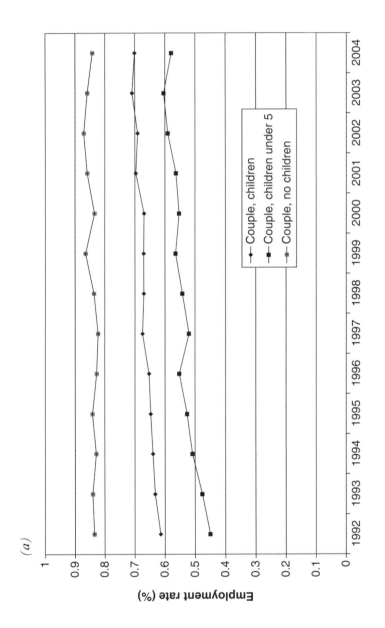

(a)

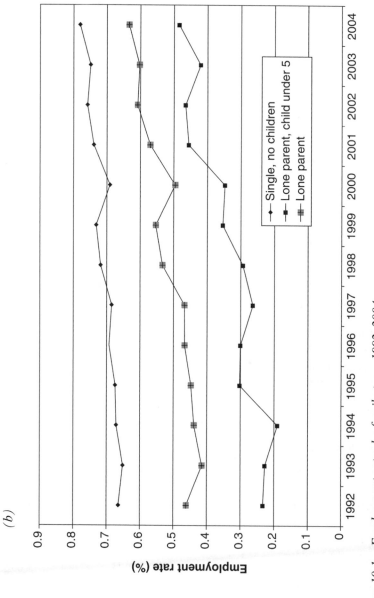

(b)

Figure 10.1 Employment rates by family type, 1992–2004

241

Table 10.1   Household work patterns (women aged 25–49, partner <65)

(a) Married and cohabiting

	Dual career (both FT)	Male FT, female PT	Male breadwinner	Female breadwinner	No earner	Sample size
All						
1993–94	0.38	0.27	0.21	0.05	0.07	3182
2003–04	0.42	0.29	0.20	0.04	0.04	2760
Change	0.04	0.02	−0.01	−0.01	−0.03	—
No dependent children						
1993–94	0.61	0.16	0.11	0.07	0.04	1213
2003–04	0.65	0.14	0.10	0.05	0.03	985
Change	0.04	−0.02	−0.01	−0.02	−0.01	—
Dependent children <16						
1993–94	0.24	0.35	0.28	0.04	0.09	1851
2003–04	0.28	0.37	0.26	0.04	0.03	1637
Change	0.04	0.02	−0.02	0.00	−0.06	—
Dependent children 12–15						
1993–94	0.40	0.36	0.13	0.05	0.06	337
2003–04	0.48	0.30	0.13	0.05	0.05	282
Change	0.08	−0.06	−0.00	0.00	−0.01	—
Dependent children 5–11						
1993–94	0.24	0.42	0.19	0.05	0.09	643
2003–04	0.29	0.42	0.20	0.05	0.03	583
Change	0.05	0.01	0.01	0.00	−0.06	—
Dependent children <5						
1993–94	0.17	0.29	0.41	0.03	0.10	871
2003–04	0.20	0.36	0.38	0.02	0.03	772
Change	0.03	0.07	−0.03	−0.01	−0.07	—

(b) Single women

	FT	PT	Not working	sample Size
All				
1993–94	0.52	0.14	0.34	1,041
2003–04	0.57	0.19	0.24	882
Change	0.05	−0.05	−0.10	—
No dependent children				
1993–94	0.73	0.09	0.18	602
2003–04	0.78	0.09	0.13	509
Change	0.05	0.00	−0.05	—

Table 10.1 (continued)

(b) Single women (continued)

	FT	PT	Not working	sample Size
Dependent children <16				
1993–94	0.23	0.19	0.58	407
2003–04	0.28	0.34	0.39	358
Change	0.05	0.15	−0.19	—
Dependent children 11–16				
1993–94	0.40	0.30	0.30	73
2003–04	0.42	0.30	0.28	94
Change	0.02	0.00	−0.02	—
Dependent children 5–11				
1993–94	0.28	0.20	0.53	197
2003–04	0.25	0.38	0.37	178
Change	−0.03	0.18	−0.16	—
Dependent children <5				
1993–94	0.08	0.13	0.79	137
2003–04	0.16	0.29	0.55	86
Change	0.08	0.16	−0.24	—

Source: British Household Panel Survey.

paid work hours and a fall in hours of unpaid work particularly among those with young children. It is notable, too, that hours of both paid and unpaid work tend be marginally lower for single women, although this is likely to reflect at least in part lower employment rates.

Of course aggregate changes mask large variations in hours of work across families with different employment patterns. Table 10.3 disaggregates hours of employment for couples and single women for all, households where the women work part-time and men full-time, and households where both work full-time. Panel (b) reports the same information for single women (all, part-time and full-time working). Looking first at all households taken together and comparing those with and without children, it is clear that men's paid and unpaid work hours are little affected by having children; in 2003–04, on average, men with children spend an extra two hours per week on paid work but no more time on unpaid work within the home. Female time use, however, continues to be heavily influenced by the presence of children; in 2003–04 those with children spent on average 21 hours on paid work compared with 34 hours for childless women but an additional six hours on unpaid work within the home. Among male

Table 10.2   Hours of paid and unpaid work within households (women aged 25–49, partner <65)

(a) Couples

	Paid work hours			Unpaid work hours		
	Wife	Husband	Total	Wife	Husband	Total
All						
1993–94	23.4	41.4	64.8	20.8	5.7	26.5
2003–04	25.2	41.7	66.9	16.2	5.5	21.7
Change	+ 1.8	+ 0.3	+ 2.1	−4.6	−0.2	−4.8
No dependent children						
1993–94	31.9	41.6	73.5	15.1	5.5	20.6
2003–04	33.5	40.4	73.8	12.2	5.5	17.7
Change	+ 1.6	−1.2	−0.3	−2.9	0.0	−2.9
Dependent children <16						
1993–94	18.1	41.7	59.8	24.4	5.7	30.1
2003–04	20.5	42.6	63.2	18.4	5.4	23.8
Change	+ 2.4	+ 0.9	+ 3.4	−6.0	−0.3	−6.3
Children <5						
1993–94	14.9	41.8	56.7	24.7	5.9	30.6
2003–04	17.8	42.9	60.7	18.7	5.2	23.9
Change	+ 2.9	+ 1.1	+ 4.0	−6.0	−0.7	−6.7

Note: Sample sizes for couples are, for paid and unpaid work respectively, 2786 (2650) for all couples, 992 (987) for those with no children, 1663 (1648) for those with dependent children; 291 (290) for those with children and 776 (769) for women with dependent children under 5. For 1993–94 samples are 3339 (3125), 1268 (1255), 1946 (1918) and 923 (915) respectively.

(b) Single women

	All		No children		Children <16		Children <5s	
	Paid	Unpaid	Paid	Unpaid	Paid	Unpaid	Paid	Unpaid
1993–94	24.5	15.1	32.8	9.3	13.0	23.0	5.8	25.9
2003–04	28.1	12.1	35.1	8.6	18.0	17.1	13.0	18.3
Change	3.6	−3.0	2.3	−0.7	5.0	−5.9	7.2	−7.6

Note: Samples sizes for single women for paid and unpaid work respectively are 841 (831) for all single women, 606 (599) for those with no children, 318 (312) for those with dependent children and 68 (67) for women with dependent children under 5. For 1993–94 samples are 1047 (1029), 510 (506), 409 (398) and 137 (134) respectively.

Source: British Household Panel Survey.

breadwinner families gender divisions are, unsurprisingly, stronger. Most notable here is that these men work longer paid hours than in dual-earner families, particularly when children are present. Where women work part-time the division of household work remains similar to where women do not work at all, with women now working 20 hours a week in paid employment, but spending four hours less on housework compared with those not working at all. Finally in 'dual-career' couples, where both partners work full-time, women spend an average of 41 hours per week in paid work. While hours are marginally lower for those with children, the data suggests that there is little accommodation in paid working hours for women who have children. Instead, adjustments in working hours come about by women moving into part-time work and working substantially fewer work hours, or out of the labour force altogether. While full-time working mothers are employed for shorter hours than their partners (39 compared with 46 hours in 2003–04) they continue to do the bulk of the housework (14 hours compared with seven), suggesting strong gender divisions remain, even where both men and women work full-time. Indeed, while women in dual full-time earner households contribute towards 46 per cent of all paid hours of work, they do 70 per cent of housework hours. Even where women are the main breadwinner (with non-working partners) men do not take on the role of being the main worker within the home.

There are also some notable changes over time. As Figure 10.2 shows, there has been a sharp fall in wives' housework hours over the past 15 years and, looking within household types in Table 10.3, it is clear that this decline is not just a result of increasing employment; women are working less within the home, whether not working or working full- or part-time. These changes could indicate that women's negotiating position has improved at home, or be a result of an increase in wealth which may mean that more households are investing in labour saving devices or hiring paid help.

Panel (b) of Table 10.3 shows hours of paid and unpaid work carried out by single women. One of the most notable findings here is that single women spend less time on household chores than those that are married, regardless of employment status. Comparing partnered and single mothers it is notable, too, that hours of paid work are lower for single mothers (mainly because single mothers are less likely to be in work). However, there are notable changes in paid hours over time, with single parents' average hours of paid work increasing by four hours per week from 1993–94, while for the majority of working lone parents, who are employed part-time hours, paid work rose from an average of 16 to 20 hours per week. Single parents working full-time put in an average of 40 hours per week and, while this is marginally longer than the time spent in paid work by full-time employed partnered mothers, the fact that single parents spend less time on

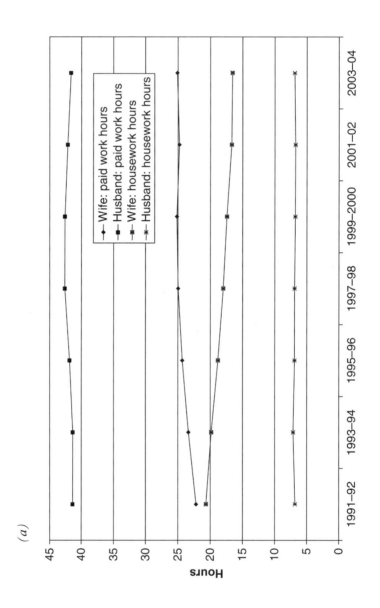

(a)

(b)

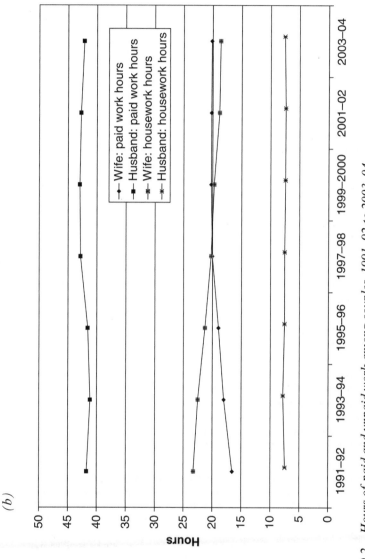

Legend:
- Wife: paid work hours
- Husband: paid work hours
- Wife: housework hours
- Husband: housework hours

Figure 10.2   Hours of paid and unpaid work among couples, 1991–92 to 2003–04

247

Table 10.3   Work hours by family work patterns

(a) Couples

	All		No children		Dependent children <16	
	Wife	Husband	Wife	Husband	Wife	Husband
1993–94						
All						
Hours paid work	23.4	41.4	31.9	41.6	18.1	41.7
Hours unpaid work	20.8	5.7	15.1	5.5	24.4	5.7
Male breadwinner						
Hours paid work	—	48.3	—	47.1	—	48.7
Hours unpaid work	28.3	4.3	25.7	4.7	29.0	4.2
Male FT, female PT						
Hours paid work	18.3	48.6	19.9	47.8	17.7	48.9
Hours unpaid work	23.6	4.8	20.6	4.6	24.5	4.8
Both working FT						
Hours paid work	41.4	48.0	41.9	45.4	39.6	48.4
Hours unpaid work	13.7	5.4	10.9	5.2	16.8	5.8
2003–04						
All						
Hours paid work	25.2	41.7	33.5	40.4	20.5	42.6
Hours unpaid work	16.2	5.5	12.2	5.5	18.4	5.4
Male breadwinner						
Hours paid work	—	46.9	—	45.3	—	47.2
Hours unpaid work	22.1	4.2	19.9	4.2	22.9	4.1
Male FT, female PT						
Hours paid work	19.5	46.7	22.4	46.5	18.9	46.7
Hours unpaid work	18.3	4.5	15.1	4.3	19.0	4.6
Dual career (both work FT)						
Hours paid work	40.8	45.8	41.9	45.4	39.1	46.2
Hours unpaid work	12.1	5.8	10.9	5.2	13.6	6.6

Notes: Sample sizes for all couples are, for paid and unpaid work respectively, in 2003–04 are 2786 (2650) for all work types, 763 (755) for male breadwinner families, 558 (554) for male FT female PT, and 1131 (1125) for dual-career families. For 1993–94 respective samples are 3339 (3125), 675 (665), 848 (839) and 751 (724). Sample sizes for all couples without children are, for paid and unpaid work respectively, in 2003–04 are 992 (987) for all work types, 241 (237) for male breadwinner families, 81 (81) for male FT female PT, and 1131 (1125) for dual-career families. For 1993–94 respective samples are 1268 (1255), 125 (123), 181 (181) and 649 (644). Sample sizes for all couples with children are, for paid and unpaid work respectively, in 2003–04 are 1663 (1648) for all work types, 451 (447) for male breadwinner families, 587 (581) for male FT female PT, and 426 (421) for dual-career families. For 1993–94 respective samples are 1946 (1918), 527 (519), 633 (625) and 430 (429).

Table 10.3   (continued)

(b) Single women

	All	No children	Dependent children <16
1993–94			
All			
Hours paid work	24.5	32.8	13.8
Hours unpaid work	15.1	9.3	22.7
Working PT			
Hours paid work	17.0	19.9	16.0
Hours unpaid work	16.2	11.2	19.1
Working FT			
Hours paid work	42.3	42.6	40.3
Hours unpaid work	8.4	7.0	11.6
2003–04			
All			
Hours paid work	28.1	35.1	18.0
Hours unpaid work	12.1	8.6	17.3
Working PT			
Hours paid work	19.8	21.6	19.8
Hours unpaid work	14.0	15.9	15.2
Working FT			
Hours paid work	42.0	42.4	40.3
Hours unpaid work	8.4	7.7	11.6

Notes: Sample sizes for all in 2003–04 are 841 (831) all, 167 (164) PT and 498 (497) FT. For those without children respective samples are 606 (599) for all, 50 (48) PT and 397 (397) FT. For those with dependent children under 16 samples are 331 (325) for all, 117 (116) PT, 101 (100) FT. Sample sizes for 1993–94 for all are 1047 (1029) all, 145 (139) PT, 567 (562) FT. For those without children they are 510 (506) for all, 55 (55) PT and 450 (447) FT. For those with dependent children in 1993–94 samples are 441 (430) for all, 90 (84) PT and 117 (115) FT.

Source: British Household Panel Survey.

household chores meant that in 2003–04 their overall work burden was slightly lower than that of 'dual-career' married mothers.

Relative Earnings

The gap in pay between men and women has narrowed substantially over recent decades for those working full-time, falling from 29 per cent in 1975 to 17 per cent in 2005.[3] For those working part-time the picture has been substantially different, with the pay gap remaining stubbornly at around 40 per cent over the past 30 years. These changes in relative wages, together with rising female employment, have had a substantial impact on the relative contribution of husbands and wives to household income. These within household changes in the relative earnings of couples are summarised in Table 10.4 for all working couples (panel a) and separately for those in which the wife works part-time (panel b) and full-time (panel c).

In 2003–04 three-quarters of wives worked and, where both partners worked, the earnings contribution of the median woman to the weekly

Table 10.4   Household employment and relative earnings, wives aged 25–49

(a) All (both partners employed)

	% working wives	Wives' median share of husbands earnings		% wives' earnings > husbands'	
		Hourly	Weekly	Hourly	Weekly
All					
1993–94	70	76	51	29	18
2003–04	75	77	55	31	20
No dependent children					
1993–94	85	83	71	34	26
2003–04	88	84	75	36	29
Dependent children <16					
1993–94	61	67	35	25	11
2003–04	68	73	43	27	14

(b) Wife works PT (partner FT)

	% PT wives	Wives' median share of husbands earnings		% wives' earnings > husbands'	
		Hourly	Weekly	Hourly	Weekly
All					
1993–94	30	60	23	20	2
2003–04	31	61	27	18	4
No dependent children					
1993–94	18	59	24	23	5
2003–04	16	54	27	7	3
Dependent children <16					
1993–94	37	61	23	20	1
2003–04	39	63	27	20	5

Table 10.4   (continued)

(c) Both FT

	% FT wives	Wives' median share of husbands earnings		% wives' earnings > husbands'	
		Hourly	Weekly	Hourly	Weekly
All					
1993–94	40	84	74	35	28
2003–04	45	87	78	38	29
No dependent children					
1993–94	67	87	81	38	31
2003–04	72	91	85	41	33
Dependent children <16					
1993–84	24	80	64	32	23
2003–04	29	83	75	35	23

Notes: In (a) sample sizes for all in 1993–94 are 1937 hourly wages (1993 weekly); 855 (876) for those with children; and 1082 (1117) for the childless. Sample sizes for all in 2003–04 were 1770 hourly wages (1825 weekly), 718 (735) for those with children and 1052 (1090) for those without children. In (b), were women work PT, sample sizes for all in 1993–94 are 761 hourly wages (773 weekly), 607 (614) for those with children and 159 (159) for the childless. Sample sizes for all in 2003–04 were 663 hourly wages (667 weekly), 556 (557) for those with children and 107 (110) for those without children. In (c), were women work FT, sample sizes for all in 1993–94 are 1053 hourly wages (1053 weekly), 380 (380) for those with children and 673 (673) for the childless. Sample sizes for all in 2003–04 were 991 hourly wages (991 weekly), 410 (410) for those with children and 581 (581) for those without children.

Source: British Household Panel Survey.

family budget stood at 55 per cent of their partners' earnings (or just over one-third of total family earnings). This relatively low earnings share is a reflection both of the relative low pay of women and the fact that women on average work fewer hours than men. To adjust for hours, relative hourly pay is also reported and shows that in 2003–04 women earned an hourly wage equivalent to 77 per cent of their partners. This may be a better reflection of women's potential to contribute to household earnings and a potentially important factor (in addition to actual earnings shares) in determining her bargaining position within the household. There is also a large variation in the share of women's earnings contribution to the family budget; in 2003–04 one-in-five women had greater weekly earnings than their partners while the share with greater hourly pay was 31 per cent. Over the preceding decade, while there has been a notable rise in the average share of earnings of women relative to men, particularly for those with children, there has been no real rise in the proportion of women out-earning their partners. This partly may reflect the fact that while employment has risen for partnered women, as women typically work shorter hours than their partners, even when working full-time, the rise in relative pay has not led to women being more likely to out-earn their partner.

This picture once again varies substantially for those with and without children; among couples without dependent children earnings of women stand at 75 per cent of male weekly pay and 84 per cent of hourly earnings while around one-third have earnings greater than their partners. On the other hand, for those with dependent children wives' median share of weekly earnings is just 43 per cent and median hourly pay stands at 73 per cent. The second and third panels of Table 10.4 look at the relative earnings for couples where the women work part-time and full-time respectively. Part-timers, with or without children, have low earnings relative to their partners with hourly pay falling to a ratio of 61 per cent (while weekly earnings were just 27 per cent). But the gap between men and women closes considerably when only full-time employees are considered, rising to close to 78 per cent of male weekly earnings and 87 per cent of hourly pay. Those with children continue to earn a relatively smaller wage share even while working full-time; 75 per cent of partners' weekly pay (compared to 85 per cent for those with no children) and 83 per cent of hourly pay (compared to 75 per cent).

UNPAID WORK WITHIN THE HOME

As female employment has risen the number of hours available for household work has fallen. In this section we ask whether, in response to these changes: (1) what has happened to total housework hours; (2) have women's housework hours fallen and (3) are men now contributing a greater share. A number of studies have looked at changes in housework hours over time. In the USA influential work by Fuchs (1986; 1988) suggested that, in spite of a fall in the pay gap, there was no improvement in the 'welfare gap' between men and women between 1960 and 1986 because gains from improved work opportunities were accompanied by a large rise in the total number of hours (both paid and unpaid) worked. However, this research was based on projections from a single time use survey. Comparing data from two time use studies Manchester and Stapleton (1991) have found a fall in total hours of work in the USA. In the UK, Jenkins and O'Leary (1997) find big changes in the composition of women's work hours (with a switch towards paid work), but relative stability in the total number of hours worked between 1974–75 and 1987. Their results also suggest some switch from traditional gender roles within households, with a universal increase in domestic work for men and a universal decrease for women. Similar findings are reported by Gershuny and Robinson (1988). Results reported in Table 10.3 show a similar picture between 1993–94 and 2003–04 for the UK, with a continued rise in hours of paid work and decline in hours of housework among women but only a very small compensating rise in time spent on housework by men and no change in paid work. For women in couples average total hours have fallen because the increase in hours of paid work (from 23 to 25 hours) has been more than offset by a decline in the amount of time spent on unpaid work (from 21 to 16 hours) leading to an overall fall in hours worked per week of almost three hours. As we have already seen these changes in women's hours of work were particularly manifest for those with children. In this section these changes are investigated further, looking at the division of different types of household tasks and the influence of hours of paid work and relative earnings on the division of labour.

Summary evidence on the division of household tasks is reported in Table 10.5. In families with a 'male breadwinner' or where women work part-time the majority of household tasks are done by women. Indeed, there is little difference in the division of labour for non-working and part-time working women; both employment types show a clear division of household labour. Yet even where there is a less clear division of paid work, where both partners work full-time, women still carry the primary responsibility for grocery shopping, cooking, cleaning and washing/ironing in half of all households. Tasks are shared in only around one-third of these families and men take on main responsibility for household tasks in a small minority of families. Paid help is one possible response to women working, and while 7 per cent of families pay for a cleaner in dual-career families (compared to 3 per cent in families where women do not work or work part-time) other household tasks are rarely contracted out. For childcare, while over half of all families share responsibility for childcare arrangements when both work full-time it remains the case that the when a child is ill the responsibility for their care remains primarily with mothers (and rarely with fathers) even when both partners are full-time employed.

To further quantify the relationship between hours of paid work and housework, Figure 10.3 shows how the time husbands and wives spend on unpaid work varies with wives' working hours. Note however that this measure of unpaid work includes only time spent on household chores and does not include time spent caring for children. Results are reported for 1992 and 2004. Wives' unpaid work hours fall substantially beyond 30 hours of paid work, while husbands' work hours show a small increase as

Table 10.5   Household tasks and wives' paid work, 1999–2004

	Mostly self	Mostly partner	Shared	Paid help	Other	Sample size
1. Grocery shopping						
All	57.0	10.5	32.2		0.4	8766
MBW	65.7	7.4	26.5		0.4	1763
Wife PT	67.9	6.6	25.4		0.1	2302
Both working FT	50.6	11.9	37.3		0.3	3571
2. Cooks						
All	60.8	11.4	26.9		0.9	8766
MBW	79.4	4.9	15.2		0.5	1763
Wife PT	76.7	5.0	18.1		0.2	2302
Both working FT	48.3	15.7	34.8		1.1	3571
3. Cleans						
All	66.6	5.2	22.2	5.3	0.7	8766
MBW	81.3	2.6	11.9	3.0	1.2	1763
Wife PT	81.1	2.6	12.6	3.1	0.6	2302
Both working FT	55.1	6.4	30.8	6.7	0.9	3571
4. Washing/ironing						
All	74.8	4.5	18.6	1.2	0.9	8766
MBW	87.6	2.2	8.3	1.4	0.6	1763
Wife PT	87.0	1.7	9.7	0.8	0.8	2302
Both working FT	67.4	4.9	25.3	1.5	0.9	3571
5. Nurses sick child						
All	70.9	9.7			19.4	3467
MBW	79.4	6.4			14.2	243
Wife PT	77.8	7.1			15.0	1674
Both working FT	59.4	11.7			28.9	1190
6. Responsible for childcare						
All	68.3	2.4	28.4		0.8	4919
MBW	81.5	6.4	11.7		0.4	1409
Wife PT	69.0	5.3	25.4		0.3	1671
Both working FT	40.3	3.4	54.0		2.3	1200

Source: British Household Panel Survey. Data is pooled for all years from 1999 to 2004.

their wives work more hours. However, women's unpaid hours remain substantially greater than those of their partners, although we do observe some decline in this gap over time mainly because women's housework hours have fallen. The relationship between the share of husbands' hours of paid work (relative to total hours) and the share of his contribution to total housework hours are graphed in Figure 10.4. A clear pattern emerges here: where husbands specialise in working in the labour market, contributing more than half of husbands' and wives' total hours of paid work, they do only a small share of the housework which further declines as specialisation increases. But even when women and men work the same hours men contribute just one-third of total housework hours. As men's share of paid work declines further their contribution to unpaid work does tend to rise, but the average contribution never rises to more than around 45 per cent of all housework hours. An exception is where men do no paid work at all; in this case they contribute an even smaller share of housework hours, just one-quarter of the total. This may support notions of 'identity' as a driving force behind observed patterns of male and female work behaviour; the loss of male identity associated with not working may be compensated for by a declining contribution to (female) household tasks.

While Becker's (1991) theories of specialisation explain how men and women may allocate their time to paid and unpaid work, more recent theories emphasise bargaining within marriage with the bargaining power of each party being strongly dependent on their outside options. As female wages rise the negotiating position of women is strengthened and this may impact on the division of labour within the home. A woman's ability to command resources (in the form of earnings), rather than just her allocation of time, will in this case effect the division of domestic labour. Raw data on earnings shares of husbands and wives are reported in Table 10.6. For wives, as earnings rise relative to those of their husbands', housework hours fall. There are differences however between those with and without children: for those with no children hours do not vary greatly with earnings, for those with children on the other hard there is a clear fall in housework hours, up until the point that male and female earnings are roughly equal but as earnings shares rise further women tend to do increasing housework hours. This finding is in line with a number of US studies. Bittman et al. (2003), for example, found that women decrease their housework hours as earnings rise up until the point at which they contribute equally (in line with exchange-bargaining theory). However, where women earn more than their partners they also are found to do more housework. Similar empirical findings are reported by Akerlof and Kranton (2000) who suggest that this result can be explained by notions of identity; women who earn more than their partners lose utility (or satisfaction) because of this reversal of gender roles and in order to restore identity women respond by taking on a greater share of housework. The male share of total housework hours is plotted against the male share of paid work hours in Figure 10.5. As with working hours, men's contribution to total housework hours rises as the share of their contribution to family earnings

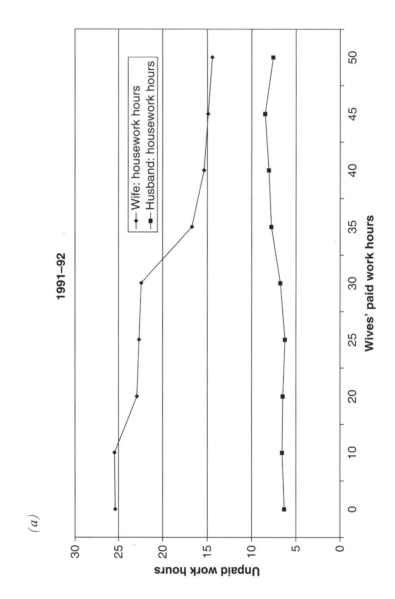

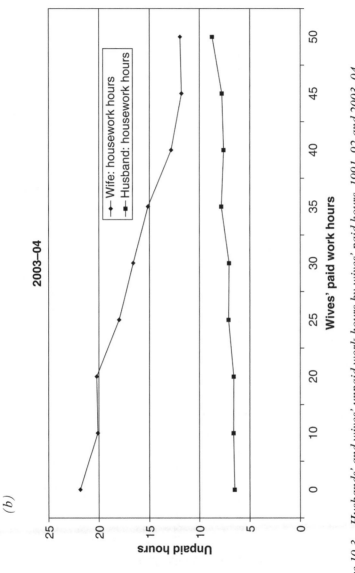

Figure 10.3   Husbands' and wives' unpaid work hours by wives' paid hours, 1991–92 and 2003–04

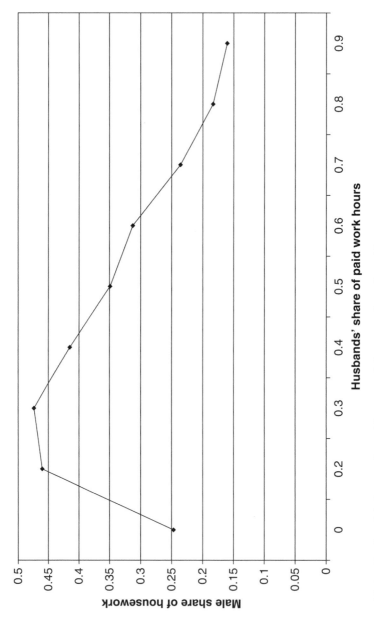

Figure 10.4 Husbands' shares of total housework hours and total paid hours

Table 10.6   Hours of housework and relative weekly earnings, 2003–04

Share of partner's weekly earnings	Hours Housework					
	All		No dependent children		Dependent children <16	
	Wife	Husband	Wife	Husband	Wife	Husband
<50%	18	5	14	4	19	5
50–75%	13	6	11	6	15	6
75–90%	12	6	10	5	14	6
90–100%	12	6	9	5	15	7
100–110%	11	6	9	6	12	7
110–120%	11	6	10	6	13	6
120% +	11	6	9	5	14	7
Sample size	2795		991		1804	

Source: British Household Panel Survey.

falls up until the point where men earn 20 per cent of total earnings (at which point their share of housework rises to 40 per cent). Below this point men's share of the housework again declines. As with the share of paid work hours, this story is again consistent with female gains, due to increased bargaining power, up until the point at which there is gender role reversal at which point the identity theory suggested by Akerlof and Kranton appears to lead to an increased contribution of women within the home.

Most empirical studies on household work look at the number of hours individuals spend on unpaid tasks taking into account variations by age, employment and the presence of dependent children. However, time use studies in particular rarely collect information on both partners in the household. Coverman (1985) suggests that factors which influence the division of housework include (1) resources (including education and earnings) both in absolute terms and relative to spouses, (2) attitudes towards gender roles and (3) the availability of time. Presser (1994) provides a detailed discussion of the motivation for inclusion of these controls, and a similar set of explanatory variables are used by Hersch and Stratton (1994). In order to examine the joint effect of a range of factors on the share of household work, we estimate a tobit model over the period 1992 to 2004, with men's share of total housework hours the dependent variable and a set of employment, demographic and income variables included as explanatory variables.[4] This model is similar to that estimated by Akerlof and Kranton (2000). We also include a series of year of birth

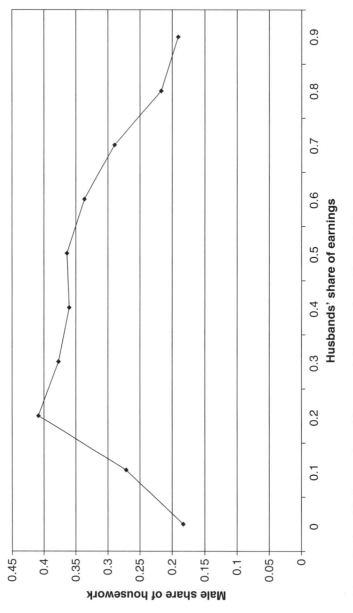

Figure 10.5 Husbands' shares of total housework hours and total household earnings

Table 10.7 Marginal effects from a tobit model of the share of husbands in total housework hours

	Model 1	Model 2	Model 3
Share of work hours	−0.06***	—	−.11***
Share of weekly earnings	—	−0.33***	—
Ratio of male/female hourly earnings	—	—	−.02***
Total family earnings (log)	0.03***	0.04***	0.04***
Wife's education (omitted category below A level)			
Degree	0.06***	0.04***	0.06***
As-Higher	0.03***	0.02***	0.03***
Employment			
Male spouse not employed	0.14***	0.13***	0.10***
Wife not working	−0.13***	−0.32***	−0.16***
Women's age (grouped, omitted category 25–29)			
30–34	−0.00	−0.00	−0.00
35–39	−0.02*	−0.04**	−0.03**
40–44	−0.02	−0.02**	−0.02**
45–49	−0.03**	−0.04***	−0.05***
Birth cohort (omitted category 1940s)			
1950–59	0.02**	0.01	0.01
1960–69	0.07***	0.04***	0.04**
1970–1980	0.08***	0.04***	0.05***
Age of youngest child (compared with no children)			
Youngest <5	−0.04***	−0.03***	−0.04***
Youngest 5–10	−0.04***	−0.02***	−0.03***
Youngest 11–16	−0.04***	−0.03***	−0.03***
Observations	7200	6370	6334

Note: *** Significant at 10%; ** significant at 5%; *** significant at 1%.

Source: British Household Panel Survey.

cohort dummies as these may influence the division of housework if cultural norms and attitudes have changed across generations.

The marginal effects from the tobit model of the share of men's contribution to total housework hours are reported in Table 10.7. The reported coefficients can be interpreted as the change in the share of housework resulting from a unit change in the independent variables at their mean values. The results show that men do a larger share of housework when total family earnings are higher and where women are better educated, younger and employed. Over and above age, year of birth matters with those born in more recent decades contributing substantially more unpaid labour than earlier generations; the partners of women born in the 1970s contribute around 8 per cent more to the share of household chores than those born in the 1950s. As expected, having children is associated with men doing a smaller share of household chores, mostly because the increase in total housework associated with having children is done almost entirely by women. Of most interest here are the coefficients on the share of work hours and relative earnings. The findings reported here confirm our descriptive results showing that men who contribute a greater share of paid work hours do a smaller share of housework. But, relative earnings have an even larger effect, with increased weekly earnings shares of men being associated with a very large reduction in housework shares. Model 3 reports results when both relative hourly pay and hours of work are modelled together; both have an important influence on men's contribution to household work, with housework shares falling both as relative hours and earnings rise.

The reported results suggest that there have been some important cultural changes over time, with the partners of women born in the 1960s and 1970s making a substantially greater contribution to household chores compared to women born earlier. These changes in behaviour may suggest that there has been a reduction in gender stereotyping over time. To investigate this further we look at the contribution of boys and girls within the home using data from the 2002 to 2004 youth files of the BHPS. This suggests that boys and girls still grow up making very different contributions to household work. Table 10.8 reports basic descriptive statistics from the BHPS youth files. Clear differences between genders emerge with 36 per cent of boys doing little or no housework compared with 23 per cent of girls, while 11 per cent of boys spend more than four hours doing housework each week compare with 18 per cent of girls.

We have already seen that when women do more paid work there is very little compensating increase in the amount of time spent on unpaid work within the home by their partners. While a minority of households do buy in paid help when wives work, this is not the case for the vast majority. Could it be the case that instead of husbands doing more, more housework is instead being done by children? In the second and third panels of Table 10.8 we report young peoples' housework hours in two- and one-parent families by employment status. In two-parent families strong gender divisions between girls and boys remain, with these differences being particularly stark in male breadwinner families. While children do more housework when there mothers work, these differences are relatively small. But children in lone-parent families behave quite

Table 10.8 *Young people's (aged 11–16) contribution to household work, 2001–04*

(a) All young people

Doing/helping with housework	Boys %	Girls %
Don't do/less 1 hr	36	23
1–3 hours	53	59
4–6 hours	9	14
7 or more hours	2	4
Sample size	763	798

(b) Young people in two-parent families and parental employment

Doing/helping with housework	All		Male Breadwinner		Wife PT		Wife FT	
	Boys %	Girls %	Boys %	Girls %	Boys %	Girls %	Boys %	Girls %
Don't do/less 1 hr	35	22	37	14	34	25	33	19
1–3 hours	54	59	54	70	55	57	55	60
4+ hours	10	19	9	16	11	18	12	20
Sample size	609	647	125	112	205	235	212	227

(c) Young people in lone-parent families and parental employment

Doing/helping with housework	All		Not working		Working	
	Boys %	Girls %	Boys %	Girls %	Boys %	Girls %
Don't do/less 1 hr	40	26	55	33	26	22
1–3 hours	47	60	28	52	63	66
4+ hours	13	14	17	16	11	13
Sample size	154	151	69	61	85	90

Source: British Household Panel Survey youth files, data pooled for years 2001–2004.

differently: while children in lone-parent families do less on average than those in two-parent families, their contribution within the home is strongly dependent on whether their mothers work. And while for non-working lone parents there is a large gender gap in the contribution of boys and girls to household chores, once their parent goes to work their contribution to the home rises markedly, particularly for boys, and the gender gap all but disappears. This is the case whether their parent works full- or part-time.

CONCLUSIONS

This chapter has looked at the effect of the rapid rise in women's economic position in the labour market on patterns of household employment, hours of paid and unpaid work, and the division of tasks within the home. Since 1992 improved labour market opportunities for women have led to a continued decline in the 'male breadwinner' model of household employment and a rise in 'dual-earner' families. Almost all this change has occurred within families with children and has been dominated by increases in dual-earning families where both partners work full-time. The net effect of rising female employment has been a large rise in the number of hours of labour market work within families, although wide variations between families remain. How have these changes affected the division of unpaid labour within the home? Results presented here show that there has been a five-hour fall in the total number of hours spent on housework each week, mainly because women are spending less time on unpaid work (and there is no evidence of a compensating rise in the number of unpaid hours carried out by men). Most striking, however, is that the observed decline in wives' unpaid hours has more than fully offset the rise in the number of hours they spend in paid work.

Of course, aggregate changes may mask variations across different family types. Taking account of differences in employment patterns declining housework hours appear to be not just a result of rising employment; it is also the case that women are working less within the home whether not employed, or employed part- or full-time. Looking in greater depth at patterns of specialisation, while among male breadwinner families and in those families where women work part-time, gender divisions in paid and unpaid work are unsurprisingly strong. It is also the case that clear gender divisions in unpaid work remain even when both partners work full-time. A more detailed analysis shows that when husbands specialise in labour market work, contributing more than half of the families' total hours of paid work, they do only a small share of housework. But even when women and men work the same number of paid hours, men's contribution to housework rises to just one-third of the total. Indeed, as roles are reversed in the labour market, with men's share of labour market hours falling below 50 per cent, their contribution to household hours rises but never goes beyond 45 per cent of total unpaid hours. An exception is where men do no paid work. In this case they contribute an even smaller share of housework hours, just one-quarter of the total, suggesting that notions of 'identity' may play an important role in driving observed patterns of male and female work behaviour.

When do men contribute more within the home? On average men's housework shares rise with total family earnings and where their wives are younger and better educated. Men's housework contribution is additionally influenced heavily both by shares of hours of paid work and shares of earnings: men who contribute a greater share of paid work hours or have greater earnings power than their wives do a much smaller share of housework. Having children is of enormous importance too, and associated with men doing a much smaller share of household chores, mostly because the increase in total housework associated with having children is done almost entirely by women.

How do single women compare with those with partners? Results reported here suggest that both hours of paid and unpaid work tend be marginally lower for single women. For those with children this is particularly true, mainly because single mothers are much less likely to be in work. Yet when single parents work full-time they put in an average of 40 hours per week, and while this is marginally longer than the time spent in paid work by full-time employed partnered mothers, the fact that single parents spent less time on household chores meant that in 2003–04 their overall work burden was slightly lower than that of 'dual-career' married mothers.

The evidence presented in this chapter has shown that for women the past decade has seen profound changes in women's work hours. While the evidence suggests that there has been some decline in 'specialisation', in 2003–04 male and female patterns of work remained strongly gendered, with women undertaking 75 per cent of housework hours within the family but 38 per cent of hours of paid work. For men there is little evidence of changes in average hours of work, inside or out of the home, over the last decade. Instead it is women's work behaviour that has changed, with these changes being particularly profound for those with children. However, the assumption that children only affect women's time use remains largely true; for women who work full-time there is little accommodation in their working hours if they have children and, instead, mothers tend to adjust their work patterns either by leaving the labour market altogether or moving to part-time work. While the evidence presented suggests that patterns of work within the home have been relatively slow to adjust to changes in women's labour market position, it does appear to be the case that there has been greater progress among more recent generations; the partners of women born in the 1970s contributed around 8 per cent more to the share of household chores than those born in the 1950s. This may suggest some optimism for the future. However, substantial gender stereotyping remains, as evidence from the housework contributions of 11- to 15-year-old boys and girls shows. Finally, the evidence presented from the BHPS suggests that the rise in women's paid work hours has been accompanied by a decline in total unpaid work hours. The resulting fall in the overall burden of work may lead to benefits for both women and children if the decline in unpaid work hours has allowed mothers to spend more time with their children.

NOTES

1. Source: Labour Force Survey.
2. See, for example, *Observer*, 26 May 2002.
3. Sources: 1975, New Earnings Survey; 2005, Annual Survey of Hours and Earnings.
4. The tobit model is a special case of censored regression model where the dependent variable is in this case censored, lying between the values of zero and one.

REFERENCES

Akerlof, G.A. and R.E. Kranton (2000), 'Economics and identity', *Quarterly Journal of Economics*, **115**(3), 715–53.

Becker, G. (1991), *A Treatise on the Family*, Cambridge, MA: Harvard University Press.

Bittman, M., P. England and N. Folbre (2003), 'When does gender trump money? Bargaining and time in household work', *American Journal of Sociology*, **109**(1), 186–214.

Bonke, J (2005), 'Paid work and unpaid work: diary information versus questionnaire information', *Social Indicator Research*, **70**, 349–68.

Coverman, S. (1985), 'Explaining husbands' participation in domestic labor', *The Sociological Quarterly*, **26**(1), 81–97.

Fuchs, V. (1986), 'His and hers: gender differences in work and income, 1959–1979', *Journal of Labor Economics*, **4**(3), pt 2 (July), S245–S272, Journal of Labor Economics Conference Volume.

Fuchs, V. (1988), *Women's Quest for Economic Equality*, Cambridge, MA: Harvard University Press.

Gershuny, J. and J. Robinson (1988), 'Historical changes in the household division of Labour', *Demography*, **25**(4), 537–52.

Gershuny, J., M. Bittman and J. Brice (2005), 'Exit, voice, and suffering: do couples adapt to changing employment patterns?', *Journal of Marriage and Family*, **67**(3), 656–65.

Harkness, S., S. Machin and J. Waldfogel (1997), 'Evaluating the pin money hypothesis: the relationship between women's labour market activity, family income and poverty in Britain', *Journal of Population Economics*, **10**(2), 137–58.

Hersch, J. and L. Stratton (1994), 'Housework, wages, and the division of housework time for employed spouses', *American Economic Review*, **84**(2), 120–25.

Jenkins, S.J. and N.C. O'Leary (1997), 'Gender differentials in domestic work, market work, and total work time: UK time budget survey evidence for 1974/5 and 1987', *Scottish Journal of Political Economy*, **44**(2), 153–64.

Kitterød, R.H. and T.H. Lyngstad (2005), 'Diary versus questionnaire information on time spent on housework – the case of Norway', *Electronic International Journal of Time Use Research*, **2**, 13–32.

Manchester, J.M. and D.C. Stapleton (1991), 'On measuring the progress of women's quest for economic equality', *Journal of Human Resources*, **26**(3), 562–80.

Observer (2002), 'Hewitt: end this macho work culture', by G. Hinsliff, 26 May, http://observer.guardian.co.UK/politics/story/o,,722397,00.html (accessed 27 January 2008).

Office for National Statistics (1975), *New Earnings Survey*, Office for National Statistics, UK.

Office for National Statistics (2005), *Annual Survey of Hours and Earnings*, Office for National Statistics, UK.

Organisation for Economic Co-operation and Development (OECD) (2002), *Employment Outlook*, Paris: OECD.

Pollak, R.A. (2007), 'Family bargaining and taxes: a prolegomenon to the analysis of joint taxation', IZA Discussion Paper No. 3109, available at SSRN: http://ssrn.com/abstract=1029916 (accessed 29 January 2008).

Presser, H.B. (1994), 'Employment schedules among dual-earner spouses and the division of household labor by gender', *American Sociological Review*, **59**, 348–64.

11. Work–family balance policies: issues and development in the UK 1997–2005 in comparative perspective

Jane Lewis

INTRODUCTION: WORK–FAMILY BALANCE AS A POLICY PROBLEM

The way in which adult men and women balance their family and employment responsibilities was historically considered to be a private responsibility. However, many continental European countries accepted a role for the state in helping to 'reconcile' work and family long before the UK, which has only begun to see this issue as territory for state intervention since 1998. All Western countries have experienced more public debate about the issue of work–family balance, including the USA where the state has intervened least but where literature on the 'crisis of care' and the 'time squeeze' is most common.[1] And in European Union (EU) member states over the past decade this policy field has been one of the few to show expansion cross-nationally (Daly 2005).

Indeed, what is happening at the family and the household level in terms of changes in the behaviour of men and women and the nature of the contributions they make to family life is increasingly driving policy. For household-level change has been linked to a number of interrelated concerns about changes in family form and family instability, about low fertility and population ageing, and about the welfare of children, alongside the perceived need to maximise male and female labour market participation in order to promote competitiveness and growth.

The relationship between paid work and social provision has always been central to the development of modern welfare states. At the beginning of the twentieth century the nature of the relationship was hammered out only in respect of men; women and children were treated as dependents and it was assumed that women would take primary responsibility for housework and carework. Changes in the contributions to families made by women, especially in the form of increased earnings, have thrown the whole basis of the welfare settlement at the household level into question. The consequences of family and labour market change may be conceptualised in terms of 'new social risks' (Bonoli 2005), which turn on how the care of children and other dependents will be accomplished in the new circumstances, and, increasingly, how people will be enabled to have the number of children they want.[2]

In this context it is possible to see how state policies that help people to fulfil their responsibilities as carers for dependent family members and as paid workers by providing care services or leaves to carry out caring responsibilities, are seen as serving a wide – probably impossibly wide (Dex 2003) – range of policy goals: addressing the challenges of an ageing society (by enabling women to work and thereby improving the dependency ratio), and falling fertility rates (thought to be exacerbated by lack of supports for women as workers). In some places work–family reconciliation has been seen additionally as the best way of tackling child poverty (in the UK, by encouraging and enabling mothers – especially lone mothers – to work), and children's educational achievement (in the UK and Germany, by promoting high-quality early learning in nursery settings). Some of governments' interventions have also focused on galvanising employers to put in place some form of what used to be called 'family-friendly' policies in respect of working time, and what are now more likely to be called 'work–life balance' policies.

Policy-makers often refer to work–family balance issues either in gender-neutral terms, or as ways of making it possible for women to reconcile work and family responsibilities, and thus increase their labour market participation. The push towards the resulting 'adult worker model family' (Lewis, J. 2001), in which women and men are responsible for participating in the labour market, is a trend common to all Western countries. It has been made particularly explicit at the EU level (Lewis 2006), where setting benchmarks for the provision of formal childcare services in member states, for example, was conceptualised instrumentally as a way of achieving the targets for female labour force participation. But women have continued to bear the brunt of care work in families in all Western countries; women have changed their labour market behaviour much faster and to a much greater degree than men have changed their participation in domestic work (Gershuny 2000). If gender equality is to enter the frame as a policy goal, this means that work–family balance policies must also address the role of men as fathers. This chapter explores, first, the wider context for policy development in this field, looking both at the existing models for combining work and family responsibilities in different Western countries and the evidence we have as to how men and women want to balance paid and unpaid work. It then looks more specifically at the gender issues in work–family balance policy development and particularly at the problem of deciding what might constitute gender equality in this policy area, and the possibilities for an effective 'policy package'. Finally, it outlines what has happened in the UK since 1997, the tensions that exist between the policies pursued, and the extent to which polices are likely to further gender equality.

CONTEXT: EXISTING MODELS OF PROVISION

Work–family balance policies have grown up in very different ways in different countries, in respect of their form, extent and concentration. For example, the UK has historically done more to provide care for elderly people than for children, whereas in France, Belgium and Italy the reverse has been the case. Furthermore, the *policy logics* underpinning various *policy packages* differ considerably from country to country.

Only in the USA and in some of the Nordic countries have policies been based on the assumption that men and women will be fully engaged in the labour market. However, ways of reconciling work and family look very different in these two parts of the world. In the US case, the obligation to enter the labour market is embedded in an ungenerous welfare system, whereas in Scandinavia, it is supported by an extensive range of care entitlements in respect of children and older people. The Nordic model treats women as workers, but then makes allowance for difference, grafting on transfers and services in respect of care work for partnered and unpartnered mothers alike. Hobson (2004) has described the Swedish variant as a 'gender participation model', focusing as it does on promoting gender equality in employment and providing 'supports' via cash (for parental leaves) and services in the form of care for children and elderly dependents.[3]

Thus, the USA operates a fiercely gender-neutral, equality-defined-as-sameness adult worker model, with very few supports for care work,[4] although the market provides good access to affordable (but not necessarily good quality) childcare. Schmid (2000) has referred to this market provision as the reinvention of domestic service, using, as it often does, migrant workers. Scandinavia operates what is in practice, but not in name, a gender-differentiated 'supported adult worker model', with high penetration of services for the care of children and elderly people, and cash transfers in respect of parental leave. As a result, moderately high proportions of women work (long) part-time hours, exercising their right to work a six-hour day when they have pre-school children, as well as leaving the labour market for up to three years if they have a second child within two years of the first child. It must also be noted that the Swedish labour market is the most sexually segregated in the Western world. Swedish women have more choice about combining work and care, but at the expense of inequality in respect of vertical labour market segregation. The introduction of the 'daddy quota' in the Scandinavian countries, whereby men are obliged to take part of the parental leave allocation (usually a month or two) or lose it altogether, was aimed at promoting greater gender equality in unpaid work, something that would also begin to tackle labour market inequalities (Leira 1998).

Other Western European countries have moved substantially towards assuming the existence of an adult worker model family, but in practice still operate a model in which women who work part-time are only partially economically autonomous. Thus the Netherlands and the UK have changed the nature of entitlements for lone-mother families, such that women with school-age children are encouraged to seek employment, the main motives being the wish on the part of governments to address the issue of child poverty and to limit public expenditure on cash benefits for this group. However, incentives for the female partners of unemployed and employed men to enter the labour market are ambiguous in the UK, where the operation of a welfare system for adults that relies on means-tested social assistance rather than social insurance (Rake 2000). Reform of the tax/benefit system such that low-paid jobs are subsidised via tax credits (similar in principle more than in practice to the USA's earned income tax credit), have served to extend the hours of part-time work, but the vast majority of mothers of young children in the UK (and in Germany and the Netherlands) continue to work relatively short part-time hours (the 2004 European Social Survey shows over a quarter of mothers with children under 12 work under 20 hours in these countries).[5] Cash benefits have recently been made available via the tax credit system for the purchase of childcare, mainly to lone parents, but 45 per cent of childcare in the UK is funded by parents, compared, for example, to 23 per cent in former West Germany, and there is no paid, parental leave and only limited, poorly paid, paternity leave in the UK. Thus, while the UK has opted to move towards a 'supported' rather than an 'unsupported' adult worker model since 1997, much more attention has been paid to investing in childcare services, which are more likely to result in women 'choosing' to enter employment (Lewis, J. 2002). In the Netherlands, part-time work is still explicitly the preferred way of reconciling work and family for men and women in terms of the policy discourse and survey evidence on revealed preferences (Knijn 2004). In Germany, too, providing women (but not men) with the 'choice' to work *or* care remains an important part of the political debate (Ostner 2004).

   Labour market policies, particularly those regarding working time, have
increasingly been recognised as a crucial part of the policy logic informing
work–family reconciliation (Dex 2003; Lewis, S. 2002). However, notwithstanding the European Commission's (EC's) 1993 Directive limiting
working hours, the organisation of working time remains largely the pre-
rogative of employers. For example, while in Sweden, the Netherlands and
Germany parents have the right to reduce their working hours, in the UK,
parents with children under 6 have a weaker right to *request* flexible
working hours. The UK also retains the right to an individual opt-out from
the EC's 1993 Directive and thus may work more than 48 hours a week.
This is important because in the UK, perhaps in order to compensate in
what remains, relative to other Western European countries, a low-wage
economy, men with young dependent children work the longest hours in the
EU. The more flexible labour markets of the English-speaking countries
also have higher rates of 'shift parenting' (Dex et al. 2005; La Valle et al.
2002). In addition, low-wage, flexible labour markets have implications for
the welfare of carers in the formal sector. The welfare trade-offs and the
politics of choice in respect of care are complicated, and have the potential
to pit men against women, carers against care-receivers, and carers against
non-carers.
   It is possible to discern ideas about what is appropriate for women in particular to do in respect of work and care in all these different kinds of
arrangements. The choices that men and women make in respect of balancing work and care are structured to some extent – it is very difficult to determine how much – by social policies. In some countries the desire to promote
an adult worker model family is stronger in respect of some groups of
women (particularly lone mothers) than in others. In the USA and
Scandinavia the assumption that all adults will be in the labour market is
strongest. But in Scandinavia, sufficient 'policy supports' in the form of cash
compensation for care are provided to permit women to choose to care, and
these countries effectively operate a 'one-and-three-quarter-earner model
family'. To the extent that the 'policy supports' are gender neutral, men are
also permitted to choose to care, but labour market segregation means that
men are likely, as in other countries, to be in better paying, private sector
jobs and, again as is the case elsewhere, to experience work cultures that are
often unsympathetic to leaves for caring (hereafter referred to as 'care
leaves'). In the USA, women can choose to work (there is an ample supply
of affordable, but not necessarily high-quality, childcare), but it is much
harder to choose to care. In the UK and the Netherlands, the pendulum shift
in the treatment of lone mothers – from mothers to workers – has affected
the behaviour of this group of women, and in these countries and in
Germany recent increases in social expenditure on care have been focused

as much or more on service rather than cash provision, with the aim of promoting female employment more generally. However, part-time work remains the main way of reconciling work and family in these countries.

GENDER ISSUES AND WORK–FAMILY BALANCE POLICIES

Work–family balance involves the distribution of paid and unpaid work and is an inherently gendered issue, which necessarily raises the question of what people want as well as what the goals of governments are. This is a very vexed issue. Hakim (2000) argues that women's position in the labour market is a function of their preferences and that structural constraints are becoming less significant. If Hakim's conclusion that behaviour is a matter of revealed preferences is correct, then there are no policy issues in respect of gender equality. However, her emphasis on the importance of 'choice' and her assumptions regarding the stability of preferences has been subjected to fierce criticism (for example, Crompton 2006; McRae 2003). There is evidence of a gap between actual and preferred working hours for men and for women in couple families with children under 6 in all EU15 countries, with some evidence that both men and women prefer to work 'long part-time' hours (OECD 2001: 135–7). On the other hand, in the UK, there is little evidence of the demand for flexible working being linked to family responsibilities (Hogarth et al. 2001; MacInnes 2005). In addition, a 2004 Eurobarometer survey of 5688 men over 18 in EU15 found that 84 per cent had either not taken or were not thinking of taking parental leave, which seems to cast doubt over the extent to which men want to change the balance they have between paid and unpaid work.

These kinds of data are enormously hard to interpret. People can report views that appear to be incompatible, and their meanings are often difficult to unravel. For example, fathers' lobby groups, such as – in the UK – fathers 4justice, campaign for absent fathers to have more contact with their children, but this leaves open what kind of care they envisage providing. In the case of mothers, it has been suggested that they may have a different sense of personal entitlement from fathers (Major 1993), which may make them disinclined to express dissatisfaction with the gendered division of work.[6] Preferences interpreted as simple 'wants' are unlikely to account either for behaviour or for what people say they would like to happen, because they are culturally, socially and economically embedded. Thus men and women may be expressing ideas about their own identities, about the 'proper thing to do' (Finch 1989), and about their assessment of what the options are. In the case of childcare in the UK, for example, they may believe that provision in their neighbourhood may be either too expensive or of insufficiently high quality, because historically it is likely to have been so. There is evidence to suggest that some groups of women do attach greater importance to their role as mothers than to their role as workers (see, for example, Duncan and Edwards, 1999, on lone mothers in the UK). In addition, cultural differences between countries exist (Pfau-Effinger 1998); Trzcinski (2000) has suggested that Germany has taken a 'different route' to equality, due to the widespread desire expressed by mothers to stay at home. Furthermore, individuals may have different ideas as to what constitutes equality at different points in their life course (Rapoport et al. 2002).

Thus choice is likely to be important, but it is also likely to be embedded in a range of structural factors and personal experiences. It is difficult to justify the assumption that people's behaviour necessarily reflects what they want to happen. Thus the *terms and conditions* under which the shift to an adult worker model family takes place are likely to be important. State policies are but one determinant of those terms and conditions, and a causal relationship between them and behaviour is remarkably difficult to demonstrate. However, different policy options do have different incentive and disincentive effects regarding the allocation of paid and unpaid work, as the next section shows, and are likely to have a more determining role the more co-ordinated and coherent the policy package (Hantrais 2004: 184). First, though, we need to consider the additionally vexed issue of what might constitute gender equality in terms of work–family balance.

The goals of governments in promoting work–family balance are diverse, but gender equality in and for itself is rarely at the top of the list. Indeed, in the UK, it has been hardly articulated at all; policy documents have striven for gender neutrality rather than gender equality. It is very difficult to define gender equality in the context of work–family balance policies. The age-old problem of equality-as-sameness or equality-as-difference is central to this problem. If the aim is sameness, in the context of work–family balance this translates for feminists into an equal division of paid and unpaid work between men and women: a citizen worker/carer model. This has been espoused by Fraser (1997) on the basis of philosophical argument, and by Gornick and Meyers (2003) as a result of their empirical research. However, for policy-makers, equality as sameness is as likely to be construed in terms of making women more like men, especially in respect of the male career model. But if equality consists of recognising difference or diversity, then policy should seek to reward women's disproportionate amount of care work, albeit at the risk of perpetuating this work as women's responsibility.

Both the definitions of equality in terms of sameness and difference focus on the outcomes we might wish to see. But this starting point is difficult in respect of family policies because they tend to be more value-laden than other social policies (Strohmeir 2002: 346). Hertz (1999) noted the extent to which the whole idea of balancing work and family may be a euphemism for competing ideologies about childrearing. Using cross-national evidence, Kremer (2005) has also stressed the importance of different ideals of mothering, in respect of childcare, at different times in different countries (for example, professional, surrogate mothering, or parental sharing) and their influence on policy-makers. It is certainly note-worthy that most Western and Northern European welfare states rely on ideas about best practice in terms of caring for children, so that, usually, some form of leave (taken mainly by mothers) will cover the child's early years, followed by extensive provision of childcare services. An exception is Finland, where, notwithstanding the existence of long 'home-care leaves' (introduced during the period of economic crisis in the early 1990s), parents have the right to choose between formal, institutional childcare provision and leaves for children under 3 (OECD 2005). Such a policy is more likely to provide the opportunity for making a 'genuine choice' between paid and unpaid work.

Governments are concerned to provide 'choice' in modern social provision and, not surprisingly, are reluctant to make policy that might be construed as prescribing behaviour within the private sphere of the family, although in many countries there has been notably less reluctance to prescribe behaviour in the case of lone mothers. However, the meaning of 'choice' in this policy field is often value-laden. As Morgan and Zippel (2003) have pointed out, right-wing parties in continental Europe have often justified policies that provide cash for care, usually via parental leave programmes, in terms of giving women more choice as to whether to work or care. It is women who tend to use these benefits to stay at home, especially if they are low paid and have low educational qualifications, thus the policy ends up supporting a more traditional gendered division of work. The right-of-centre Danish government abandoned 'daddy leave' in 2002 on the grounds that it interfered with men's freedom to choose (in fact this was not the case: daddy leave is a 'use it or lose it' policy and is thus compatible with the goal of providing a genuine choice to work or care). Given the difficulties in interpreting what people want by way of work–family balance, together with the difficulties in prioritising any form of gender equality within most governments' work–family balance policies, it may be strategic for those concerned about gender equality, as well democratic, to focus on inputs and to aim for policies that maximise *genuine* choice for men and women in respect of work–family balance.

But a gender equality strategy in the field of 'work and family reconciliation' has to face the difficult issue of what Baldock and Hadlow (2004) have termed the 'male veto'. Is it possible or desirable to 'force' men to do more unpaid work? 'Compulsion to care' threatens the moral qualities of attentiveness, responsibility, competence and responsiveness identified by the feminist theorists of care (for example, Tronto 1993). Yet men's choice not to care affects women's choices on whether and how to combine paid and unpaid work. If care is a universal human need (Nussbaum 1999; Sen 1999), then it has to be done and warrants a central place in policy-making. Arguably, it has to be possible for anyone to choose to do it, as a matter of both principle and pragmatic policy-making. For, given that informal care usually involves emotion and love *as well as* labour, and passive 'watching over' *as well as* active tending, it is highly unlikely that it will be possible fully to commodify it. In other words, policy must make it possible to exercise what Sen (1999) terms 'real agency freedom' – a genuine choice to do carework (Lewis and Giullari 2005). Policies such as 'daddy leave', which provide an incentive for men to choose to care (because the time set aside for the father to take leave will be lost to the family if he does not take it) thus acquire considerable significance. Work–family policies that take gender equality seriously must address the issue of what happens at the household level, and it may be, as Bianchi and Casper (2004) have suggested, that further enlargement of choices for women depends on men changing their behaviour, and in particular on changes to the male career norm (see also Lewis, S. 2001).

Real or genuine choice to engage in paid and unpaid work for men and women requires a policy package that addresses the possibility of first, being able to care, which requires care leaves that are paid, and/or reduced or more flexible working hours; and, second, the possibility of being able to work, which requires the provision of care services and/or money to buy services. Because work–family balance policies have many goals, governments will often tend to put their policy eggs in a single basket, depending on current priorities. Thus, at EU and member-state levels, the desire to increase female labour market participation, in order to maximise competitiveness and growth and as a means of tackling child poverty, has meant that since the late 1990s much more attention has focused on the provision of childcare services, which are more likely to encourage women into the labour market. In 2002, the Barcelona Council set targets for the provision of childcare services to reach 90 per cent of children between 3 and school age and 33 per cent of under 3s. Care services are likely to be the most effective work–family balance policy for stimulating women's entry to the labour market.

Indeed, much of the increase in state intervention in this policy field has been directed towards what the continental European literature has called 'work–family reconciliation' measures for *women*, to enable them to combine paid and unpaid work. But Windebank (2001) has argued that these kinds of state policies make it possible for men to continue to avoid taking care responsibilities – care is effectively shared between women and the state, which means also that women continue to be disadvantaged in the labour market. In the Scandinavian countries, where there are generous childcare leaves, taken predominantly by women, there are also very high levels of gender segregation in the labour market. In addition, Crompton and Lyonette (2005) have pointed out that there are high levels of stress in relation to work–family balance in France, a country with very good child-care coverage, which they attribute to the lack of engagement by men in domestic work.

In the English-speaking countries, there has been considerable effort on the part of academics and, in the UK, by policy-makers to broaden the terms of debate to 'work–life balance', in an effort to include consideration of leisure (for example, Warren 2004; Perrons 2000); to include all workers, not only those with children; to make the argument that the new approach is about 'working smart' not working less (Wise 2003); and to include more actors than the state, particularly employers. In the US, Gambles et al. (2006) have used a new descriptor for this approach: 'work–personal life harmonisation'. It is an approach that has been concerned most about working hours at the level of the firm, and has not promoted measures, such as daddy leaves, which aim to change men's behaviour in relation to care work. However, first, it is no more possible to place reliance on one set of actors – employers – than on one set of policies. As the OECD (2001) has reported, in countries with good state provisions on leave in general, firms did little, but where the state did nothing, firms failed to fill the gap (see also, den Dulk 2001). Brandth and Kvande (2001) also concluded on the basis of their research in Norway that state initiatives on parental leave to encourage fathers to take care of young children are crucial to changing workplace culture. Second, a focus on only one dimension of work–family balance policy is unlikely to succeed. The length of working hours are also very important. In the UK, the fathers of young children are the most likely to work very long hours (Bishop 2004; Lewis et al. 2008) and policies to address this issue, as well as policies to encourage more flexible working hours, are essential to securing gender equality. In short, time and money to enable the choice to care are both crucial.

CHANGES IN UK WORK–FAMILY BALANCE POLICIES SINCE 1997

The UK government has not put its policy eggs in a single basket. It has developed policies on services, leaves and working hours. One of its main concerns, certainly post-2000, has been to promote choice for parents. However, securing gender equality has not been an explicit priority in building the policy, and this is reflected in the nature of all three dimensions and in the tensions between and within them.

The various types of work–family balance policies present different problems and possibilities for gender equality. Childcare services offer women in particular the chance to enter the labour market, but much depends on their accessibility, affordability and quality. In the UK, historically, childcare provision has been deficient in all three respects, which affects the willingness of mothers even to consider using it. Given that research on the household division of resources has showed that the costs of childcare tend to be set against the mother's rather than the family's income (Brannen and Moss 1987; Harkness 2003), the high cost of childcare can be a particularly large obstacle. Leaves to care can be short or long, and compensated at high or low rates. Long, low-paid leaves have been shown to disadvantage women in the workforce, especially in respect of wage levels (Ekberg 2004), and to be taken disproportionately by low-educated women (Fagnani and Letablier 2004). Galtry and Callister's (2005) review of the evidence shows that the optimum leave for mothers, in respect of maximising re-entry to the labour market and minimising loss of income, to be six months (but that children's health and developmental interests lie in longer leaves; see also, Gregg and Waldfogel 2005). Galtry and Callister have sought to reconcile this conflict by concluding that the best compromise may be a six-month leave for the mother followed by a six-month leave for the father.

Similarly, flexible ways of working may advantage or disadvantage women. Part-time work in the UK has been shown to have a seriously detrimental effect on the gender wage gap (Manning and Petrongolo 2005), while other forms of flexibility can have either negative implications for employees, for example, when they take the form of non-standard working hours with little or no choice for the employee, or can be positive when they offer the employee greater control (Rubery et al. 1998). As Le Bihan and Martin (2005) have shown, parents, in particular, need control over their working time and 'predictable flexibility'.

In respect of childcare provision, in 1997 the UK was near the bottom of the EU league tables. The vast majority of childcare was provided either informally or by childminders. Free institutional provision tended to be reserved for 'children at risk' and was otherwise expensive (Land and Lewis 1998; Randall 2000). Labour's first major policy initiative centred on childcare, with the launch of a National Childcare Strategy in 1998 (DfEE 1998), and investment in childcare services has continued to be a major commitment in Labour's subsequent terms of government, with further expansion planned up to 2010. A commitment to increasing nursery school provision for 4-year-olds had been made by both the Conservatives and Labour in response to the 1995 Select Committee Report on mothers' employment (HC, 1995). However, the Conservatives had fought shy of legislative commitment, while Labour's 1998 strategy document set out an ambitious plan for funding 'early years learning' for both 3- and 4-year-olds, focusing especially on disadvantaged areas. Nevertheless, there was substantial continuity in respect of government support for a mixed economy of provision, with private and voluntary providers expected to play the major part.

Since 1998 policy has consistently aimed to increase provision. The hours of free nursery care have been expanded from 12.5 per week in 1998, rising to 15 hours by 2010, with a goal of 20 hours. Longer hours of opening (wraparound care) for children aged 3–14 years have also been promised in the new 10-year strategy announced in 2004 (HMT et al. 2004). Expenditure has amounted to about £2.4 billion on the supply-side for childcare for the under 5s (HC 2005: annex A) and about £650 million on the demand-side (Brewer et al. 2005; HMT et al. 2004). Childcare services are the part of the work–family balance (WFB) policy package that have attracted perhaps the most commentary; particularly in relation to the reliance on the private and voluntary sector for provision, the sustainability of this provision (especially in poor neighbourhoods), the amount of choice that parents actually have, the continued very high cost of childcare compared with continental European countries, the low qualifications of the childcare workforce and the difficulties in securing labour supply, the degree of success that has been achieved in targeting poor children, and the attention paid to early learning rather than more holistic approaches to childcare (Land 2002; Lewis 2003; Moss 2006; Penn and Randall 2005).

In respect of policies providing time to care, the UK had – in common with all Western European countries – long-standing provision for paid maternity leave, but unlike its European neighbours, no provision for other types of leave, particularly parental and paternity leaves. Labour's 1997 election manifesto commitment to sign up to the European Social Chapter meant that it had to implement the European Directive on Parental Leave (96/34/EC), which it did at the level of minimal compliance. Thirteen weeks unpaid parental leave was made available to parents of children under 6, if they had worked for their employers for one year. The leave must be taken in blocks of one week up to a maximum of four weeks a year. However, the right to leave was extended via paternity and adoption leaves from April 2003, going beyond what was required by the European Directive. The two-week paternity leave is paid at the level of flat rate statutory maternity pay. While the introduction of these leaves was new, the most dramatic policy development came in respect of maternity leave, which has been significantly extended, and statutory maternity pay, which has been raised from £55.70 per week in 1997 to £108.85 by 2006 (HMT 2005). Between 1999 and 2005, over £800 million was spent annually on maternity pay, and there has been a new annual cost of £57 million for paternity pay and £10 million for adoption pay over the same period. The 2006 Work and Families Act increased paid maternity leave with the possibility of the father taking around six months as 'additional paternity leave', with low levels of compensation, if the mother returns to work. This corresponds to Galtry and Callister's (2005) model in terms of length of leave for mothers and fathers (see above). In comparison with continental Europe, the UK has the longest maternity leave (Deven and Moss 2002), but has made little inroad into the more difficult territory of paid leave for fathers.

Finally, in respect of working hours, Labour's 1997 election manifesto stressed its commitment to 'fairness at work' and included 'the rights of employees not be forced to work more than 48 hours a week' (Labour 1997: 21). However, the individual opt-out to the 1993 European Directive on working time negotiated by the Conservative government to permit individuals to work longer than a 48-hour week, has not been rescinded. This is significant because British fathers have among the longest working hours in Europe, which constrains the time they can spend on care work and the time their partners can spend on paid work. While at the EU level the debate about working time moved from a narrow health and safety focus to one of work and family reconciliation, in the UK the reverse happened, with the government stating that 'the Working Time Directive, which has a health and safety basis, is an inappropriate vehicle for dealing with work–family balance issues' (DTI 2004: 1). Rather, Labour sought to promote flexible working patterns, first in response to another European Directive on part-time work (97/81/EC), but using non-binding guidance rather than legislation. However, in 2001, Labour decided to depart from the strong voluntarist tradition in British industrial relations (Fagan and Lallement 2000) and to introduce 'light touch' legislation to establish a 'right to request' flexible working patterns for the parents of children under six, now extended to all carers and likely to be extended to the parents of older children (DTI 2005). Other European countries, for example, Germany and the Netherlands, as well as the Scandinavian countries, have established a firm right to reduce working hours, although comparative evaluations show UK policy to have been relatively successful (Hegewisch 2005).

However, government's central concern has remained the balance between paid work and family responsibilities. The objectives have been both economic and social. The economic objective has encompassed both the desire to increase employment as a means to greater growth and competitiveness, and to take seriously the 'business case'. The social objective puts family first, which has also meant increasing employment as a means to social inclusion and tackling child poverty, but which has increasingly led to proposals regarding working time and time to care in particular that are difficult to square with the business case (CBI 2005). Indeed, the role envisaged for the state has varied in respect of the different dimensions of WFB policy and over time. Policy has been built incrementally in all three fields, with considerable effort given to bringing employers onside and consulting with 'parents' representatives' (mainly from third sector organisations). While the decision to tackle care leave in respect of children, childcare services and working hours constitutes the kind of policy package that is necessary to tackle gender equality, the tensions between and within the different parts of the policy, which have prioritised different policy goals, pose problems for its achievement.

The distinctive British pattern of long working hours for men and short working hours for women has been addressed only through exhortation – rather than statutory change on hours or wage replacement for fathers' leaves. Labour decided to maintain the individual opt-out from the EU Working Time Directive and instead promoted flexible working patterns. The right to request more flexibility and the various kinds of leave on offer to parents have been taken up primarily by mothers. Furthermore, by 2004, the government seemed to have settled on making provision for the 'parental' care of children – effectively by mothers – during the first year, and investing in childcare in order to make (women's) labour market participation and children's early learning easier once children reach the age of 3. The policy prescription for 1- and 2-year-olds is still unclear, just as the academic evidence as to what might be best is also mixed for this group of children. But the UK government has reached a reasonably coherent and not dissimilar policy strategy to most of its Northern and many of its Western European neighbours in seeking to underpin a pattern of family care during the child's very early years, followed by institutional care provision that enables women to enter the labour market.

Nevertheless, as an explicit policy driver, gender equality has taken a back seat. Labour has tackled the different dimensions of policy – in respect of working time and caring time, and service provision – that are necessary if real choice is to be promoted for men and women. But while the UK government has made work–family balance a matter of public policy concern, the major policy documents have insisted that parents must make their own choices about what constitutes an appropriate balance. Indeed, most documents use gender-neutral language throughout and refer to the importance of individual choice; there is little public recognition of the extent to which men's choices affect those taken by women. To this extent, work–family balance remains a matter for purely private decision-making in the UK.

NOTES

1. For example, Schorr (2001), Skocpol (2000), Heyman (2000) and Hewlett (1991).
2. European Foundation for the Improvement of Living and Working Conditions (2004) identified the gap between actual and desired family size as a problem.
3. See also Korpi's (2000) typology of family policy, which is based on the extent to which family policies promote female employment.
4. Equality-as-sameness has a long historical tradition in the USA and has been supported by feminists, who in the early twentieth century were not inclined to support even basic legal recognition of carework in the form of maternity leave (Wikander et al. 1995). There are, however, tax allowances for childcare.
5. Bishop (2004) also notes that while in France, Denmark and Sweden, the usual hours worked by (all) men and women are similar, in the UK there are major differences, with men working longer hours and women most commonly working 16–20 and 31–35 hours.
6. Hochschild (1990) and Coltrane (1996) have explored other possible explanations as to why women are do not more openly express dissatisfaction, centring on complicated couple dynamics involving expectations and 'economies of gratitude'.

REFERENCES

Baldock, J. and J. Hadlow (2004), 'Managing the family: productivity, scheduling and the male veto', *Social Policy and Administration*, **38**(6), 706–20.

Bianchi, S.M. and L.M. Casper (2004), 'The stalled revolution: gender and time allocation in the US', paper given to the International Conference on Work and Family, CRFR, University of Edinburgh, 30 June–2 July.

Bishop, K. (2004), 'Working time patterns in the UK, France, Denmark and Sweden', *Labour Market Trends*, March, 113–22.

Bonoli, G. (2005), 'The politics of the new social policies: providing coverage against new social risks in mature welfare states', *Policy and Politics*, **33**(3), 431–49.

Brandth, B. and E. Kvande (2001), 'Flexible work and flexible fathers', *Work Employment and Society*, **15**(2), 251–67.

Brannen, J. and P. Moss (1987), 'Dual-earner households: women's financial contributions after the birth of the first child', in J. Brannen and G. Wilson (eds), *Give and Take in Families. Studies in Resource Distribution*, London: Unwin Hyman.

Brewer, M., C. Crawford and L. Dearden (2005), 'Reforms to childcare policy', in R. Chote, C. Emmerson, D. Miles and Z. Oldfield (eds), *Green Budget*, London: Institute for fiscal Studies.

Coltrane, S. (1996), *Family Man: Fatherhood, Housework and Gender Equality*, Oxford: Oxford University Press.

Confederation of British Industry (CBI) (2005), *Second Reading Briefing on Work and Families Bill*, December, London: CBI.

Crompton, R. (2006), *Employment and the Family*, Cambridge: Cambridge University Press.

Crompton, R. and C. Lyonette (2005), 'Work–life "balance" in Britain and Europe', *The British Journal of Sociology*, **56**(4), 601–20.

Daly, M. (2005), 'Changing family life in Europe: significance for state and society', *European Societies*, **7**(3), 379–98.

Den Dulk, L. (2001), *Work–Family Arrangements in Organisations. A Cross-National Study on the Netherlands, the UK and Sweden*, Amsterdam: Rozenberg.

Department for Education and Employment (DfEE) (1998), *Meeting the Childcare Challenge*, Cm 3959, Norwich: The Stationery Office.

Department of Trade and Industry (DTI) (2004), *UK Response to Commission's 2003 Re-examination of Directive 93/104/EC*, London: DTI.

Department of Trade and Industry (DTI) (2005), *Work and Families: Choice and Flexibility*, Discussion Document, DTI.

Deven, F. and P. Moss (2002), 'Leave arrangements for parents: overview and future outlook', *Community, Work and Family*, **5**(3), 237–55.

Dex, S. (2003), *Work and Family in the Twenty-First Century*, York: Joseph Rowntree Foundation.

Dex, S., D. Hawkes, H. Joshi and K. Ward (2005), 'Parents' employment and child-care', in S. Dex and H. Joshi (eds), *Children of the 21st Century: From Birth to Nine Months*, Bristol: Policy Press.

Duncan, S. and R. Edwards (1999), *Lone Mothers, Paid Work and Gendered Moral Rationalities*, Basingstoke: Macmillan.

Ekberg, J. (2004), 'Sharing responsibility? Short and long-term effects of Sweden's "daddy month" reform', paper given to DTI, London, 27 May.

European Foundation for the Improvement of Living and Working Conditions (2004), *Fertility and family Issues in an Enlarged Europe*, Luxembourg: Office for the Official Publications of the European Communities.

Fagan, C. and M. Lallement (2000), 'Working time, social integration and transitional labour markets', in J. O'Reilly, I. Cebrian and M. Lallement (eds), *Working-Time Changes. Social Integration through Transitional Labour Markets*, Cheltenham: Edward Elgar.

Fagnani, J. and M.-T. Letablier (2004), 'Work and family life balance: the impact of the 35-hour laws in France', *Work, Employment and Society*, **18**(3), 551–72.

Finch, J. (1989), *Family Obligations and Social Change*, Cambridge: Polity Press.

Fraser, N. (1997), *Justice Interruptus. Critical Reflections on the 'Post-Socialist' Condition*, London: Routledge.

Galtry, J. and P. Callister (2005), 'Assessing the optimal length of parental leave for child and parental well-being: how can research inform policy?', *Journal of Family Issues*, **26**(2), 219–46.

Gambles, R., S. Lewis and R. Rapoport (2006), *The Myth of Work–life Balance: The Challenge of our Time for Men, Women and Societies*, Chichester: Wiley.

Gershuny, J. (2000), *Changing Times: Work and Leisure in Post-industrial Society*, Oxford: Oxford University Press.

Gornick, J. and M. Meyers M. (2003), *Families that Work: Policies for Reconciling Parenthood and Employment*, New York: Russell Sage.

Gregg, P. and J. Waldfogel (2005), 'Symposium on parental leave, early maternal employment and child outcomes: introduction', *The Economic Journal*, **115**, February, F1–F6.

Hakim, C. (2000), *Work–Lifestyle Choices in the Twenty-first Century: Preference Theory*, Oxford: Oxford University Press.

Hantrais, L. (2004), *Family Policy Matters. Responding to Family Change in Europe*, Bristol: Policy Press.

Harkness, S. (2003), 'The household division of labour: changes in families allocation of paid and unpaid work, 1992–2002', in R. Dickens and P. Gregg (eds), *The Labour Market under New Labour*, Basingstoke: Palgrave.

Hegewisch, A. (2005), 'Individual working time rights in Germany and the UK: how a little law can go a long way', in A. Hegewisch (ed.), *Working Time for Working Families: Europe and the United States*, Washington, DC: Friedrich-Ebert-Stiftung.

Her Majesty's Treasury (HMT) (2005), *Pre-Budget Report*, London: Treasury.

Her Majesty's Treasury, Department for Education and Skills, Department for Work and Pensions and Department of Trade and Industry (HMT, DfES, DWP and DTI) (2004), *Choice for Parents, the Best Start for Children: A Ten Year Strategy for Childcare*, London: Treasury.

Hertz, R. (1999), 'Working to place family at the center of life: dual-earner and single-parent strategies', *Annals of the American Academy of Political Science*, **562**, March, 16–31.

Hewlett, S.A. (1991), *When the Bough Breaks: The Cost of Neglecting our Children*, New York: Basic Books.

Heyman, J. (2000), *The Widening Gap. Why America's Working Families Are in Jeopardy and What Can Be Done about It*, New York: Basic Books.

Hobson, B. (2004), 'The individualised worker, the gender participatory and the gender equity models in Sweden', *Social Policy and Society*, **3**(1), 75–84.

Hochschild, A. (1990), *The Double Shift*, London: Piatkus.

Hogarth, T., C. Hasluck and G. Pierre (2001), *Work–Life Balance 2000: Results from the Baseline Study*, Research Report RR249, London: Department for Education and Employment.

House of Commons (HC) (1995), *Second Special Report*, Employment Committee, 1994–5 Session, HC 457, Hansard.

House of Commons (HC) (2005), *Ninth Report*, Education and Skills Select Committee, 2004–5 Session, HC 40, Hansard.

Knijn, T. (2004), 'Challenges and risks of individualisation in the Netherlands', *Social Policy and Society*, **3**(1), 57–66.

Korpi, W. (2000), 'Faces of inequality: gender, class, and patterns of inequalities in different types of welfare states', *Social Politics*, **7**(2), 127–91.

Kremer, M. (2005), 'How welfare states care: culture, gender and citizenship in Europe', unpublished PhD thesis, University of Utrecht.

La Valle, I., S. Arthur, C. Millward, J. Scott and M. Clayden (2002), *Happy Families? Atypical Work and its Influence on Family Life*, Bristol: Policy Press.

Labour (1997), *New Labour because Britain Deserves Better*, election manifesto, www.labour-party.org.uk/1997/1997-labour-manifesto.shtml (accessed on 12 April 2005).

Land, H. (2002), *Meeting the Child Poverty Challenge: Why Universal Childcare is Key to Ending Child Poverty, Facing the Future*, Policy Papers 3, London: Daycare Trust.

Land, H. and J. Lewis (1998), 'Gender, care and the changing role of the state in the UK', in J. Lewis (ed.), *Gender, Social Care and Welfare State Restructuring in Europe*, Aldershot: Ashgate.

Le Bihan, B. and C. Martin (2005), 'Atypical working hours: consequences for childcare arrangements', in T. Kroger and J. Sipila (eds), *Overstretched: Families Up Against the Demands of Work and Care*, Oxford: Blackwell, pp. 9–33.

Leira, A. (1998), 'Caring as social right: cash for child care and daddy leave', *Social Politics*, **5**(3), 362–79.

Lewis, J. (2001), 'The decline of the male breadwinner model: the implications for work and care', *Social Politics*, **8**(2), 152–70.

Lewis, J. (2002), 'Gender and welfare state change', *European Societies*, **4**(4), 331–57.

Lewis, J. (2003), 'Developing early years childcare in England, 1997–2002: the choices for (working) mothers', *Social Policy and Administration*, **37**(3), 219–39.

Lewis, J. (2006), 'Work–family reconciliation, equal opportunities, and social policies: the interpretation of policy trajectories at the EU level and the meaning of gender equality', *Journal of European Public Policy*, **13**(3), 420–37.

Lewis, J. and S. Giullari (2005), 'The adult worker model family, gender equality and care: the search for new policy principles and the possibilities and problems of a capabilities approach', *Economy and Society*, **34**(1), 76–104.

Lewis, S. (2001), 'Restructuring workplace cultures: the ultimate work–family challenge?', *Women in Management Review*, **16**(1), 21–30.

Lewis, S. (2002), 'Work and family issues old and new', in R.J. Burke and D.L. Nelson (eds), *Advancing Women's Careers: Research and Practice*, Oxford: Blackwell.

Lewis, J., M. Campbell and C. Huerta (2008), 'Patterns of paid and unpaid work in Western Europe', *Journal of European Social Policy*, **18**(1), 21–37.

MacInnes, J. (2005), 'Work–life balance and the demand for reduction in working hours: evidence from the British Social Attitudes Survey 2002', *British Journal of Industrial Relations*, **43**(2), 273–95.

Major, B. (1993), 'Gender, entitlement, and the distribution of family labor', *Journal of Social Issues*, **49**(3), 141–59.

Manning, A. and B. Petrongolo (2005), *The Part-Time Pay Penalty*, London: DTI.

McRae, S. (2003), 'Constraints and choices in mothers' employment careers', *British Journal of Sociology*, **53**(3), 317–38.

Morgan, K. and K. Zippel (2003), 'Paid to care. The origins and effects of care leave policies in Western Europe', *Social Politics*, **10**(1), 45–85.

Moss, P. (2006), 'From a childcare to a pedagogical discourse – or putting care in its place', in J. Lewis, (ed.), *Children in the Context of Family and Welfare State Change*, Cheltenham: Edward Elgar.

Nussbaum, M. (1999), *Sex and Social Justice*, Oxford: Oxford University Press.

Organisation for Economic Co-operation and Development (OECD) (2001), *Employment Outlook 2001*, Paris: OECD.

Organisation for Economic Co-operation and Development (OECD) (2005), *Babies and Bosses: Reconciling Work and Family Life*, vol. 4, Paris: OECD.

Ostner, I. (2004), ' "Individualisation" – the origins of the concept and its impact on German social policies', *Social Policy and Society*, **3**(1), 47–56.

Penn, H. and V. Randall (2005), 'Childcare policy and local partnerships under Labour', *Journal of Social Policy*, **34**(1), 79–97.

Perrons, D. (2000), 'Care, paid work and leisure: rounding the triangle', *Feminist Economics*, **6**(1), 105–14.

Pfau-Effinger, B. (1998), 'Gender cultures and the gender arrangement – a theoretical framework for cross-national comparisons on gender', *The European Journal of Social Sciences*, **11**(2), 147–66.

Rake, K. (2000), 'Gender and New Labour's social policy', *Journal of Social Policy*, **30**(2), 209–32.

Randall, V. (2000), *The Politics of Child Daycare in Britain*, Oxford: Oxford University Press.

Rapoport, R., L. Bailyn, J.K. Fletcher and B.H. Pruitt (2002), *Beyond World – Family Balance, Advancing Gender Equity and Workplace Performance*, San Francisco: Josey Bass.

Rubery, J., M. Smith and C. Fagan (1998), 'National working-time regimes and equal opportunities', *Feminist Economics*, **4**(1), 71–101.

Schmid, G. (2000), 'Transitional labour markets', in B. Marin, D. Meulders and D.J. Snower (eds), *Innovative Employment Initiatives*, Aldershot: Ashgate.

Schor, J. (2001), *The Overworked American*, New York: Basic Books.

Sen, A. (1999), *Development as Freedom*, New York: Knopf.

Skocpol, T. (2000), *The Missing Middle: Working Families and the Future of American Social Policy*, New York: W.W. Norton.

Strohmeir, K.P. (2002), 'Family policy – how does it work?', in F.-X. Kaufman, A. Kuijsten, H.-J. Schulze and K.P. Strohmeier (eds), *Family Life and Family Policies in Europe*, vol. 2, Oxford: Oxford University Press, pp. 321–62.

Tronto, J. (1993), *Moral Boundaries: A Political Argument for and Ethic of Care*, London: Routledge.

Trzcinski, E. (2000), 'Family policy in Germany: a feminist dilemma?', *Feminist Economics*, **6**(1), 21–44.

Warren, T. (2004), 'Working part-time: achieving a successful "work–life" balance?', *British Journal of Sociology*, **55**(1), 99–122.

Wikander, U., A. Kessler Harris and J. Lewis (eds) (1995), *Protecting Women. Labor Legislation in Europe, the US and Australia, 1880–1900*, Urbana, IL: University of Illinois Press.

Windebank, J. (2001), 'Dual-earner couples in Britain and France: gender divisions of domestic labour and parenting work in different welfare states', *Work, Employment and Society*, **15**(2), 269–90.

Wise, S. (2003), *Work–Life Balance Literature and Research Review*, London: DTI.

PART IV

Ways Forward

12. Women and work in the UK: the need for a modernisation of labour market institutions

Jill Rubery

In 1994 the Organisation for Economic Co-operation and Development (OECD 1994) made the argument that a new gender contract and a new set of labour market arrangements were needed to fit with changing patterns of women's employment and household formation. That argument added a new dimension to the gender equality debate: promoting gender equality was to be regarded as not only an issue of social justice but also a means of modernising the economy and welfare systems (Humphries and Rubery 1995; Rubery et al. 2003a; 2003b). This approach has been developed through the commitment to gender mainstreaming of public policy made at the Beijing World Conference on women. Gender mainstreaming is a tool that can be used to determine whether current institutional arrangements are fit for purpose, once the interests of women as well as men are taken into account (Council of Europe 1998; Rees 1998). The argument presented in this chapter is that labour market institutions in the UK need to be modernised and upgraded to match the changing aspirations of women, to promote a more productive economy and to reduce risks of poverty and social exclusion. Such a modernisation process obviously involves costs for individuals or groups, as is the case with any process of change. It must be remembered that maintaining the status quo also implies costs, not just for individual women concerned but also for the economy. These costs include both those of underutilised potential, if women are unable to work at their full capacity (Bruegel and Perrons 1995; Grant et al. 2005), and of welfare dependency, if current institutional arrangements increase risks of social exclusion among women (Esping-Andersen et al. 2002).

To identify the changes that are needed in the UK economy to achieve the objectives of both a more productive and a more gender equal society, use can be made of international comparisons to generate valuable and concrete examples of alternative modes of organising work, employment and welfare. In developing an international comparative perspective it is important to recognise that on some dimensions and variables women in the UK may be relatively favourably situated, even if on other dimensions the UK performance is poor. Furthermore, experience in other contexts does not necessarily provide pointers to simple or easy solutions. Indeed, in all societies gender equality remains an aspiration rather than a full achievement. Nevertheless, significant examples can be extracted from these international comparisons where the worst problems of gender inequality have been at least modified. Such comparisons may open up a wider range of policy options and choices than are apparent when issues are considered from within the confines of one particular labour market.

INTERNATIONAL COMPARISONS: A CHECKLIST

Gender equality can be measured with respect to a range of indicators relating to different dimensions of equality (Plantenga and Hansen 1999). Table 12.1 compares the UK to European average standards for five main dimensions of gender equality: access to employment, education and careers, pay and job quality, independence in tax and benefits and work–life balance/support for parenthood. To assess equality along these dimensions a range of indicators can be used and the UK can be seen to score relatively well on some indicators, in relation to European average standards, including, for example, high female employment rates, low female unemployment rates, high female participation and performance in education, good opportunities for women to develop initial careers, early introduction of independent taxation for women, awareness of equal pay issues among policy-makers and, in particular, trade unions and plentiful opportunities to work non-standard hours (see Table 12.1 and Figure 12.1).

While at first glance this may appear to be a pretty impressive list of good performance attributes, a more detailed investigation reveals problems even with these positive indicators. On the female employment rate, the UK scores much higher when a headcount basis is used than when these data are calculated on a full-time equivalent basis, owing to a high share of part-time work among women in the UK. Women's share of the volume of employment is therefore not as high as that indicated by employment rate levels. Unemployment rates tend to be lower for women than for men in the UK. However, this gender disparity in favour of women may be a consequence of the poor quality of jobs available to the unemployed; research showed in the mid-1990s (Gregg and Wadsworth 1995) that only second income earners in households, that is not prime breadwinners, were in a position to take the low-paid and often part-time jobs on offer. The working tax credit system was in fact introduced by New Labour so that prime earners in

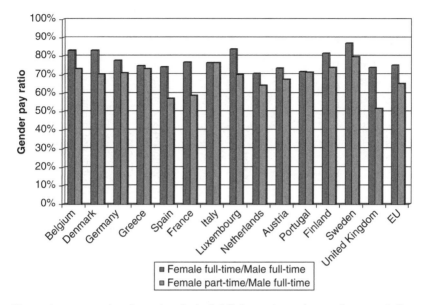

Figure 12.1 *Women's relative average pay in full-time and part-time work (private sector)*

households would find it worthwhile to take the low-paid jobs on offer. However, there is still limited evidence that the male unemployed have been induced to move into jobs previously regarded as primarily women's work – that is, part-time jobs in the service sector. Furthermore, although independent taxation for women was established relatively early on in the UK, the spread of household-based tax credit systems has compromised this development, at least for some low-income households.

A more positive picture emerges with respect to the opportunities provided for women as a result of the particular characteristics of the education system. The tendency for higher education to be completed at a relatively young age in the UK undoubtedly assists women in establishing themselves in careers before the age at which motherhood can no longer be postponed. In many continental European countries careers of higher-educated women are hardly under way before the age of 30, in part as a consequence of extended education but also, in some cases, due to high unemployment among graduates. On the other hand, the focus on early

Table 12.1 Dimensions to equality of women in work: assessment of the performance of the UK relative to other EU member states

Dimensions to equality of women in work	Do well	European comparison	Do badly	European comparison
Access to employment	High female employment rate Low female unemployment rate	UK fifth highest female employment rate in EU15/EU25 UK second lowest female unemployment rate in EU15/25	High share of part-time jobs that are primarily low paid Most jobs for unemployed are low paid and part-time	Third highest share of women in part-time work EU15/EU25 (Eurostat 2006) Low unemployment may be due to low access to unemployment benefit/availability of part-time work
Education and careers	Women account for around 54% tertiary students (Eurostat 2005) Earlier graduation allows for early establishment of careers	Female student share higher than for Germany, Netherlands, Austria Bologna process – harmonising degree programmes in Europe more around UK model	Lower continuity of careers for higher educated Greater emphasis on achievement at young age in UK	70% higher educated women with children worked continuously 1994–98 cf EU average 77% (OECD 2002) Later starts to careers in many other European countries but possibility of promotion at later age may be higher (Crompton et al. 1991)

Pay and job quality	Trade union awareness of equal pay issues	UK has a number of significant examples of trade union initiatives on equal pay especially in public sector; more active than many other EU countries	Gender pay gap – especially for part-timers	Largest gender pay gap for part-timers (see Figure 12.1) Netherlands pays holiday and sick pay to part-timers based on actual earnings/hours not contractual earnings/hours
			Pay inequality	Women face larger penalties for being concentrated a bottom of labour market (OECD 2002)
Independence in tax and benefits	Independent taxation	Many European countries and low especially Germany have joint taxation – disincentive to participation	Low entitlements to benefits especially for low earners due to threshold below which national insurance is not payable	Entitlements greater in some other European countries – for example, citizenship pensions in Netherlands, Sweden – higher share of female unemployed entitled to benefits (Rubery et al. 1998: table 5.1)
			Low levels of basic benefits – reliance on household means testing for benefits	UK lowest replacement rate for basis unemployment benefits except for Italy (Rubery et al. 1998: table 5.5)
			Employment – conditional benefits – tax credits – creates new disincentives to participation for spouses	Belgium has introduced employment – conditional benefit based on individual earnings not household earnings

Table 12.1 (continued)

Dimensions to equality of women in work	Do well	European comparison	Do badly	European comparison
Work–life balance/support for parenthood	Opportunities to work part-time	Second highest part-time employment rate for women in EU15/25	WLB through unequal gender division of labour	UK – full-time male/part-time female household model seen as norm as both men and women work long full-time hours– but in France more dual-earner couples both work full-time but <40 hours (Eurostat 2002)
			Many part-time jobs involve flexible scheduling; many full-time jobs involve long hours of work	High level of 24/7 working (Woodland et al. 2003) and moves in that direction; part-time employment is associated with long opening hours (Woodland et al. 2003: 39). Longest employee full-time hours in Europe (Kodz et al. 2003)
			Expensive and uncertain provision of childcare	Right to childcare in Sweden and Finland; Sweden includes costs of childcare in making work pay policies and adjusts costs of childcare to keep down marginal rate of 'tax'

Source: CEC (2006) and publications of the European Group of Experts on Gender and Employment (http://mbs.ac.uk/ewerc/egge) unless otherwise stated.

success in careers in the UK may well increase the penalties for both fathers and mothers who choose to hold back on their careers during the period when their children are young. Indeed, the focus on early starts to careers may also restrict opportunities for women returning to the labour market, confining them to lower grade jobs with limited promotion prospects, even though they still have the majority of their working lives ahead of them.

Another point in the checklist in the UK's favour is the evidence of greater awareness of equal pay issues than is found in many continental European countries. The UK has a much higher level of legal cases related to equal pay and many of these cases are supported by trade unions and collective bargainers in order to set new precedents with respect to pay structures and practices. Equal pay issues have thus become central to trade union strategies. However, the use of the law to obtain leverage in collective bargaining could be interpreted as an indicator of overall weakness of trade unions within the UK labour market.

The checklist of positive indicators in relation to European average standards is more than outweighed by a longer list where the UK scores are low. The negative indicators refer in particular to the quality of jobs available, especially for women working part-time and for women who are not highly educated. These problems of poor job quality are associated with problems faced by mothers in making transitions back into employment and are manifest in a high gender pay gap, particularly for part-timers (see Figure 12.1).[1] In the UK, the high levels of wage inequality means that women who take jobs lower down the pay hierarchy, in order to fit with their domestic requirements, also have to accept a larger pay penalty than when women 'trade down' in those societies where there is less wage inequality between the top and the bottom of the labour market (Blau and Kahn 1992). This is not just a temporary effect while children are young; indeed there is evidence of a long-term scarring effect of taking part-time jobs, in part related to this occupational downgrading (Olsen and Walby 2004; Walby and Olsen 2002). Working part-time also often leads to a lack of individual entitlements to social protection, such as unemployment benefits and pension entitlements, as part-time workers may earn below the threshold for making national insurance contributions. Thus, despite a good record with respect to independent taxation in the UK, women still often lack independent rights to benefits, particularly pensions and unemployment benefits. In low-income households eligible for working tax credit, women are even discouraged from participation as second income earners in the labour market owing to high rates of withdrawal of the tax benefit.

The UK also scores poorly on issues related to work–life balance, including low-paid leave entitlements and limited and relatively expensive child-care, even if the provision under both headings has improved recently

(Fagan and Hebson 2005). The high share of women in low-paid part-time jobs, particularly mothers of young children, may also be in part accounted for by the long-hours of work expected in many full-time jobs (Kodz et al. 2003). This long-hours culture not only prevents them returning themselves to full-time work, but also creates barriers to the development of part-time work opportunities within those jobs that require full-timers to work many additional hours, often on an unpaid basis. Part-time jobs in the UK are therefore more often found in specific enclaves, designed as part-time jobs to meet the flexibility demands of employers, instead of being 'reduced hours jobs' within standard full-time job areas. Thus while the opportunities to work non-standard or flexible hours are plentiful in the UK, there are also strong pressures on employees on both full-time and part-time contracts to work flexibly according to the dictates of management.

The consequences of these combinations of welfare policies, labour market structures and household arrangements are that, despite the apparent high level of integration of women into the wage economy, in practice women remain highly economically dependent – either on their partners or on means-tested benefits provided by the state if their partnership ends. Particular problems arise from the concentration of women in low-paid part-time jobs, the long hours of work in full-time jobs that act as a barrier both to staying in full-time work and to the creation of quality part-time work, the limited pension provision for those not employed on a continuous basis in large organisations and, finally, the increasing focus on means-tested benefits – including the new tax credit systems – that reinforce women's economic dependence on partners and/or the state in low-income households. There is strong prima facie evidence, therefore, that there is a need for modernisation of the labour market and welfare institutions for both reasons of economic efficiency and for social justice: women in the UK are not yet fulfilling their full potential in the labour market and remain vulnerable to social exclusion and poverty.

In developing the case for a rethinking of current labour market and welfare policy, international comparisons can be used both to underpin the case for change and to challenge some common beliefs about the possibilities for improvements to gender equality. For example, a common perception is that there is a trade-off between levels of pay and benefits for part-time work and the size of the part-time jobs sector.[2] However a consideration of experience in the Netherlands suggests that this is not a universal rule. In the Netherlands the gap between full- and part-timers' pay and benefits is much lower than in the UK but the rate of part-time working is even higher. Indeed, in general the pay penalties for part-time work can be seen to be lower in the rest of the EU (Figure 12.1 and CEC 2002) and therefore the low pay associated with part-time work in the UK is not an inevitable feature of non-standard working hours. Similarly, the high dependency found for women working part-time in the UK is the outcome of particular systems of welfare organisation; for example, in the Netherlands and Sweden there are citizenship rights to pensions, not dependent upon work histories (Ginn and Arber 1998; Rubery et al. 1998). The challenge of designing tax and benefits systems so as not to disadvantage second income earners or mothers has been addressed differently in different societies; for example in Belgium in-work benefits similar to the working tax credit have been introduced but based on individual not household earners; and in Sweden the costs of state provided childcare borne by the parents are adjusted explicitly so as not to deter the second earner from re-entering the labour market. There is no presumption here that policies implemented in one societal context can be easily or appropriately transferred to the UK context, but the benefits of international comparisons is at least to open up the agenda for possible policy approaches and solutions to problems that are too often regarded as inevitable outcomes of the working of a market system.

MODERNISATION OF THE WELFARE AND LABOUR MARKET SYSTEM

The poor performance of the UK on many dimensions of gender equality points to the need to modernise the institutional arrangements and systems to promote gender equality. This needs to be done in a holistic way so that the benefits of changes and renewed investment in some areas are not lost because of myopia or perverse incentives in other areas. A prime example of the failure to develop and build on investment in one area because of a lack of reform in another area is found in the underutilisation of the potential of female graduates. Women in the UK account for over half of higher education students but policies to adjust the workplace to improve retention of those who wish to become mothers are often dismissed as too costly, taking into account employers' costs in the short term. The failure to capitalise on the investments in a productive labour force is not taken into account (Breugel and Perrons 1995). Another example of problems where policy areas are not joined up is in respect of policy to reduce poverty and social exclusion. Women also constitute the group most at risk from poverty in old age and are particularly vulnerable to falling into poverty in prime age. It is women who tend to lose contact with the labour market or trade down to lower-level jobs to meet family commitments, thereby leaving themselves exposed to falling into poverty if the family or household unit breaks down. However, working tax credits actively discourage women as second income earners from entering employment, thereby promoting disconnection from the labour market. There is strong evidence that women are less likely to enter poverty and to become welfare dependent at the point of marital break-up if they are already in the labour market (Lister 2005). This lack of joined-up policy has major implications for the policy to take children out of poverty, as women are both more likely to take children into poverty with them and, conversely, to spend more of their own income on the welfare of children. These two examples suggests that there may be a need to rethink both the organisation of labour markets and the organisation of welfare systems to promote the productivity of the economy and to reduce social exclusion. In some areas of economic organisation – for example, the public services – it is well recognised in government circles that the so-called 'modernisation' of the service involves changes that will disrupt vested interests and cause problems of adjustment for employers and employees. Indeed, such disruption is frequently cited by New Labour as one of the main objectives of the modernisation agenda.

Not all change is therefore automatically dismissed by policy-makers as undesirable. Yet when the case for equal opportunities is promoted, there seems to be a desire to find modes of change that impinge as little as possible on the current ways of doing things both in employing organisations and in state policy fields. While advocating a joined-up or holistic approach to the modernisation question, to facilitate discussion we divide the policy domain into three main areas: pay, the organisation of work, time and careers, and welfare and employment regimes. Under each policy area we provide some brief empirical information before analysing the major problems for gender equality and identifying possible policy options.

MODERNISING PAY STRUCTURES

Wage inequality is relatively high in the UK. The impact of this wage inequality on the gender pay gap has been estimated by the OECD using a technique developed by Juhn et al. (1993) and applied inter alia by Blau and Kahn (1992) and the OECD (2002). According to OECD calculations, the UK's gender pay gap was over 6 percentage points above the EU average, but if the gap were to be adjusted for the difference in the UK's wage structures compared with the EU average wage structure, it would only have been some 2 percentage points above the EU average. In contrast, in the Netherlands the gender pay gap is around 4 percentage points above the

Table 12.2   *Women's pay in female-dominated jobs relative to total average male full-time earnings*

Occupation	Percentage of total average male full-time earnings		
	Full-time	Part-time	All
Sales/shop assistants			
Australia	58.8	57.2	57.8
Canada	55.6	52.5	—
France	59.0	59.0	59.0
Germany	46.4	—	—
Norway	64.0	62.4	63.0
United Kingdom	47.3	43.5	44.4
United States	52.2	50.7	50.4
Professional nurses			
Australia	102.6	106.2	104.2
Canada	94.4	—	97.1
Germany	75.4	—	—
Norway	86.0	91.1	88.2
United Kingdom	96.0	92.0	94.3
United States	146.4	123.6	131.0
Nursing assistants/auxiliaries			
Canada	62.6	—	65.3
France	72.9	72.0	72.7
Germany	51.4	—	—
Norway	73.6	79.8	77.2
United Kingdom	63.3	62.2	62.8
United States	51.8	63.1	55.2

Source: OECD (1998: tables 2.4 and 2.5) based on Grimshaw and Rubery (1997: tables 13 and 14 and appendix table 5).

EU average, but if the Netherlands had the same wage structure as the EU as a whole, in contrast to its current more egalitarian wage structure, its gender pay gap could rise to around 9 percentage points above the EU average. These two examples illustrate the importance of the overall wage structure for gender pay equality.

The impact of differences in pay penalties imposed on those at the bottom of the labour market is also indicated in Table 12.2 which shows the relative pay in female-dominated jobs in seven advanced countries in a study conducted for the OECD in 1997 (OECD 1998). Pay here is shown as a percentage of men's full-time earnings and it is notable that low-skilled full-time jobs, including sales and shop assistants and nursing assistants

Table 12.3   Typology of education-earnings profiles by gender

	Relative size of education-earnings pay-off			
	High for all workers	Low for all workers	High for men, low for women	Low for men, very low for women
Highly educated women earn more than average male full-time pay	Luxembourg Austria Portugal	Denmark Germany Finland Sweden	Italy	—
Highly educated women earn less than average male full-time pay	—	Greece UK	France Netherlands Spain	Belgium

Source: Rubery et al. (2005a).

and auxiliaries, were much lower paid in the UK, the USA and Germany than in the more egalitarian Norway, and also lower than in France, Australia and to some extent Canada. However, one consequence of the more compressed wage structure in Norway is a relatively low level of pay for full-time professional nurses compared with that found in the UK and the USA (although the pay for nurses in Germany is even lower). These results suggest that national pay structures reward different groups of women differently; the UK structure may provide reasonable levels of pay for those in higher-skilled and professional jobs but imposes very high penalties on those at the bottom of the labour market, where most women remain concentrated.

The differences in pay structures between advanced societies indicates that efforts to break down the gender pay gap into those parts of the gap 'explained' by variations in productive factors such as education and experience and those 'explained' by factors such as discrimination are unlikely to provide robust or consistent results, certainly not across countries (see Grimshaw and Rubery 2002 for a review of these issues) and that, at the very least, they need to be adjusted using the Juhn et al. (1993) procedure mentioned above. We know that earnings are in all countries correlated with education and experience but the actual rate of return on education and experience varies between countries – both overall and by sector and by gender (see Table 12.3). Moreover, as women have increased both their education and experience – through more continuous working – the importance of gaps in 'productive factors', in explaining the gender pay gap, has tended to decline and the importance of other factors has increased, with limited change taking place in the actual size of the overall gap (Rubery et al. 2005a).

New Labour explicitly recognised that there were problems with the level of pay at the bottom of the labour market when it introduced both a minimum wage and working tax credits to enable people to move off benefits and into work. However, no particular explanation has been put forward for the low wages prevailing at the bottom of the UK labour market. The emphasis on working tax credits for first earners in a household but not for second income earners or young people on low pay, has reinforced a view that it is acceptable to pay wages that are insufficient to meet minimum substance needs of an employee, even when employed on a full-time basis. While the gap is to be made up by the state in the case of the main breadwinner, the implication is that the family will step into support female second income earners and young people (McLaughlin 1995). The possibility that the low wages in this segment are not so much caused by low productivity of the workforce but by embedded gender discrimination and a tendency to undervalue women's work has effectively not been countenanced by policy-makers. This is surprising in the light of women's dominance of this employment segment and the widespread recognition – evident in debates on the gender pay gap – that pay discrimination against women is still present in the UK and is therefore likely to be present also for low wage female workers where the power of monopsonistic employers is likely to be greatest. We also know that the practice of low pay breeds poor employment and training practices. If labour is considered cheap, organisations may take little trouble to ensure that employees are effectively trained and motivated. Part-time workers are much less likely to be offered training than full-time workers (Arulampalam and Booth 1997; OECD 2004). Furthermore, the opportunity to pay low wages promotes the development of more segregated and fragmented systems of work; outsourcing of low-skilled jobs may appear particularly advantageous if there are opportunities to reduce pay levels and to minimise the likelihood of equal pay claims. These tendencies will reinforce gender divisions in the pay structure and prevent women being able to move towards economic self-sufficiency.

The national minimum wage has done something to protect pay at the bottom of the labour market, particularly over the period where the minimum has risen faster than average earnings. However, the Low Pay Commission in 2006 believed that the case for further above average increases is less clear as the national minimum wage is likely to be insufficient to reduce pay inequality at the bottom end of the labour market. An even larger problem exists in developing policies to reduce the rampant inequalities developing at the top end of the labour market. This form of inequality only contributes to the size of the gender pay gap if the gap is measured by reference to mean earnings not to median earnings. The government now prefers the latter, possibly because of the more favourable picture it presents.

Some Policy Recommendations

To modernise the pay structure we need to consider policies to address the two main problems faced in the UK, namely

- wide earnings inequality
- the interaction of segregation and low pay in UK.

Wage inequality

Action on wage inequality is required at both ends of the distribution. To address issues of low pay, serious consideration needs to be given to raising the level of a minimum wage towards what could be considered a living wage. Such an approach has found some favour in the USA where the lack of both a stable family structure and a strong welfare state makes workers, including women, increasingly reliant on their own earnings for survival (Figart et al. 2002). Living wage campaigns are beginning in the UK, particularly in London, and provide a means of starting a debate on how to eradicate the legacy of women's pay as pin money from the economy (Harkness et al. 1997).

Policies that could promote pay moderation for the higher skilled are likely to be more indirect as at present there are no direct tools to influence pay at the top end of the labour market. Countries where there is less pay inequality may benefit from strong social norms against excessive pay but such norms appear to have broken down in the UK. One factor behind the increasing wage inequality in the UK may be the pressure on higher level staff to work more and more hours; this reduces the talent pool for such jobs, thereby pushing up the wage rate, as anyone with domestic responsibilities may feel unable to apply. Furthermore those expected to work unreasonable hours are themselves likely to put pressure on employers to reward them with high pay. We now need to consider how to reverse this vicious circle, whereby a small group of people absorb more of the pay and more of the available work. The notion of a scarcity of talent should be rejected at a time when women's own investments in education are being underutilised. Another policy approach is to introduce more transparency into the wage system by preventing employers requiring pay levels to be confidential and by promoting the publication of the full range of pay levels by job category and gender. Greater transparency could be a trigger for the development of stronger social norms with respect to the appropriate levels of pay dispersion.

Low pay and segregation

The interaction between low pay and segregation needs addressing through three main policy approaches. First, there is a need to promote the re-evaluation of women's work, an approach that has been applied recently in the public sector through the negotiation of single pay spines. The second policy approach must be to promote opportunities for continuity of employment within the same job even when a change in the number or scheduling of hours is required. This policy is being pursued through the right to request flexible working, as we discuss further below, but at present it does not provide a parallel right to request a return to full-time hours once domestic circumstances change again. The third policy that needs developing in this area is to provide opportunities to use either hypothetical comparators or comparators outside of the employing organisation for the application of equal pay legislation. The concentration of women in organisations dominated by part-time low-paid work significantly curtails the effectiveness of the legislation which provides for equal pay for work of equal value, as the law is only at present allowed to be applied within a workplace where there are relevant male comparators employed. Here there is a need for change in European legislation but the issue is particularly urgent in the UK, where the individual organisation has much more power over wage determination due to the effective absence of sector-based collective bargaining.

To avoid further intensification of the links between segregation and low pay, the incentives for and pressure towards fragmentation and outsourcing need to be modified. This implies, in particular, reconsidering the policy preference for public sector work to be contracted out, to limit the likelihood of the development of a two-tier workforce in which women dominate in the lower tier. One way that the incentives to outsource could be reduced or the consequences of outsourcing mitigated is, as proposed in the Kingsmill report (2002) and in the trade union campaigns against a two-tier workforce, to both protect the equal pay grading for outsourced staff and to extend the protection of terms and conditions to all new hires. The argument in favour of reducing incentives to outsourcing is not only based on social justice for the workers involved but that it may also promote efficiency. Policy towards outsourcing is still based on the assumption that there is an untapped supply of readily available and reliable labour for low-paid part-time jobs, even when these jobs are stressful and demanding, such as in the care sector. However, women's lives are changing and more women are both acquiring higher education and remaining in continuous careers, thereby reducing the supply of women returners for sectors such as social care (Eborall 2003). There is a need therefore to persuade employers not to seek an easy way out of problems of recruitment – by subcontracting to the private sector or agen-cies – but instead to approach problems of lack of labour supply through strategies to improve the image of the occupation through higher pay and improved career and training opportunities. This practice, to some extent, has been adopted recently in the National Health Service (NHS), where they have embarked upon a skills escalator programme for low-skilled workers, at the same time as extending the protection of the NHS minimum wage to private sector subcontractor employees (Grimshaw and Carroll 2005).

MODERNISING WORK, TIME AND CAREER STRUCTURES

Two characteristics of the UK labour market system have particular impli-cations for women's position in the labour market. These include the long-hours culture that prevails in the UK and the practice of age discrimination in hiring and promotions.

Long-hours Culture

As we have already argued, the long-hours culture acts to promote the culture of income inequality. Research suggests a positive link between high earnings and long hours, with long hours of unpaid overtime being associated with a higher chance of promotion in the next period (Kodz et al. 2003). The long-hours culture feeds a process whereby the higher paid are expected to work more and therefore are more likely to put pressure on for yet higher compensation; this restricts opportunities to employ more staff and to share out responsibilities across a wider spec-trum of the workforce, including women. Employer expectations that key employees will have total commitment to work thus lies at the heart of the problem of promoting both gender inequality and a reasonable work–life balance (Rubery et al. 2005b). These arrangements also inhibit the devel-opment of quality part-time jobs as the meaning of part-time work is unclear in a context where full-timers are expected to work outside of standard hours without additional compensation. Where these expecta-tions are linked to extended opening and operating hours, the opportu-nity needs to be taken to create job shares for managers and supervisors, rather than extending a single manager's responsibilities outside of a normal working week. The '24/7' society should be used to expand oppor-tunities for non-standard hours and for new ways of working and not for creating unmanageable workloads. Such developments not only create barriers for women taking up higher-level jobs but also restrict opportunities for couples to agree upon and implement a more equitable sharing of domestic tasks.

Some Policy Recommendations

The abolition of the voluntary opt out from UK working time regulations is the first and most important policy measure that needs to be taken to tackle the long-hours culture. Another possible step towards a change in approach might be to rule that expectations that staff on full-time contracts should work both flexibly and beyond a standard week should not be considered grounds for refusing a request made under the right to request flexible or reduced hours provisions. The policy agenda must be to rebuild social norms that work can and should be confined within reasonable bounds, and action needs to be taken to roll back the tendency for all hours to be potentially available to employers.

Age Discrimination

The UK's higher education system results in most students graduating by age 21 or 22. This early entry for graduates into employment provides women with a good start in the labour market, compared to societies where both extended education and in some cases problems of unemployment for graduates limits the opportunity to become established in a career before it is necessary to consider seriously having children. However, there is some evidence – which requires further research – that the UK tends to continue to place a high premium on employees achieving promotions up a career ladder at a young age (Crompton et al. 1991). The UK has moved away from a seniority-based approach to promotion but, while time served is clearly neither an efficient nor equitable way of selecting people for higher jobs, there is a clear danger that the opposite practice is being adopted, that of not promoting people once they have passed a certain age. To the extent that age discrimination is prevalent, the effect is to reduce opportunities for those returning from a break, both in terms of entry-level job options and prospects within those jobs. Even those who stay in work but limit their work efforts during the time of heavy domestic demands may find their future opportunities are proportionately curtailed. Such factors can exacerbate problems of developing a more gender-equitable domestic division of labour, as there may be a high price to pay by men if they agree to limit their work commitments during particular time periods when key promotion decisions are made.

Some Policy Recommendations

The implementation of age discrimination legislation needs to take into account these interactions between gender equality and age discrimination. One possibility would be for employers to be asked to demonstrate that there are opportunities for promotion and entry-level recruitment across the age spectrum. Diversity policies need to be expanded to include age diversity as well as other dimensions.

MODERNISING THE WELFARE AND EMPLOYMENT REGIME

As we have argued, the organisation of the welfare and employment system in the UK still tends to reinforce women's economic dependence on the family or the state, despite the evidence of women's willingness to invest in education and to integrate into the labour market. Three factors can be identified that reinforce this mismatch between current institutional arrangements and women's aspirations. First, the notion of a 'male breadwinner' model of the family and household is still embedded in benefits and tax credit systems, even if income tax has been individualised. Secondly, the costs of motherhood in the UK are still high and largely borne by women, rather than the household. These costs include low maternity pay, which therefore presumes that women can and should rely on their partner's income and increases the need for male partners to seek to earn 'a family wage'. The recent extension of paid leave in the UK is still based on a low weekly benefit (Fagan and Hebson 2005), so that, although it provides women and families with some extra resources, it certainly does not do much to reduce dependence. The costs of motherhood are further increased by the difficulties of returning to full-time work in a context where full-time work involves long hours and there is a lack of affordable childcare. Contrary to the situation in Sweden, where women and men can take their paid paternity leave on a part-time basis thereby providing some compensation for reduced hours, in the UK there is no compensation for lost income due to reduced hours and, moreover, many part-time jobs are lower paid on an hourly basis then full-time work (CEC 2002; OECD 1998). Entering part-time work, which is often the only option available, also leads to long-term 'scarring effects', on both earnings and benefit entitlements, associated with segregation into low-skilled jobs (Olsen and Walby 2004; Walby and Olsen 2002). This tendency to push the costs of having children on to mothers, and thereby encourage mothers to become either disconnected from the labour market or to pursue segregated careers in low-paid part-time jobs, has particular impacts on women who become single parents if their partnership fails and reduces their opportunities to become independent of the support of ex-partners or the state.

The tendency for discontinuous careers and for significant periods of part-time work also has consequences for access to pensions. The government is changing the state pension system (see below) to improve women's rights but there is the further problem that good pension rights in the UK really depend upon employer schemes. Women may already be disadvantaged by being employed – at least in the private sector – in organisations with lower-quality or no schemes. However, the new approach to pensions in the private sector, based on defined contribution schemes, will further penalise those who reduce hours/pay or take breaks early in their careers, as investments made at an early age in careers – exactly when women tend to work less – will be the most productive.

Some Policy Recommendations

Action needs to be taken to reduce the costs borne by mothers in both the labour market and in entitlements to benefits. There are four main principles that need to be adopted through the UK welfare systems in order to promote greater gender equality. First, the extent of targeted benefits, based on household means-testing, needs to be reduced to limit the disincentives to women to enter employment in low-income households. Use of the household rather than the individual as the unit of analysis in welfare policy evaluation tends to ignore intra-household inequalities and the fact that many households prove to be unstable over time, so that it does matter in a material sense whether both partners are attached to the labour market. Other countries are much less reliant on household means-testing. Belgium, as we have already noted, has introduced a new tax credit based on individual earnings. Objections that such an approach is too costly might lead to a reconsideration of the appropriate level of minimum wages; the UK system provides a form of subsidy to employers paying wages too low to cover costs of subsistence and it might be better to combine an individualised tax credit system with higher guaranteed hourly earnings so that incentives for employers to upgrade the productivity of their work environment and workers is not removed by policies that allow the less efficient employers to be subsidised.

A second but linked type of reform is to base benefit entitlements more on citizenship than on employment history. In the Netherlands and Sweden pensions are linked more to citizenship. The UK is reducing the number of years needed for a full contribution with the objective of radically increasing the number of women who are eligible for a full state pension and from

2012 the state pension is again to be index linked to earnings, such that it should provide over time a better level of benefit. However, it will still need to be combined with household means-tested additional benefits to bring pension recipients above the poverty line.

If the likelihood of further improved state pensions is discounted, then the third area for reform relates to private pensions. Here the government needs to find some way of assisting those who work reduced hours over the period of when they have responsibility for young children from missing out on important contributions to pension schemes at key stages; this could be included as part of a parental leave scheme package where those on reduced hours could have pension contributions made up to full-time hours, for example.

This leads to the fourth point that welfare reforms are required to reduce the costs borne by mothers, in the interests both of gender equality and of maintaining or improving fertility rates. One key to this is to provide high benefit levels for those taking maternity or parental leave; this is a strategy currently being pursued in Germany owing to concerns about low levels of fertility among higher educated women who have the most to lose when taking low-paid parental leave. In Sweden, as we have already noted, the fact that women can retain their economic independence, while reducing their work commitments by using their maternity and parental leave in a flexible way to provide compensation for loss of pay owing to reduced hours of working, has the additional benefit of reducing pressure on male partners to earn a family wage. In the UK, maternity pay is only available if mothers are absent from employment and not as a top-up to part-time working. Furthermore, the new right to request flexible working when responsible for a child under six does not provide the right to request a return to full-time work, unlike in Sweden where hours can be reduced without prejudice to the opportunity to return to full-time work until a child is 8.

CONCLUSIONS

Improving the position of women in work is an objective fully justified on grounds of social justice. Pursuing the social justice objective should also provide the bonus of helping to update and modernise the UK's employment and welfare institutions. The outcome in principle should be an opportunity to base economic and social policy on more equitable and more appropriate models of social organisation, more in line with citizens' aspirations and behaviour. There is a need, therefore, to identify those institutional arrangements that promote and reflect an outdated and discriminatory model of women as economic dependents and to take action to avoid women being trapped in low-paid and insecure parts of the labour market. The mismatch between labour market institutions and changing gender roles increases the risks of promoting a low-productivity economy that wastes the investments made in women's education and heightens the likelihood of social exclusion and poverty, particularly in old age and for single parents and their children. Alongside these arguments, examples have been presented of best practice from a range of European countries, to make clear that current institutional arrangements and customary practices in the UK are not the only options available. There is not one model of social and economic organisation that has solved all the problems of gender inequality, but by drawing upon examples across the spectrum of different social and labour market arrangements, it is possible to build up a picture of policy approaches that could be adopted that both promote gender equality and align our labour market and welfare institutions more with the needs of citizens – both male and female – over the life course.

NOTES

1. In a study by the European Commission, the UK was the only member state out of the EU15 to have a significant penalty for working part-time , even after controlling for education, experience, gender, and so on. (CEC 2002)
2. This is contrary to, for example, arguments put forward by the then Conservative government when the part-time directive giving equality of rights was first passed in Brussels where a major decline in part-time work opportunities was predicted if part-timers were to be given equal rights with full-timers.

REFERENCES

Arulampalam, W. and A. Booth (1997), *Labour Market Flexibility and Skills Acquisition: Is There a Trade-off?*, Programme on Labour Market Dynamics in a Changing Environment, Institute for Labour Research, University of Essex, Discussion Paper Series, No. 97 13 August.

Blau, F. and L. Kahn (1992), 'The gender earnings gap: learning from international comparisons', *American Economic Review*, **82**(2), 533–8.

Bruegel, I. and D. Perrons (1995), 'Where do the costs of unequal treatment for women fall? An analysis of the incidence of the costs of unequal pay and sex discrimination in the UK', in J. Humphries and J. Rubery (eds), *The Economics of Equal Opportunities*, Manchester: Equal Opportunities Commission, pp. 155–74.

Commission of the European Communities (CEC) (2002), *Employment in Europe 2002: Recent Trends and Prospects*, Luxembourg: Office for Official Publications of the European Communities.

Commission of the European Communities (CEC) (2006), *Indicators for Monitoring the Employment Guidelines Including Indicators for Additional*

Employment Analysis, Luxembourg: Office for Official Publications of the European Communities, http://ec.europa.eu/employment_social/employment_ strategy/pdf/indicatorsendnov_en.pdf (accessed on 17 January 2008).

Council of Europe (1998), *Gender mainstreaming: conceptual framework, methodology and presentation of good practices*, final report of activities of the Group of Specialists on Mainstreaming, EG-S-MS (98) 2, Strasbourg.

Crompton, R., L. Hantrais, N. Le Feuvre and P. Walters (1991), *Women in Professional Occupations in France and Britain*, Brussels: CEC, DGV.

Eborall, C. (2003), *The State of the Social Care Workforce in England*, Leeds: Topss England, www.topssengland.net/files/vol1%20TopssEnglandwkfce2003re65A. doc (accessed on 17 January 2008).

Esping-Andersen, G., D. Gallie, A. Hemerick and J. Myles (2002), *Why We Need a New Welfare State*, Oxford: Oxford University Press.

Eurostat (2002), *Statistics in Focus*, 9/2002, Women and men reconciling work and family life, Population and social conditions theme 3, Luxembourg: Office for Official Publications of the European Communities, http://epp.eurostat. ec.europa.eu/cache/ITY_OFFPUB/KS-NK-02-009/EN/KS-NK-02-009-EN.PDF (accessed on 17 January 2008).

Eurostat (2005), *Statistics in Focus*, 19/2005, 17 million tertiary students in the European Union, Population and social conditions, Luxembourg: Office for Official Publications of the European Communities, http://epp.eurostat. ec.europa.eu/cache/ITY_OFFPUB/KS-NK-05-019/EN/KS-NK-05-019-EN.PDF (accessed on 17 January 2008).

Eurostat (2006), *Statistics in Focus*, 11/2006, Labour market latest trends, 4th quarter 2005 data, Increasing trend for the employment rate, Luxembourg: Office for Official Publications of the European Communities, http://epp.eurostat. ec.europa.eu/cache/ITY_OFFPUB/KS-NK-06-011/EN/KS-NK-06-011-EN.PDF (accessed on 17 January 2008).

Fagan, C. and G. Hebson (2005), '*Making work pay' debates from a gender perspective: a comparative review of some recent policy reforms in thirty European countries,* The co-ordinators', report for the EU Expert Group on Gender, Social Inclusion and Employment Expert Group (EGGSIE) to the Equal Opportunities Unit, Employment Directorate (DGV) European Commission, http://ec. europa.eu/employment_social/publications/2006/ke6905836_en.pdf (accessed on 17 January 2008).

Figart, D., E. Mutari and M. Power (2002), *Living Wages, Equal Wages*, IAFFE Advances in Feminist Economics, London: Routledge.

Ginn, J. and S. Arber (1998), 'How does part-time work lead to low pension income', in J. O'Reilly and C. Fagan (eds), *Part-time Prospects*, London: Routledge, pp. 156–73.

Grant, L., S. Yeandle and L. Buckner (2005), *Working Below Potential: Women and Part-Time Work*, EOC Working Paper Series, No. 40.

Gregg, P. and J. Wadsworth (1995), 'Gender, households and access to employment', in J. Humphries and J. Rubery (eds), *The Economics of Equal Opportunities*, Manchester: Equal Opportunities Commission, pp. 345–64.

Grimshaw, D. and M. Carroll (2005), 'Healthcare sector report: the UK report', produced for the Russell Sage Foundation project, 'Low-Wage Work in Europe' EWERC, Manchester Business School, University of Manchester.

Grimshaw, D. and J. Rubery (2002), 'The adjusted gender pay gap: a critical appraisal of standard decomposition techniques', Paper for the Equal

Opportunities Unit in the European Commission, March, Group of Experts on Gender and Employment, the Equal Opportunities Unit in the European Commission, http://www.mbs.ac.uk/research/europeanemployment/projects/gendersocial/documents/EPEpolitical%20paper.pdf (accessed 17 January 2008).

Harkness, S., S. Machin and J. Waldfogel (1997), 'Evaluating the pin money hypothesis: the relationship between women's labour market activity, family income and poverty in Britain', *Journal of Population Economics*, **10**(2), 137–58.

Humphries, J. and J. Rubery (eds) (1995), *The Economics of Equal Opportunities*, Manchester: Equal Opportunities Commission.

Juhn, C., K. Murphy and B. Pierce (1993), 'Wage inequality and the rise in returns to skill', *Journal of Political Economy*, **101**(3), 410–42.

Kingsmill, D. (2002), *The Kingsmill Review of Women's Employment and Pay*, www.womenandequalityunit.gov.uk/pay/kingsmill/kingsmill_review_report.pdf (accessed 17 January 2008).

Kodz, J., S. Davis, D. Lain, M. Strebler, J. Rick, P. Bates, J. Cummings, N. Meager, D. Anxo, S. Gineste, R. Trinczek and S. Pamer (2003), *Working Long Hours: A Review of the Evidence*, Department of Trade and Industry Employment Relations Research Series No. 16, London: DTI, http://www.berr.gov.uk/files/file 11543.pdf (accessed 17 January 2008).

Lister, R. (2005), 'The links between women's and children's poverty in women's budget group', *Women's and Children's Poverty: Making the Links*, www.wbg.org.uk/documents/WBGWomensandchildrenspoverty.pdf (accessed 17 January 2008).

McLaughlin, E. (1995), 'Gender and egalitarianism in the British welfare state', in J. Humphries and J. Rubery (eds), *The Economics of Equal Opportunities*, Manchester: Equal Opportunities Commission, pp. 291–312.

Olsen, W. and S. Walby (2004), *Modelling Gender Pay Gaps*, Manchester: EOC.

Organisation for Economic Co-operation and Development (OECD) (1994), *Women and Structural Change. New Perspectives*, Paris: OECD.

Organisation for Economic Co-operation and Development (OECD) (1998), 'The concentration of women's employment and relative occupational pay', in OECD, *The Future of Female-Dominated Occupations*, OECD: Paris, pp. 15–47.

Organisation for Economic Co-operation and Development (OECD) (2002), *Employment Outlook*, Paris: OECD.

Organisation for Economic Co-operation and Development (OECD) (2004), *Employment Outlook*, Paris: OECD.

Plantenga, J. and J. Hansen (1999), 'Assessing equal opportunities in the European Union', *International Labour Review*, **138**(4), 351–79.

Rees, T. (1998), *Mainstreaming Equality in the European Union: Education, Training and Labour Market Policies*, London: Routledge.

Rubery, J., M. Smith, C. Fagan and D. Grimshaw (1998), *Women and European Employment*, London: Routledge.

Rubery, J., D. Grimshaw and H. Figueiredo (2002), *The Gender Pay Gap and Gender Mainstreaming Pay Policy in EU Member States*, European Expert Group on Gender and Employment Report to the Equal Opportunities Unit, DG Employment, http://mbs.ac.uk/ewerc/egge

Rubery, J., C. Fagan, D. Grimshaw, J. Humphries and M. Smith (2003a), 'Equal opportunities as a productive factor', in B. Burchell, S. Deakin, J. Rubery and J. Michie (eds), *Systems of Production: Markets, Organizations and Performance*, London: Routledge, pp. 236–62.

Rubery, J., M. Smith, H. Figueiredo, C. Fagan and D. Grimshaw (2003b), *Gender Mainstreaming and the European Employment Strategy and Social Inclusion Process*, European Expert Group on Gender and Employment Report to the Equal Opportunities Unit, DG Employment, http://mbs.ac.uk/research/europeanemployment/projects/gendersocial/documents/NapEmp_Inc2003.pdf (accessed 17 January 2008).

Rubery, J., D. Grimshaw and H. Figueiredo (2005a), 'How to close the gender pay gap in Europe: towards the gender mainstreaming of pay policy', *Industrial Relations Journal*, **36**(3), 184–213.

Rubery, J., K. Ward and D. Grimshaw (2005b), 'The changing employment relationship and the implications for quality part-time work', *Labour and Industry*, **15**(3), 7–28.

Walby, S. and W. Olsen (2002), *The Impact of Women's Position in the Labour Market on Pay and Implications for UK Productivity*, report to the Women and Equality Unit, London: Department of Trade and Industry.

Woodland, S., N. Simmonds, M. Thornby, R. Fitzgerald and A. McGee (2003), *The Second Work–Life Balance Study: Results from the Employer Survey*, Employment Relations Research Series No. 22, London: National Centre For Social Research.

13. The regulation of women's pay: from individual rights to reflexive law?

Simon Deakin and Colm McLaughlin

1 INTRODUCTION

Legislation mandating equality of pay between women and men was among the earliest forms of sex discrimination legislation to be adopted in Britain. The Equal Pay Act 1970 pre-dated the more general prohibition on sex discrimination in employment by five years. It was introduced prior to the UK's membership of the European Community (EC) and at a point when the EC, although it had a treaty provision governing pay equality between women and men, had no directive on the subject, and prior to the judgments of the European Court of Justice which opened up the field of equality law in the course of the 1970s. If the model for the UK Act was more American than European, the federal Congress having passed an equal pay law in 1963 and the more extensive Civil Rights Act in 1965, the British measure was, in important respects, *sui generis*. It relied on a combination of individual claims and collective dispute resolution mechanisms to achieve its objectives, and was initially successful in combining legal remedies and pre-existing features of the industrial relations system to close the pay gap. In the 1980s and 1990s, when collective bargaining was being eclipsed, individual litigation increasingly took its place, encouraged by developments in European Union (EU) law and backed by strategic support from the Equal Opportunities Commission (EOC) in key cases.[1] This did not simply lead to the radical reshaping of equal pay law, but had far-reaching consequences for payment systems and for industrial relations more generally, not least in bringing into the open tensions between unions and their own members. In part because of these destabilising effects, the model embodied in the 1970 Act is increasingly being questioned: the law is, at one and the same time, highly complex and difficult to apply, while apparently contributing little to the further narrowing of the pay gap. As a result there is a growing debate about whether a shift in regulatory strategy is needed, away from direct legal enforcement to a more flexible approach, based around the concept of 'reflexive law'.

This chapter considers the nature of the shift which may now be taking place, against the backdrop of the evolution of equal pay law over the past four decades, and recent reviews of the legislation which have set out the case for change. Section 2 provides an overview of the different regulatory approaches adopted in the course of the legislation's development, culminating in the proposals set out in the 2007 *Discrimination Law Review*. Section 3 links the proposals in the 2007 *Review* to the wider debate on the role of 'reflexive regulation' in employment and company law and section 4 provides an assessment of whether reflexive approaches are likely to work in the equal pay area. Section 5 concludes.

2 THE EVOLUTION OF REGULATORY STRATEGIES IN THE FIELD OF EQUAL PAY

The Equal Pay Act 1970 gave an individual worker the right to bring a claim against her employer for equality of pay with a comparator of the opposite sex who was employed in the same 'employment' and 'establishment' as she was. The legal mechanism by which a successful claim took effect was the insertion into the applicant's contract of an 'equality clause' which harmonised her terms and conditions of employment with those of her chosen comparator. The Act, although passed in 1970, did not come into force until 1975, during which time many payment structures, particularly at sector level, were amended voluntarily through collective bargaining. In addition, the compulsory arbitration procedure which was provided for by section 3 of the Act enabled unions to bring claims for the realignment of discriminatory pay structures to the Central Arbitration Committee (CAC), which had the power to amend entire collective agreements and similar arrangements at sector or company level. Econometric analysis conducted in the mid-1970s suggested that the narrowing of the pay gap which occurred at this time – average hourly wages rose to around 70 per cent of men's by the end of the 1970s, compared with around 60 per cent at the start – was the result of a combination of the legal mechanisms set out in the Act and implementation of the equality principle through centralised pay bargaining (Zabalza and Tzannatos 1985).

Nevertheless, following several landmark decisions of the European Court of Justice (ECJ) in the course of the 1970s and the passage of the Equal Pay Directive in 1975, UK law was seen to be out of line with the requirements of European Community law, and the Equal Pay Act was amended in 1983 to allow claims for equality in the case of work of 'equal value' in addition to the existing categories of 'like work' and 'work rated as equivalent' under a voluntary job evaluation scheme. The amendment was effected in a highly complex way and it took some considerable time for the litigation which followed to establish clear parameters for equal pay claims. Repeated references to the ECJ, given financial and logistic support by the EOC, led to significant extensions (or perhaps clarifications) of the law in relation to pension rights, the position of part-time and fixed-term workers, and the scope of employers' defences (see Deakin and Morris 2005: 576–9). Although this litigation-led approach was successful in reshaping the law, the process was often protracted (some cases took over a decade to resolve) and induced considerable uncertainty for collective agreements and pension schemes.

One reason for the prominence accorded to individual claims at this time was the diminishing role played by collective bargaining. The collective arbitration route set out in section 3 of the Act was effectively blocked off by the Court of Appeal's 1979 decision in the *Hy-Mac* case, which decided that the CAC's powers were confined to cases of direct discrimination (in effect, payment structures which were based directly on the criterion of gender) and did not extend to cases of indirect discrimination (payment structures which resulted in different outcomes by sex by virtue of occupational segregation). Although the ECJ later held (in 1982) that this decision had placed the UK in breach of EC law, amendments made to sex discrimination legislation in the mid-1980s, rather than restoring the pre-*Hy-Mac* meaning of section 3, repealed that provision altogether, putting in its place a largely symbolic and practically ineffective measure for declaring void provisions of collective agreements or similar payment structures which contravened the prohibition on discrimination (see Deakin and Morris 2005: 692–3). Thus, from the early 1980s onwards, individual litigation was the only effective route by which the equal pay principle could be implemented. Although legal victories were often the catalyst for collective agreements which led to large-scale realignments of payment structures, the decline in union power in this period undermined the potential role of collective bargaining in implementing the goals of legislation. Then, in the early 2000s, a series of court decisions allowed individual litigants to challenge deals struck by unions and employers and to claim compensation from unions themselves in cases where they were held to have failed to pay due regard to the equality principle in balancing competing claims of groups of workers (Dickens 2007: 483).

At the same time, a substantial gender pay gap remained. Women's average hourly earnings had reached 75 per cent of men's by 1988 and the figure rose to 79 per cent by 1992 and 82 per cent by 2000 (see Deakin and Morris 2005: 583 and the sources cited there). In the early 2000s it was largely static, with a further narrowing being attributed not to equal pay law but to the introduction from 1999 of the national minimum wage (DCLG 2007: 9). As a result, attention began to turn to alternative and more proactive modes of addressing pay discrimination. In part this took the form of a growing recognition that the Equal Pay Act's focus on the workplace addressed only one part of the problem, and a belief that assumptions about the gendered nature of the division of labour should be challenged through changes to the law governing maternity and paternity rights and by reforms to the tax-benefit system (see Fredman 1997), an agenda which was then taken up in the area of 'work and families' legislation (Deakin and Morris 2005: 696–713). In the field of equal pay law itself, 'proactive approaches' put forward included those placing positive duties on organisations to take action to overcome institutional discrimination inherent in their policies and practices, rather than leaving it up to individuals to lay claims. It was argued that these methods would reduce reliance on confrontational litigation and shift the emphasis to one of changing organisational behaviour and attitudes (Hepple et al. 2000; O'Cinneide 2003).

One proactive method for addressing pay discrimination that began to be widely advocated at this time was that of mandatory equal pay reviews, as part of a wider reconsideration of the role of regulatory strategies in discrimination law (Hepple et al. 2000). The underlying assumption was that pay discrimination is mostly systemic and unseen, and as such can only be identified through a systematic analysis of job roles, responsibilities and remuneration. Thus, the argument was made that employers should be obligated to examine their pay systems and identify and rectify any gender-based wage differentials they uncover. This approach was first adopted in Ontario under its 1987 Pay Equity Act (McColgan 1997), and this lead was then followed in a number of other jurisdictions, including Quebec, Sweden and, most recently, Finland.

In the UK, a significant step in the same direction was taken when the Equal Pay Task Force, which was set up by the EOC in 1999 to explore the pay gap 30 years after the introduction of the Equal Pay Act, recommended that employers should be required to conduct equal pay reviews on a regular basis. The task force took the view that 'the vast majority of employers do not believe they have a gender pay gap and therefore do not believe an equal pay review is necessary'; legislation was needed to make reviews mandatory since 'the overwhelming evidence to date is that [employers] will not [introduce them] voluntarily' (Equal Pay Task Force 2001: xi).

However, the official government response since then has been to reject compulsion in favour of public policy support to encourage employers to undertake a pay review. Thus, two months after the release of the Equal Pay Task Force Report, the government commissioned Denise Kingsmill to undertake a very similar review into women's pay and employment, but the terms of reference were limited to examining and reporting on *non-legislative* proposals for reducing the pay gap (Kingsmill 2001). Given this, it is not surprising that Kingsmill recommended a voluntarist rather than mandatory approach to getting employers to undertake pay reviews. Significantly, part of the reasoning offered was that for the private sector, and in particular large companies with stock exchange listings, a combination of reputational effects and shareholder activism would put companies under pressures to reform their practices. Here, Kingsmill used the language of corporate social responsibility (CSR) to argue that private sector companies would recognise the business case for reform. The main drivers would be the risk and cost of reputational damage from gender bias, including loss of shareholder confidence and the fragmentation of companies' consumer base; the high expense of equal pay litigation; and costs stemming from an inability to recruit and retain high-calibre employees. A different approach was suggested for the public sector, where commercial pressures would not apply to the same degree: Kingsmill recommended compulsory employment and pay reviews for public sector organisations, with the findings of reviews to influence the public procurement process.

The issue of pay reviews was considered again only a few years later by the Women and Work Commission (2006). The commission had a wide remit, which included a consideration of the issue of gender stereotyping and other broader causes of occupational segregation. In relation to pay reviews, the commission's terms of reference did include consideration of the case for making pay reviews mandatory through legislation. The commission recommended a voluntarist approach, however, for the reason that its members were unable to reach consensus on the need for compulsion. Thus, the report simply outlined the arguments for and against pay reviews without taking a position, and recommended a series of measures intended to raise awareness, promote best practice and build employer capacity to address equality issues. In common with the Kingsmill report, the commission recommended a mandatory approach in the public sector.

Following on from the recommendations of these successive reports various public policy supports were put in place in the 2000s to encourage firms to examine their pay systems, as well as to address the issue of gender equity in the workplace more generally. The government launched the so-called Castle Awards to encourage and reward firms that displayed excellence in addressing equal pay, and it began working with a number of networks of 'fair pay champions' such as Opportunity Now to promote best practice. The EOC published various documents to encourage and assist firms conduct an equal pay review. One of these was the *Code of Practice on Equal Pay* (EOC 2003) which set out best practice on compliance with legislation. It stressed that the best way for firms to avoid equal pay litigation was to conduct regular equal pay reviews in consultation with their employees. In 2003, the equal pay questionnaire came into effect, which allowed individual employees to request information from their employer if they thought they were not receiving equal pay. These combined steps were considered to have raised the profile of equal pay reviews in the private sector by the mid-2000s (Neathey et al. 2005).

In the public sector, all civil service departments and agencies were required to draw up an equal pay action plan in 2003, and in 2006 the *Civil Service Reward Principles* (The Civil Service 2006) were released, one of which targeted equal pay and the need to eliminate pay discrimination. Local authorities were required to conduct a pay review by 2007 under the 2004 National Joint Council pay agreement. In addition, the public sector gender equality duty, which became law in April 2007, required public authorities to take active steps to promote gender equality and eliminate gender discrimination. This placed obligations on public bodies to further examine their pay and employment systems. At the same time, several high-profile equal pay cases involving local authorities highlighted the penalties involved for unequal pay and further raised the profile of the equal pay issue.

The Discrimination Law Review of 2007 may well prove to be a turning point in the debate. At the time of writing the review was only a consultation document, but it set out a clear vision for the future of anti-discrimination law in the UK, with the government's position on certain issues very clear. And in the area of equal pay reviews, the influence of both the Kingsmill report and the Women and Work Commission was clear. Thus, no consultation was invited over this issue, with the *Review* arguing that the likely costs of enforced pay reviews would outweigh the benefits, and as such, would 'contravene better regulation principles'. Instead, it favoured an approach based on 'promoting the spread of good practice' as well as mechanisms to increase the 'reputational benefits' for firms that undertake them voluntarily (DCLG 2007: paras 3.7–3.8).

However, the *Review* was not confined to equal pay or indeed to sex discrimination law, but covered legal issues arising from the full range of anti-discrimination provisions (sex, race, disability, age, gender reassignment, sexual orientation, and religion or belief), one of its objectives being to provide a framework for a new Single Equality Act. Its broad approach can be described as one based on 'reflexive regulation', as McCrudden (2007: 360) has suggested: various elements in the report, 'when taken together, amount . . . to the partial adoption of reflexive regulation which . . . is quite different in significant respects from those methods of anti-discrimination regulation that have gone before'. These elements ranged from a new emphasis on the business case for equality, to references to the diffusion of good practice in contradistinction to enforcement strategies based on strict legal compliance, and to the role of engagement with stakeholders. Specific proposals included amendments to the law to allow greater scope for positive action by employers in favour of workforce diversity, and the replacement of specific aspects of the duty of public sector bodies to promote equality with a more general test of proportionality.

3 THE MEANING OF 'REFLEXIVE REGULATION'

What, then, is reflexive regulation? It is perhaps easier to say what it is not. It is generally contrasted to, on the one hand, 'command-and-control' forms of regulation which are based on prescriptive and detailed controls and supported by penal or civil sanctions for non-compliance; and, on the other, deregulation of the kind which removes statutory controls altogether in favour of a return to individual freedom of contract or (which may amount to the same thing) market-based governance. The critique of the command-and-control approach maintains that there are limits to the effectiveness of legal regulation in the face of alternative sources of norms beyond the law. These alternatives range from relatively formal systems of self-regulation, such as collective bargaining or financial codes of conduct, to informal social norms and tacit conventions which may shape behaviour in particular contexts. The idea can be expressed more formally using the language of autopoiesis or systems theory, which posits a radical separation of the legal system from the social sub-systems which it is seeking to regulate (Teubner 1992). Legal rules, it is suggested, rely on linguistic forms and institutional processes which are particular to the legal system itself and translate incompletely, at best, into the economic or organisational contexts in which legal rules are intended to be applied. The more detailed and prescriptive attempts at regulation are, the less successful they tend to be in achieving their desired goals, a phenomenon which feeds back into the legal system in the form of the 'juridification' of law, implying the over-specification of rules and excessive detail and complexity in the form of the law, particularly legislation.

More positively, the theory also emphasises the possibilities of matching legal rules more effectively to the various tasks which regulation is called on to perform. 'Reflexive law' can, it is argued, be designed in such a way as to stimulate self-regulation of the kind which will fulfil policy objectives. Reflexive law is therefore associated, to some degree, with a shift from

substantive to procedural norms. Legal interventions are often characterised as reflexive when they make use of default rules and other quasi-
optional forms of regulation. These allow the parties to self-regulatory
arrangements – for example, trade unions and employers in the context of
collective bargaining – to vary the terms of statutory norms, which, as a
result, cease to be completely mandatory. In this way the application of the
law is tailored to local conditions. In such fields as working time, equal
treatment of part-time and fixed-term workers and information and consultation of employees, legislation sets default rules which can be varied by
agreement – so called 'bargained statutory adjustments' (Davies and
Kilpatrick 2004) – but only if certain conditions are met. In a sense, the law
has been 'proceduralised' – a standard which was previously substantive, in
the sense (for example) of setting an absolute limit to working time, is now,
in part at least, procedural. The law is no longer exclusively concerned with
setting the contents of the relevant norm, but also with stipulating the procedure by which the norm can be modified.

Reflexive law also has a hybrid quality which is suggested by the way it
combines sanctions of different types. The influential 'pyramid of enforcement' model developed by Ayres and Braithwaite (1992) and extended to
discrimination law by Hepple et al. (2000) presupposes that hard sanctions,
possibly penal ones, must be exercised if all else fails. The model assumes
that the application of legal sanctions will hardly ever have to occur – these
are the few cases occupying the apex of the 'pyramid' – but it is important
that the possibility should exist in order to maintain the stability of the
overall structure. Many apparent cases of financial self-regulation depend
on the existence, as a matter of last resort, of hard sanctions of this kind.

A common thread uniting the different conceptions of reflexive law is the
idea that the role of the law is to promote a learning process around the question of 'what works best' as a route to achieving social or economic policy
goals. Thus the law recognises or validates a range of potential solutions,
while at the same time using benchmarking procedures and other deliberative mechanisms to set up a series of tests for determining their relative
success or failure. In order for such deliberative strategies to be effective,
some have argued that attention has to be given to the issue of the 'frame':
'the hypothesis of reflexive governance holds that the conditions under which
a deliberative process may succeed can be identified, and once identified,
must be affirmatively created, rather than taken for granted' (De Schutter
and Deakin 2005: 3). In that sense, reflexive regulation is governance by
design, rather than a process left entirely to the forces of spontaneous order.

At the same time there are limits to what can be achieved by design alone.
For reflexive strategies to be effective, institutions and mechanisms must be
in place, beyond the law, to receive and translate reflexive legal norms in a

way which makes their implementation effective. In theoretical terms, this presupposes the existence of bridging institutions which assist the 'structural coupling' of the legal system with the organisational and market contexts in which the rules are intended to be applied. Such institutions may include, in the employment law context, collective bargaining or other possible forms of workplace-based deliberation such as employee consultation (Barnard et al. 2003). Thus another critical issue is whether social institutions have the capacity to play the role ascribed to them by reflexive regulatory strategies. To the extent that they do not, the law may have to undertake a capacity building role.

The debate over the role of CSR provides an illustration of this point. In principle, CSR can be quite effectively integrated into a reflexive approach to regulation. Corporate social responsibility involves an appeal to companies to go 'beyond compliance' since by doing so they can better preserve their competitiveness and prepare themselves to deal with future shocks. The business case for CSR intersects with the regulatory argument for limiting the role of the law to that of providing a framework which will reward those organisations which can most effectively internalise their social costs. One of the regulatory techniques associated with this approach is the use of disclosure rules and reporting requirements to generate a flow of information about the way in which companies handle the issue of externalities. This issue has appeared on the policy agenda in the UK as a result of the protracted debate over the introduction of a statutory 'operating and financial review' (OFR) which would require large companies to produce annual reports on how they were dealing with various aspects of their social and environmental performance. The somewhat diluted form of this provision which was eventually brought into force by the Companies Act 2006, the 'business review', is, despite the changes made after the government abandoned the OFR in 2005, a measure with the potential to stimulate processes of benchmarking and peer review, when coupled with the active participation of social actors in the evaluation process. Changes in pensions law have also been introduced with the aim of stimulating a greater interest in social and environmental issues on the part of institutional investors; legislation requiring pension funds to disclose their voting policy and to state the extent to which social, ethical and environmental investment matters are taken into consideration, came into force in the UK in 2001. The Association of British Insurers has taken the view that this requirement has had a 'significant and wide-ranging impact on the investment community . . . [and has] added significantly to the growing Socially Responsible Investment (SRI) movement' (ABI 2001: 13). These measures can therefore be seen as 'capacity building' mechanisms in the sense identified by reflexive theory.

How successful is this strategy likely to be in the context of discrimination law, and equal pay in particular?

4   THE PROSPECTS FOR THE REFLEXIVE REGULATION OF PAY INEQUALITY: THEORY AND EVIDENCE

As we have seen, a core aspect of the theory of reflexive law is the rejection of models based on spontaneous order. Reflexive approaches, far from advocating complete deregulation, contemplate a version of 'market steering' which presupposes a role for the legal 'frame'. Two dimensions of this problem are critical: the appropriate role of sanctions, and the role of the law in capacity building. Here we first examine the empirical research, before discussing whether a voluntary approach to equal pay adequately addresses either of these dimensions.

The empirical research suggests that a voluntary approach has had limited impact in persuading private sector firms to conduct pay reviews. The EOC commissioned four surveys between 2002 and 2005 looking at the extent of equal pay reviews among organisations (Adams et al. 2006; Brett and Milsome 2004; Neathey et al. 2003; Schäfer et al. 2005). While there was some increase in the number of large (500-plus employees) private sector firms that had conducted an equal pay review between 2003 (14 per cent) and 2004 (33 per cent), in the 2005 survey this figured was almost unchanged (34 per cent). More than half of large private sector firms reported no past equal pay review activity, nor any intention to conduct one in the future, and only 5 per cent had an equal pay review in progress. Once small and medium-sized organisations were included the picture was even less positive. Eighty-two per cent of organisations in the 2005 survey had not conducted an equal pay review, did not have one in progress and did not intend to conduct one (Adams et al. 2006). These survey results are supported by data in the 2004 Workplace Employment Relations Survey (WERS), which showed only 24 per cent of firms were monitoring their recruitment and selection, only 10 per cent were monitoring promotion, and only 7 per cent were reviewing their relative pay rates for indirect gender discrimination (Kersley et al. 2006).

There is therefore little reason to revise the view of the Equal Pay Task Force in 2001, to the effect that the majority of employers do not think that they have pay equity issues to resolve, a conclusion that the EOC has also reached in now advocating for equal pay reviews to be made mandatory.

From a theoretical perspective, the issue of the 'frame' is concerned with the role of legal rules in setting appropriate incentives for self-regulation. From this point of view, and in the light of the evidence concerning voluntary audits, making pay audits mandatory should be considered as a viable option here. This would not amount to committing employers to any particular outcome, but it would require them to undertake a regular review process and to disclose the results. Enforced audits are therefore comparable to mandatory disclosure rules which in other contexts (such as corporate governance) are seen as playing a vital role in stimulating learning without dictating the final form of solutions arrived at by employers.

Evidence from Ontario illustrates that such learning can take place, but only when the right 'frame' is in place. Here, mandatory pay reviews have had only limited success due to a lack of monitoring, which has meant high levels of non-compliance (Baker and Fortin 2000) and manipulation of the process by employers where unions are not involved (McColgan 1993). The most successful reflexive governance seems to occur in organisations where strong unions exist and the process is jointly managed. The Canadian Pay Equity Task Force (2004) notes that both employers and unions in such firms report that they have gained a greater appreciation of the skills involved in many traditional female roles as a result of conducting job evaluations and that there have been self-worth benefits for the workers themselves in having the skills involved in their work identified and acknowledged. The report also notes that jointly conducted pay reviews have often led to better industrial relations, in contrast to the adversarialism that a complaints-based system engenders. In some cases, unions have reached agreements where they bargained away the statutory requirement to conduct a pay review (breaching the legislation) in exchange for more generous pay rises for female-dominated jobs (McColgan 1993).

This last point raises an important issue in the debate over self-regulation in the employment law field, and that is how to protect appropriate voluntary arrangements from external legal challenge. In the case of 'bargained statutory adjustments', as we have seen earlier, this involves giving priority to collective or workforce agreements over statutory standards as long as certain procedural safeguards are met. The 2007 *Review* considered adopting a similar scheme for equal pay, in the form of an 'equal pay moratorium'. This would mean that 'where an employer carries out an equal pay review and identifies gender inequalities in their pay systems, they would have a set period free from legal challenge, within which to rectify discriminatory pay policies and practices' (DCLG 2007: para. 3.23). But while acknowledging that this move would 'have the advantage of helping employers to address the issue of equal pay', the *Review* came down against it on the grounds that to dilute individual rights in this way might run counter to EU law, as well as leading to uncertainty about the position of individuals if the issue of pay inequality were not effectively reviewed during a moratorium (DCLG 2007: para. 3.24).

In rejecting the case for equal pay moratoria, the *Review* gave little encouragement to collective solutions at workplace level. Research suggests that such solutions will not emerge 'spontaneously' if the right conditions are not put in place at the level of the legislative 'frame'. Barnard et al. (2003) looked at the way in which employers were achieving flexibility in the application of the legislation implementing the Working Time Directive. They found that very little use was being made of the collective routes to working time flexibility – those based on collective or workforce agreements – given the ease with which employers could impose opt-outs on individual workers. The wide derogation allowed by the legislation for individual agreements meant that an opportunity had been lost to generate a process of collective learning, based on deliberation at workplace level. As a result, the legislation had had little impact in changing prevailing organisational practices: most employers continued to rely on a mixture of long working hours to meet peaks in demand, while employees remained dependent on overtime earnings to supplement their pay.

In defence of the *Review*, the issue of how to reconcile individual claims with collective procedures is not straightforward. The history of equal pay legislation suggests that the two routes can be complementary; as noted above, litigation often provided the catalyst for collective agreements which brought about significant progress in removing institutionalised disadvantage in relation to pay and other employment conditions. More recently, however, clear tensions have surfaced. In *Allen* v *GMB* (2005) an employment tribunal ruled that the union had acted in a discriminatory fashion in concluding a collective agreement which purported to implement the equal pay principle, and awarded damages to the applicants. Although the ruling was reversed on appeal, the *Allen* litigation represents a direct challenge to collective approaches; there is now less room for collective agreements to balance the interests of different workforce groups, and any attempt to trade off the implementation of the equality principle against other union interests (such as the preservation of employment, a real concern in the public sector) would be fraught with difficulty from a legal perspective. Nor does the potential liability of unions end there. In one week alone in the summer of 2007, several thousand claims were issued against trade unions alleging negligence in the way equal pay cases had been handled.[2]

These developments suggest that litigation-based routes towards enforcement show no signs of diminishing in importance in the UK system, and that having been complementary to self-regulatory approaches based on collective bargaining in the past, they now have the potential to undermine the capacity of unions to act in the equal pay field. One of the preconditions for the success of a reflexive strategy, namely the presence of effective employee representation at workplace level, is looking less secure by the day.

Perhaps the continuing demise of collective bargaining matters less when alternative mechanisms, in the area of corporate governance, are taken into account. But to take this view would be, at best, naive. The proactive role for the shareholder activism which Kingsmill emphasised has yet to be realised. In part this is because of the troubled legislative history of attempts to extend corporate reporting requirements on employment issues; the government's abrogation of the OFR in December 2005, followed by its partial rebirth in the form of the business review, has both diluted and delayed the implementation of new disclosure rules. But there is also empirical evidence that institutional supports for shareholder activism of the kind envisaged by Kingsmill are lacking (Deakin and Hobbs 2007). Notwithstanding the growth of interest in SRI, it remains a niche segment of asset management. Pension funds, although legally required to disclose how far CSR affects their investment strategies, are also constrained by fiduciary law and by financial regulations in the degree to which they can direct fund managers to take employment issues into account when making voting or investment decisions. Uncertainty affecting the funding of many defined benefit pension funds, coupled with an increasing degree of stock market turbulence, have meant that many funds still pay little regard to CSR issues within the wider context of their obligation to maximise returns to scheme members.

5 CONCLUSION

This chapter has considered the evolution of regulatory strategies in the area of equal pay between women and men since the inception of equal pay legislation in the 1970s. There is a case for saying that the legislation was most successful in the first years of its operation when an interventionist legal strategy was linked to the use of collective bargaining to put the equality principle into practice. Of course, this was also the point at which some of the more egregious examples of pay discrimination – including separate grades in job evaluation schemes and collective agreements for women and men – could be easily identified and rectified. However, the failure of the legislation to go on to deal with indirect sex discrimination, arising from occupational segregation, was due not to inherent difficulty of applying the law in this area, but more straightforwardly to the weakening and then removal of the collective arbitration mechanism which had been contained in section 3 of the Act. The individual claims route which came to the fore in the 1980s and 1990s produced some spectacular legal victories which led to fundamental changes in the content and structure of equality law, but led to an ever more complex body of legislation which, in turn, contained the potential for seriously destabilising existing payment structures. While this could, from one point of view, be justified as an inevitable feature of the application of the equality principle to established procedures, a more fundamental critique would point to the dangers inherent in growing employer resistance to the aims of the law and union disenchantment with the prevailing approach to its enforcement.

It against this background that the case for reflexive regulation has come to the fore as a way of making the operation of equal pay legislation more effective in practice. 'Reflexive' approaches involve a shift from litigation-based and other 'hard law' strategies to a range of self-regulatory mechanisms and proactive measures for embedding the equality principle in organisational practice. A discussion about the role of such mechanisms has been going on since the early 2000s in the context of pay audits. The *Discrimination Law Review* of 2007 marked a potentially significant step in extending reflexive techniques, which have been widely used elsewhere in the labour law field, to equality law as a whole. However, the recommendations made by the *Review* in the area of equal pay reflected certain ambiguities which are inherent in the concept of reflexive law, and highlight certain of its limitations.

The ambiguity of reflexive law relates to a lack of clarity concerning the relationship between mandatory law and flexible enforcement mechanisms. It is inherent in theories of reflexive law, and in much of the practice over the past decade or so since the idea started to gain acceptance, that legal sanctions have to be deployable as a matter of last resort if legal changes are to have an impact on practice. This means, conversely, that self-regulatory solutions must be accorded some protection from the impact of more direct legal intervention once they pass certain thresholds of acceptability. This is the approach used in the context of 'bargained statutory adjustments' in the area of working time law and the default options which operate in relation to employee representation. But in the current context of equal pay law, these routes are not available, and the option of promoting equal pay reviews by securing them from legal challenge was ruled out in the Review itself. The limitations of reflexive law derive from the dependence of this technique on social institutions beyond the legal system which, in the manner of 'bridging mechanisms', can assist in the translation of legal norms into workplace and organisational practice. A reflexive strategy is unlikely to be effective in the context of equal pay law at a time when collective bargaining is being undermined by a number of factors including equal pay litigation itself, and when the institutional preconditions for alternative 'bridging mechanisms', such as shareholder activism, do not yet exist. For all that, it seems that discrimination law is currently taking a reflexive turn. It remains to be seen whether this will make the law more effective and workable in practice.

NOTES

1. The Equal Opportunities Commission ceased to exist in October 2007 and became part of the newly formed Commission for Equality and Human Rights (CEHR).
2. 'Who's best at getting equal pay for women?', *Observer*, 12 August 2007.

REFERENCES

Adams, L., K. Carter and S. Schäfer (2006), *Equal Pay Reviews Survey 2005*, Manchester: Equal Opportunities Commission.

Association of British Insurers (ABI) (2001), *Investing in Social Responsibility: Risks and Opportunities*, London, Association of British Insurers.

Ayres, I. and J. Braithwaite (1992), *Responsive Regulation: Transcending the Deregulation Debate*, Oxford: Oxford University Press.

Baker, M. and N. Fortin (2000), 'Does comparable worth work in a decentralized labor market?', NBER Working Paper No. 7937, National Bureau of Economic Research, Cambridge, MA.

Barnard, C., S. Deakin and R. Hobbs (2003), 'Opting-out of the 48-week: employer necessity or individual choice? An empirical study of the operation of Article 18(1)(b) of the Working Time Directive in the UK', *Industrial Law Journal*, **32**, 223–52.

Brett, S. and S. Milsome (2004), *Monitoring Progress on Equal Pay Reviews*, Manchester: Equal Opportunities Commission.

Canadian Pay Equity Task Force (2004), *Pay Equity: A New Approach to a Fundamental Right*, Ottawa: Department of Justice.

The Civil Service (2006), *Civil Service Reward Principles*, http://www.civilservice.gov.uk/documents/doc/pay_reward/reward_principles.doc (accessed 10 August 2007).

Davies, P. and C. Kilpatrick (2004), 'UK worker representation after single channel', *Industrial Law Journal*, **33**, 121–51.

De Schutter, O. and S. Deakin (2005), 'Introduction: reflexive governance and the dilemmas of social regulation', in O. De Schutter and S. Deakin (eds), *Social Rights and Market Forces: Is the Open Coordination of Employment and Social Policies the Future of Social Europe?*, Brussels: Bruylant, pp. 1–17.

Deakin, S. and R. Hobbs (2007), 'False dawn for CSR? Shifts in regulatory policy and the response of the corporate and financial sectors in Britain', *Corporate Governance: An International Review*, **15**, 68–76.

Deakin, S. and G. Morris (2005), *Labour Law*, 4th edn, Oxford: Hart Publishing.

Department for Communities and Local Government (DCLG) (2007), *Discrimination Law Review. A Framework for Fairness: Proposals for a Single Equality Bill for Great Britain*, London: Department for Communities and Local Government.

Dickens, L. (2007), 'The road is long: thirty years of equality legislation in Britain', *British Journal of Industrial Relations*, **45**, 463–94.

Equal Opportunities Commission (EOC) (2003), *Code of Practice on Equal Pay*, Manchester: Equal Opportunities Commission.

Equal Pay Task Force (2001), *Just Pay*, Manchester: Equal Opportunities Commission.

Fredman, S. (1997), *Women and the Law*, Oxford: Oxford University Press.

Hepple, B., M. Coussey and T. Choudhury (2000), *Equality: A New Framework – Report of the Independent Review of the Enforcement of UK Anti-Discrimination Legislation*, Oxford: Hart Publishing.

Kersley, B., C. Alpin, J. Forth, A. Bryson, H. Bewley, G. Dix and S. Oxenbridge (2006), *Inside the Workplace: Findings from the 2004 Workplace Employment Relations Survey*, Abingdon: Routledge.

Kingsmill, D. (2001), *Review of Women's Employment and Pay*, London: DTI.

McColgan, A. (1993), 'Legislating equal pay? Lessons from Canada', *Industrial Law Journal*, **22**(4), 269–86.

McColgan, A. (1997), *Just Wages for Women*, Oxford: Clarendon Press.

McCrudden, C. (2007), 'Equality legislation and reflexive regulation: a response to the Discrimination Law Review's Consultative Paper', *Industrial Law Journal*, **36**(3), 255–60.

Neathey, F., S. Dench and L. Thomson (2003), *Monitoring Progress Towards Pay Equality*, Manchester: Equal Opportunities Commission.

Neathey, F., R. Willison, K. Akroyd, J. Regan and D. Hill (2005), *Equal Pay Reviews in Practice*, Manchester: Equal Opportunities Commission.

O'Cinneide, C. (2003), *Taking Equal Opportunities Seriously: The Extension of Positive Duties to Promote Equality*, London: Equality and Diversity Forum.

Schäfer, S., M. Winterbotham and F. McAndrew (2005), *Equal Pay Reviews Survey 2004*, Manchester: Equal Opportunities Commission.

Teubner, G. (1992), *Law as an Autopoietic System*, Oxford: Blackwell.

Women and Work Commission (2006), *Shaping a Fairer Future*, London: Women and Equality Unit.

Zabalza, A. and Z. Tzannatos (1985), *Women and Equal Pay: The Effects of Legislation on Female Employment and Wages in Britain*, Cambridge: Cambridge University Press.

14. Migration, employment and gender divisions of labour

Linda McDowell, Adina Batnitzky and Sarah Dyer

INTRODUCTION

Transnational movements are perhaps *the* defining characteristic of the global capitalism that characterises the new millennium. Flows – of people, money, ideas and information – have transformed the global political economy, creating new links between localities, regions and nation states. Although accurate figures are impossible to compile, about 200 million people are now migrants, the largest absolute number in history (Smith 2006: 9). Facilitated by developments in transport and communication technologies, people are now able to cross vast distances relatively easily and relatively inexpensively. Perhaps more significantly, these technologies permit them to retain contacts with the 'homeland'. The Internet, cheap telephone rates, low budget flights, all mean that what was once – for migrants from say Poland to Chicago in the late nineteenth and early twentieth centuries – a permanent movement, involving the severance of ties to those left behind, has become less permanent. It seems that a new stage in migration – although historical continuities are also clear – has begun: transnationalism, involving living between two (or more) places.

In this chapter we explore the shape and meaning of transnationalism and its implications for gender relations, before turning to the particular position of migrant workers in the British labour market. First, we set the scene with a brief assessment of the scale and directions of contemporary movements.

THE SCALE AND PATTERN OF TRANSNATIONAL MOVEMENTS

Global patterns of migration are complex and historically variable, depending on changing political circumstances, natural events such as famine or flooding and changes in the legal instruments regulating the movement of people between nation states.[1] The International Labour Organization estimates that 60 to 65 million people currently are economically active in a country other than their own. Luxembourg has the largest percentage of foreign-born labour (67 per cent), followed by Australia, Canada and Switzerland, who all have more than 15 per cent. The lowest Organisation for Economic Co-operation and Development (OECD) levels are to be found in Japan (0.2 per cent). If family members and estimated numbers of irregular labour migrants are included, this figure rises to 120 million.

These official figures exclude migrants who enter countries on clandestine or irregular bases. The International Organisation of Migration estimates that between one third and a half of all migrants into developed economies are irregular. In 2001, about 12 million people in the USA are thought to be irregular migrants: a larger number than all the people who passed through immigration control at Ellis Island in the first 60 years of its operation. In the European Union (EU), the number of irregular migrants in 1999 was about half a million (this was before the expansion of the EU in 2004 and in 2007 which reduced irregular entry). The gender breakdown of these migrants is not easy to establish either, as not all countries collect relevant figures. It is clear, however, that the proportion of women among economic migrants is increasing and is now approximately half of all legal entrants. Women no longer enter mainly as dependents, as part of family groups or under family reunification schemes, but as workers in their own right. They move into jobs in many parts of the economy in receiving societies but particularly into stereotypically 'female' jobs in forms of personal care, including nursing, care assistants, nannies, maids and domestic servants, as well as into retail, food processing and agriculture (Ehrenreich and Hochschild 2003). We look at the position of migrant workers in the British labour market in more detail below. For all these transnational workers, for men as well as women, their legal position and constitutional status typically give them fewer rights than 'native' workers, positioning them as a potentially exploitable and vulnerable labour force. Recognising that women are migrants in their own right, rather than moving as part of a family group, has raised new questions for feminist researchers about the production of gendered identities in different sites and locations – both particular nation states and sites such as the home, the workplace and the locality – and about women's capacity to resist both old and newer forms of oppression, as well as questions about women's role in transmitting and reproducing memories and myths of the homeland among diasporic communities (Mahler and Pessar 2006; Sinke 2006).

One of the most interesting elements of the growth of transnational migration is the changing attitudes of 'exporting' economies to the movement of their citizens elsewhere. Instead of being seen as an inevitable loss of key workers, many nation states now see transnational migrants as a valuable resource in two distinct ways. First, financial remittances from migrants have become an important resource for cash-starved economies in the south, supporting both individual families and infrastructure and other forms of investment in the 'home' nation (Hernandez and Coutin 2006; Lianos 1997; Massey and Parrado 1994; Maurer 2003). It has been estimated that, in 2003, remittances by migrants accounted for $80 billion worldwide (Kapur and McHale 2003, and quoted in Hernandez and Coutin 2006) – a sum exceeding foreign aid transfers from North to South. Governments in both origin and destination societies have begun to transform banking structures so that a larger proportion of remittances passes through official, rather than informal, channels. The expansion of remittances fits well with contemporary neoliberal policies with their emphasis on the values of independence and self-support and may, paradoxically, lead to reduced investment in welfare and social provision in the exporting economies, as well as less direct financial aid from governments in the affluent west. Second, migrants increasingly are seen not as lost to the nation but as citizens temporarily elsewhere, whose growing expertise is valuable, which will, if they return, bring new skills to the exporting nations. Indeed, some national governments – the Philippines, Mexico and Morocco are good examples – now see the export of people rather than goods as an economic development policy and have put in place agreements to supply labour for shortages identified by Western economies that permit the entry of their nationals under special arrangements. Both these trends have gender-specific implications, especially as women are often the group targeted for 'export'. The pressure on migrant families to support relatives and dependents left behind may mean an inadequate standard of living for the households that have migrated, increasing the need for all the adult members of the household to enter the labour market, and thus their susceptibility to exploitation, as well as restricting opportunities to undertake further education or vocational training for upward social mobility (Wong 2006). Under the sets of programmes introduced to increase the export of labour, specific female-dominated jobs and professions are often targeted – nursing and domestic service are common examples – leading to the loss of female members of households and to what has been termed transnational mothering or mothering at a distance, where women with child-rearing responsibilities are forced to leave their children in the care of others (Hochschild 2001; Hondagneu-Sotelo 2001). Here remittances connect the two features of transnational migration just identified.

THEORISING MIGRATION: DIASPORIC IDENTITIES, THIRD SPACES AND NEW FORMS OF BELONGING

In this section we focus on the consequences of mobility for constructing a sense of self and group identity, for maintaining a sense of the old self and connections with 'home', as well as for constructing new forms of identity in a new location. This issue – the extent to which transnational migrants construct, re-create or hold on to older forms of identity, whether based on ethnicity, nationality or religion – currently is the focus of a difficult debate about the consequences of migration within the UK. It affects not only migrants' sense of themselves, but also their willingness to enter and suitability for particular sectors of the labour market.

The growth and scale of international movement, and its consequences for both sending and host societies, have become increasingly significant for debates about belonging, social changes, citizenship and ethnicity. These shifts have been captured in theoretical literatures in migration studies in the terms diaspora and transnationalism. In its broadest sense, the term diaspora captures the consequences of migration, displacement, immigration and exile for all peoples who have become dislocated from their homelands. There is, inevitably, a debate about the impact of migration on both 'diasporic' and indigenous communities. Questions such as how a group comes to be situated in official discourses about 'One' and the 'Other', about the nature and impact of state policies and how social and institutional structures of regulation affect different groups and their position within economies and societies have been addressed. Here the work of Stuart Hall (1990; 1992), has been influential. He argues against an essentialist view of 'home' among both migrant and indigenous groups, suggesting instead that both groups are affected by migration and insisting on positive as well as negative impacts of migration and settlement for migrants and the communities among which they live. Terms such as 'hybridity' and 'creolisation', or the more neutral term 'heterogeneity', have been used to capture continuous processes of change amongst diverse communities, creating a new, often contested, cultural construction of nationality and belonging to a nation, that challenges taken-for-granted associations between place and identity (Gilroy 1987; 1993; Gupta 1992; Low and Lawrence-Zuniga 2003; Ong 1999).

It is clear, however, whether claims to an authentic identity, or notions of travelling, hybrid or translated identities are held by theorists and by migrants themselves, that there remain significant axes of differentiation and contestation within migrant communities with important labour market effects. Differences based on class, gender, age or sexual identity divide and structure the lives of migrants in exile, as they did 'at home', and yet community elders – typically men – often speak for communities in exile. As a consequence, the images and myths of homeland and national identity that are so significant in constructing versions of solidarity in migration/exile often depend on ignoring differentials of power based on gender, sexuality or class position. However, women have an important place in transmitting the narratives of belonging elsewhere that are an important part of the maintenance of a separate identity among many migrant groups. To unpick the differences and inequalities that divide, as well as unite, immigrant communities, feminist scholars of diaspora (Brah 1996) have developed more complex notions of identity based on multiple forms of identification, in which the intersections of nationality, disloca-tion, race, and gender, as well as age and generation, are recognised.

Transnational Theory

More recently, a variant of this vein of theorising about migration and its consequences – transnational theory – has become influential (Portes 2001; Smith 2006; Smith and Guarnizo 1998; Vertovec 1999). Here the emphasis is even more explicitly on both ends of the migration chain. Transnational theory reflects a wider recognition that, in an increasingly globalised world, contacts and travel between places have become common. As Aiwa Ong (1999) has documented, repeated or circulatory migration, especially among the rich and footloose is now common, and migrants maintain economic and social links, through investment, busi-ness and social networks, across two or more societies. This has important methodological implications for analysts of labour migration, as multi-sited work is now necessary. Further, this approach encourages the inte-gration of political economy and situated ethnography, exploring both structural circumstances and individual behaviours, global shifts and local lives, creating what Michael Burawoy (Burawoy et al. 2000) has termed the practice of 'global ethnography'. But the idea of living across borders also raises complex issues. This complexity is problematic for individuals, who are often torn by ambivalent ideas of belonging or not belonging, as Anne-Marie Fortier (2000) has explored among post-war Italian migrants to London. It also challenges conventional concepts of citizenship, trad-itionally tied to the rights and obligations of individuals within a single nation state. The rise of transnational identities, even the acknowledge-ment of dual-citizenship rights, challenges this model of political obedi-ence to a single nation state. Some theorists have perhaps optimistically seen the prospect of a new form of cosmopolitanism in these shifts in iden-tity and multiple political allegiances. Whatever the eventual outcome in terms of institutional forms of belonging, it is clear that the growing diversity of migrants within host societies and their continuing adherence to forms of ethnicised identities raises urgent questions for notions of citizenship and nationhood (Favell 2001; Hanson and Weil 2000; Joppke and Lukes 1999; Kymlicka 1995; Soysal 1994) that are at the heart of contemporary policy decisions in many industrial nations.

MIGRANTS' LOCATION IN RECEIVING SOCIETIES: WHERE MIGRANTS END UP IN THE UK

In 2001, just over 10 per cent of the population living in the UK, was born elsewhere. People from what might be termed Empire India (India, Pakistan and Bangladesh), the Irish Republic, the EU (before expansion in 2004), the Caribbean Islands and the USA and Canada (in descending order) are the largest groups among this foreign-born population (Dorling and Thomas 2004). This figure does not include the entire ethnic minority population living in the UK, as the children of earlier generations of migrants were born in the UK. London is the most significant location for incomers. Here there are 16 boroughs where less than a half but more than a third of all residents in 2001 were born outside England. There are no other areas in England where this is the case, despite the significant number of foreign-born and ethnic minority populations in certain wards within some northern towns and cities.

The nature and extent of migration into the UK has changed over the twentieth century (Paul 1997; Winder 2004). Before the Second World War, the number of UK residents born outside the UK remained small. Migrants were in the main from other European societies, especially from Ireland and from parts of Central and Eastern Europe, although small numbers of Black African and Chinese people had lived in certain British cities for centuries. From the mid-century onwards, the origins of migrants changed. From the early 1950s, migrants from former British colonies were recruited first to meet labour shortages in key industries and, later, the demands for low-wage labour in expanding industries and the public sector. These migrants, because of their skin colour, were visibly different from both the native population and earlier migrant communities, discriminated against because of their appearance and yet, paradoxically, with close ties to Britain as they were, in the main, British citizens. It is also important to remember that, at the same time, more skilled migrants, both from post-colonial societies – doctors from India, for example, and nurses from the Caribbean, as well as from the USA, Australia, Canada, New Zealand and South Africa who were, in the main, white – entered the UK as skilled workers. Since the expansion of the European Union in May 2004, the nature of in-migration has changed again as migrants from former Communist states in Eastern Europe, especially from Poland, are now numerically significant. For these migrants, language rather than skin colour marks them out as different from the 'native' population.

Almost all nations have formal and informal mechanisms that construct a migrant underclass, in which economic migrants are recruited for a limited set of low-wage, often dead-end jobs in a limited range of sectors, typically in agriculture, manufacturing and parts of the service sector such as retail and hospitality. In some countries, migrants are explicitly restricted to temporary residence, with no rights to settle in the receiving society. These migrants are literally transnational – forced to return to their own or a third country when their visas expire. In other cases, migrants may have a series of more limited rights to residence, or even rights of citizenship, but nevertheless they are constructed as cheap labour and are over-represented in jobs at the bottom end of the pay and status hierarchy. Migrant workers are rendered 'cheap' through the manipulation of racial, gender and national stereotypes, as well as through labour market and government policies that operate selectively to include and exclude particular migrants groups from, for example, welfare policies or portray them in popular dis-courses as welfare cheats or as stealing jobs/undercutting wages. Here femi-nist analyses have been useful is showing how the social construction of migrant women as, variously, naturally caring or as socially backward, positions them as exploitable labour in advanced industrial economies or as illegitimate welfare claimants.

In Britain, one of the consequences of the intersection of ethnic origin and skin colour is a clear pattern of racialised segregation in the labour market (Blackwell 2003). Migrants from the Caribbean, recruited from the late 1940s onwards, were directed towards particular jobs. Women from the Caribbean, atypically, often found themselves in more secure jobs than their male counterparts, working in the National Health Service (NHS) and London Transport, for example. Other women migrants found work in the manufacturing sector which was less secure but relatively well paid and, because these women usually were employed on a full-time basis, their average weekly earnings were often higher than those of white women. For women and men from South Asia, who entered Britain from the 1970s, life tended to be harder. These migrants, especially those from rural parts of the Indian sub-continent, found that the combination of lacking skills valued in the UK, deindustrialisation from the mid-1970s and discrimination resulted in their concentration into particularly low-status and poorly paid jobs. National labour market statistics reveal significant differences between people from ethnic minority groups and the majority population.[2] Thus, people from Black and minority ethnic (BME) groups have lower levels of labour market participation than white people (59 per cent in 2001 compared with 75 per cent), higher levels of unemployment, especially among minority youth, lower average incomes and lower levels of occupational attainment and progression (CRE 2006). In 2002, when the unemployment rate for all white people was about 4 per cent, for the Black Caribbean and Black African population it was 10 per cent and 11 per cent respectively, 8 per cent for people of Pakistani origin and 11 per cent for the Bangladeshi group.

The patterns of low participation and job segregation, mirrored by low incomes, are exacerbated for women by the intersection of marked gender divisions of labour that also affect white British women, and by religious and cultural barriers to women's employment, especially among Muslim communities. The Labour Force Survey shows that for men, the differential in employment rates between the white and BME population is just under 20 per cent; for women the differential is 45 per cent.

Social Segregation and Education

Although the degree of ethnic segregation has not reached the level experienced in the US, the UK is nevertheless characterized by high levels of social segregation that result in disparate educational and employment outcomes (Burgess et al. 2005; Peach 2005; 2006). The gap between white and ethnic minority employment rates is narrowest – just over 10 per cent – in the more economically prosperous parts of the UK – in the south-east of England, as well as in the eastern and south-west economic planning regions, and significantly higher in less prosperous northern regions where deindustrialisation since the 1970s still has a marked effect. However, even within the more prosperous regions, especially in the South East, the minority and migrant population is significantly spatially segregated into the poorest and most deprived areas. Indeed nationally, over 70 per cent of the minority population lives in the 88 most deprived districts. This segregation is reflected in patterns of school attendance and attainment where BME children are more likely to leave school at 16 and less likely to do well in school leaving examinations. Here gender disparities are also evident but in this case it is young men, especially of Caribbean, African, Bangladeshi and Asian origins who are most likely to do poorly in examinations. They are also more likely to attend schools with a high proportion of children from minority and migrant groups, reflecting the patterns of spatial segregation in British cities.

In the last two or so years, the growing evidence of segregation among certain minority groups, especially the most disadvantaged, has led to a reassessment of British policy instruments towards the minority population.

This debate reached the press when the head of the Commission for Racial Equality, Trevor Phillips (2005), suggested that Britain was 'sleepwalking to segregation': in danger of mirroring US urban ghettos. It is clear that spatial segregation has an important effect on access to the labour market, as well as to other locally based resources, including education. Whatever the statistical evidence for Phillips's claim about ghetto formation in the UK (and this is disputed), there is no doubt that a new discourse around the dangers of separatism, especially among the Muslim population, has come to dominate both policy-making and popular media considerations of the connections between ethnicity and religious fundamentalism, between young unemployed men and urban unrest. This debate, which we do not discuss here, centres on both migrant and British-born Muslims and is entirely different from the other significant area of contention in current discussion of migrant workers' impact on the labour market – the economic effects of the growth of migration from the new EU accession states (see Anderson et al. 2006).

THE IMPACTS OF EU ENLARGEMENT ON LABOUR MARKET SEGMENTATION

In May 2004 the European Union expanded significantly in terms of member states – from 15 to 25 – and in population – to more than 500 million people (an increase of 28 per cent). Eight of the new member states, jointly referred to as the A8 members (Czech Republic, Estonia, Hungary, Latvia, Lithuania, Poland, Slovakia and Slovenia: the other two accession states are Malta and Cyprus) formerly were part of the USSR or within its sphere of influence. Despite significant economic change in these states, the overall standard of living remains low compared to the 15 'old' EU members, unemployment rates are significantly higher and income inequalities have increased since 1991. One of the most difficult issues raised during the accession negotiations was how to tackle fears of the existing member states that these new, less-privileged citizens would immediately migrate westwards on accession. Once in the West, it was assumed that either they would swell the unemployment figures or take the jobs of poorly qualified natives, as well as constitute a politically awkward enclave population.

The resolution of these fears about an overwhelming stream of migrants from the East was reached in a decision that each of the old member states might decide its own terms of entry, as well as the employment, residence and other social rights to be extended to new EU citizens, for a period of up to seven years after the Accession Treaty. Ireland, Sweden and the UK were the only three of the EU15 member states that granted immediate labour market access to A8 nationals,[3] followed two years later by the relaxation of restrictions by France and Germany. In the UK, the main impetus behind the liberal entry scheme was severe labour market shortages, especially in the south-east of England, mainly in low-wage public services as well as in a range of occupations in the health service including nursing. Rather than a completely free entry scheme, however, the UK established a Worker Registration Scheme (WRS) which imposes obligations on both the migrant workers and their employers. After a year's registration, workers become eligible for a European Economic Area (EEA) residence permit and are entitled to state benefits. By the end of June 2006, 447 000 workers had registered, 62 per cent of whom were Polish. There is no way of knowing, of course, how many A8 migrants were working without registering, nor what the total number of A8 workers in the UK is, as the registration requirement applies only to employees and to the first 12 months of employment in the UK. Further, applicants are not required to deregister when they cease employment and/or leave the country.

It is clear, then, that the WRS figures are a significant underestimate. There may be, for example, as many as 1 million Poles currently resident in the UK (estimated by the Polish news magazine *Polityka* in 2006) although the official figures are much lower – about 60 000 Poles already lived in the UK before accession in 2004 (Gilpin et al. 2006). However, there is no doubt that the number of people of Central and East European origin now in the UK has increased significantly since May 2004. Although the Poles are the numerically dominant group, Lithuanians and Latvians have the greatest propensity to enter the UK labour market, relative to the total population in their home country. When Bulgaria and Rumania also joined the EU in January 2007, more severe entry restrictions were placed on their citizens, in part in a response to the large number of A8 entrants who had preceded them. For this second group of new Europeans, only the self-employed and a small number of employees, in the main in agriculture and food processing, were permitted to work.

The new migrants from Europe are young, single and without dependents (at least at the time that they entered the UK). Eighty-two per cent of the new Europeans were aged between 18 and 34, 93 per cent had no dependents and almost 60 per cent were men (Home Office 2006). In almost all cases, these migrants were attracted to the UK because of severe labour shortages in the British economy, especially in low-paid jobs. Many of the pre-2004 migrants from the A8 states came, for example, under different schemes to fill vacancies in agriculture, construction, retail and hospitality, and research commissioned by the Home Office (Gilpin et al. 2006) found that new entrants work in similar sectors, many of them in jobs considerably below their skill levels. Most registered for work in hospitality and catering, agriculture, manufacturing and in food, fish and meat processing (Home Office 2006: 1). Anderson et al. (2006) found that for employers, the main advantage of these workers was their capacity for hard work in jobs that British workers tend to find unacceptable. A8 migrants were regarded by employers as generally good and reliable, and often as superior to migrants form elsewhere because of their motivation and commitment. Thus, the entry of these new migrants disrupts many of the conventional associations outlined earlier. They are white, young and relatively independent and, although it is not possible to tell yet whether they will stay either in low-paid jobs or indeed in the UK, they constitute a new reserve army of labour for employers.

Fourteen per cent of all A8 migrants who registered between May 2004 and June 2006 were based in London, many of them finding work in hotels and restaurants, pubs and clubss. As part of a larger study (McDowell et al. 2007), we undertook a series of interviews in a large west London hotel – Bellman International (BI) (a pseudonym) – to explore the extent of employment of A8 nationals, their working conditions and the class, gender and racialised divisions of labour that are developing as a new source of migrant workers became available. Workers in all sections of the hotel – from the front office to housekeeping, including security and catering – were interviewed. The hotel relied to a great extent on migrant labour. Almost 90 per cent of the workers employed in 2006 were not born in the UK. However, we found an extreme gender and ethnic division of labour with marked differences in the origins of workers employed in different parts of the hotel.

The most evident impact of EU enlargement was in the housekeeping division. Here we found that a previously mainly Vietnamese staff had been almost entirely replaced by Polish women, typically recruited through and employed by employment agencies. They registered for work after arrival in London, or used personal contacts among the Polish community to find a job. These workers were poorly paid – on basic minimum wages – ineligible for a range of benefits that permanent employees had access to, and were further distinguished from direct employees by their uniform. Their terms and conditions of employment were poor – they had few rights and no guaranteed hours of employment. Room cleaning, for example, is demanding, and payment was based on the number of rooms to be cleaned in a specified period. Agency staff, of whom Teresa, a young Polish woman was one, were required to clean 16 rooms each shift and were allocated between 20 minutes and half an hour for each room, although as Teresa noted, it often takes longer: 'very dirty room, one hour is cleaning this room because everything is oh my God! Family, it's one room and family, the children . . . many children and all the rooms, it's oh my God!'.

While there was no additional remuneration for the standard set of 16 rooms, paid overtime was often available – 'because sometimes the supervisor ask me "you more rooms, you want?", maybe sometimes it's busy, they ask help'. Although Teresa finds it hard to refuse, room attendants are not obliged to clean additional rooms: 'sometimes they can say if they are, don't know, feel bad or they are tired, they can say "I don't want to take extra rooms"'. However, when the hotel is not at full occupancy, room attendants are not guaranteed their full quota and are paid accordingly – a labour practice that unsurprisingly generated resentment. Further, cleaning is physically demanding and employees are prone to injuries from strain and lifting, as well as adverse reactions to chemicals (Seifert and Messing 2006; Søgaard et al. 2006). The young women we interviewed told us that the work was demeaning, demanding and unpleasant. Customers treated them as if they were invisible, rooms were often left in an unpleasant state and the chemical cleaners that they were required to use often irritated their skin. For the hotel, of course, agency workers such as these Polish women brought advantages – not only in terms of low costs but also flexibility. The agency could be asked to terminate the employment of unsuitable workers, whereas reliable agency workers could be tested and then offered more permanent employment. Judith, the Head of Housekeeping explains why she uses agency employees:

> Most of the agency staff who work with us are really nice girls and they get on with what they need to get on with, and they don't give you problems, but for somebody who does, it's much easier to phone the agency and say 'look, this is the third time we're speaking, if this candidate doesn't pull up their socks. We're going to move them on', and so . . . being through an agency, it's wonderful.

The second area of the hotel where a marked ethnic and gender division of labour was evident was in the catering division, where we found a concentration of young Indian men employed in a range of positions from basic tasks in the kitchens such as washing up, though cooking in different categories and the more visible jobs of waiting in the dining rooms. These men were recruited and employed by BI in an entirely different way to the Polish housekeeping staff. In the main, they were recruited in India on a management trainee scheme, which required experience in different divisions within the hotel. They were direct hotel employees, although temporary, on time-limited visas arranged by BI. Their basic rate of pay was higher than for the Polish women. What both groups had in common was their youth and their impermanence – neither group intended to stay long at BI but for the Indian men their job was a step onto a career ladder, whereas for the Polish women it was casual work to make a basic living while looking for something better. Relationships between the two groups were limited – they worked in different areas of the hotel and on different shift patterns. However, resentment and contested relationships were evident. The Indian men felt their gender and language skills should bring them preferential treatment, whereas some of the new EU employees felt their skin colour should mark them as superior in a racialised hierarchy within the hotel. A man from Hungary, working in room service, suggested 'this government gives too much power to other people who's not belong to the European Community, you know what I mean?' he went on to argue:

> It's a kind of ethnic thing . . . a lot of Indian people, there's a lot of Indian people working there and they think they are Gods and they can do everything when they want. You have to stay shut up, that's it . . . I went to school for four years to learn this and they come in from out of nowhere, they come in and they can do the same job as me, how come? This is a kind of shame on myself, you know?

Several of the Polish women room attendants also expressed hostility towards Indian employees. But the racism was not all one way. British-born employees of the hotel were in a minority (although mainly in supervisory positions) and some of them expressed negative views of the Polish staff. Overall, however, as A8 migrants are white-skinned in a largely white country, they clearly did not expect to suffer discrimination.

This example illustrates the ways in which complex relations between gender, class, ethnicity, skin colour and employment contracts, produce segmented labour markets that concentrate most new migrants in the UK into poorly paid and undesirable sectors of the service economy but also create and re-create hierarchies of suitability for different slots in the job market based on distinctions between different categories of migrants. At different periods of time in the post-war history of British migration, new workers from distinctive parts of the world find themselves exploited and segregated. To conclude we consider recent policy responses to economic migration.

CONCLUSIONS: MULTICULTURALISM, COHESION AND INCLUSION AND THEIR LABOUR MARKET IMPLICATIONS

For policy-makers, in countries that rely on migration to meet labour shortages, a set of dilemmas lie in the need to both assess the impact of migrants and justify their position within the nation. Heated debates rage about economic advantages and disadvantages of migration, as adherents and

opponents of open-door policies argue about the relative merits and consequences of a new pool of labour, its impact on wages, and the extent of
dependency of new migrants and their families on social services. Debates
about the social impact of migrants hinge on sets of racialised assumptions
about ways of life and 'difference' from a mythical 'Britishness'. It is clear
that economic migrants who enter a society legally and who contribute
through their labour and through their financial contributions as taxation
and general spending add to the overall economic good. However, it is also
clear that the nature of the rights to which they are entitled, and especially
to formal citizenship and its associated set of benefits, affects the 'costs' of
a migrant labour force for the host society. Where migrants are in the main
'guest workers' – entrants to a society on a temporary basis, expected to
return 'home' in some specified time period – then their rights to social
welfare provisions in particular and to the full set of entitlements of a citizen
may be limited. As a consequence, the changing ways in which migrants are
constructed and whether or not they are seen as having full rights makes a
difference to their labour market position, their ability to move between jobs
and their scope for resisting exploitation. For this reason we end with a brief
consideration of the ways in which economic migrants have been treated
during the past decades through an exploration of the changing ideology of
what was once termed 'assimilation'. This notion is perhaps best captured
in that vivid US concept 'the melting pot'. A full assimilation policy assumes
that incomers will at some stage be eligible for the full set of rights and will
become indistinguishable, at least in the legal or formal sense, from other
citizens. What is more problematic is the extent to which cultural differences
might remain and, more importantly, be recognised by the receiving society.

As Castles and Miller (2003) have documented, in countries such as the
USA, Australia and the UK, where the permanent settlement of economic
migrants (asylum seekers and refugees raise different questions) has been
recognised and to a large degree encouraged, there has been a shift over
time from policies of individual assimilation, based on an idealised notion
of a good citizen, to the acceptance, at least in official discourse, of some
degree of long-term cultural difference. This acceptance has resulted in the
granting of minority and cultural rights in particular social arenas and to
a wider acceptance of a politics based on the concept of multiculturalism.
In this discourse, migrants' customs and cultural attitudes are accepted as
equal but different to those of the majority community. Thus the older versions of assimilation, which in the UK, the USA and Australasia, seemed
to incomers to demand conformity to an imagined set of white, Anglo-
Saxon Protestant norms, are challenged and policies of diversity put in the
place of policies based on a singular version of equality. In the labour
market, this has had an interesting impact, allowing questions about

ethnicity, religion, clothing and other cultural habits to become part of the discourse of workplace-based rights. Other western states have maintained a version of assimilation as an ideal, insisting on adherence to a secular version of human rights, as in France, and so have banned, for example, visible displays of religious adherence in the workplace. In both versions, however, migrants are constructed as different, as visible 'Others'. Whereas this multiculturalism is celebrated in the UK (at least in official rhetoric, if not in practice), in societies in which assimilationist policies are emphasised, visibly different migrants tend to become positioned as marginalised ethnic minorities and suffer greater workplace disadvantage. However, in the UK there have recently been a number of interesting cases, based on the (lack of) recognition of diversity in the workplace, that have challenged the version of multiculturalism outlined above. A Muslim woman working as a classroom assistant was denied the right to wear the niqab – a full version of concealing clothes including the face veil – at the school where she worked, and a check-in assistant at Heathrow Airport was (initially) prevented from wearing a visible symbol of her religion (a necklace that was a crucifix). In part, this retreat from the recognition, even celebration, of diversity in the workplace, is a response to the changing political situation in the UK, especially since the terrorist attacks in London in 2005 which have severely tested the rhetoric of multiculturalism.

Fears about divided communities, spatial segregation and the high unemployment rates – especially of minority young men – in the inner areas of many British towns and cities are now reflected in a new discourse of community cohesion, as joint projects between majority and minority groups are emphasised as the way to mutual understanding and greater tolerance and a new emphasis on what is termed the 'managed migration' of economic migrants into the UK. This latter shift has resulted in the restriction of the rights to both enter and work within the UK of migrants from what used to be the traditional sending countries, especially those of the former colonies, in proposals to rely more heavily on migrants from the new Eastern European members of the EU. It seems, then, as if the once proud boast that Britain was a nation that accepted strangers is turning into a xenophobic panic about the links between identity, religion and terrorism, focused primarily on the Muslim population but also on other categories of migrant in a combination of nasty racist rhetorics in which, for example, the Bulgarians are constructed as thugs and gangsters and the Romanians as uncivilised Roma or gypsy people. In this climate it is clear that only some of the latest economic migrants – the majority, but not all, white-skinned East and Central Europeans – have a significant advantage in their efforts to obtain work and make a living in post-millennium Britain, whereas non-white migrants as a group, but Muslims in particular, suffer from growing exclusion both from and within Britain. The more optimistic versions of hybrid identities, outlined earlier, seem a distant dream in Britain today as poverty, inequality and confinement to low wage jobs are the prospect for all but highly skilled migrants. And yet, in an ageing country where the white 'native' population increasingly demands the services – of care, hospitality, welfare provision – that depend on a migrant labour force, it is clear that economic migration will remain an essential part of economic planning for many years to come.

NOTES

1. Space restrictions do not allow discussion of refugees and asylum seekers, who are a significant and growing part of transnational movements in the new millennium.
2. Of course, not all members of minority groups are migrants, in the sense of being born abroad, but these figures reveal the consequences of past migration and continuing inequality.
3. In January 2007, Bulgaria and Romania also joined the EU but this time access to British labour markets was refused. Nationals from these two states at present may live but not work in the UK.

REFERENCES

Anderson, B., M. Ruhs, B. Rogaly and S. Spencer (2006), 'Fair enough? Central and East European migrants in low-wage employment in the UK', *COMPAS*, Oxford www.compas.ox.ac.uk/changing status (accessed January 2008).

Blackwell, L. (2003), 'Gender and ethnicity at work: occupational segregation and disadvantage in the 1991 British Census', *Sociology*, **37**, 713–31.

Brah, A. (1996), *Cartographies of Diaspora: Contesting Identities*, London: Routledge.

Burawoy, M., J. Blum, S. George, Z. Gilie, T. Gowan, L. Haney, M. Klawiter, S. Lopez, S. O-Riain and M. Thayer (2000), *Global ethnography: forces, connections and imaginations in a postmodern world*, Berkeley, CA and London: University of California Press.

Burgess, S., D. Wilson and R. Lupton (2005), 'Parallel lives? Ethnic segregation in schools and neighbourhoods', *Urban Studies*, **42**(7), 1027–56.

Castles, S. and M. Miller (2003), *The Age of Migration: International Population Movements in the Modern World*, 3rd edn, London: Palgrave Macmillan.

Commission for Racial Equality (CRE) (2006), 'Statistics: labour market', www.cre.gov.uk/research/statistics_labour.html (accessed 20 October 2006).

Dorling, D. and B. Thomas (2004), *People and Places: A 2001 Census Atlas of the UK*, Bristol: Policy Press.

Ehrenreich, B. and A. Hochschild (eds) (2003), *Global Woman: Nannies, Maids and Sex Workers in the New Economy*, London: Granta.

Favell, A. (2001), *Philosophies of Integration: Immigration and the Idea of Citizenship in France and Britain*, 2nd edn, London: Palgrave.

Fortier, A.-M. (2000), *Migrant Belongings: Memory, Space, Identity*, Oxford: Berg.

Gilpin, N., M. Henty, S. Lemos, J. Portes and C. Bullen (2006), 'The impact of free movement of workers from Central and Eastern Europe on the UK labour market', *Working Paper No. 29, Department of Work and Pensions*, Leeds: Corporate Document Services for HMSO.

Gilroy, P. (1987), *There Ain't No Black in the Union Jack*, London: Routledge.

Gilroy, P. (1993), *The Black Atlantic: Modernity and Double Consciousness*, Cambridge, MA: Harvard University Press.

Gupta, A. (1992), 'The song of the non-aligned world: transnational identities and the reinscription of space in late capitalism', *Cultural Anthropology*, **13**, 63–79.

Hall, S. (1990), 'Cultural identity and diaspora in Rutherford', in J. Rutherford (ed.), *Identity, Community, Culture, Difference*, London: Lawrence and Wishart, pp. 222–37.

Hall, S. (1992), 'New ethnicities', in J. Donald and A. Rattansi (eds), *'Race', Culture and Difference*, London: Sage.

Hansen, R. and P. Weil (eds) (2000), *Towards a European Nationality: Citizenship, Immigration and Nationality Law in the EU*, London: Macmillan.

Hernandez, E. and S. Coutin (2006), 'Remitting subjects: migrants, money and states', *Economy and Society*, **35**(2), 185–208.

Hochschild, A. (2001), 'Global care chains and emotional surplus value', in W. Hutton and A. Giddens (eds), *On the Edge: Living with Global Capitalism*, London: Vintage, pp. 130–46.

Home Office (2006), *Accession Monitoring Report: May 2004–June 2006*, a joint online report by the Home Office, Department of Work and Pensions, HM Revenue and Customs and Department for Communities and Local Government, www.ind.homeoffice.gov.uk/ind/en/home/0/reports/accession_monitoring.html (accessed January 2008).

Hondagneu- Sotelo, P. (2001), *Doméstica: Immigrant Workers Cleaning and Caring in the Shadows of Affluence*, Berkeley, CA and London: University of California Press.

Joppke, C. and S. Lukes (eds) (1999), *Multicultural Questions*, Oxford: Oxford University Press.

Kapur, D. and J. McHale (2003), 'Migration's new payoff', *Foreign Policy*, **139**, 48–57.

Kymlicka, W. (1995), *Multicultural Citizenship*, Oxford: Oxford University Press.

Lianos, T.P. (1997), 'Factors determining migrant remittances: the case of Greece', *International Migration Review*, **31**, 72–87.

Low, S. and D. Lawrence-Zuniga (eds) (2003), *The Anthropology of Space and Place: Locating Culture*, Oxford: Blackwell.

Mahler, S.J. and P.R. Pessar (2006), 'Gender matters: ethnographers bring gender from the periphery toward the core of migration studies', *International Migration Review*, **40**, 27–63.

Massey, D.S. and E. Parrado (1994), 'Migradollars: the remittances and savings of Mexican migrants to the USA', *Population Research and Policy Review*, **13**, 3–30.

Maurer, B. (2003), 'Uncanny exchanges: the possibilities and failures of "making change" with alternative monetary forms', *Environment and Planning D: Society and Space*, **21**, 317–40.

McDowell, L., A. Batnitzky and S. Dyer (2007), 'Division, segmentation and inter-pellation: the embodied labours of migrant workers in a Greater London hotel', *Economic Geography*, **83**(1), 1–26.

Ong, A. (1999), *Flexible Citizenship: the Cultural Logics of Transnationality*, Durham, NC and London: Duke University Press.

Paul, K. (1997), *Whitewashing Britain: Race and Citizenship in the Postwar Era*, Ithaca, NY: Cornell University Press.

Peach, C. (2005), 'The ghetto and the ethnic enclave', in D.P. Varady (ed.), *Desegregating the City: Ghettos, Enclaves and Inequalities*, Albany, NY: State University of New York Press, pp. 31–48.

Peach, C. (2006), 'Muslims in the 2001 Census of England and Wales: gender and economic advantage', *Ethnic and Racial Studies*, **29**(4), 629–55.

Phillips, T. (2005), 'After 7/7: sleepwalking towards segregation', speech given on 22 September to Manchester Council for Community Relations, www.cre.gov.uk (accessed May 2007).

Portes, A. (2001), 'The debates and significance of immigrant transnationalism', *Global Networks: A Journal of Transnational Affairs*, **1**, 181–94.

Seifert, A.M. and K. Messing (2006), 'Cleaning up after globalisation: an ergonomic analysis of work activity of hotel cleaners', *Antipode*, **38**, 557–78.

Sinke, S.M. (2006), 'Gender and migration: historical perspectives', *International Migration Review*, **40**, 82–103.

Smith, M.P. and L.E. Guarnizo (eds) (1998), *Transnationalism from Below*, Brunswick, NJ: Transaction.

Smith, R.C. (2006), *Mexican New York: Transnational Lives of New Migrants*, Berkeley, CA and London: University of California Press.

Søgaard, K., A. Blangsted, A. Herod and L. Finsen (2006), 'Work design and the labouring body: examining the impacts of work organisation on Danish cleaners' health', *Antipode*, **38**, 579–602.

Soysal, Y. (1994), *Limits of Citizenship: Migrants and Postnational Membership in Europe*, Chicago, IL: Chicago University Press.

Vertovec, S. (1999), 'Conceiving and studying transnationalism', *Ethnic and Racial Studies*, **22**(2), 446–62.

Winder, R. (2004), *Bloody Foreigners: The Story of Immigration to Britain*, London: Abacus.

Wong, M. (2006), 'The gendered politics of remittances in Ghanaian transnational families', *Economic Geography*, **82**, 355–81.

15. Policy on care: a help or a hindrance to gender equality?

Susan Himmelweit

Economies need to provide both for the production of goods and services and for the provision of care. Traditionally, in the UK as elsewhere, provision for these dual needs has been posited on a gender division of labour; with men taking on employment, earning enough to keep a wife and family, while women, financially supported by such a 'family' wage, provide care for children, the old and the infirm, as part of their unpaid labour of running a home and family. In practice, men's and women's lives never universally fitted this model, with many women needing to take employment either because there was no man to support them and their children or because the man expected to do so did not earn enough. Although the reason behind the existence of much social policy was the fact that the male breadwinner/female carer model did not provide for all, the model nevertheless has had a powerful effect in shaping policy and retains powerful hold even now on public discourse and the imagination of policy-makers.

In particular, financial support for caring, through the Married Man's (subsequently 'Married Couple's') tax allowance, was until very recently based on supporting a family that was presumed to consist of a single (male) breadwinner who needed to be able financially to support a non-earning (female) carer.[1] Though such tax allowances were always a badly targeted way to subsidise the cost of caring, depending as they did on marital status alone, not on the existence or number of dependents needing care, tax allowances for marriage were abolished in the UK only in 2000 (and even now continue in a modified form for those over 70).[2]

Public services for the care of children, outside the exceptional conditions of wartime, were generally restricted to those with special needs or from families seen as unable to cope. For those on very low incomes, childcare had been indirectly and somewhat intermittently subsidised through a childcare disregard on some benefits (Kiernan et al. 1998: 268, 272). These subsidies became explicit, more generous and were extended to more families by New Labour in 1999 and again in 2003 with the introduction and reform of Tax Credits, along with the National Childcare Strategy launched in 1998 to expand childcare services. But it was only in the 2005 general election that childcare first surfaced as an electoral issue, with all major parties making pledges to ensure its wider availability.

Similarly gendered assumptions, based on the male breadwinner/female carer model, that had been built into allowances for the disabled and their carers have only recently been lifted. It used to be the case that a married woman who could perform normal household duties was not entitled to any disability payments (because she should not need to take employment), and married women were denied the right to claim any allowances for carers (because their husbands were presumed to be financially supporting them anyway). These restrictions were removed only in 1988 and 1986 respectively. In recent years the care of elderly people and those with disabilities has become as pressing a political issue as childcare, as reports of care homes closing, care standards falling and local authorities failing to fund all but the most severe care needs have surfaced.

These changes in policy and the current policy interest in care are belated and insufficiently far reaching responses to women's increasing participation in the labour force since the mid-twentieth century, a trend that has accelerated greatly in the years since 1980, as the earlier chapters in this book document. This sea change has rendered the male breadwinner/female carer model in need of serious amendment. However, much less has changed in the gender division of labour over care, so that it is women and those that they care for that have been primarily affected by the lag in public perceptions and in policy responses.

WOMEN'S LABOUR FORCE PARTICIPATION AND THE PARTIAL COMMODIFICATION OF DOMESTIC LABOUR

One reason behind the movement of women into the workforce has been the growing availability of commodity substitutes for many of the products of domestic labour, particularly for those that could be mass-produced for the market at higher productivity than in the home, such as clothing or pre-prepared food. Similarly, developments in household technology have reduced the time needed to provide many domestic services, including washing and cleaning. Despite rising standards, these developments have meant that a 'housewife' taking employment needs to spend a diminishing fraction of her wages to replace an increasing proportion, though not all, of what she would have previously produced at home. Another way to put this is that the 'opportunity cost' of time spent at home on domestic labour has risen along with the purchasing power of the wage that could otherwise be earned. Further, as the standard of living of the average household has risen, so have expectations, so that families that rely on the income of only one earner have increasingly fallen behind the two-earner family, or in the UK, typically, the one-and-a-half earner family that has become the norm (Lewis 2001).

But domestic labour was not abolished in this process. The remaining unpaid work was coped with by a 'second shift' still performed disproportionately by women. The gender division between paid and unpaid work in the UK has remained particularly unequal with disproportionately male full-time employment, taking the longest hours in Europe, coexisting with a large sector of disproportionately female relatively short hours' part-time employment. In the UK, while nearly all men work full-time and a smaller proportion of women do so than in the rest of Europe, a large proportion of women combine domestic labour with part-time work, entrenching that traditional division of labour but in a different form. The results of this are well known. The UK has one of the largest gender pay gaps in Europe, because part-time work is largely low-quality work, in occupations that are low paid anyway but even worse paid when part-time, and most part-time workers are working below their potential, with consequent loss of skills to the economy (Women and Equality Unit 2006). In all European countries women are more likely than men to work part-time and to take an unequal share of caring responsibilities. However, it is only in the UK, where gender disparities in working hours are exceptionally wide, that women pay such a large labour market penalty for working part-time (Commission of the European Communities 2007; Grimshaw 2007; Himmelweit and Land 2007; Manning and Petrongolo 2005).

The pressures of rising productivity that shifted previous domestic production out of the home mean that what remains behind is the care of people, the aspect of domestic labour that cannot be so easily commodified (for reasons which will be explored below). Present or past caring responsibilities now provide effectively the only restriction to labour market participation for able-bodied people of working age. This is officially recognised in policies such as the European Employment Strategy which has target employment rates of 67 per cent rising to 70 per cent in 2010 for the population of working age of all member countries, backed up by specific employment rate targets for women (of 57 per cent rising to 60 per cent in 2010) and for older workers (of 50 per cent in 2010), the two groups whose members are most likely to be caring for others (European Commission 2005). Not only women, but increasingly older people of both sexes are more likely than men and younger people to be unpaid carers in the domestic sector. Care, in other words, is the last frontier in the commodification of labour power; it is care that is preventing the economic activity rates of women and older people rising to meet those of younger men.

In the UK, at least, it is women with higher earning potential who have tended to stay in the labour force even when they have caring responsibilities (Joshi and Davies 2000; Rake 2000). Lower-skilled women are more likely to take time out of the labour force, and many reduce their hours of employment to care for others. If these women are to stay in the workforce, or increase their hours of employment, how to provide care will become an increasingly pressing private and public issue. Already, demographic change, increasing lifespan and the rising costs of providing care, are provoking the UK government to say it needs a new 'contract over care' (Lewis 2007). Nevertheless, if policy is to encourage the movement of women into the labour force and if, in particular, if it is to encourage those with currently lower-earning potential into employment, more not less state support for care will be needed. Otherwise existing inequalities between women and men, or more exactly between those with and those without caring responsibilities that restrict their labour market participation, will increase, as will the effect of an increasingly unequal distribution of earnings on the life chances of the former (Himmelweit 2007).

DIFFICULTIES IN THE COMMODIFICATION OF CARE

Care is an object of social policy because the commodification of care cannot be the relatively smooth market-led process that attended the commodification of other aspects of domestic labour, in which both the well paid and the lower paid could eventually find affordable substitutes for their own domestic labour. This is because care differs from most economic goods and services traded on the market, including most of those others that were previously provided domestically, in at least three crucial respects.

First, without lowering standards, the productivity of caring cannot be raised substantially through mass production. This process was crucial in the commodification of other domestically produced goods, where standards and productivity could generally rise simultaneously. This is because caring, as well as performing physical activities, is the development of a relationship between a carer and the person cared for. This limits how many people can be cared for at the same time. While this limit may be different for different caring relationships, after a certain point spreading care over more people becomes synonymous with reducing quality. Indeed, what in other industries would be seen as measures of high productivity are specifically taken as indices of low quality when it comes to care.

The forces of innovation and competition that increase productivity in most other industries can do so to a much more limited extent in care. Increasing productivity elsewhere in the economy results in a rising opportunity cost of care, as the time taken to deliver care does not fall nearly as fast, if at all, as that required to produce a typical bundle of other goods and services. This is not caused by inefficiency (or rising standards) in the provision of care, nor increasing numbers of people needing care, but is an inherent effect of the relational nature of care. It applies at the macro-level of society as a whole, across both the paid and unpaid economies, and to individuals deciding how best to use their time. Increasing productivity causing wages to rise elsewhere in the economy raises the price of paid care at a similar rate, modified only to the extent that wage rises in caring differ from those in other industries. Those unpaid carers who would have to pay for full replacement care if they entered the labour market find the costs of doing so rising in line with the growing opportunity cost of staying at home, making them no more able to afford paid care but more likely to want to take employment.

The second reason why the transfer of care into the paid economy, if left to the market forces alone, cannot be as smooth a process as it was for other products of domestic labour is that people who need care cannot in general be flexible about when and where that care is provided. A child too young to look after itself needs 24-hour supervision as do many people with disabilities. Older children, those with lesser disabilities and the elderly may not have quite such continual needs, but there is still a rhythm to their needs through the day, which limits flexibility as to when and where their care can be delivered. Carers are often therefore restricted in where and when they can pursue other activities, including paid employment, restricting their labour market opportunities. In the UK, part-time employment has developed as an opportunity for both employers and potential workers to make use of gaps in the day free of caring responsibilities, such as during the school day for mothers of older children, or when others are around to provide care. Employers have seized these opportunities because they could pay less to workers whose bargaining power in the labour market was reduced by having to find employment that fitted around their caring responsibilities. The part-time pay penalty, which as we have seen is particularly high in the UK, is at least in part a result of carers having to pay a price in lower wages for the flexibility they require of employers to meet their own 'inflexibility'.

The third reason why the transfer of care to the paid economy cannot be left to market forces alone, and is therefore an object of social policy, is that the need for care and the ability to provide it are both unequally distributed. Further, because incomes are unequally distributed and not according to care needs, inequality exists not only in the ability to provide care

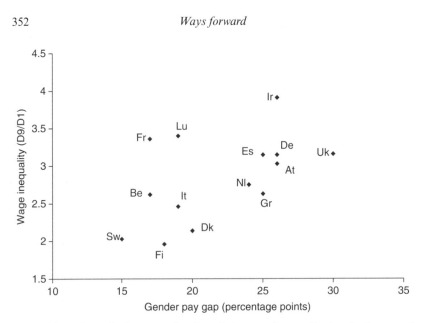

Note: * Wage inequality is measured as the ratio between the cut-off points for the top and bottom deciles of the distribution of hourly wages. The gender pay gap in unadjusted form is given as the difference between average gross hourly earnings of male and of female paid employees as a percentage of average gross hourly earnings of male paid employees.

Source: Eurostat Structure of Earnings Survey.

Figure 15.1   Wage inequality and gender pay gaps for the EU15*

directly, but also in the financial resources needed to pay for care by other means. The allocation of caring responsibilities for others is highly gendered and does not necessarily entail the time or income to carry out those responsibilities. Once caring responsibilities are taken on, they do not diminish through lack of resources to meet them. In practice, caring responsibilities often make people poorer, by restricting their time to make use of economic opportunities, in particular to enter the labour market. The more unequal incomes are, and given the gendered allocation of such responsibilities, the greater that inequality is between men and women, the more people will have difficulty meeting caring responsibilities unaided.

POLICY TO HELP WITH CARE AND GENDER INEQUALITIES

The overall level of inequality in earnings and the gender pay gap are closely related (Blau and Kahn 1999; 2003). Figure 15.1 shows that the UK, which in 2002 had the highest gender pay gap of the 15 countries of the European Community, also had one of the highest levels of overall wage inequality (Grimshaw 2007; Plantenga and Remery 2005). These measures are related because whatever it is that leads to women having fewer opportunities than men to climb up the wage hierarchy will have a more significant effect on the gender wage gap the greater the level of overall wage inequality. The gender wage gap, in turn, then affects the number of women and other unpaid carers who cannot afford to move into employment because their wages are insufficient to pay for substitute care. On the other hand, if paid carers are particularly badly remunerated, and in most countries carers are paid at rates well below the median, then a greater dispersion of income might lead to more people being able to afford their services. Either way, the distribution of wages will impact on the numbers of carers needing financial assistance to enter the labour market and, as we shall see, on the cost of providing such assistance.

The aim of this chapter is to assess the effect on gender inequalities of various ways in which social policy can provide for care. To do so it is important therefore to look at the effects of various solutions not only on *gender* inequalities within and between caring and employment, but also on the *overall* level of wage inequality too, since that will determine how effective policy can be in reducing gender inequalities. If wage inequality continues to rise, it will continue to reproduce inequalities between those who succeed and those who do not succeed within the labour market, magnifying any handicap that caring responsibilities provide and making it far harder to challenge gender divisions within the home.

Policy options basically fall into two types according to how they cope with the care that still needs to be provided when someone with caring responsibilities enters or increases their hours of employment. Some solutions focus on enabling some or all of that care to be performed by family members without leaving their jobs, by reducing the incompatibility of 'informal' unpaid care with employment. Such policies may enable either all workers or just those with specific caring responsibilities to limit or reschedule their working time, either on a regular basis or for particular periods when care needs are at their most acute. Other solutions involve shifting care into the paid economy by subsidising its provision by others, directly or indirectly through the market, or by state provision of care as a public service.

Which of these solutions is adopted can have significant implications for a number of areas of concern, notably on the quality of care received by children and adults. For example, formal childcare can have significant impacts, largely positive but some negative, on cognitive and behavioural outcomes for pre-school children (Belsky et al. 2007; Sylva et al. 2004).

However, the focus of this chapter is specifically on the implications for gender inequality. All types of policy on care can be carried out in ways that either reduce or reinforce gender inequalities and wage inequalities more generally. This has implications not only for the desirability of such solutions, but also for their sustainability and eventual cost.

REDUCING WORKING TIME

Whether policies that enable all workers to limit their working hours increase or decrease gender inequalities depends on what happens to working time as a result. Existing gender inequalities in both employment and caring will be exacerbated if such policies result in women but not men limiting their working hours. On the other hand, policies that limit working hours for everyone can enable men as well as women to participate in care, reducing gender gaps in both caring responsibilities and employment.

Take, for example, the application in the UK of the EU Working Time Directive (WTD) which limits the total number of hours per week that employees can be required to work on a regular basis. The UK, unlike other EU members, allows individual employees to opt-out of the WTD and agree to work longer hours. The UK has the most dispersed distribution of working hours in Europe, with not only the highest concentration of people working long hours, but also a heavy concentration of people employed for short part-time hours (EOC 2004). The UK government likes to claim that this shows that it has one of the most flexible labour markets in Europe and that the UK's opt-out to the EU WTD has been essential in achieving this. It defends the opt-out on the grounds of individual choice but does not explicitly recognise that one worker's 'choice' to work long hours may result in their partner's choices with respect to employment being heavily curtailed. The government does recognise the interdependence of working hours in saying that some families may 'choose' to have one parent working long hours in order to enable the other to work short hours, or not at all, and care for their children, but it does not explore the potential contradictions with respect to individual choice that such a notion of 'choice' by a family entails (DTI 2004).

Long full-time working hours in the UK, for women as well as men, make it difficult for parents of young children to both work full-time. Combine this with a large gender pay gap and expensive childcare provision, and it makes more financial sense for women to reduce and men to increase their working hours, reinforcing gender divisions and confining women to part-time work, where their skills are often underused. That this particular labour market niche of low-quality part-time work exists in the UK is thus both cause and consequence of the UK's long full-time working hours and its large gender pay gap. Women's part-time working also does little to challenge the poor availability of affordable childcare since women earning little in relatively flexible jobs will not tend to use it. The long-term consequences for women's lifetime employment prospects are severe, and particularly so because of the overall level of inequality in the UK labour market. Just one year of part-time employment can result in a woman earning up to 10 per cent less per hour even 15 years later (Francesconi and Gosling 2005).

Compare this with the situation in the Scandinavian countries of the EU, where full-time working hours are much shorter than in the UK but both men and women tend to work full-time, and in the Netherlands, where there is a significant level of part-time working but increasingly by men as well as women. Neither have the individual opt-out to the WTD, and in both there is greater equality between men and women in the distribution of hours across paid and unpaid work, less of a gender pay gap and greater sharing of caring roles than in the UK (Anxo et al. 2007; Plantenga 1997).

This suggests that policies to limit working hours have to be universal and mandatory if they are to be effective in reducing gender inequalities. Otherwise employers will still be able to expect full-time workers to work long hours, making the sharing of caring responsibilities and working time within a couple difficult. Given current gender norms and the pay gap, it will be women who take the jobs with shorter hours, which will remain characterised by low-quality work and poor pay, because filled predominately by women of low labour market bargaining power. This in turn will damage women's longer-term career prospects and weaken their bargaining power in changing the division of caring responsibilities within the home. Conversely men, through a lack of time spent in the home, will fail to develop the awareness and skills that would enable them to take a more equal share in those caring responsibilities.

Thus making working hours a matter of individual choice (in reality an absence of policy on working hours) does nothing to challenge gender inequalities and, indeed, reinforces them. In a world in which labour market inequality in general is widening, without any control on working hours those with caring responsibilities will increasingly be left behind, unable to compete on the same terms with those whose labour market engagement is unconstrained in this way. This would be a cause for concern even if there was not such a clear gender division entailed, but that such a division between workers reinforces traditional gender norms only intensifies its unequalising effect.

FLEXIBLE WORKING

Instead of regulating working hours, an alternative approach, which the UK government has been pursuing, is to allow some categories of workers with caring responsibilities to work 'flexibly', that is, to vary their conditions of employment by reducing their working time, shifting it around the day or from workplace to home. Reducing hours entails a loss of income, though shifting working time should not. Such a right could be instituted in various forms and indeed many have argued that it should have more teeth than the UK's present 'right to request' that does not test the reason for an employer's refusal but just specifies the process of consideration that has to be followed, although in practice most requests are fully (60 per cent) or partially (18 per cent) agreed to (Department of Trade and Industry 2007: 57). A significant issue is whether this right should be available to all workers or only to those with particular types of caring responsibilities such as parents of children under 6 or children with disabilities (as initially in the UK), or to carers of adult relatives (to whom it was extended in April 2007), or to parents of older children (as many campaigners would like).

The problem with such rights, if they cannot be enforced on employers and are not backed up by anti-discrimination legislation, is that they can increase gender inequalities, by enabling employers to make those who take up this option pay for it in other ways. For example, employers who are more flexible in order to attract staff are often forced to be so because they pay so badly; they would no longer be able to recruit staff if those better-paying employers with whom they compete in the labour market also had to grant flexibility to their workers. Without the right being generalised and employees protected from discrimination if they make use of it, employers who grant flexibility may be able to be worse employers in other respects.[3] This is especially true in the UK where part-time work has traditionally been poor-quality work attracting a high pay penalty. This reduces the fall-back position for any worker trying to negotiate flexible working.

Whatever the legal status of any right to flexible working, its availability can increase gender inequalities if women make use of the right more than men and, for reasons given above, with a large gender pay gap reinforcing current gender norms, it will be women who take up these opportunities more than men. Such a right can also lead to discrimination against all women, not just against those who take up the right, if they are thought more likely to ask for flexible working or would be more difficult to refuse – employers in the UK, particularly in the private sector, currently decline more requests from men (24 per cent) than from women (10 per cent) (DTI 2007: 58). It can also increase gender inequalities if the conditions of flexible working are themselves too inflexible, so that those who take up flexible working cannot easily return to a 'normal' contract and have their employment prospects permanently reduced as a result. This is particularly important for carers of older people whose future needs are likely to be less predictable than those of children. Again the larger labour market inequalities, the greater the cost of these career penalties and thus the greater the effect on gender inequalities.

On the other hand, flexible working can enable women to stay employed under existing terms of employment through intensive care periods, reducing gender inequality in both labour market participation and the conditions of employment. By reducing the supply of labour into poorly paid, low-quality part-time employment, it should also erode the part-time pay penalty, and the de-skilling of the majority of women who change jobs in order to work family-friendly hours. This would be a significant step in reducing pay inequality and consequent disincentives to challenging traditional gender roles within couples. A reasonably high level of uptake might also mean more men consider the possibility of working flexibly.

PARENTAL AND CARING LEAVE

A third prong of policy to enable workers to combine employment with caring responsibilities is to introduce job-protected leave from employment to cover periods in which caring needs are particularly acute. These include maternity, paternity and parental leaves, which can be either paid or unpaid. In the UK there is currently no specific provision for leave for carers of adults, although both they and parents have a right to unpaid leave to cover emergencies, such as when the people they are caring for are sick and/or existing caring arrangements break down. Other countries do have forms of paid leave for carers of adults; for example, both Denmark and Sweden provide paid leave to care for sick adults under certain conditions, though in the case of Denmark the leave is conditional on employers' agreement (Moss and Deven 2002).

The institution of maternity leave, by enabling women to remain employed through childbirth, has been an important plank of feminist demands, and remains so in Australia and the USA, the only two advanced capitalist countries not to have statutory paid maternity leave. Without any such leave, the cost of motherhood to women would be much higher, since women giving birth would have to quit the labour market and subsequently re-enter it, probably on worse terms. In so far as it helps keep women employed throughout intensive care provision, the existence of leave for specific caring needs is important, therefore, in reducing gender inequalities. And in so far as such leave is paid, and thus keeps the income of those who take it from falling too far behind those who do not, it reduces gender inequalities in income too.

However, beyond its mere existence, the terms and conditions of maternity leave can have substantial effect on whether those gender inequalities are intensified or reduced. Although short periods of leave may not have material effects on labour market prospects, longer periods of leave may put workers at a disadvantage, with reduced promotion prospects. Further, the perception that women but not men are likely to take long periods of leave may lead to discrimination against women in recruitment. Again the larger labour market inequalities, the greater the cost of these career penalties and thus the greater the effect on gender inequalities. While policy should outlaw discrimination against those who take up their leave entitlements, if leave is taken for long periods by one sex only, it will exacerbate gender inequalities both in employment and in the ability of men and women to contribute equally to the care of family members. Patterns of unequal sharing in caring responsibilities can be set up during parental leave that become entrenched long after both partners have returned to employment, reinforcing traditional gender inequalities.

The important issue then is to create conditions under which inequality in uptake of leave between the sexes is reduced. Leave that can only be taken by women obviously does not fulfil that requirement. There is no equality case for having leave that is specifically for women beyond the period required for recovery from childbirth. Transferable maternity leave, as proposed by the UK government, is a step better than this, but the government's own projections suggested that take-up by men of leave transferred in this way would be minimal, only 4–8 per cent of those eligible (DTI 2006).

There are two ways to make non-gendered parental leave available: as an individual right for both parents and as a family right that parents can decide to allocate between them as they wish. Most Scandinavian countries now have some combination of the two, with a portion that can be allocated to either parent, and a portion of leave that can be taken by each parent alone; the latter leave is generally known as 'daddy leave', even though there is in practice at least an equivalent amount of 'mummy leave'. And it is the allocation to the father that is talked about as 'compulsory', or rather as being granted on a 'take it or leave it basis', in recognition that it is only the restriction that a portion be taken by the father that is in practice binding. This may, of course, change in the future.

Evidence on the uptake of daddy leave has been encouraging. For example, in Iceland where, since 2000, fathers have three months' leave, mothers have three months and parents have three months to share as they wish, 90 per cent of fathers take advantage of their right. This is giving fathers a substantial amount of time to assume caring responsibilities for their young children and, although they are taking considerably less time out of the labour market than women (on average 97 days annually compared with women's 180 days), it is still a significant amount of time for which employers will have to make similar sort of provision that they do for mothers taking leave. Such a parental leave system should be less likely to lead to systematic labour disadvantage for women than one in which only women take an amount of leave that can lead to significant disruption at the workplace and the amount of parental leave taken by men is comparable to that taken for annual leave. Indeed, a study of the effect of Iceland's leave system indicates that, although it is too early for any evaluation of effects on the gender pay gap, it 'has levelled the status of men and women in the labour market' (Gíslason 2007: 3). In Sweden where the total amount of leave is longer, but the amount that can only be taken by each partner is less, the proportion of leave taken by fathers is much lower, at only about 17 per cent of all parental leave days (Duvander et al. 2006).

There is also the issue of the relative cost of mothers or fathers taking leave. Given the gender pay gap, parents may not be able to afford the loss of a male wage if parental leave is paid at too low a rate. If it is paid at *any* flat rate there will be an incentive for the lower-earning parent to take any leave which is transferable. Systems that are earnings-related at a high rate of replacement pay are the only ones that do not discourage men from taking leave and thus can challenge traditional gender roles. Earnings-related parental pay is found most frequently in systems funded by earnings-related national insurance, where it is clear that those who gain more have contributed more, as in Sweden where parents on leave receive 80 per cent of their average salary up to a ceiling. That is also the case where leave is paid out of progressive general income tax, but in residual welfare systems, such as the UK, payments are more likely to be flat rate or even means tested.

Poorly paid leave not only discourages take-up, particularly by men; it also disadvantages those who take up the leave by reducing their income. As a result income inequalities between men and women and any consequent inequalities in bargaining power within households are exacerbated during the period of leave. Such power imbalances may persist in the longer term, reinforcing traditional gender divisions in employment, caring responsibilities and domestic tasks long after both partners have returned to employment.

A number of studies have concluded that for fathers to take a reasonable amount of leave, a system of maternity/paternity/parental leave requires: that the rights be independent, with some non-transferable time available only to the father (or to each parent), that it should be paid a rate high enough to be comparable with male earnings, and that there should be flexibility in the ways it is taken, both with respect to whether it is taken full- or part-time and as to when in the child's life it is taken, especially after the age of six months (Carlsen 1998; Deven and Moss 2005; Math and Meiland 2004; Moss and Deven 2006).

ALLOWANCES TO SUPPORT INFORMAL CARE

A final form in which policy can support informal care is by paying allowances to otherwise unpaid carers of adults or parents, unconnected with employment rights, to enable them to take time out of employment. In the UK, someone caring for a person receiving disability payments with a mid to high care requirement for at least 35 hours a week can claim Carer's Allowance, a small payment that is supposed partially to compensate the carer for loss of earnings, providing any remaining earnings are below a threshold (equivalent to roughly 15 hours per week at minimum wage rates). However, neither parents nor other relatives, unless the latter are registered childminders, can get payments for looking after able-bodied children. In some countries parents can receive payments for looking after their own children. For example, Finland, France and Norway have instituted such payments partly as compensation for not using state-provided childcare and to ease pressure on existing provision.

Whether such payments are good for women has been a matter of debate among feminists (Himmelweit et al. 2004). On the one hand, many women who are currently looking after their children full-time would have an income in their own right and others might welcome the opportunity to look after their children themselves. Further, such payments can be seen as recognition of informal care, and by extension of women's unpaid labour more generally.

However, unless such payments were high, their take-up would inevitably be both gender and class divided, since those with low earning power and less fulfilling employment will be more likely to take them up. But the consequent interruptions in employment history would only intensify such divisions, both between men and women and among women. Differential take-up would also intensify class divisions in care arrangements, destroying the potential for social cohesion that universal use of public childcare can provide. In France since the introduction of such payments the children of the poor are underrepresented in the *écoles maternelles*, attendance at which used to be more evenly spread across classes (Fagnani 1999). Such payments to mothers at home would therefore also be likely to entrench the pattern by which mothers with the lowest earning power pay the highest costs for having children because they take longest time out of the labour market (Joshi and Davies 2000; Rake 2000).

POLICIES TO SHIFT CARE INTO THE PAID ECONOMY

The alternative approach is to develop policies to enable some aspects of care to be provided by paid workers outside the family. Such policies, if successful, can promote gender equality in employment by enabling women to take employment and for longer hours than would be possible if reliant only on themselves or family members for the provision of care. The use of paid care may also be part of a solution which includes more equal sharing of care work between men and women, which is both more possible and more likely if the total quantity of care the family needs to provide is not too large, and therefore sharing is less disruptive of men's employment and other uses of time.

This policy has been at the heart of the Scandinavian approach to gender equality that, as we have seen, supports both parents to remain in full-time, though not long hours, employment by providing high-quality childcare. The so-called 'Dutch Solution' of encouraging high-quality part-time employment *both* by fathers and mothers has also been supported by providing high-quality childcare. Although this solution has by no means been universally adopted, the Netherlands, as we have seen, does have a larger proportion of men in part-time employment than other EU countries (Plantenga 1997). Such policies are likely to be more successful if they are part of a wider equality programme that includes training and re-evaluation of women's work, so that more women find employment worthwhile.

On the other hand, the use of paid care can increase gender inequality if it enables gender roles to go unchallenged when women take employment. The very small immediate effect that women's employment has on their partners' contribution to domestic labour, and anecdotal and time-use evidence about how little childcare men do in France, where childcare provision for working mothers is excellent, suggests that this could be a meaningful consideration (European Commission 2004).

Paid care provision can also increase gender inequality if the paid carers themselves are badly paid, since they are predominately women. Because of the difficulty of raising productivity, employers in the care sector have limited options if they are unable to pass on rising costs: all they can do is lower the quality of provision or attempt to hold wage rises below those enjoyed in the rest of the economy. However, rising demand for care services is likely to restrict the ability of employers in both the childcare and

social care sectors to hold down wages except by employing a larger proportion of untrained workers and recruiting from groups, such as immigrants, that may be more willing to work for low wages. Governments have
from time to time supported such processes by allowing immigrants to
work under inferior conditions or by diluting training requirements in the
face of labour shortages. All these practices work against gender equality,
as well as the quality of care provision.

Policy that makes the opposite response to rising costs and labour shortages and improves conditions in the care industry, by instituting a proper
career structure, backed up by well-funded training, would make a
significant contribution to improving gender equality. This would be both
through improved pay in the female-dominated care sector (which might
then become less female dominated), and through resulting better quality
care provision encouraging more women to use paid care to improve their
own position in the labour market. The quality of care provided, although
primarily an issue of improving the experience of those receiving care (and
potentially raising developmental outcomes for children), is also relevant
to promoting gender equality in so far as low quality care provision is less
likely to overcome resistance to its use.

Enabling all those with caring responsibilities to enter employment
would require public spending to keep up with rising costs in the care sector.
The cost to the public purse would undoubtedly be high and would depend
not only on the costs of care provision but also on the level of inequality in
the economy, for the wider the dispersion in wage levels, the more people
will need subsidised care and the less they will be able to contribute to its
cost if employment is to be affordable. Because the costs of care are usually
set against a woman's wages in assessing affordability and most paid carers
are women, in practice it is the level of inequality within women's wages
that is the most relevant here.

DIFFERENT WAYS OF SUPPORTING PAID CARE

Policy can support the development of care services in two ways, by enabling
parents and those needing care to purchase care from other providers, and/or
by the state itself providing care services. In the first case, the state's role is to
encourage the development of a market in the provision of care services.
Usually this is by subsidising those who would not otherwise be able to pay
for care themselves, as for example the UK government's Working Tax Credit
does by providing up to 80 per cent of the costs of childcare to low- to
middle-income lone parents in employment and dual-earner couples.
Different ways of providing subsidies may result in increasing the number of

childminders and helpers directly employed by those needing care or in the growth of the private-for-profit care sector and/or the 'third-sector' of not-for-profit providers.

Subsidies to the purchase of care can fail to reduce inequalities if they do not generate a sufficient market for care services. This is most likely to happen in areas with high costs but also high levels of poverty, such as in some areas of London, where government subsidies through tax credits have been insufficient to enable poorer parents to afford childcare, so additional help with costs and subsidies directly to providers have been needed. Subsidies also have a tendency to run behind rising costs and needs. The more that is the case, the harder it will be for them to make a real impact on gender inequality.

The alternative approach is to provide care as a public service. This approach has not been favoured by the current UK government which sees market-based solutions as most likely to provide high-quality provision and value for money. It therefore provides demand-side subsidies to child-care through the Working Tax Credit, and favours the use of direct payments rather than the provision of services by local authorities for adults needing care. For some care services, costs may be reduced by market competition, but in thinking about effects on gender equality, the fact that the market tends to generate uneven coverage may be particularly important, for it is likely to be in those areas in which women's wages are lowest that the market is mostly likely to underprovide.

Public sector care provision may also have the advantage of better protecting the conditions of employment of care workers. Training provision is likely to be superior to that provided by private sector employers, who have little incentive to train workers in an industry with a very high turnover rate, while those employed directly may not be able to afford to pay for training themselves. The distinction between the more standardised conditions of employment that are found in the public sector and those of private sector provision may be particularly acute when looking at those employed through direct payments (payments to people with disabilities to spend on employing carers themselves rather than using public services). Experience in the USA shows that little or no regulation may result in the state-funded expansion of a 'grey economy' of mainly immigrant care workers (Gilbert 2002). Unlike in other European countries, the proposed expansion of the direct payment scheme in the UK offers minimal regulation of the employment of personal carers (Ungerson 2004). Part of the appeal of direct payments to the government is that this move from public to unregulated small-scale private provision may save money on inappropriate services that are insufficiently tailored to recipients. However, if direct payments do reduce costs, that may be as much through deregulation undermining care workers' ability to keep their pay in line with wages elsewhere in the economy. And, unless gender norms change, these workers will be predominately women. This illustrates neatly the dilemma in devising policy on care to reduce gender inequalities. Policies that enable one set of women, mothers or carers, to take employment by providing substitute care, unless they are generously funded, may be able to do so only by worsening the inequalities faced by another groups of women, paid child and social care workers.

OVERALL CONSIDERATIONS

We have seen that policy on care can in practice work to reduce or exacerbate gender inequalities. Similar issues have come up in considering different policies. First, given existing gender norms, providing too much 'choice' may work against gender equality; this is because choices that people make about caring responsibilities are made in the context of families where gender norms and power imbalances are often at their most acute. Thus, giving families choice may make equality less attainable for women than if more uniform good practice were to be encouraged. It is notable that in countries with more equality, such as those in Scandinavia, there is also more homogeneity in the caring and employment solutions that governments support and families adopt. The promotion of gender equality will require gender norms to change. We have seen in parental leave an example of where some restrictions as to who takes it can be an important step in challenging unequal gender norms. Conversely, the UK's interpretation of the Working Time Directive gives an example of where apparently maximising individual freedom can reinforce stark gender inequalities in working time.

However men cannot be forced to care, nor would attempting to do so be in the interests of those they care for (even if for centuries women have had little alternative). There are therefore two questions to consider in assessing the impact on gender divisions of policy that enables men or women to take time out of employment. These are, first, how gendered the uptake of such opportunities will be and, second, what disadvantages are associated with their uptake, given that under current gender norms these are more likely to impinge on women than men. These two issues are connected, for the fewer the disadvantages, the more likely men are to take them up. The policies that cause least disadvantage to those who make use of them are those that lead to little loss of income and have least effect on future prospects. These include flexible working arrangements and leave that is not too long, state-funded and paid at earnings-related rates.

Payments for informal care that are not associated with any right to return to a particular job do not fulfil this criterion and are likely to exacerbate gender divisions, by disadvantaging those who take them up. They are also the least likely to be taken up by men. The only approach that actively encourages greater equality of take-up and challenges gendered caring roles is to have non-transferable parental leave that is available as a separate non-gendered individual entitlement for each parent and is relatively well paid (Moss and Deven 2006).

Polices that tend to exacerbate gender divisions are those which, although they may be supported by many mothers, reinforce traditional gender roles by encouraging mothers in particular to take time out of the labour market for long periods. Extensions to maternity or parental leave at low rates of pay and payments to parents to look after their own children are examples of such policies. As the analysis earlier in this chapter showed, the deleterious gender effects of such policies are not removed by simply making their availability gender neutral.

Similarly, in a different context, the policies that provide most choice to those looking for substitute care may have deleterious effect on gender inequalities through the employment conditions of those who provide that care. Paid carers, nearly all women, can be particularly vulnerable workers because they may develop caring relationships with their employers and are often isolated. Public provision or regulation of private provision may indeed restrict choice, but that may be necessary to prevent the expansion of paid care entrenching or even worsening existing gender inequalities.

Second, policy on care that is effective in reducing gender inequality is expensive. This is because, unless the pay and conditions of care workers are to fall further behind those of other workers, care costs must inevitably rise. So if the aim is to promote gender inequality by bringing women into the labour market, increasing subsidies for those who cannot earn enough to purchase substitute care will be needed. Similarly, the cost of providing paid leave to workers with caring responsibilities will increase with rising wages. And both of these costs will rise faster if the success of gender equality policies means that an increasing proportion of workers have caring responsibilities and thus are more likely to need subsidised care and to take caring leave. The scale of those subsidies, in whatever form they take, will therefore need to rise even faster than the cost of care, taking an increasing share of gross domestic product (GDP).

Some of the policies that we have considered are less expensive because they involve spending less on unpaid carers, through offering only unpaid parental leave for example, or on paid carers, through deregulation or allowing the use of cheaper labour. These are the policies on care that exacerbate gender inequalities, by allowing caring responsibilities to disadvantage women in the labour market and discouraging men from sharing caring roles. Policy on caring that impacts positively on gender inequalities does not come cheap.

However, as we have seen, good policy on care is so expensive only because elsewhere in the economy increasing productivity raises real wages and expectations. With rising gross incomes, the increased tax rates that would be needed to fund even the most costly of the policies considered here would, after an initial adjustment, be compatible with rising after-tax incomes. Spending more on care in such a way that gender equality is promoted is therefore not only feasible but affordable.

NOTES

1. From 1960, the Additional Personal Allowance, for taxpayers bring up children on their own, recognised the additional caring responsibilities of lone parents, and was from the mid-1970s until its abolition in 2000 set at a level equal to the contemporary tax allowance for marriage (Kiernan et al. 1998: 254, 266).
2. At the time of writing, 2007, the Conservatives are talking about proposing tax incentives for marriage through transferable tax allowances for married couples where one member of the couple does not make full use of their personal allowance. It remains to be seen whether this proposal, which would produce significant labour market disincentives for second earners, will in fact be implemented if the Conservatives gain power.
3. In the Department of Trade and Industry's most recent work–life balance survey, although most workers said that they have suffered no deleterious consequences through working flexibly, a sizeable minority (44 per cent) reported negative consequences including 19 per cent who had received less pay. It is not clear if this means less earnings in total or a lower rate of pay (Department of Trade and Industry, 2007: 74).

REFERENCES

Anxo, D., C. Fagan, I. Cebrian and G. Moreno (2007), 'Patterns of labour market integration in Europe – a life course perspective on time policies', *Socio-economic Review*, **5**, 233–60.

Belsky, J., M. Burchinal, K. McCartney, D.L. Vandell, K.A. Clarke-Stewart and M.T. Owen (2007), 'Are there long-term effects of early childcare?', *Child Development*, **78**(2) 681–701.

Blau, F. and L. Kahn (1999), 'Analyzing the gender pay gap', *Quarterly Review of Economics & Finance*, **39**(3), 625–46.

Blau, F. and L. Kahn (2003), 'Understanding international differences in the gender pay gap', *Journal of Labor Economics*, **21**(1), 106–44.

Carlsen, S. (1998), *Men on Parental Leave – How Men Use Parental Leave in the Nordic Countries*, Copenhagen: Nordic Council of Ministers.

Commission of the European Communities (2007), *Tackling the Pay Gap between Women and Men*, COM(2007) 424, http://eur-lex.europa.eu/LexUriServ/site/en/com/2007/com2007_0424en01.pdf (accessed January 2008).

Department of Trade and Industry (DTI) (2004), *Working Time – Widening the Debate: A Preliminary Consultation on Long Hours Working in the UK and the*

Application and Operation of the Working Time Opt Out www.berr.gov.uk/files/file11782.pdf (accessed January 2008).

Department of Trade and Industry (DTI) (2006), Work and Families – *Choice and Flexibility: Additional Paternity Leave and Pay, Government Response to Consultation*, www.berr.gov.uk/files/file35584.pdf (accessed January 2008).

Department of Trade and Industry (DTI) (2007), *The Third Work–Life Balance Employee Survey: Main Findings*, Employment Relations Research Series No. 58. www.berr.gov.uk/files/file38387.pdf (accessed January 2008).

Deven, F. and P. Moss (eds) (2005), *Leave Policies and Research: A Review and Country Notes (CBGS Working Papers 2005/3)*, Brussels: CBGS.

Duvander, A.-Z., T. Ferrarini and S. Thalberg (2006), 'Swedish parental leave: achievements and reform challenges', in G. Rossi (ed.), *Reconciling Family and Work: New Challenges for Social Policies in Europe*, Rome: Franco Angelli, pp. 217–38.

Equal Opportunities Commission (EOC) (2004), *Response to the Commission to the Council. The European Parliament, the European Economic and Social Committee and the Committee of the Regions Concerning the Re-exam of Directive 93/104/EC Concerning Certain Aspects of the Organization of Working Time*, Manchester: EOC.

European Commission (2004), 'How Europeans spend their time: everyday life of women and me', Eurostat, www.unece.org/stats/gender/publications/Multi-Country/EUROSTAT/HowEuropeansSpendTheirTime.pdf (accessed January 2008).

European Commission (2005), 'European employment strategy', http://ec.europa.eu/employment_social/employment_strategy (accessed January 2008).

Fagnani, J. (1999), 'Parental leave in France', in P. Moss and F. Deven (eds), *Parental Leave: Progress or Pitfall?*, Research and Policy Issues in Europe Series, Brussels: CBGS.

Francesconi, M. and A. Gosling (2005), *Career Paths of Part-time Workers*, Working Paper Series No 19, Manchester: EOC.

Gilbert, N. (2002), *Transformations of Welfare States*, Princeton, NJ: Princeton University Press.

Gíslason, I.V. (2007), *Parental Leave in Iceland. Bringing the Fathers In*, Ásprent: Akureyri.

Grimshaw, D. (2007), 'The gender pay gap in the UK: key issues', Women's Budget Group seminar given at HM Treasury, January.

Himmelweit, S. (2007), 'The prospects for caring: economic theory and policy analysis', *Cambridge Journal of Economics*, **31**(4), 581–99.

Himmelweit, S. and H. Land (2007), *Supporting Parents and Carers*, Equal Opportunities Commission, Working Paper Series No. 63, http://83.137.212.42/sitearchive/eoc/Docs/Wp63_Supporting_parents_and_carers.rtf?page=20673 (accessed January 2008).

Himmelweit, S., B. Bergmann, K. Green, R. Albelda, The Women's Committee of One Hundred and C. Koren, (2004), 'Lone Mothers: What is to be done', *Feminist Economics*, **10**(2), 237–64.

Joshi, H. and H. Davies (2000), 'The price of parenthood and the value of children', in N. Fraser and J. Hill (eds), *Public Policy for the 21st Century: Social and Economic Essays in Memory of Henry Neuberger*, Bristol: Policy Press.

Kiernan, K., H. Land and J. Lewis (1998), *Lone Motherhood in Twentieth Century Britain*, Oxford: Oxford University Press.

Lewis, I. (2007), Interview, *Care and Health*, 15 February.

Lewis, J. (2001), 'The decline of the male breadwinner model: implications for work and care', *Social Politics*, **8**, 152–69.

Manning, A. and B. Petrongolo (2005), *The Part-Time Pay Penalty*, Women's Equality Unit and London School of Economics, CEP Discussion Paper No. 679, www.womenandequalityunit.gov.uk/research/part_time_paypenalty.pdf (accessed January 2008).

Math, A. and C. Meiland (2004), *Family-related Leave and Industrial Relations*, Dublin: European Foundation for the Improvement of Living and Working Conditions (EIROnline).

Moss, P. and F. Deven (2002), 'Leave arrangements for parents: overview and future outlook', *Community, Work & Family*, **5**(3), 237–55.

Moss, P. and F. Deven, (2006), 'Leave policies and research: a cross-national overview', *Marriage & Family Review*, **39**(3/4), 255–85.

Plantenga, J. (1997), 'The Netherlands', in M. Klein (ed.), *Part-time Work in Europe*, Frankfurt and New York: Campus Verlag.

Plantenga, J. and C. Remery (2005), *Reconciliation of Work and Private Life: A Comparative Review of Thirty European Countries*, Luxembourg: Office for Official Publications of the European Communities.

Rake, K. (ed.) (2000), *Women's Incomes over the Lifetime: A Report to the Women's Unit*, Cabinet Office, London: TSO.

Sylva, K., E. Melhuish, P. Sammons, I. Siraj-Blatchford and B. Taggart (2004), *The Effective Provision of Pre-School Education (EPPE) – The Final Report*, Project Technical Paper 12, London: DfES/Institute of Education, University of London.

Ungerson, C. (2004), 'Whose empowerment and independence? A cross-national perspective on cash-for-care schemes', *Ageing and Society*, **24**, 189–212.

Women and Equality Unit (2006), *Women and Work Commission: Shaping a Fairer Future*, www.womenandequalityunit.gov.uk/publications/wwc_shaping_fairer_future06.pdf (accessed January 2008).

Index

Titles of publications are in *italics*.

369